The art of influence
Asian propaganda

Mary Ginsberg

The British Museum

AUTHOR'S NOTE

This catalogue accompanies the exhibition at the British Museum, but does not correspond to it directly. The catalogue has images of more objects than the exhibition can accommodate, and some objects are categorized differently.

Chinese words and names are romanized using *pinyin*, except for a few names which have a generally recognized English spelling, such as Sun Yat-sen. Korean words and names use the McCune-Reischauer system.

This book is published to accompany the exhibition at the British Museum from 30 May to 1 September 2013

First published in 2013 by The British Museum Press
A division of The British Museum Company Ltd
38 Russell Square, London WC1B 3QQ
britishmuseum.org/publishing

A catalogue record for this book is available from the British Library

ISBN 978 0 7141 2474 2

Designed by Andrew Shoolbred
Printed in Italy by Printer Trento S.r.l.

The papers used by The British Museum Press are recyclable products and the manufacturing processes are expected to conform to the environmental regulations of the country of origin.

MIX
Paper from responsible sources
FSC® C015829
FSC
www.fsc.org

The majority of the images illustrated in this book are from the collection of the British Museum. Their museum registration numbers can be found in the captions or catalogue entries. Further information about the Museum and its collection can be found at britishmuseum.org.

HALF-TITLE PAGE: Chairman Mao badge. Profile of Mao Zedong on red sun-ray background. Below Mao is Tian'anmen on a background of flags and the inscription 1949–1969. (British Museum, 2004,0108.63.)
FRONTISPIECE: *Dawn of Victory* (detail), Liu Lun, 1941. (British Museum, 1980,0630,0.86.) See cat. 16.
p.6: *Read the newspaper regularly to follow current events*, Yang Yuhua, 1964. Colour poster, 77 x 52.5 cm. (British Museum 2006,0501,0.14.)

Contents

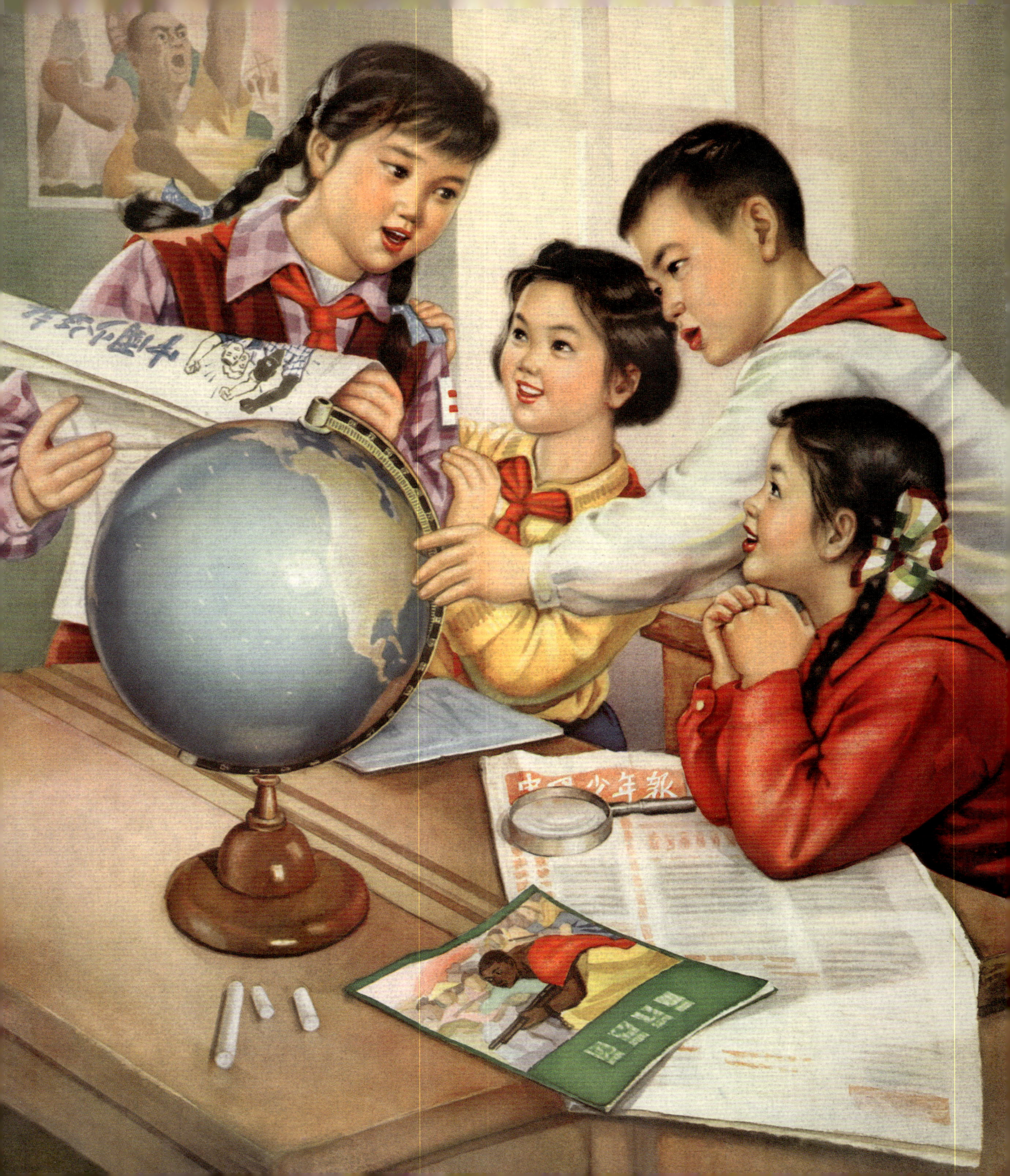
少年报

Preface

The familiar aphorism 'a picture is worth a thousand words' and similar, slightly earlier phrases came into common usage in the early twentieth century and describes perfectly the fascinating exhibition project *The art of influence: Asian propaganda*, which introduces some of the most powerful visual imagery used between 1900 and 1976 across Asia for a variety of causes. The notion that complicated ideas can be memorably and perhaps more effectively communicated through images than words lies at the heart of the increasingly popular academic field of 'visual communication' that brings together diverse approaches including the anatomy and physiology of the brain and eye, cognitive and perception theories, as well as aesthetics and semiotics. The human brain is wired to respond strongly to images, and as the author, Mary Ginsberg, demonstrates, their emotive and persuasive power has been effectively harnessed worldwide and very much in Asia during the twentieth century by individuals and agencies aiming to recruit people to a mission or adopt a prescriptive behaviour.

The British Museum, including the Department of Asia, have long collected political and social propaganda, especially since the 1980s, acquiring graphic works as well as decorated objects, such as ceramics, textiles, money and badges that chronicle many of the most complex social, revolutionary and military movements across the Asian continent. This project, a survey of some of the Museum's holdings of Asian propaganda, is the first concentrated examination of this important part of the Museum's collecting, which is ongoing. With warm gratitude I thank Mary Ginsberg, a former Museum colleague and currently a volunteer researcher, for her innovative scholarship and dedication to bringing the results of the project to the public.

The author takes us on a deeply rewarding journey introducing a broad spectrum of pictorial symbols across modern Asia, all of which embody the power to affect social change. Ginsberg sets out that before the First World War the concept of propaganda was internationally viewed in neutral terms, with its sinister connotations arising only after government manipulations tied to that war. A more impartial or nuanced view of propaganda has remained in Asia. In practice, especially in populous nations hindered by low literacy, the power of propaganda was enormous, ranging from promoting beneficial hygiene practices, to recruiting soldiers, to offering spirited social protest. Mary Ginsberg provides an insightful and cogent view of the multiple contexts and types of propaganda in Asia, exploring the aesthetic and cultural qualities of the images that light up a viewer's imagination to deliver in one quick impression a weighty message rendered clearly, simply and unforgettably.

Mary Ginsberg has accomplished a high level of clarity in the exhibition layout and accompanying explications. Her efforts have been augmented by many others whom she warmly acknowledges and whose contributions I strongly second. There are a few outside contributors I would like to credit, especially Alfreda Murck, who generously donated a Chinese teapot for the exhibition, and John Cloake and Paul Bevan for their exhibition loans. For facilitating the Museum's acquisition of the Amsterdam collection of Chinese wartime drawings and cartoons, Stefan Landsberger and Marien van der Heijden, at the International Institute of Social History, were extremely helpful and many thanks go to an unnamed donor for funding the acquisition. I am grateful to Paul Bevan, Hee-jung Lee, Andrea Shen and Keith Southwell for research, translation and support. Carolyn Wong of the Huang Yao Foundation and the Sherry Buchanan and William Spurgin Collection have generously provided images for the catalogue.

The art of influence is an exciting project that opens up new ways to understand the complex, often turbulent history of early- and mid-twentieth-century Asia. Full understanding of the images calls upon knowledge of specific cultural traditions, but the author's clear vision and explanation of the images selected here ensure that they reach across time and place creating in us awe for the power of a picture.

Jan Stuart
Keeper of the Department of Asia
The British Museum

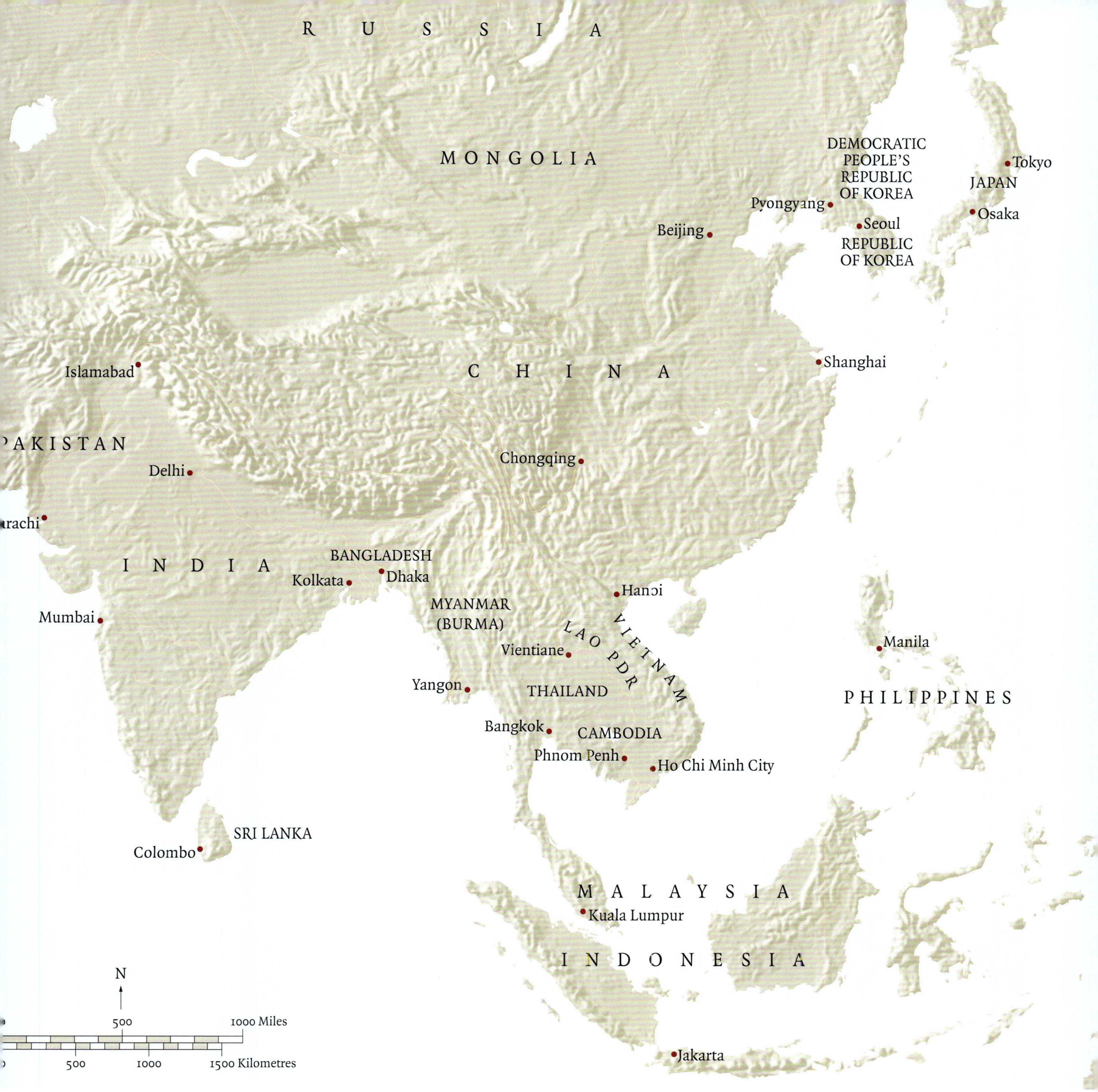
R U S S I A
MONGOLIA
DEMOCRATIC PEOPLE'S REPUBLIC OF KOREA
Tokyo
JAPAN
Pyongyang
Osaka
Seoul
Beijing
REPUBLIC OF KOREA
Shanghai
Islamabad
C H I N A
AKISTAN
Chongqing
Delhi
rachi
BANGLADESH
I N D I A
Kolkata
Dhaka
Hanoi
MYANMAR (BURMA)
Mumbai
LAO PDR
VIETNAM
Manila
Vientiane
Yangon
THAILAND
PHILIPPINES
Bangkok
CAMBODIA
Phnom Penh
Ho Chi Minh City
SRI LANKA
Colombo
M A L A Y S I A
Kuala Lumpur
I N D O N E S I A
N
500
1000 Miles
500
1000
1500 Kilometres
Jakarta

Map of Asia

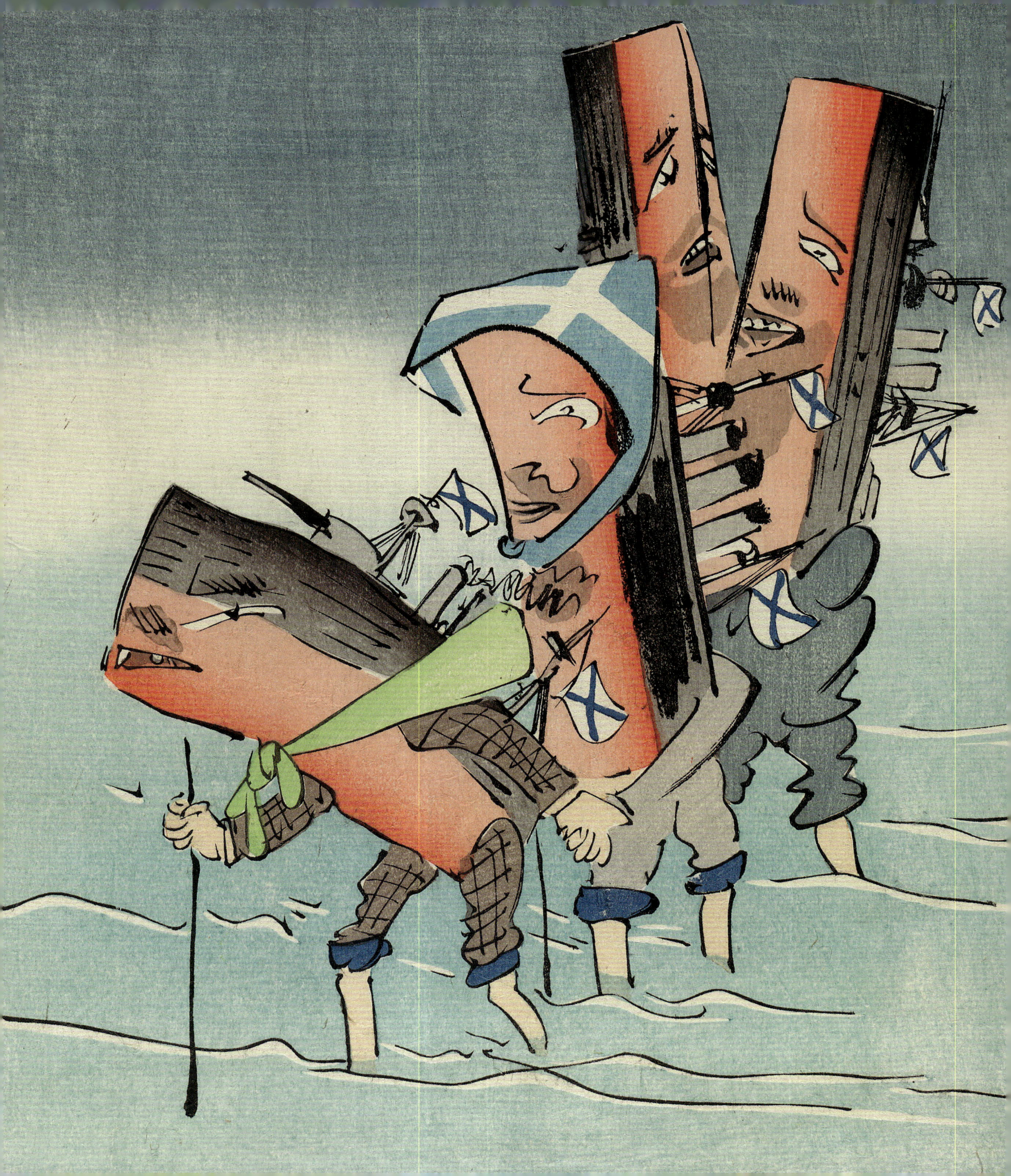

Introduction

No art, however pure, can be created or understood apart from the politics of its time.[1]

There is nothing new about propaganda in Asia. Although the medium of delivery has changed with available technology and culture, familiar messages have been transmitted for centuries.[2] 'Respect the power of your ruler' is one very early Asian example and a continual theme in propaganda. In third-century India, the Kushan kings were glorified on coins that circulated throughout their empire (fig. 1).

In fourth-century China, didactic court painting encouraged virtuous thought and loyal behaviour, just as Communist popular prints did 1,500 years later. These two artworks deliver the same message, promoting the emulation of worthy models (fig. 2).

A scene in the *Admonitions of the Instructress to the Court Ladies* illustrates the true story of Lady Feng, consort to the Han dynasty emperor Yuan (r. 48–33 BC). In 38 BC she risked her life to protect the emperor, standing between him and an escaped bear. In 1949 another virtuous woman, Zhao Guilan, was praised by Chairman Mao for risking her life to serve the state: she ran in to save a burning factory and was herself injured.[3] The first was made by a court painter for a very elite audience. The second was a popular print, reproduced from a 1951 painting, made for mass consumption. Each was produced in a style suitable to its audience, as all successful propaganda should be.[4]

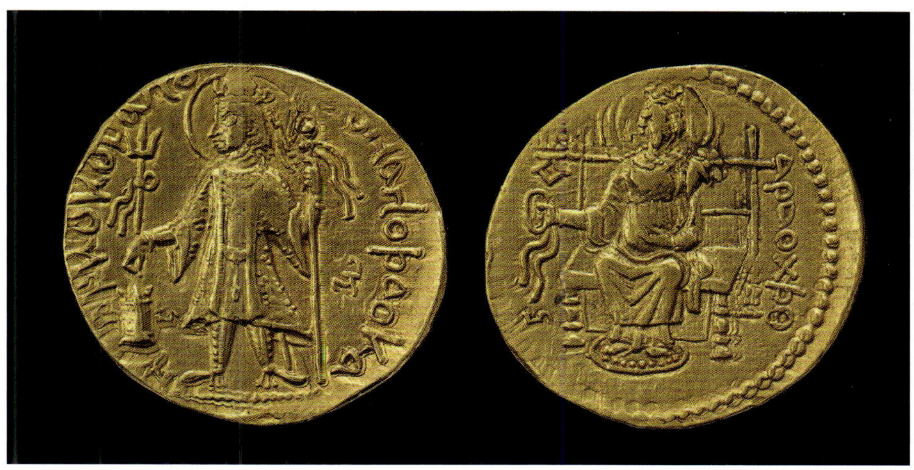

Opposite
Aimless Boats (Urouro-bune), from the series *Hurrah for Japan! One Hundred Selections, One Hundred Laughs*, Kobayashi Kiyochika, 20 March 1904. See fig. 7.

Fig. 1 (right)
Gold Kushan coin of Kanishka II, c. 229–47. Diameter 2.4 cm.
British Museum 1921,0306.12.

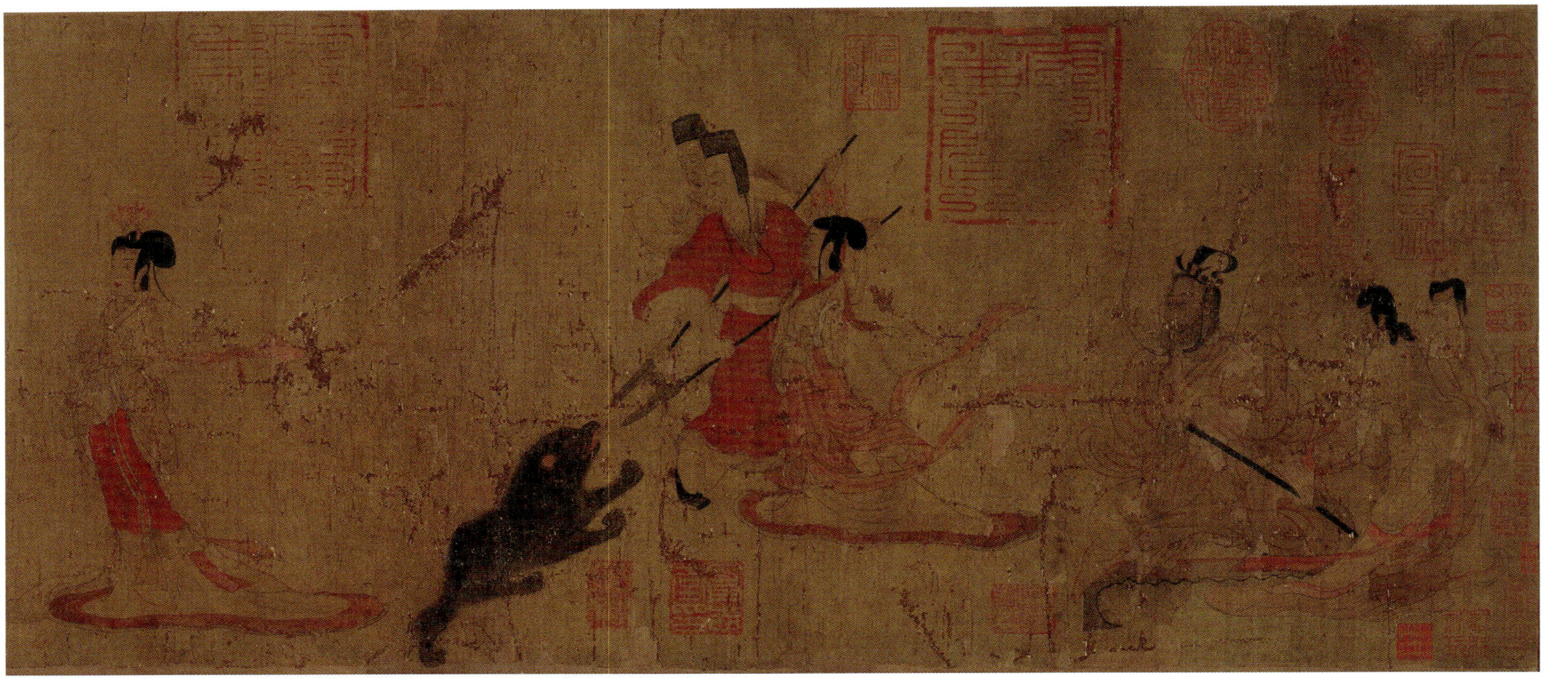

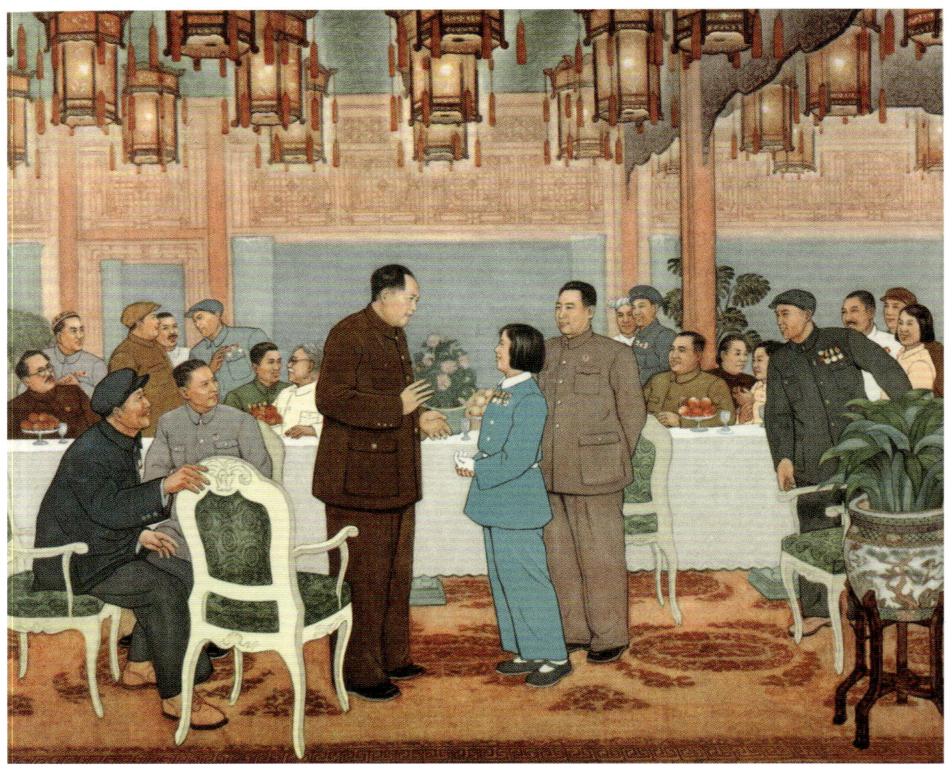

Fig. 2
Above: Scene from the *Admonitions of the Instructress to the Court Ladies* (*Nüshi zhen*), after Gu Kaizhi, probably 6th–8th century. Handscroll, ink and colours on silk, 24.37 × 343.75 cm.
British Museum 1903,0408,0.1.

Right: *Zhao Guilan at the Heroes' Reception*, Lin Gang, 1951. Coloured woodblock, 17.5 × 21.8 cm.
Private collection.

Propaganda has become a dirty word in the West. Its first use is generally ascribed to Pope Gregory XV, who established the Congregation for the Propagation of the Faith in 1622 to counter the Protestant Reformation. In the eighteenth and nineteenth centuries it was generally received as a neutral term connoting political, religious or commercial persuasion.[5] Propaganda took on the meaning of sinister manipulation during the First World War, as belligerent nations systematically censored bad news and militarized all aspects of life.

Joseph Goebbels reckoned that Germany had lost the First World War because the Allies' propaganda was more effective. Hence the National Socialists adopted many of the Allies' 'cleverest trick[s]' and developed systematically the 'virtuously mastered art' of propaganda. Goebbels wrote that propaganda was important not only in wartime, but in every area of politics, which depends on 'persuasiveness. It is no sign of wise leadership to acquaint the nation with hard facts from one day to the next . . . Propaganda in the end miraculously makes the unpopular popular, enabling even a government's most difficult decisions to secure the resolute support of the people.'[6]

A widely accepted formulation today is that of Jowett and O'Donnell, whose focus is on the purpose of propaganda. It is '*the deliberate, systematic attempt to shape perceptions, manipulate cognitions, and direct behavior to achieve a response that furthers the desired intent of the propagandist*'.[7] Particularly in wartime and revolutionary societies, propaganda is an explicit element in the mobilization of a common political culture. With reference to Japan, social historian Minami Hiroshi noted that the aim is to develop a 'group mindset', because 'Once a group mindset has been codified, individual opinions are overwhelmed by the social pressure to conform.'[8]

With these explications, it is no wonder that people equate propaganda with lies and manipulation. In many Western societies, the term is heavily loaded against Fascism and Communism, where propaganda is associated with coercion or violent suppression. However, political, corporate and pedagogical messages bombard individuals and groups in all kinds of systems. Propaganda seems to influence every aspect of collective human endeavour, and the emotive pros and cons of all this communication merit debate.

This catalogue focuses on the twentieth century in Asia, an era of almost continual war and revolution with ever-evolving styles and techniques of propaganda. The account presented here takes the relatively neutral

Fig. 3
Huang Yao, 1937–45. Although they are in the format of traditional New Year prints,[9] these wartime door gods bear modern weapons and hold Chinese flag-banners with the legend 'Defeat Japan. Revive China'. The children's discs read: 'Those who have money should donate money, those who have strength should give strength'.[10]
Ink and colours on paper, 37.5 × 27.5 cm.
Muban Foundation.

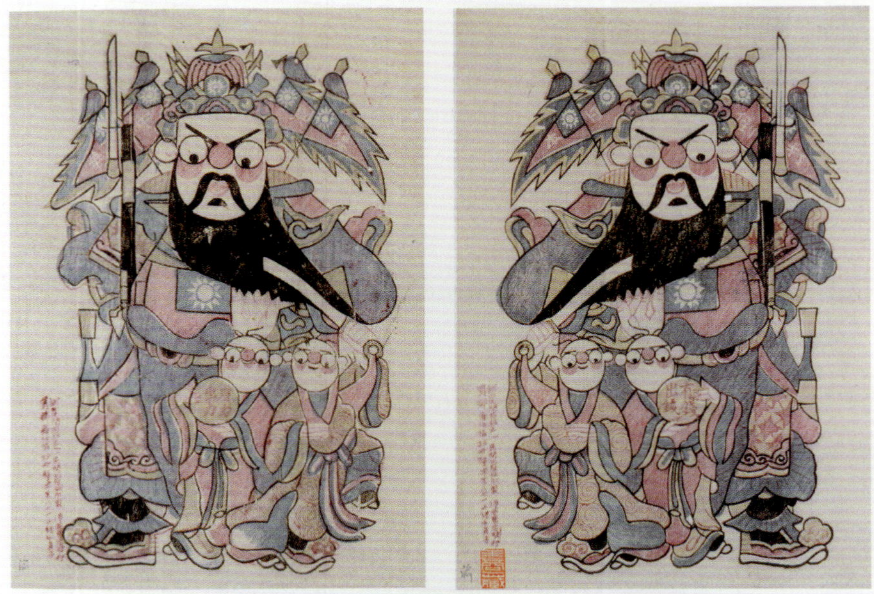

position that the main goal of propaganda – and propaganda art – is to create involvement.[11] Not all propaganda is bad; it is not always lies.[12] Propaganda aims to inspire action and belief in a common cause. It builds nations and defies enemies. It informs as well as persuades; promotes and admonishes; includes, excludes and shapes identity politics. It motivates obedience or resistance using a host of methods and modes of appeal.

Propaganda, for example, may invoke folk memory, using traditional formats and imagery to deliver a new political message (fig. 3). In the early Soviet years, the face of Vladimir Lenin (1870–1924) appeared in a red circle, icon-style: the new saint in a centuries-old stylistic form.[13] In China, Communist Party Chairman Mao Zedong (1893–1976) and Marshal Zhu De (1886–1976) replaced the Kitchen God and his wife on New Year calendar prints.[14] In rural India, too, in the 1920s and 1930s, religious imagery had a role in nationalist politics. Popular imagery has immediacy and emotion. Ritual symbols and secular motifs, vignettes of daily life, portraits of heroes – all may be used to persuade (cat. 42).

On the other hand, popular imagery often tells a different story from that sponsored by the state.[15] The Indian radical freedom fighter Bhagat Singh (1907–31) was executed for murder and conspiracy against the British king and empire. His image was and remains extremely popular in India (cat.

51), as visible as that of the 'global saint' Mahatma Gandhi (1869–1948), even in post-independence popular prints.[16] Bhagat Singh and Gandhi followed separate paths and employed different methods, but both were dissidents, fighting for Indian nationalism against colonial repression.

In fact, many of the national leaders discussed here were once outlaws. They used oppositional propaganda deliberately to expose and resist the flaws in government propaganda. The propaganda of dissent engages with manipulation, repression and inequity. The subject of political communication cannot sensibly be considered without it.

Propaganda is simple, direct and immediately understandable. It takes many forms: speech, text, graphic, film, spectacle and public art – to name a few. The influence of the medium varies with technology and audience. By the Second World War radio had achieved near-full penetration in England. Winston Churchill's wartime speeches, broadcast and published, had tremendous and lasting impact. He 'mobilized the English language and sent it into battle'.[17]

In this catalogue, however, the focus is on pictorial propaganda. Nadezhda Krupskaya (1869–1939), Lenin's wife, predicted that imagery would always have a stronger appeal than text, even when the masses became literate. For much of the twentieth century, in some Asian countries, only a small minority could read, so the image was crucial.

But is it art?[18] Some post-war Western critics argued that art should be free of politics and patronage, so that the very notion of 'propaganda art' is a contradiction in terms.[19] That thinking has given way to the realization that art – official and unofficial – reflects and is shaped by the political, social and economic circumstances of its production. Art is potentially an agent of change everywhere. In many of the revolutionary societies highlighted here, propaganda carries no negative connotation whatsoever. Cultural policy in Vietnam, for example, specifically stated: 'Art is only real art when it becomes propaganda.'[20]

Propaganda and revolutionary imagery appear as paintings and sculpture, cartoons, posters and prints; on stamps, coins and paper money; in children's textbooks and magazines and games; in design manuals and calendars; on textiles, teapots and lighters and all manner of articles for daily use. Much of this imagery is now familiar and maybe overly so, such as Chairman Mao badges or the black and red posters of China's Cultural Revolution (1966–76). Propaganda may lose its political and historical meaning and become kitsch.[21] And context is important. A patriotic print shown in 1940s Chongqing, China's wartime capital, evoked a wholly different response sixty-five years ago than it does today on the walls of a museum, or on the eBay website.

The British Museum has extraordinarily rich collections of twentieth-century propaganda art. Modern collecting at the Museum began in earnest in the late 1980s and, although political art was not specifically sought, it naturally features large in the output of countries whose cultural policy has specifically promoted propaganda.

The Chinese and Japanese collections of this material are by far the most comprehensive in the Museum's Department of Asia, covering the whole century and all media. Much of this material has been neither displayed nor published, so it has been given the lion's share of space in this exhibition and catalogue. The large collection of Vietnamese war drawings mostly cover the period 1965–75 and have been fully published and exhibited.[22] The North Korean paintings and graphics in the British Museum were mostly produced after 1990, though referring to earlier glory days; many have been published.[23] There are few works here from South Korea, as the post-war artists in the Museum's collection mostly pursued modernist rather than ideological expression.[24] The collection's Indian political prints and other works generally relate to the struggle for independence. The Department of Asia houses most of the objects in this catalogue, though the Departments of Prints & Drawings, Prehistory & Europe and Coins & Medals are also represented. A very few pieces from private collections are included to fill gaps.

The people, places and occasions portrayed in this catalogue cover the period from about 1900 up to 1976, when several events brought this tumultuous era to a close. Mao Zedong died, and the ten-year Cultural Revolution in China finally ended. The year 1976 also saw the formal unification of Vietnam after thirty years of colonial and proxy wars. Subsequently national development strategies changed, territorial conflicts persisted and some post-colonial issues were still unresolved – but the era of extreme ideology was past.

The rest of this introduction gives a very brief historical overview of the period in Asia, highlighting some important developments in propaganda art and illustrating the enormous variety of formats and styles employed. The works in the first part of the catalogue trace the narrative chronologically. The second section covers specific techniques and themes, including propaganda in daily life, women and children, and protest propaganda.

Modernization, anti-colonialism and other propaganda messages (*c.* 1900–30)

At the turn of the twentieth century many Asian countries were under the influence or outright domination of foreign powers. In 1900 the so-called Boxers in China unsuccessfully rose up against the influence of foreign missionaries and corporate interests, with the support of Cixi, the Qing dowager empress (1835–1908).[25] In the decisive battle, thousands of Chinese attacked the foreign legation in Beijing. Soldiers from an eight-nation alliance finally ended the siege (cats 8–9). The foreign powers demanded an enormous indemnity, which took China thirty-nine years to pay off.[26]

The rulers of the Qing dynasty (1644–1911) were Manchus, themselves foreigners. There were Chinese nationalists who supported the overthrow of the Qing, as illustrated in the seditious print, *Big Victory for the Han People's Army* (fig. 4). Chief among these was Sun Yat-sen (孫中山 Sun Zhongshan, 1866–1925), who became China's first president after the dynasty fell in 1911.

A rare pictorial broadsheet reports on the people and events around the uprising in Hubei province which led ultimately to the Manchu Abdication and establishment of the Republic in 1912 (fig. 5). Particularly interesting here is the portrait at the bottom of Cao Daoxin, a student who formed a corps of female soldiers.[27]

Sun Yat-sen was one of many Asian intellectuals and activists who made their way to newly modernized Japan in the early part of the twentieth century. Japan had undergone economic, military, political and educational reform under the Meiji emperor (r. 1867–1912), stunning both Asian and Western nations with its speed of development. The emperor's family are portrayed in a thoroughly Western manner in the print in fig. 6.

In 1895 Japan defeated the outmoded armed forces of China. With far greater propaganda impact, in the naval Battle of Tsushima in 1905, Japan was victorious against Russia – the first instance in the modern era of an Asian country defeating a European one.

The humorous Japanese print in fig. 7 shows the Russian navy as limping fish (aggressive Russia is usually caricatured as a bear). This triumph stimulated nationalist movements across Asia – in China, where foreign powers still controlled large territories, and in colonial India and Burma, Indochina, the Indonesian archipelago and the Philippines. By this time, however, Japan had extended its ambitions and territories and was

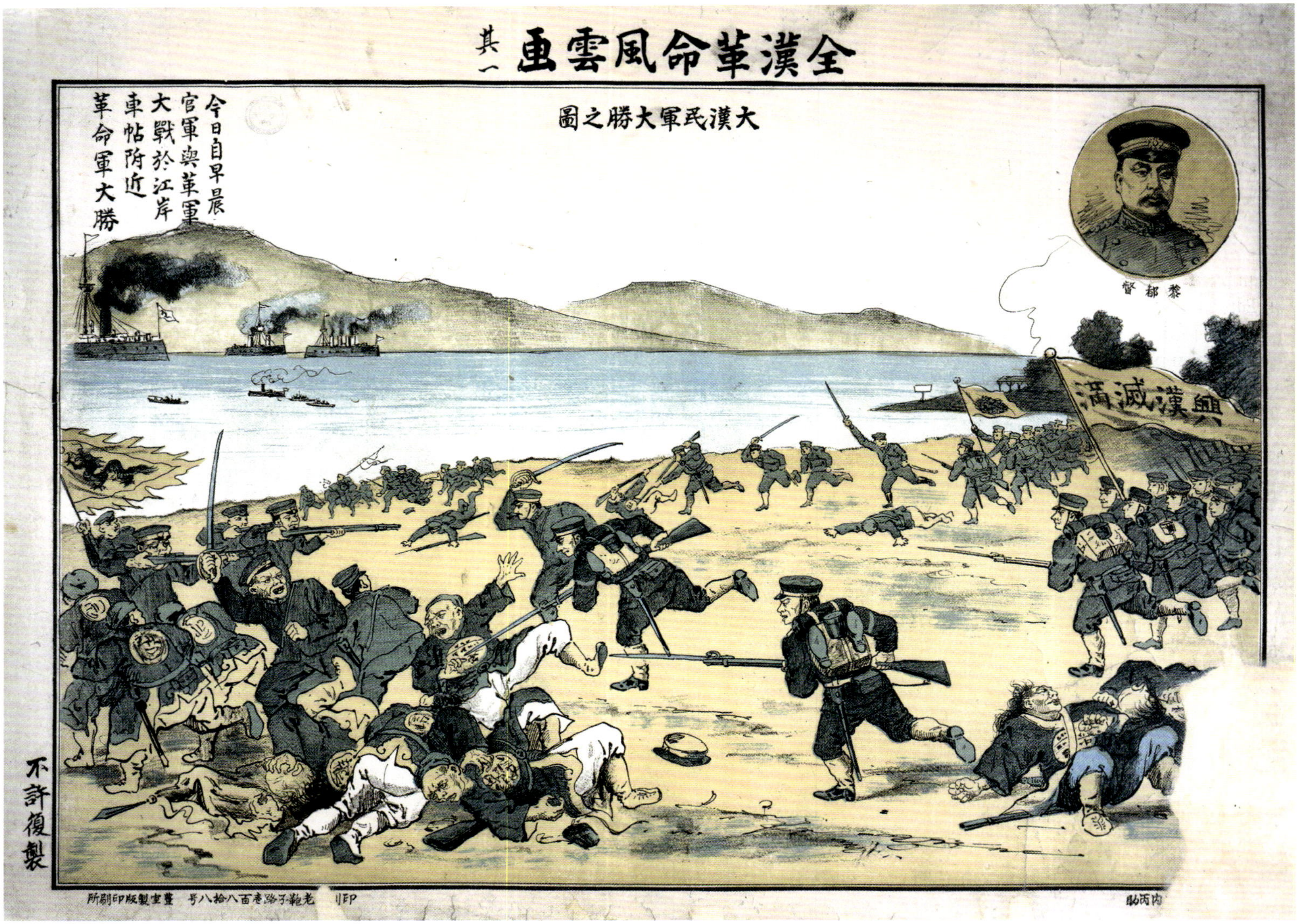

itself encountering active resistance, having acquired Formosa (Taiwan) after the 1894–5 war with China and occupied Korea in 1905.

The First World War, the 'war to end all wars', was mostly fought on the European front, but a number of Asian countries were involved. Vietnam, for example, contributed about 99,000 workers and soldiers[28] and enormous quantities of raw materials to the French effort. About 800,000 troops served from India, Burma and Nepal. Japan sided with the Allies, with a strategic eye on post-war territorial redistribution. China was

Fig. 4
Big Victory for the Han People's Army (大漢民軍勝之圖), *c.* 1900. Ink and colours on paper, 39 × 55.5 cm.
British Museum 1967,1016,0.5.4.

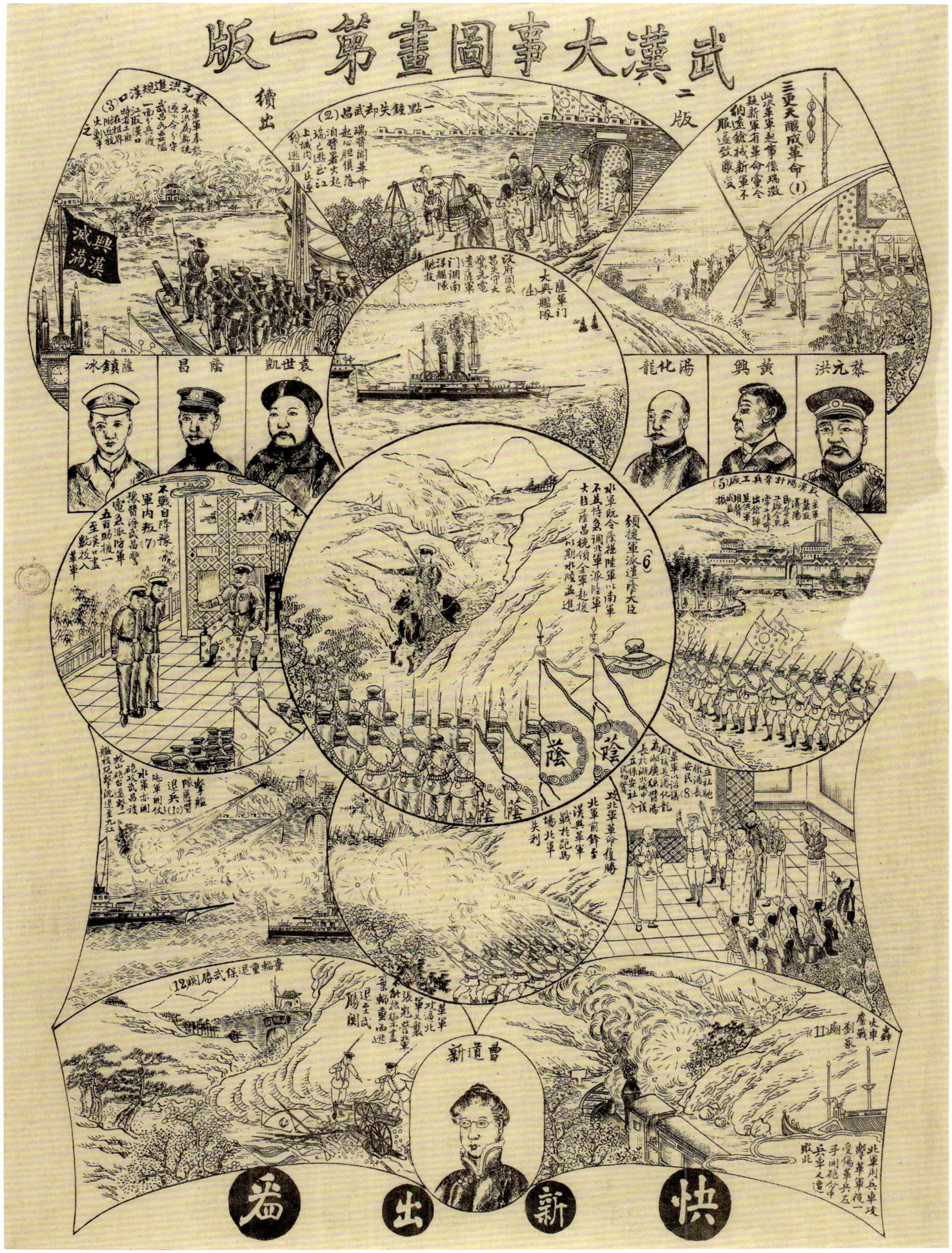

Fig. 5
Wuhan Events Pictorial, First Edition (武漢大事圖畫第一版), *c.* 1911. Ink on paper, 63.5 × 55.9 cm.
British Museum 1967,1016,0.5.3.

Fig. 6
Picture of Their Imperial Majesties and Their Imperial Highnesses (両陛下両殿下御尊影), Watanabe Tadahisa, 14 June 1900. Colour lithograph on paper, 47 × 63 cm.
British Museum 1991,0810,0.5.

Fig. 7 (opposite)
Aimless Boats (Urouro-bune), from the series *Hurrah for Japan! One Hundred Selections, One Hundred Laughs*, Kobayashi Kiyochika, 20 March 1904. Coloured woodblock print on paper, 37.1 × 25.4 cm.
British Museum 1946,0209,0.103.

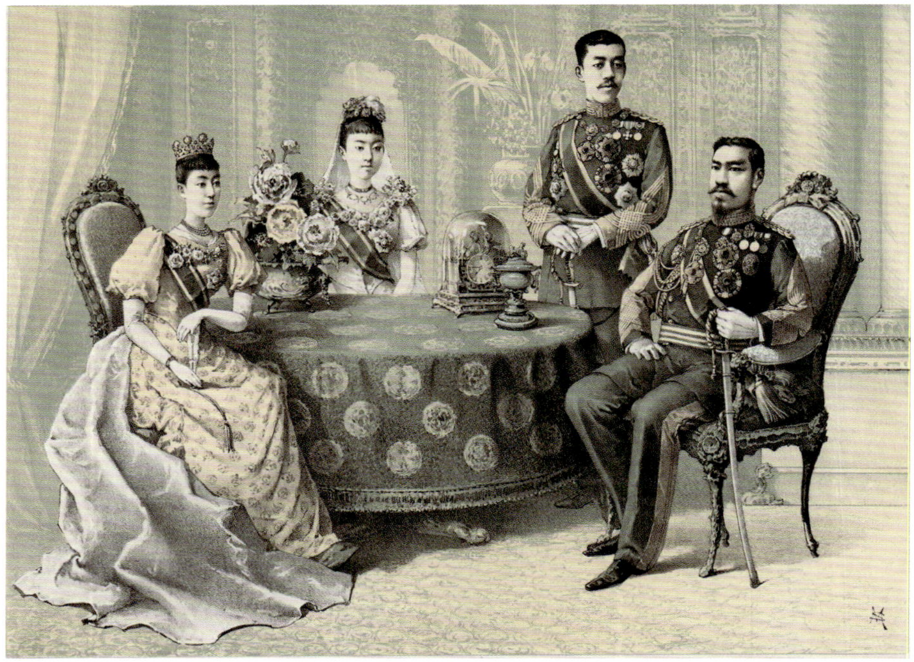

officially neutral, though 140,000 Chinese workers were sent to Britain and France in 1917.[29]

Woodrow Wilson's 'Fourteen Points' speech of 1918, with its support for national self-determination, inspired nationalist revolutionaries everywhere. The March 1st (or Samil) Movement of 1919 was one of the earliest displays of protest at Japan's occupation: a group of Korean nationalists publicly proclaimed a Declaration of Independence. They also published a list of complaints about the repressive nature of the occupation.

Nguyễn Tất Thành, better known as Ho Chi Minh (1890–1969), also acted on the Fourteen Points. He prepared an Eight-Point Plan calling for basic rights and some Vietnamese representation in the French colonial government. He tried to present this at the Paris Peace Conference in 1919, but was turned away.

At the Peace Conference, Japan was accorded the parts of Shandong previously held by Germany, thereby in a stroke politicizing a generation of Chinese students in what is known as the May Fourth Movement. This term is also employed more broadly to refer to the New Culture Movement of 1915–21. Use of the vernacular in literature, and new translations of political writings, widened enormously the group who took action in

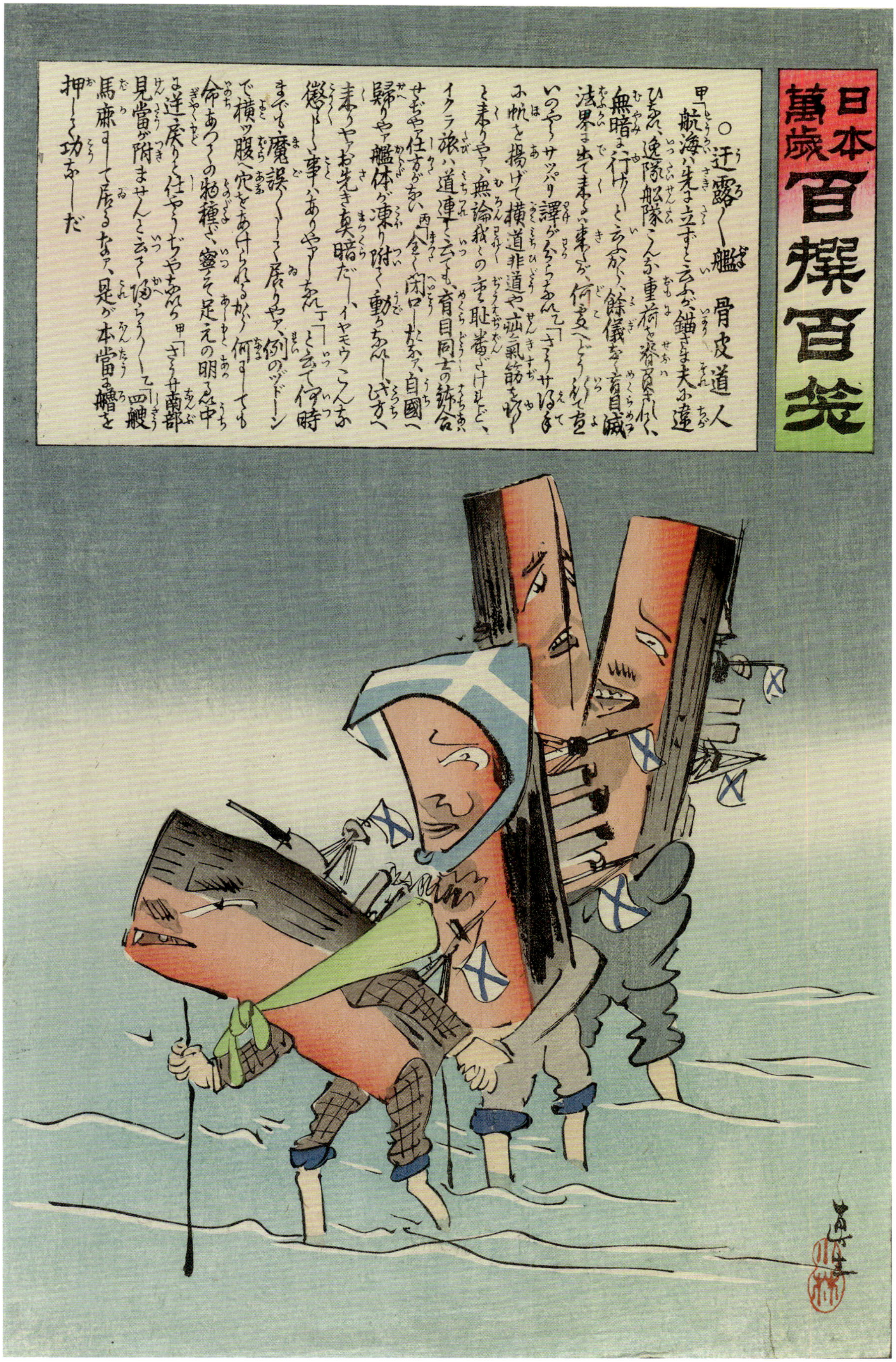
日本萬歳 百撰百笑
迂露〻艦
骨皮道人

favour of social and political reforms, and against foreign domination.

A National Products Movement (國貨運動 *guohuo yondong*) engaged every level of society. The message was promoted in graphic art and advertising, everyday objects and the establishment of National Products museums in cities all over China (fig. 8).[30] At the opening of a mammoth two-month exhibition in 1928, the nationalist leader Chiang Kai-shek (蔣介石 Jiang Jieshi, 1887–1975) declared that the government wanted 'to promote national products, revive industry and commerce', so that 'foreign products have no markets in China and everyone uses national products to destroy imperialism'.[31]

Foreign boycotts also featured in the home-rule propaganda of India and Vietnam (cats 25–6). Bal Gangadhar Tilak (1856–1920), an early activist for Indian independence, supported the Swadeshi (self-sufficiency) Movement, which began in 1905. A journalist, educator and reformer, Tilak was more radical than most of the Congress Party leaders. He provoked the colonial authorities by writing about bombs: he said they were a kind of knowledge. Small ones could be made easily and carried around. Christopher Pinney notes the parallels here with the informational flows of small printing presses, whose output made the colonial authorities increasingly nervous.[32]

One British official, for example, fixed on images of the goddess Kali as subversive (fig. 9).[33] Versions of this print had been in circulation since the 1870s. Kali stands over a recumbent Śiva, a necklace of human heads around her neck, with the hands and arms of her victims around her waist as a girdle. A very similar version from 1907–8 carries a nationalist message, though hardly apocalyptic. Advertisements around the image promote Indian-made Kali cigarettes, urging: 'Look after the interests of this country's poor and humble workers'.[34] The European-looking heads around her neck and on the ground convinced this official that the print was seditious.[35]

More explicit is the wish expressed on an intricately decorated Burmese betel box from the 1930s or 1940s (fig. 10). The inscription on the figure's banner reads, 'We shall get home rule', and the 'HO' above is likely the start of 'home rule' in English.[36]

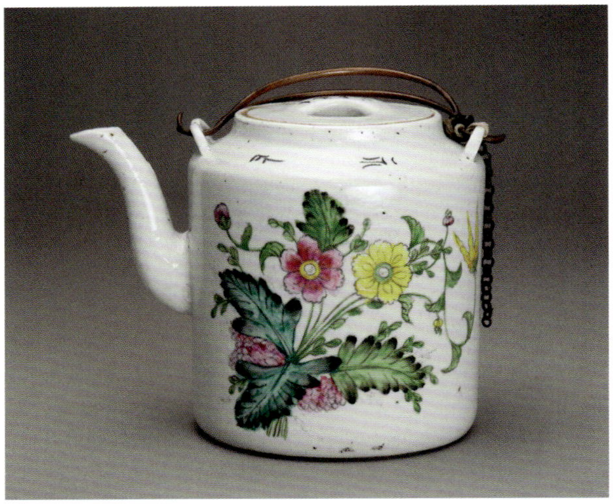

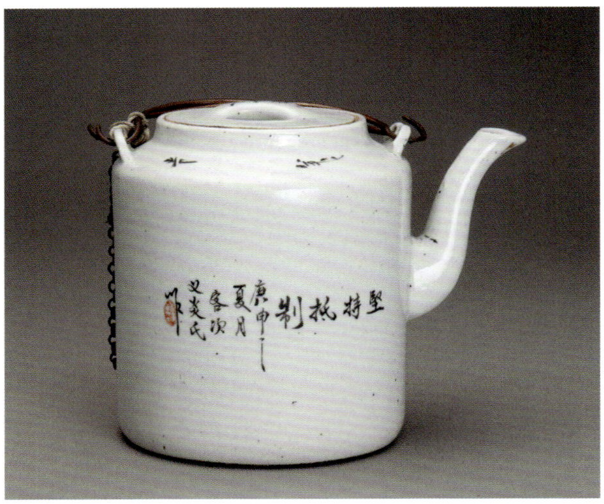

Fig. 8
'Uphold the boycott' slogan on teapot, 1920.
Hand-thrown ceramic. 13.7 × 11.9 cm.
Alfreda Murck Collection # 77/British Museum.

In 1917, the Bolsheviks overthrew the Russian government and set out to change the whole world. Marxism-Leninism was an ideology for the future. It was not a plan especially formulated for anti-colonial insurrectionists, though Marxist thought certainly attracted nationalists like Bhagat Singh and Ho Chi Minh. Raising the workers' political conscious-

Fig. 9
Kali, Chore Began Art Studio, Calcutta, *c.* 1895. Colour lithograph on paper, 40.5 × 30.7 cm.
British Museum 1950,1014,0.24.

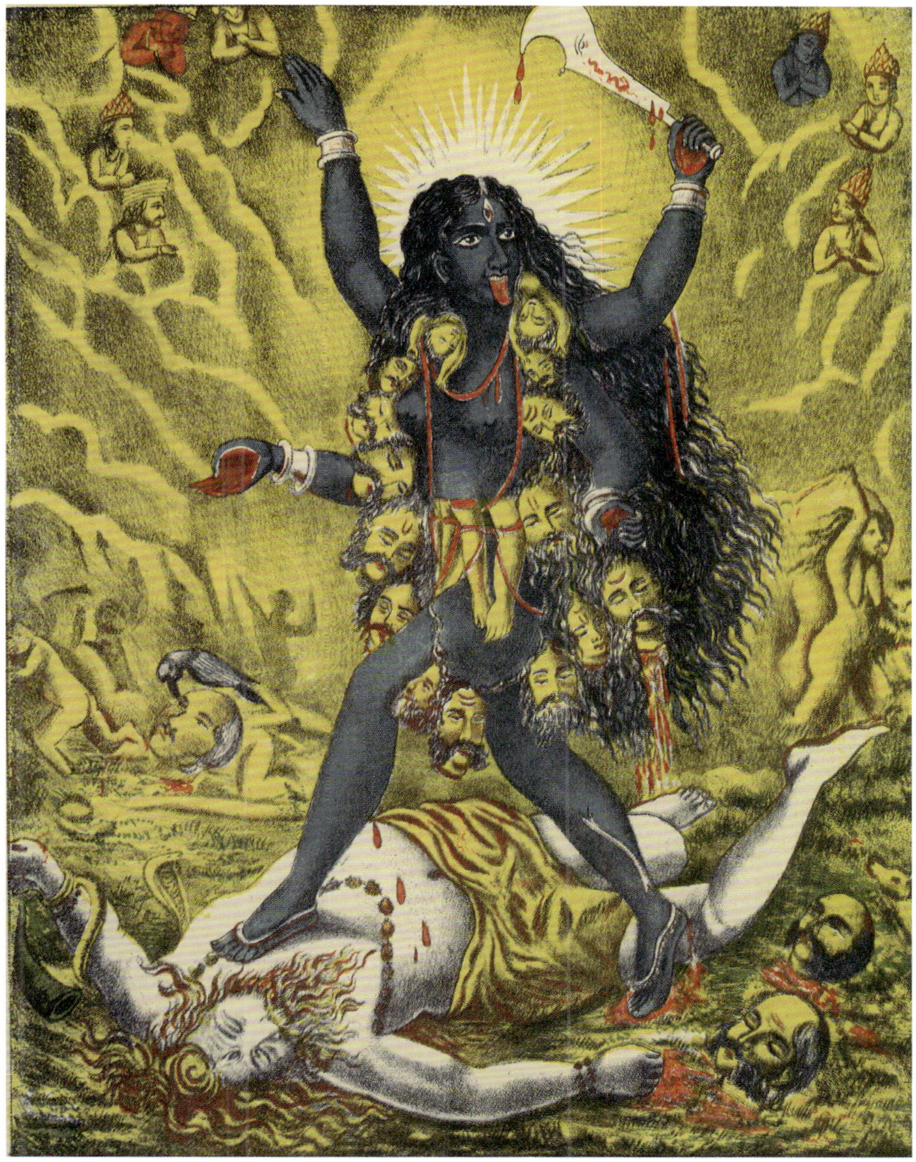

Fig. 10
Lacquered bamboo betel box, early 20th century. Diameter 21 cm.
British Museum 1998,0723.76/Isaacs 76.

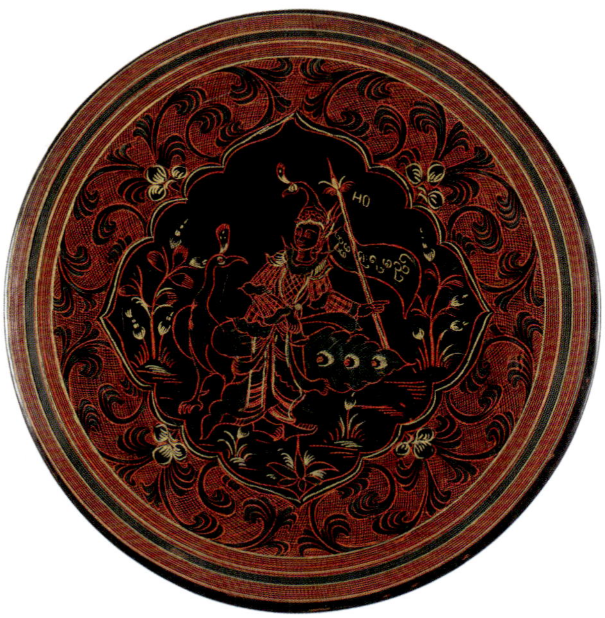

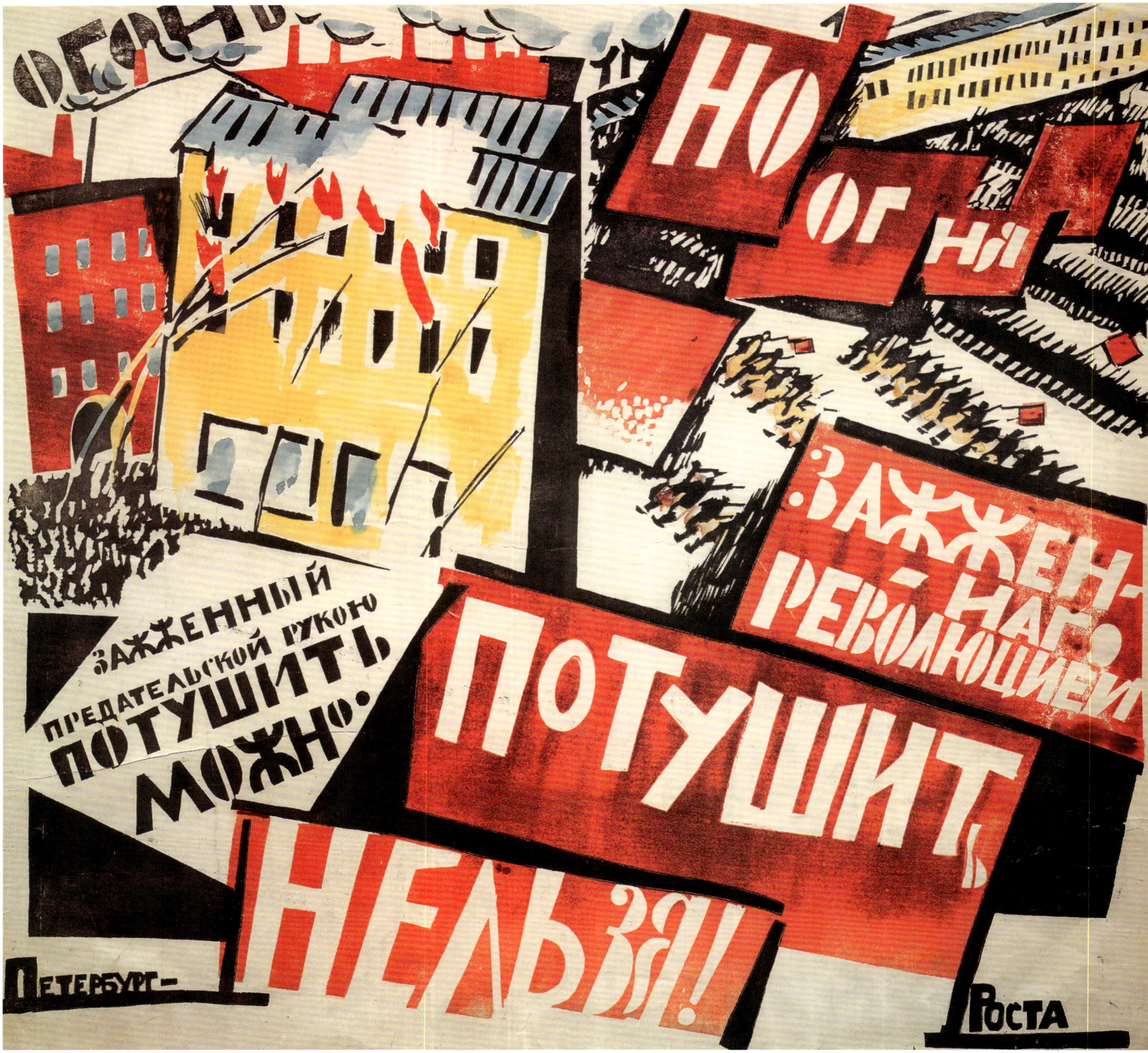
ОГОНЬ
ЗАЖЖЕННЫЙ ПРЕДАТЕЛЬСКОЙ РУКОЮ ПОТУШИТЬ МОЖНО.
НО ОГНЯ
ЗАЖЖЕН-НАГО РЕВОЛЮЦИЕЙ
ПОТУШИТЬ
НЕЛЬЗЯ!
ПЕТЕРБУРГ-
РОСТА

ness, fomenting class struggle, enjoining obedience to rules of party unity and centralization: these would lead to revolution, economic equality, social justice and the 'new Soviet man'. In the following decade, these ideas circulated in small, clandestine organizations. Communist parties were established in India in 1920, in China in 1921, in Japan in 1922, in Vietnam and Korea in 1925 and in the Philippines in 1930.

Soviet revolutionary art had an enormous influence on political movements in Asia, Europe and South America. From 1917, Soviet art and education programmes were reorganized, with enthusiastic support from artists and writers. The energy and experimentation of avant-garde movements transformed fine art, graphics and public display (fig. 11).

Under Joseph Stalin (1878–1953), however, Futurism and Suprematism soon yielded to the new ideological requirements of Socialist Realism, which became the prescribed style in Communist China, North Korea and Vietnam (cat. 36). Photomontage by Soviet Constructivists influenced war propaganda everywhere (cat. 21).

Propaganda of the Asia-Pacific War (1931–45)

In 1931 Japan seized the three provinces of north-east China (Manchuria), called it Manchukuo and installed Puyi (溥儀 1906–67), China's last emperor, as its figurehead. This encroachment stimulated all manner of literary and artistic involvement by left-wing activists. In that year, Lu Xun (魯迅 1881–1936) instigated a new direction for political art in China, known as the Modern Woodcut Movement, or Creative Print Movement. Lu Xun was arguably the most influential cultural figure in twentieth-century China. He was a writer, not an artist, but his activities made prints an instrument for social change. He published the works of the German Expressionists and Soviet printmakers he admired (cat. 2), held classes to teach the techniques of woodblock printing, and sponsored the first public exhibitions of this art in China.

Lu Xun considered woodcuts the ideal form – a practical weapon for spreading revolutionary perspective. They could be produced cheaply and in large quantity. They needed no special equipment: just a piece of wood, a knife, ink and paper. The resulting contrast of black and white was a dramatic way to illustrate real life. Unlike traditional woodblock production, where the activities of design, cutting and printing were performed by different people, the Creative Print artists did everything themselves.[37]

This was the first time artists in China were openly subversive.[38] The

Fig. 11
The fire lighted by a treacherous hand can be extinguished. However, the fire lighted by the Revolution cannot be extinguished. (Огонь зажженный предательской рукою потушить можно. Но огня зажженного революцией потушить нельзя.) Anonymous, 1921. Chromolithograph on paper, 63.5 × 71 cm.
State Russian Museum, St Petersburg.

Fig. 12
The Fire of Truth, Zhang Wanqing.
Ink on paper, 56 × 71.5 cm.
British Museum 1992,0716,0.380.

Fig. 13 (opposite)
Down with Imperialism! (打倒帝國主義!),
Li Hua, 1939–40. Woodblock print,
ink on paper, 23.2 × 19.3 cm.
British Museum 1999,0705,0.7.

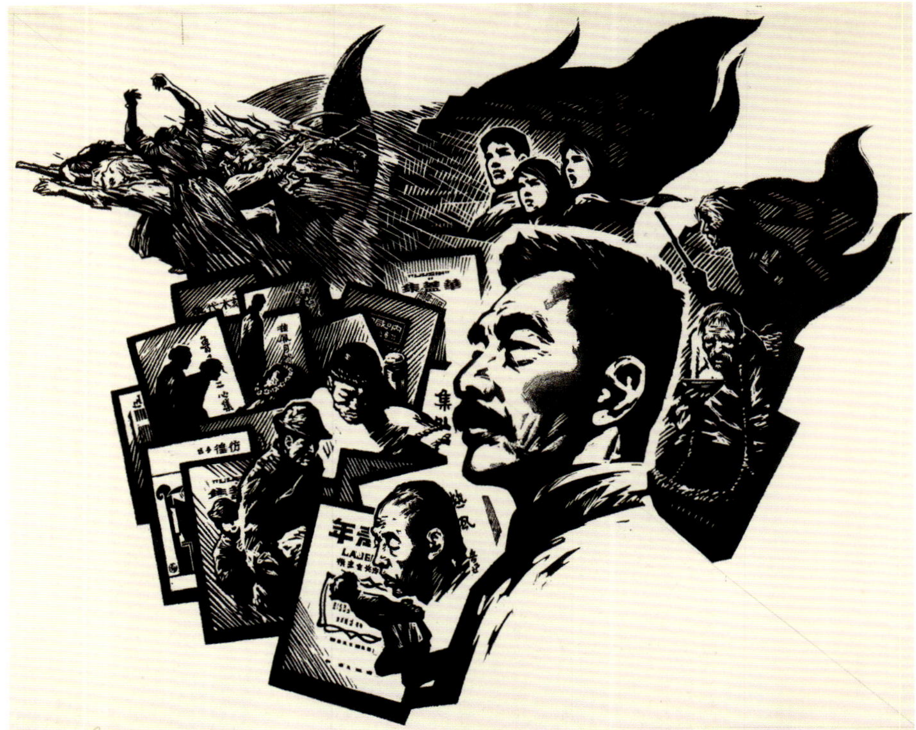

Modern Woodcut Movement was left-wing art, and in the early 1930s the government had little patience with it. Many woodcut artists and students were arrested, and some were executed. Woodcuts exposed the harsh social and political conditions of Republican China. Artists protested foreign aggression in China and the failure of the ruling Nationalist Party to resist because they were too busy fighting the Communists. In Li Hua's *Forward*, the figure rages: 'Our own hateful people act as executioners! Willing to bend their knees under the iron hooves of the imperialists. Forward! Forward! Arise, you who refuse to be slaves!'[39] (fig. 13).

Japan declared war in July 1937 and by the end of the year had invaded Shanghai, Beijing and the capital, Nanjing. During the War of Resistance, as the 1937–45 period is known in China, woodcuts were an instrument of national salvation, as Nationalists and Communists fought together under a united front.[40] More than 4,000 different prints were made (cat. 16).

Cartoons as social and political commentary had flourished since the late 1920s, but in wartime, *manhua*[41] were a weapon. A whole raft of *manhua* publications circulated, the best known being *Shanghai Manhua*

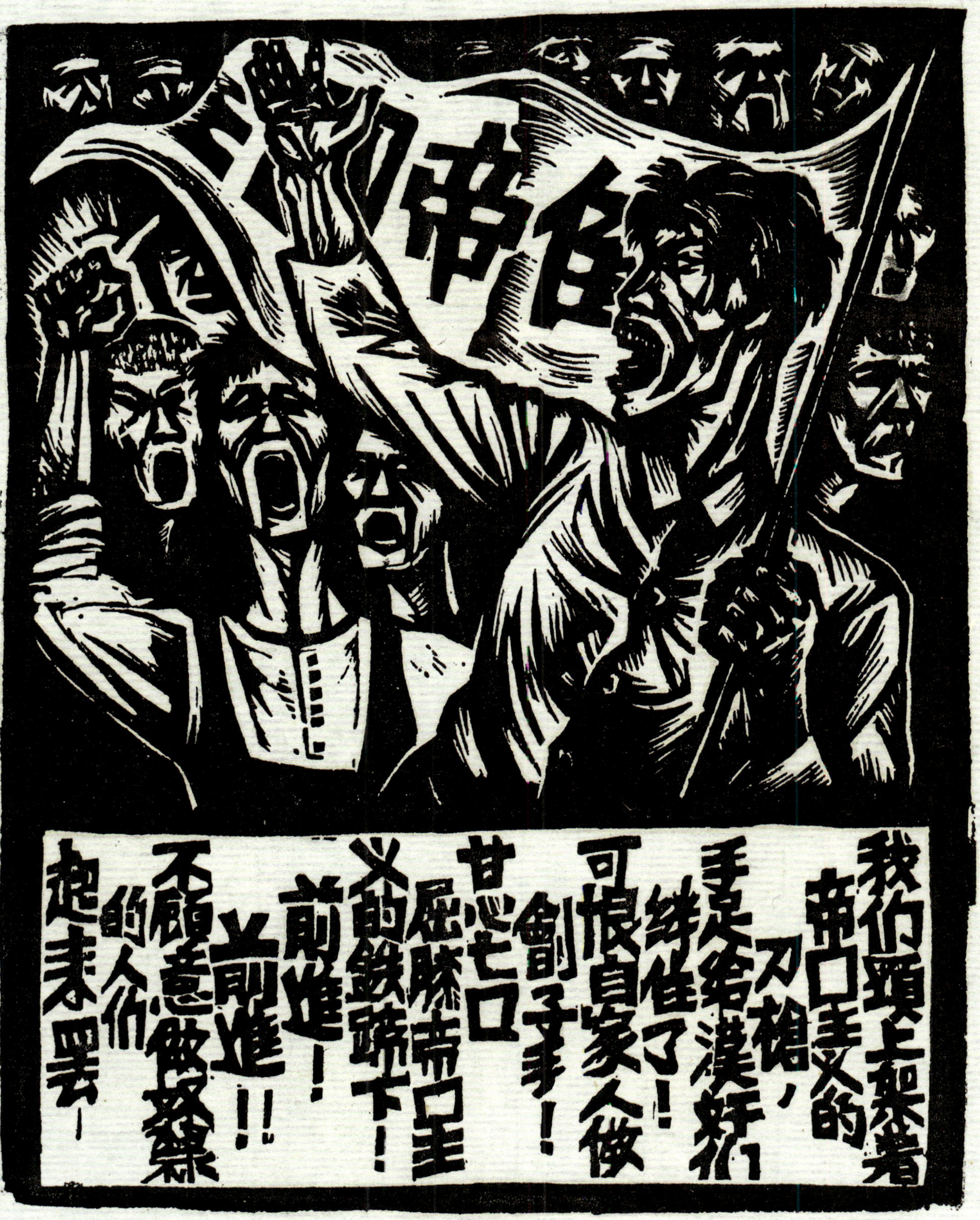
我们头上架着
帝国主义的
刀枪，
手足给汉奸们
绊住了！
可恨自家人做
刽子手！
甘心七口
屈膝帝国
义的铁蹄下！
前进！
前进！！
不顾意做奴隸
的人们
起来罢—

打倒帝国主义！

李桦

(上海漫畫) (cats 14–15) and *Shidai Manhua* (時代漫畫). Starting in 1937, several travelling propaganda teams published and exhibited thousands of cartoons to raise solders' morale and strengthen civilian resistance.[42]

Exhibitions were held abroad to increase foreign support for wartime China. Jack Chen (陈依范 Chen Yifan, 1908–95), a cartoonist and journalist trained in Moscow and Yan'an, collected cartoons, prints and drawings for shows in Europe and America in the late 1930s. His powerful skull, once published, was appropriated by propagandists in Burma and elsewhere (fig. 14).[43] In London, the exhibition catalogue was called *Five Thousand Years Young*. Most of these works are now in the British Museum.

From 1937–45, China was effectively divided into three parts. Japan occupied the eastern coastal cities and the north-east. The Guomindang (GMD) under Chiang Kai-shek moved the capital to Chongqing,[44] in Sichuan province, and controlled the interior area known as 'Free China'. The Communists, on their Long March, had reached Yan'an in 1935, establishing it as their main base and gradually increasing the 'Liberated' areas under their control.

The printmakers and cartoonists worked throughout the war, some

Opposite
Map of wartime China, 1937–45.

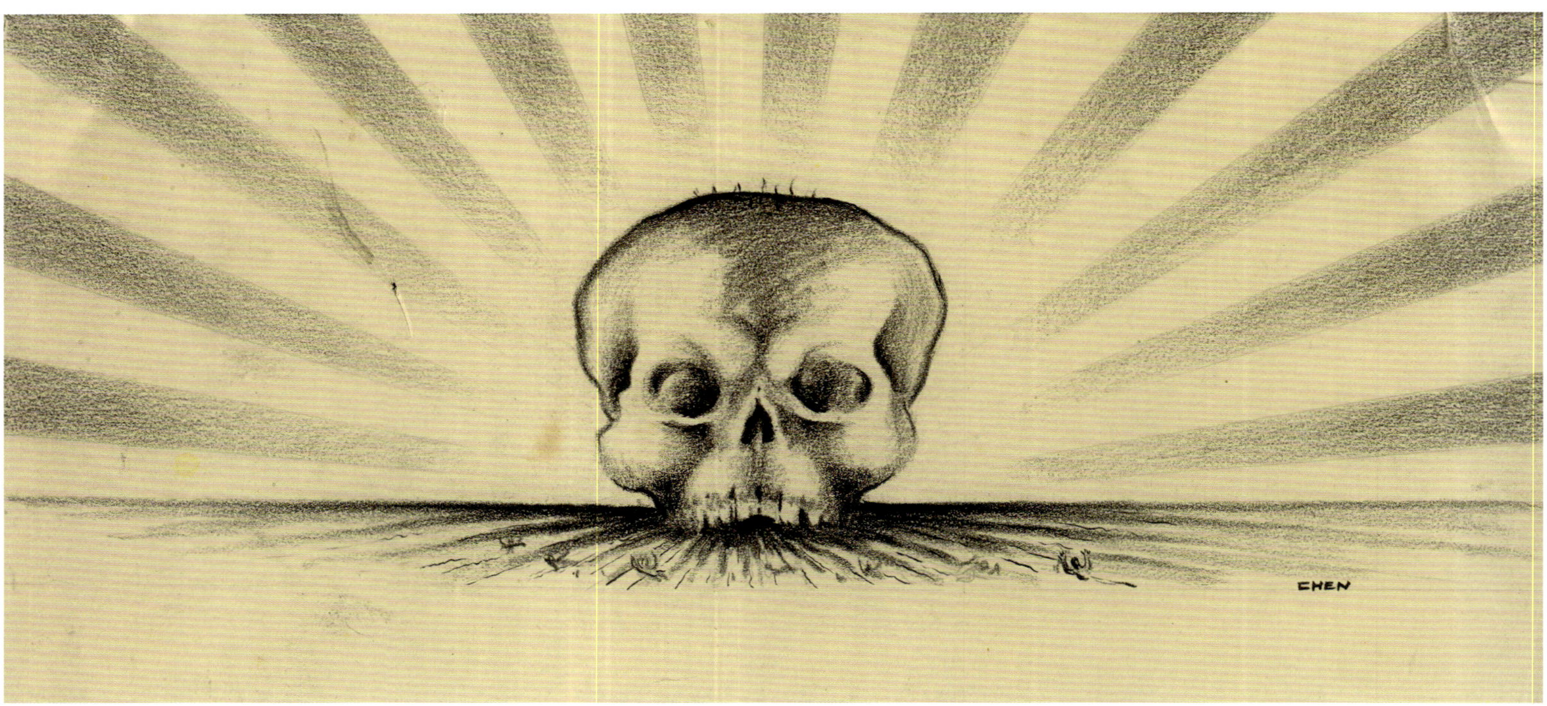

Fig. 14
Untitled drawing, Jack Chen, 1930–8.
Crayon on paper, 17.7 × 38 cm.
British Museum 2009,3022,0.3.

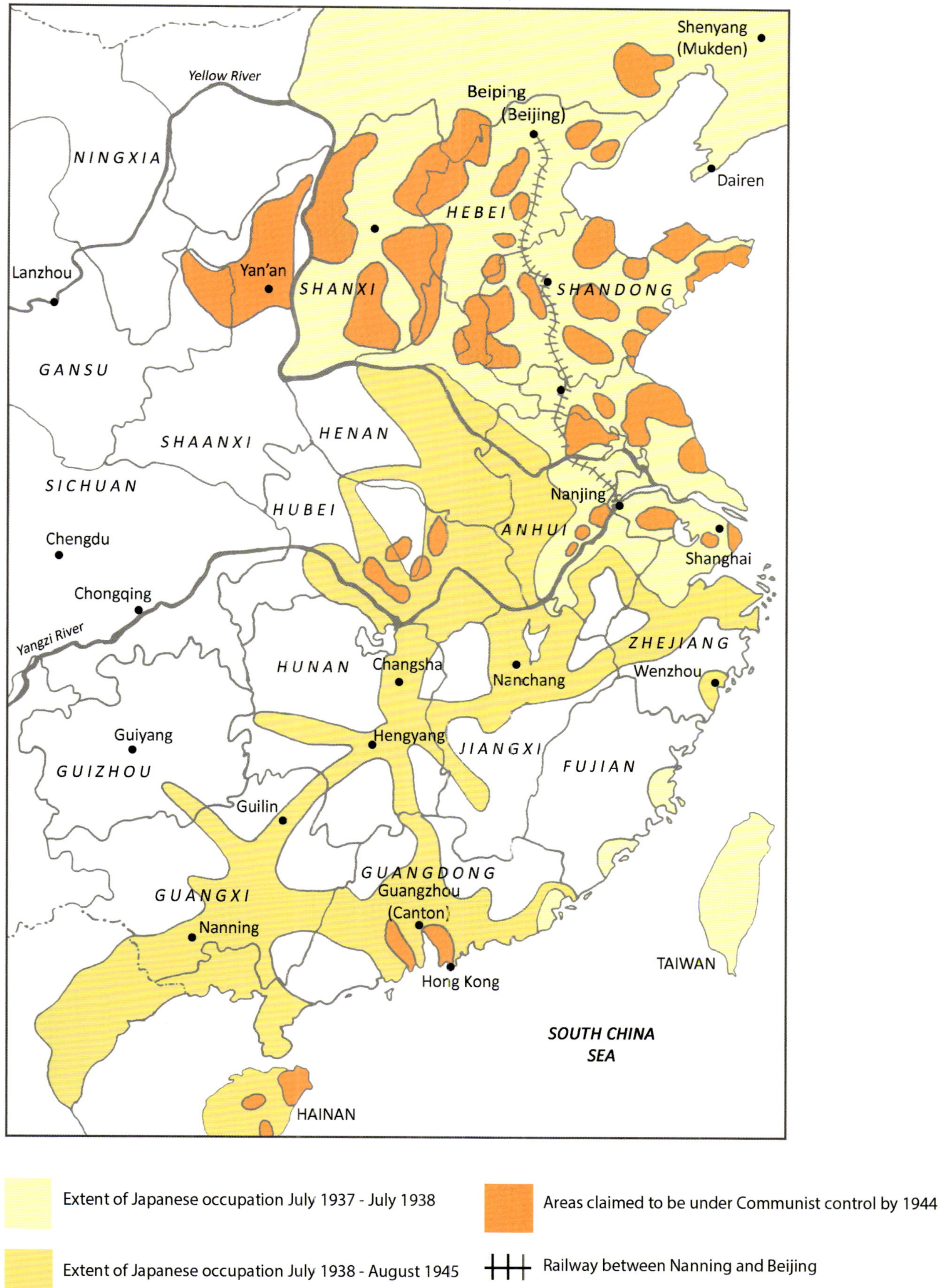
Shenyang
(Mukden)
Yellow River
Beiping
(Beijing)
Dairen
NINGXIA
HEBEI
Lanzhou
Yan'an
SHANXI
SHANDONG
GANSU
HENAN
SHAANXI
SICHUAN
Nanjing
HUBEI
ANHUI
Chengdu
Shanghai
Chongqing
Yangzi River
ZHEJIANG
HUNAN
Changsha
Nanchang
Wenzhou
Guiyang
Hengyang
JIANGXI
FUJIAN
GUIZHOU
Guilin
GUANGDONG
Guangzhou
(Canton)
GUANGXI
Nanning
Hong Kong
TAIWAN
SOUTH CHINA
SEA
HAINAN
Extent of Japanese occupation July 1937 - July 1938
Areas claimed to be under Communist control by 1944
Extent of Japanese occupation July 1938 - August 1945
Railway between Nanning and Beijing

Fig. 15
After the Drought (水旱灾之后), Yang Newei, 1943. Ink on paper, 13 × 12.3 cm.
British Museum 1980,0630,0.170.

Fig. 16
Relieve the wounded and sick soldiers (救救傷病兵), Liu Lun, 1942. Ink and light colour on paper, 25.8 × 16.4 cm.
British Museum 1980,0630,0.85.

Fig. 17 (opposite)
We Support the People's Militia (擁護咱們老百姓自己的軍隊), Gu Yuan, 1944. Reproduction of woodcut on paper, 17.8 × 12.8 cm.
British Museum 2009,3022.64.

in the GMD-controlled territory, others at Yan'an and the other base areas. Some artists, such as Qi Baishi (1864–1957), continued working in occupied cities. Most of the prints in the British Museum's Thompson Collection[45] are from 'Free China'. These celebrate patriotism and valour (cat. 16), but also record battlefield horrors and the massive social disruption of the war: streams of refugees from man-made and natural calamities, broken families and other human tragedies (figs 15 and 16).

Art in the Communist-controlled areas showed a different world of happy village life on the verge of a prosperous future, where the people and the army worked together, resisting the enemy (fig. 17).

Folk art was the prescribed style: bold, flat and brightly coloured. The red-coloured print, in the style of a papercut, is inscribed, 'Hygiene

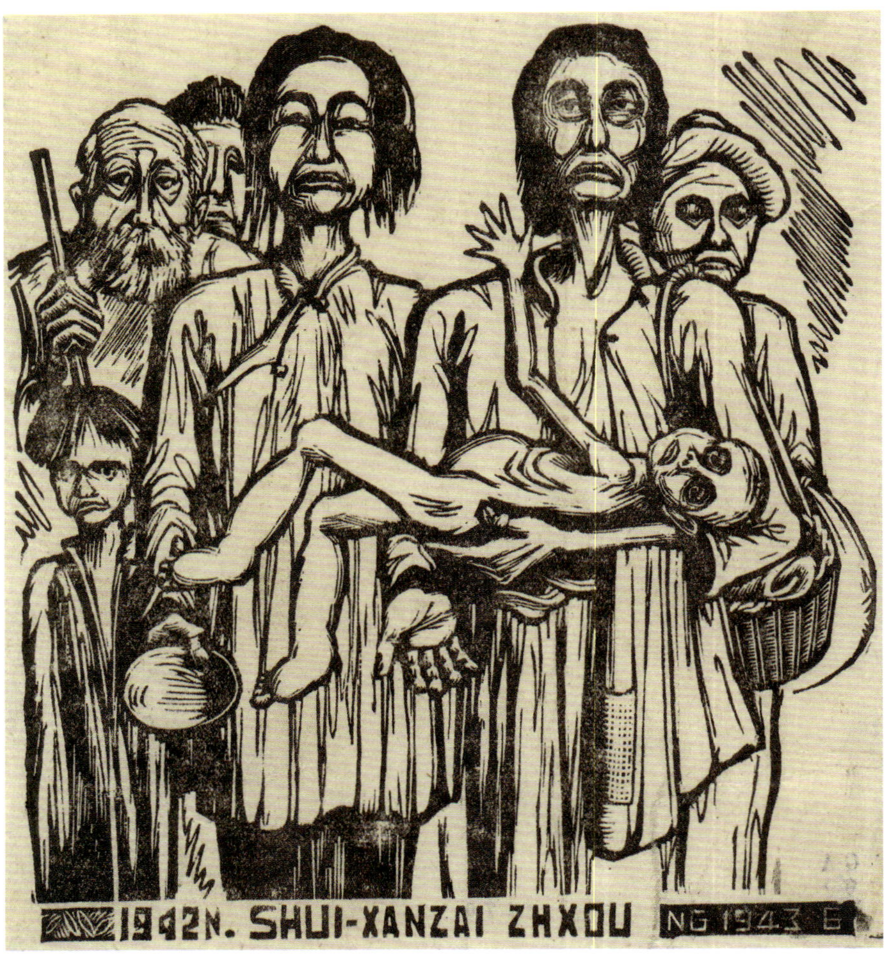

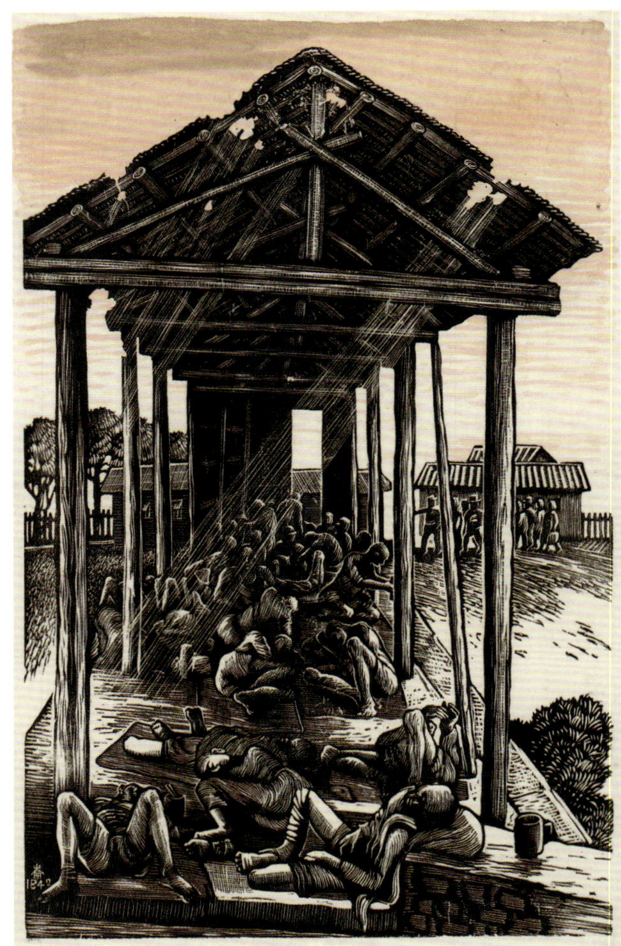

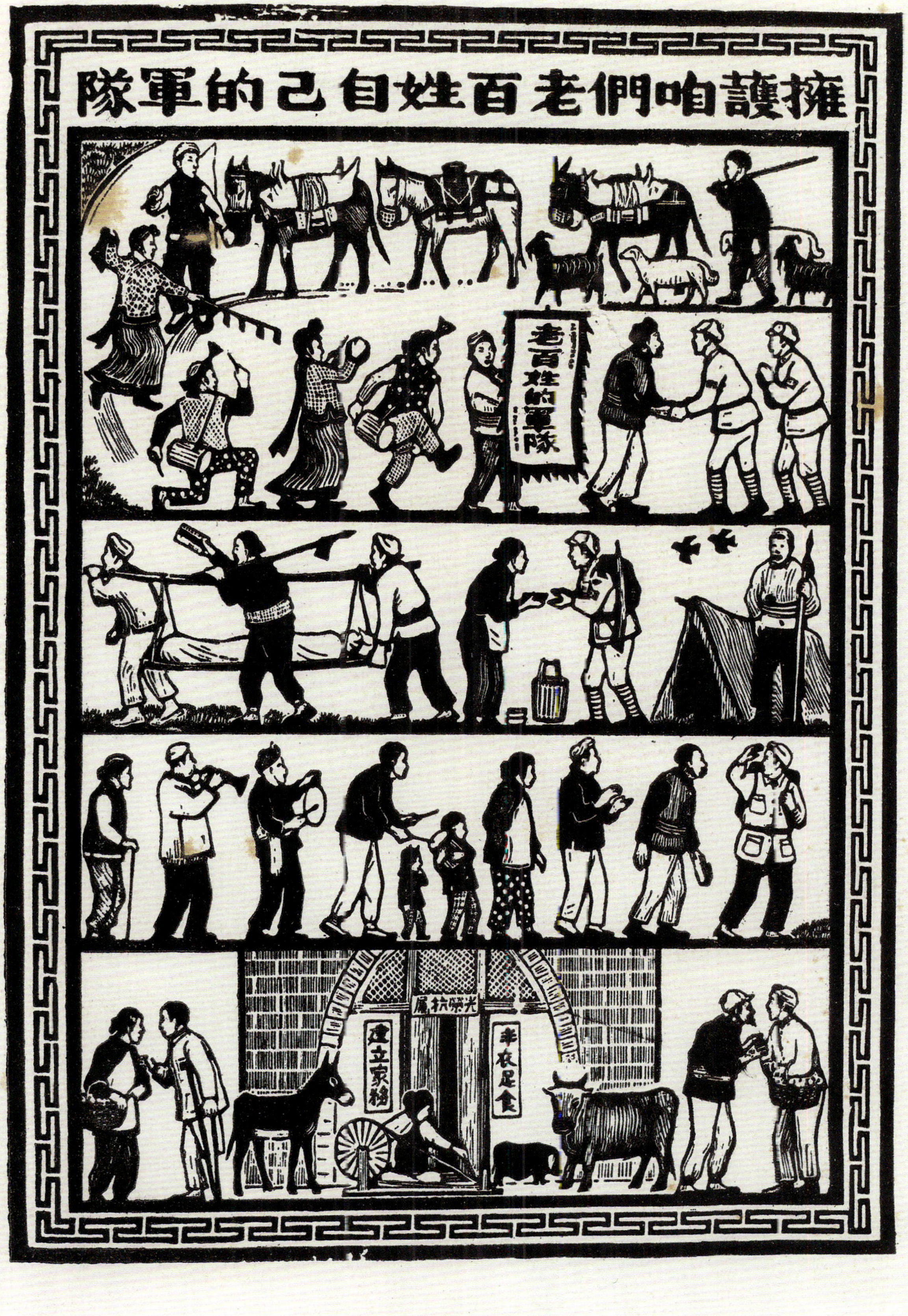
擁護咱們老百姓自己的軍隊
老百姓的軍隊
光榮抗屬
建立家務
豐衣足食

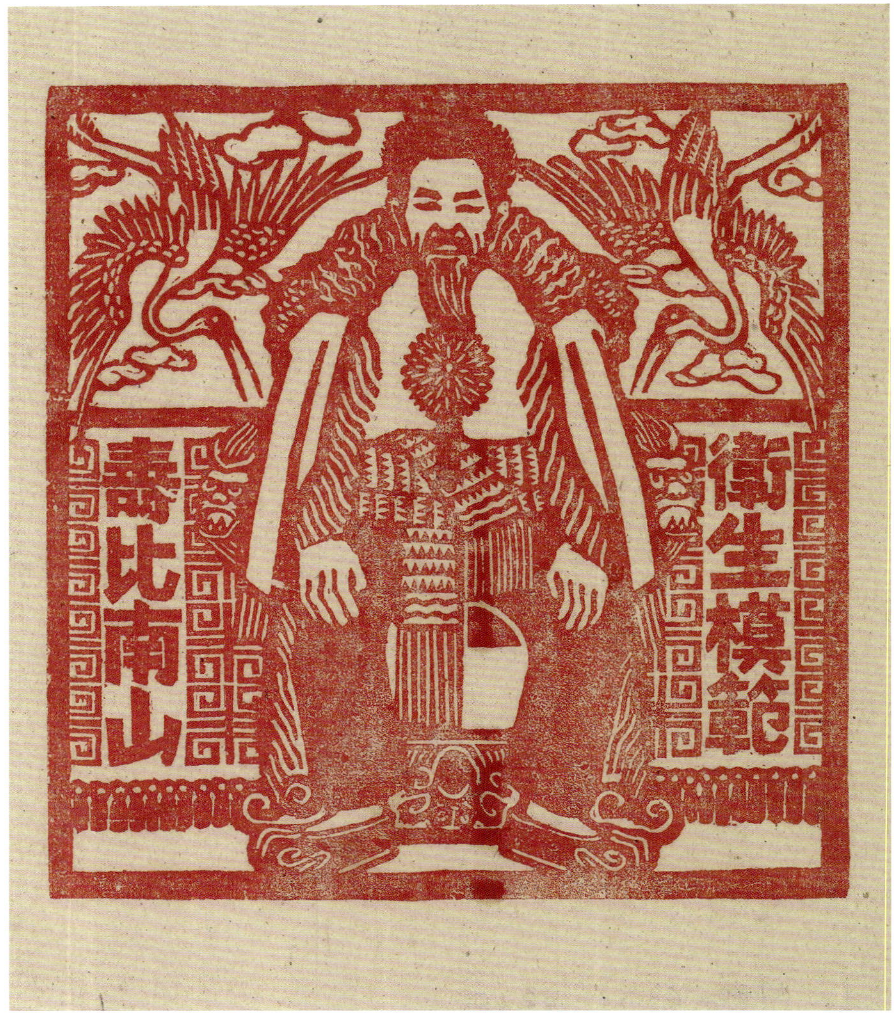

Fig. 18
New Window Decoration (新窗花),
Luo Gongliu, 1944. Woodblock print,
red ink on paper. 12.9 × 12.6 cm.
British Museum 1980,0630,0.215.

Fig. 19 (opposite)
The spring breeze lights up East Asia.
A bright bright sun shines in China.
Colour woodblock, 26.3 × 18.5 cm.
British Museum 2006,0117,0.51.

worker. Life as long as the Southern Mountain'. It uses traditional symbols such as the crane (signifying long life), while portraying a model figure whose modern hygiene practices should be emulated (fig. 18). The simple, colourful style employed by the artists in the base area was familiar and accessible to the population. The peasants' response to folk art was far more enthusiastic than to the black and white, European-inspired prints. Supply could not always keep up with the demand.[46]

The use of colourful popular prints (年畫 *nianhua*) by wartime Communist artists was inspired, at least in part, by the discovery in 1939 that Japanese artists were using the style effectively in their propaganda in the

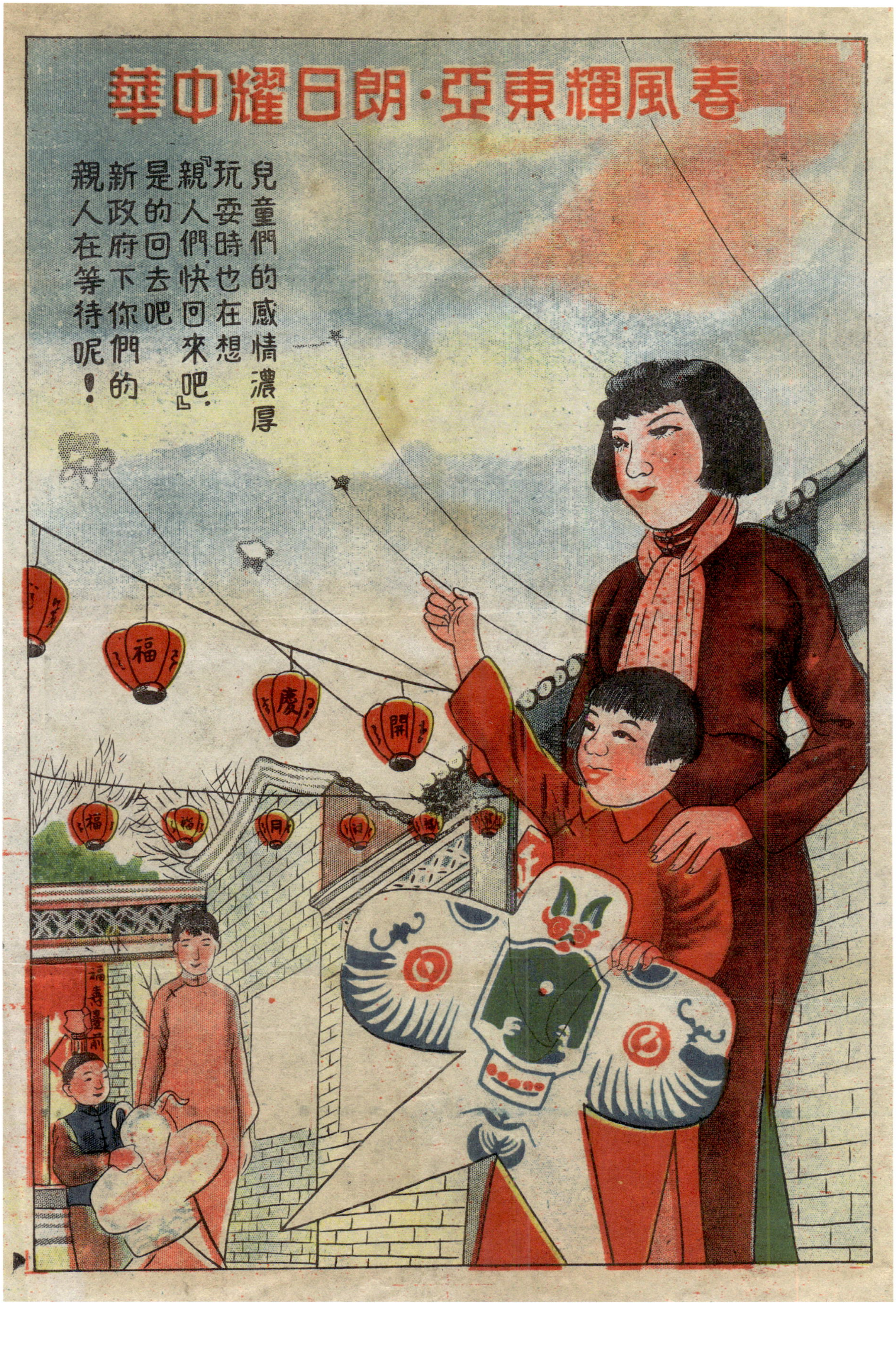
春風輝東亞·朗日耀中華
兒童們的感情濃厚
玩耍時也在想
『親人們快回來吧』
是的回去吧
新政府下你們的
親人在等待呢！
福
慶
開

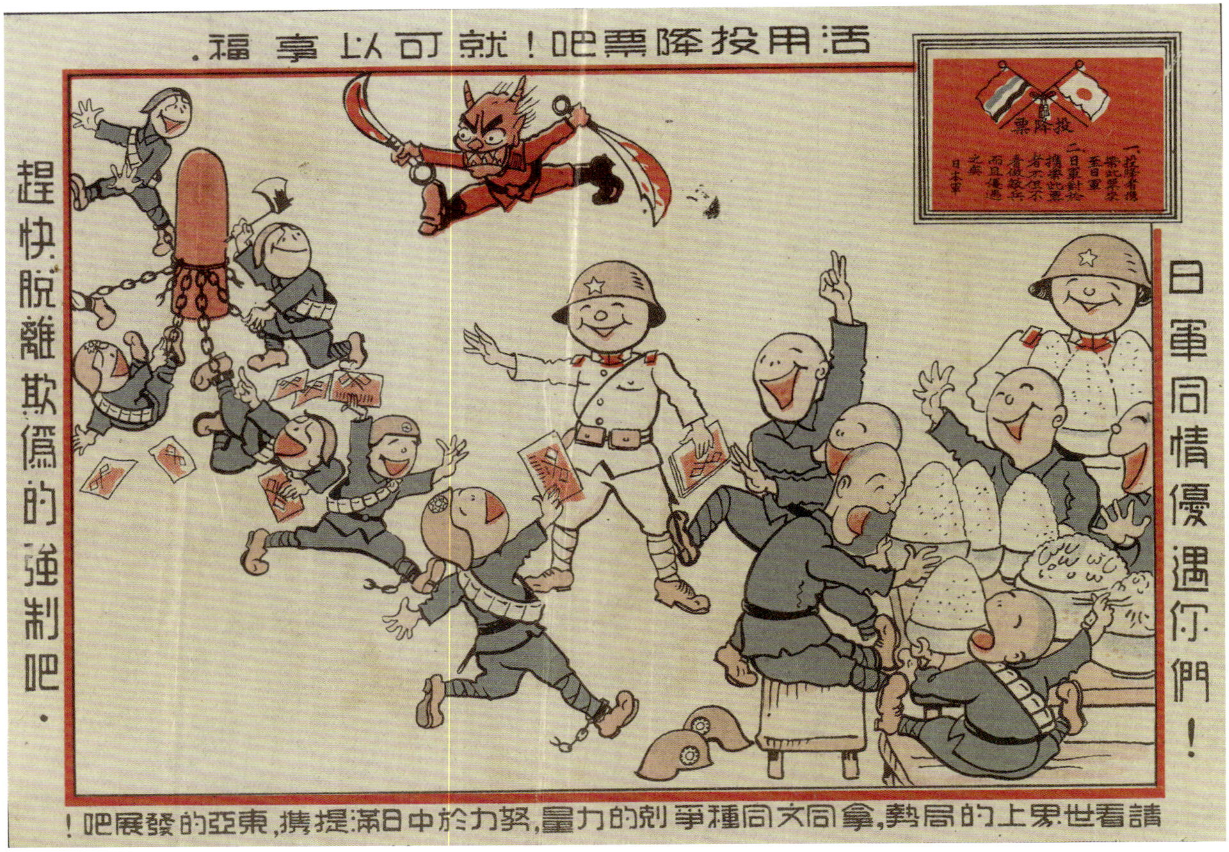

活用投降票吧！就可以享福.
趕快脫離欺僞的強制吧・
日軍同情優遇你們！
請看世界上的局勢,拿同文同種爭剋的力量,努力於中日滿提携,東亞的發展吧！

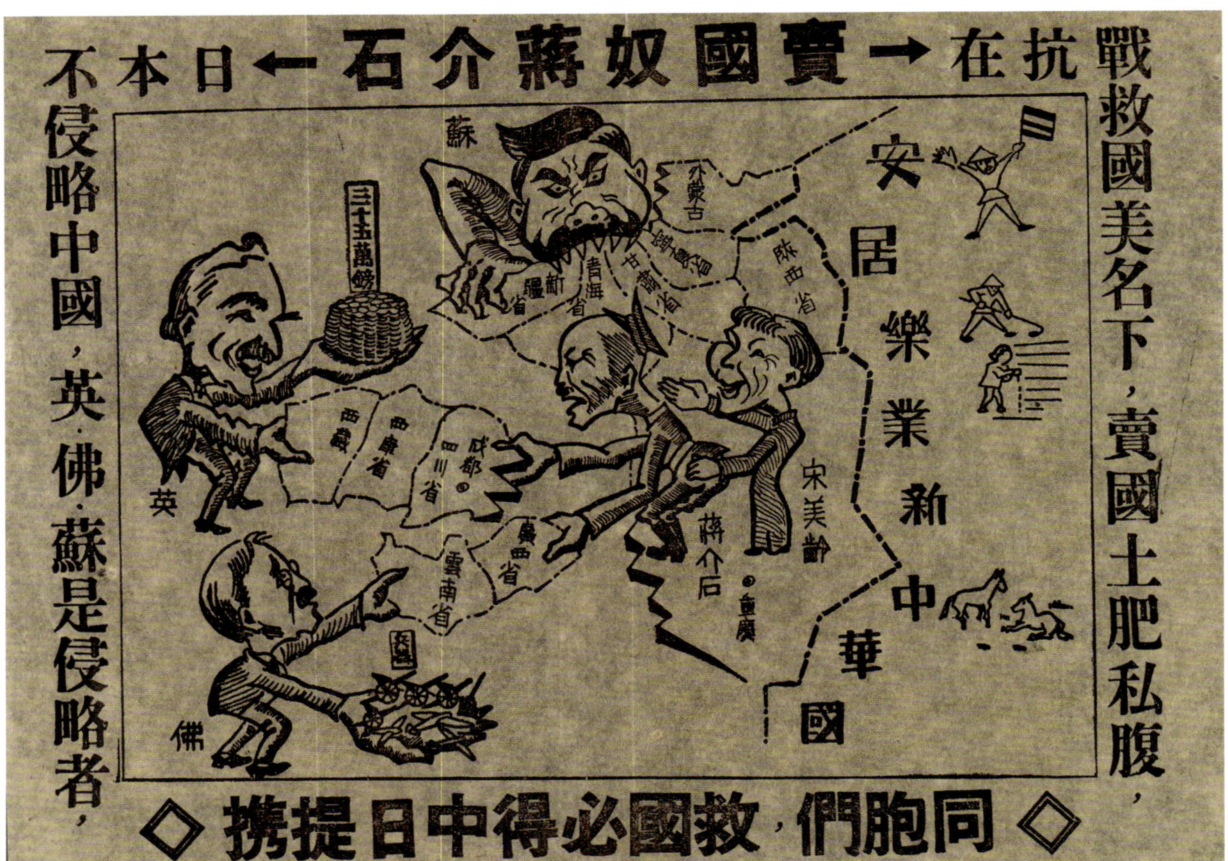

在抗戰救國美名下，賣國土肥私腹，
→賣國奴蔣介石←
日本不侵略中國，英·佛·蘇是侵略者，
◇同胞們，救國必得中日提携◇
蘇
英
佛
宋美齡
蔣介石
三十五萬鎊
安居樂業新中華國

Fig. 20
Propaganda leaflet. Ink and colours on paper, 13 × 19.5 cm.
British Museum 2006,0117,0.76.

Fig. 21
Propaganda leaflet. Ink on paper, 18.5 × 27 cm.
British Museum 2006,0117,0.05.

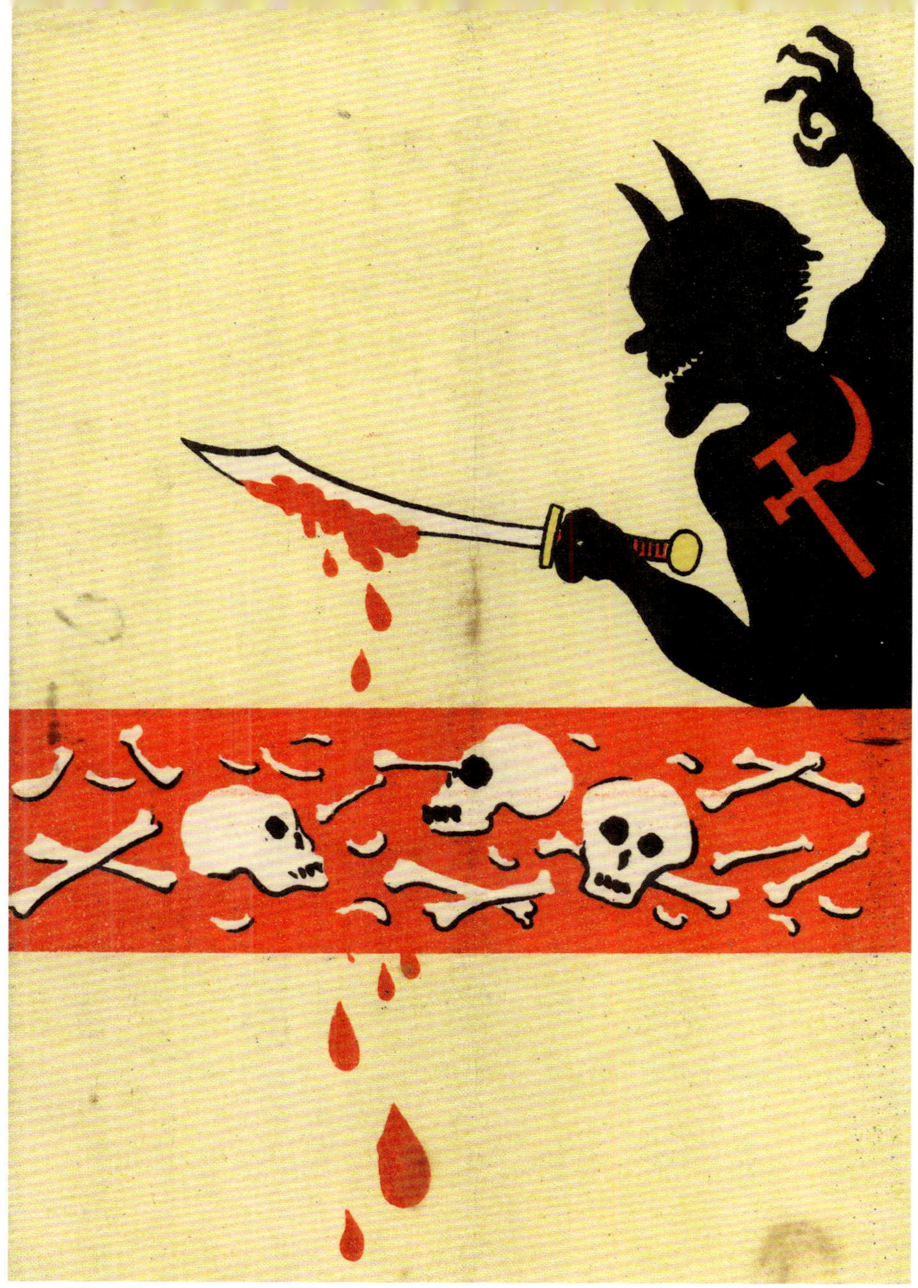

Fig. 22 (right)
Back cover of propaganda booklet, *True Stories about the Communist Bandits*. Ink and colours on paper, 19 × 13 cm.
British Museum 2006,0117,0.45.

occupied areas.[47] The Japanese propaganda war on the Chinese mainland engaged military and civilian agencies and followed several strands, positive and negative, in a wide range of styles and formats. Images created by Japanese and co-opted Chinese propaganda workers showed happy civilian life under the new regime (fig. 19). Soldiers were encouraged to change sides and become well-fed (fig. 20).

The Japanese propaganda attacked the Guomindang, claiming that Chiang Kai-shek was murdering his own people and selling China out to the Soviet Union, England and the United States (fig. 21).

The Communists were represented as equally bad or even worse than

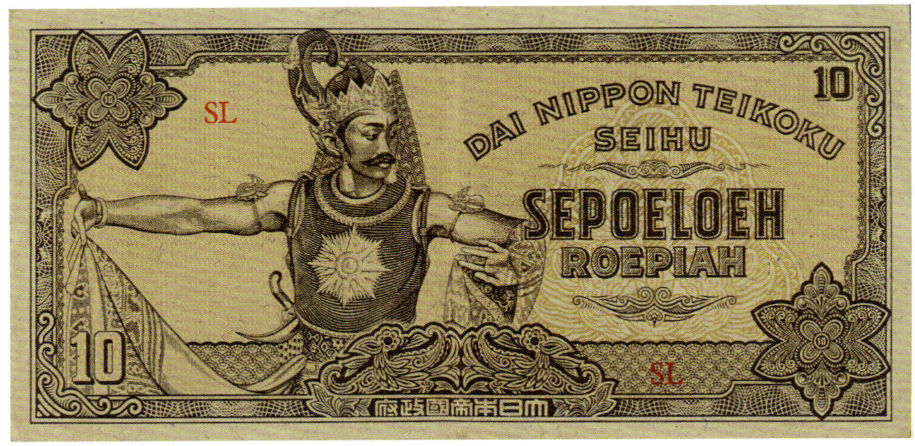

Fig. 23
Banknote, Japanese Imperial Government, 1942. Coloured inks on paper, 7.65 × 15.4 cm.
British Museum CIB,EA.215.

the Nationalists: powerful graphics and polemical texts warned against their treachery (fig. 22).

The Japanese authorities were systematic in evaluating the popular response to their own and the enemies' propaganda at home and abroad.[48] In China, they determined that Communist propaganda was more effective than that of the Nationalists and the Americans – both among the Chinese population and in turning Japanese soldiers to their cause.[49]

Propaganda campaigns were carried out in all countries where Japan sought to extend the Asian Co-Prosperity Sphere. These advance efforts were effective in some cases, where colonial populations hoped for liberation.[50]

Japan occupied the Dutch East Indies (Indonesia) from 1942 to 1945. They took over all areas of administration, including the post office and the mint (fig. 23).

Initially many Indonesians, including the nationalist Achmed Sukarno (1901–70), welcomed the Japanese, thinking their arrival would provide a route to independence. To this end, he served the occupying authorities as a propagandist and adviser.[51]

In some British colonies, too, many welcomed the Japanese in the hope of future independence. This was true in Malaya and much of Burma, but before long resistance movements arose.

In India the Congress Party leaders, Gandhi and Jawaharlal Nehru (1889–1964), linked military participation to future independence, but Churchill offered few concessions. In the end, two million Indians served

Fig. 24
Heroic Episodes from Japanese-Chinese War (支那事変武勇談). Picture book, published in Tokyo by Kōdansha, 1937. Colour lithograph on paper, 54.5 × 39.5 cm.
British Museum 2005,0610,0.1.

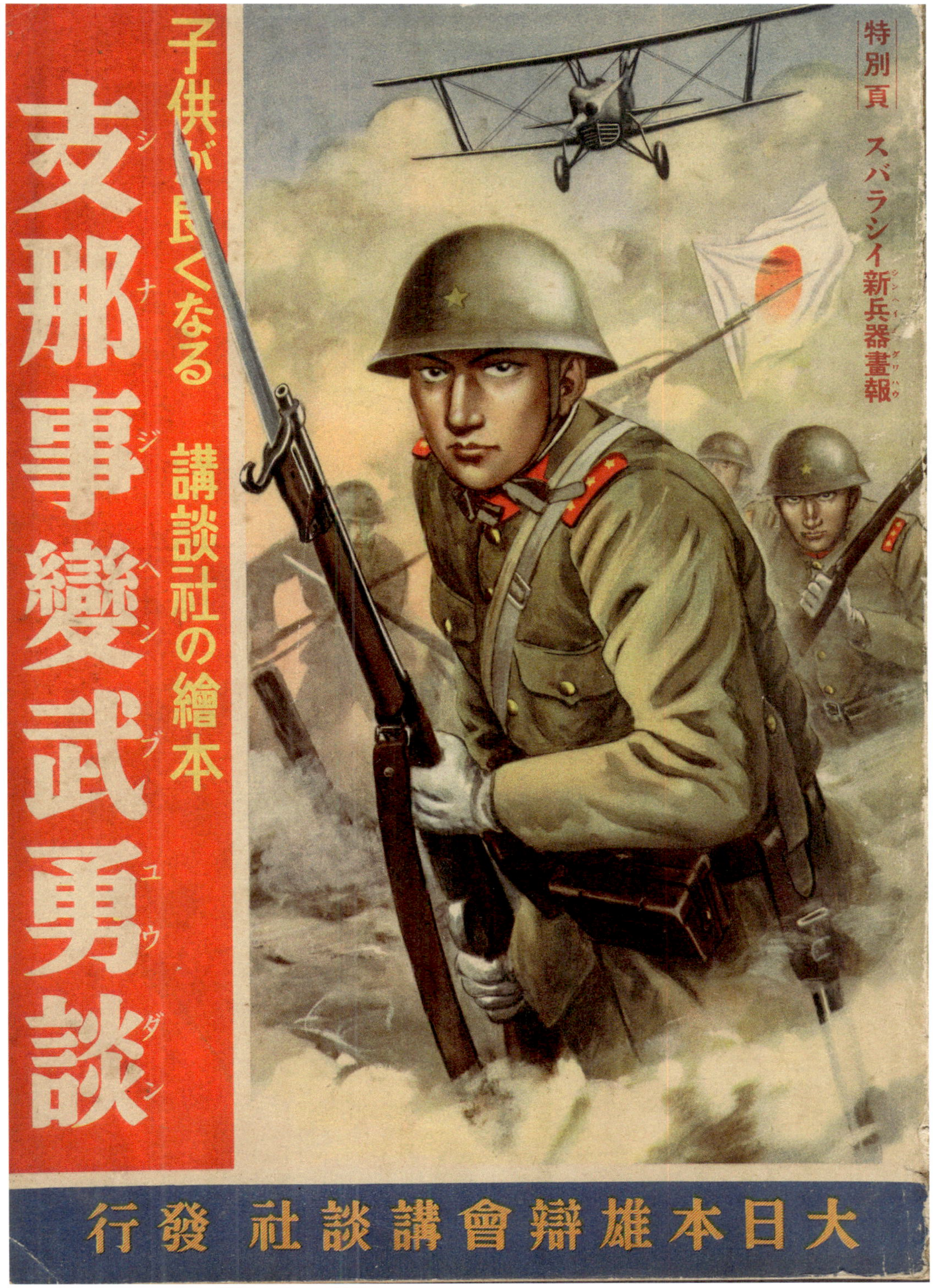

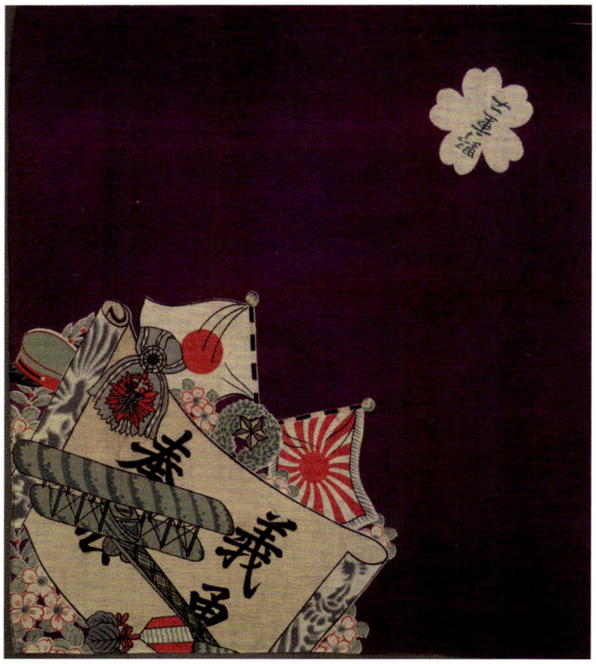

Fig. 25
Wrapping cloth, 1931–45.
Printed cotton, 72.5 x 67 cm.
Private collection.

Fig. 26 (opposite)
Subhas Chandra Bose.
Colour print, 45.5 × 32.8 cm.
British Museum 1990,0707,0.69.7.

the war effort. Gandhi's nationalist rival Subhas Chandra Bose (1897–1945?) sought backing for independence in Russia, Germany and Japan, raising an army to fight with Japan on Indian soil.[52] At a rally in 1944 he declared: 'Our victorious troops, fighting side by side with Nipponese [Japanese] troops, have pushed back the enemy and are now fighting bravely on the sacred soil of our dear motherland.' He concluded with his most famous words, 'Give me blood and I promise you freedom.'[53]

He is alleged to have died in a plane crash en route to Japan or the Soviet Union, but this is a subject of continuing controversy. Now exalted in India, Netaji ('Respected Leader') is the subject of popular prints, stories and films (fig. 26).

The propaganda effort within Japan had 'one major goal: unifying the battle front with the home front'.[54] The Japanese advance was publicized in both modern and traditional media. The British Museum has a number of rare wartime photo books and journals from Japan (cat. 21). Children's magazines celebrated heroes and encouraged frugality – as they did in Great Britain, Russia and elsewhere (fig. 24).

All commodities and practices of daily life were mobilized for the war. Military motifs and slogans decorated everyday goods, as on the wrapping textile in fig. 25, which says 'Patriotism'. [55]

Barak Kushner notes the extraordinary effectiveness of Japan's 'thought war'. It lasted more than fifteen years, had no central authority (as did, say, the Nazis) and experienced no major intellectual defections or popular revolts. 'The Japanese suffered privations, both personal and economic, yet during the fifteen-year battle for supremacy in Asia, the people of Japan remained committed to guarding and expanding its empire.'[56]

The aftermath of the war: defeat, reconstruction, civil wars and revolutions (1945–76)

On 6 August 1945 the United States dropped the world's first atomic bomb on the military and industrial port of Hiroshima. Three days later Nagasaki was the target of a second nuclear weapon. Finally the Showa emperor (r. 1926–89) agreed to surrender – announcing it himself on radio, in famously euphemistic language. Japan was defeated and exhausted. Nearly everyone was starving, millions were homeless, and about a quarter of the nation's wealth had been destroyed.[57]

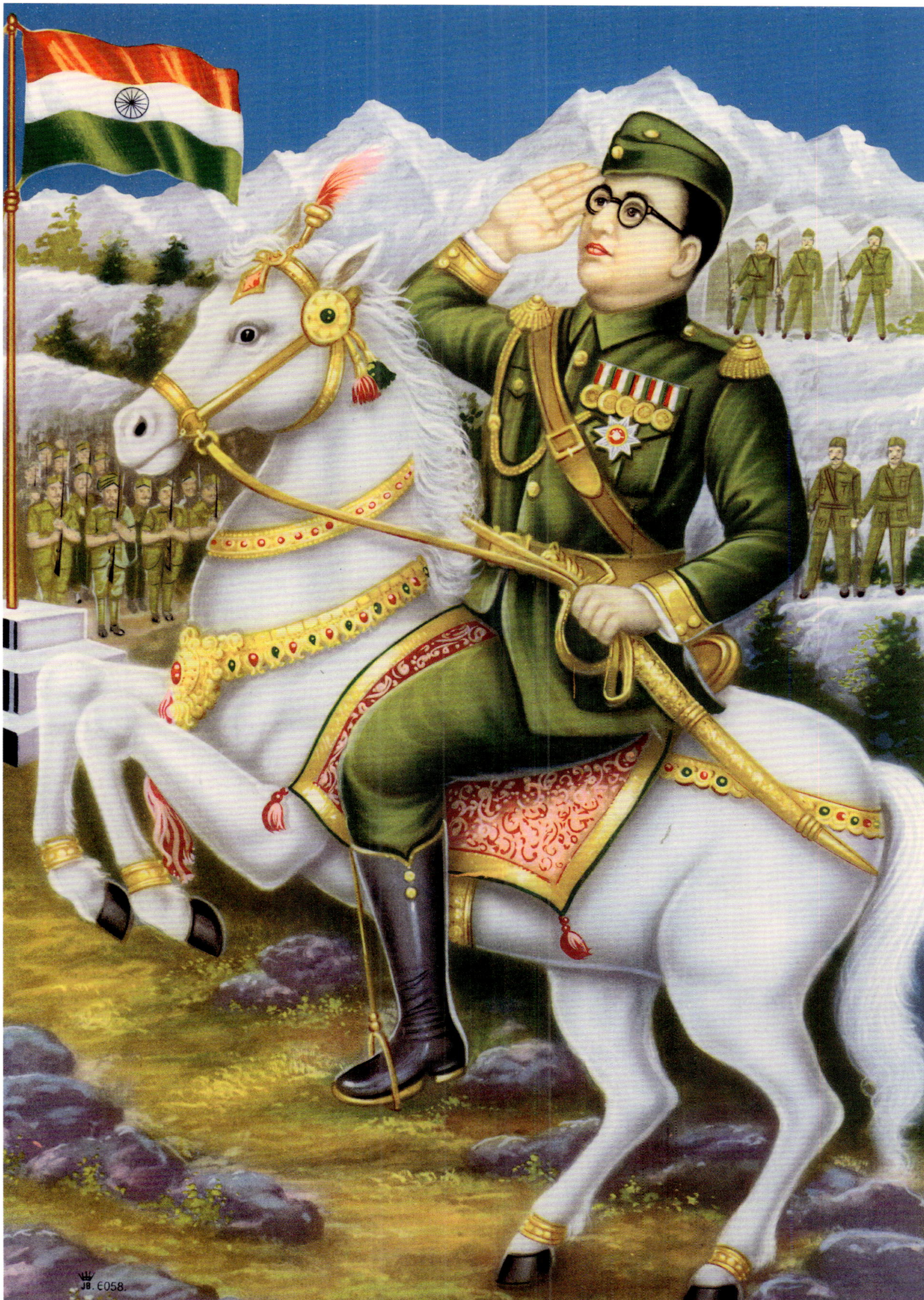
JB. E058.

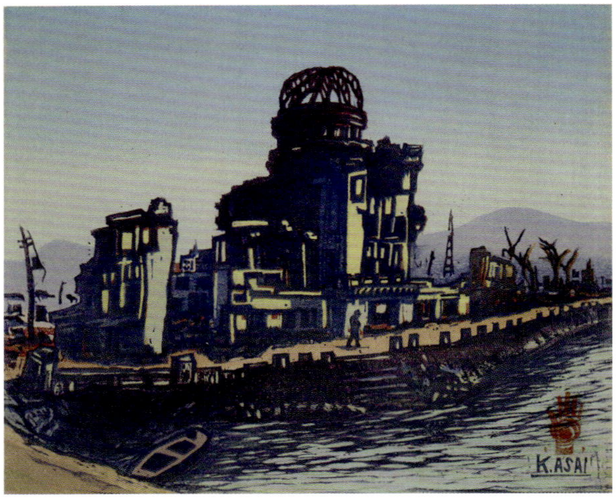

Fig. 27
Hiroshima, Asai Kiyoshi, 1950–9.
Colour woodblock print, 30 × 23.5 cm.
British Museum 1987,0316,0.9.

Fig. 28 (opposite)
Set of seven photographic postcards showing the post-war revival of Hiroshima, 1950s. Printed on paper, 9.1 × 14 cm each.
British Museum 2007,3018,3.1-7.

By the end of the year, 350,000 American troops occupied Japan under the leadership of Douglas MacArthur, whose mission was 'demilitarization and democratization'. The Supreme Command of Allied Powers (SCAP) dismantled Japan's army and reformed pre-war economic and political power structures. By around 1950, the economy was far more stable (thanks partly to the Korean War, as Japan proved vital for material supplies to South Korea).[58] As the US grew more alarmed about the spread of Communism in Asia, it firmed up its future alliance with Japan, providing for military bases in Okinawa and elsewhere.

The Occupation authorities had almost no Japanese speakers and were reliant on local administrators at all levels. Many of the wartime enemy propagandists were employed by SCAP. Propaganda was anti-military, pro-American and pro-democracy. This was an extraordinary reversal of message and was seemingly effected overnight. Kushner concluded: 'Accepting American culture became an element of postwar Japanese propaganda, . . . but the greater goal was still to rebuild Japan, using America was merely the method.'[59]

Through direct investment, priority production and expansion of international trade, economic reconstruction was attained. Cities which had been flattened, including Hiroshima and Nagasaki, were rebuilt (figs 27 and 28). By 1964, when Tokyo staged the first Asian Olympics (cat.31), the 'miracle' recovery had been achieved.

In much of Asia, the end of the Second World War brought no lasting peace. In China, the Nationalist-Communist civil war began almost immediately, putting the exhausted, devastated population through four more years of turmoil. As areas under their control expanded, the Communists implemented policies of land and wealth redistribution, new family laws and political reform (cat. 42). On 1 October 1949, Mao declared the establishment of the People's Republic.

The Socialist Realist poster commemorating that event was reproduced from a 1953 painting, which itself was based on photographs. The scene was repainted and mass-reproduced several times over the following thirty years, eliminating some figures, then putting them back in (fig. 29).[60]

The economy had been devastated by wartime destruction and inflation. The government immediately began a program of agricultural and industrial reconstruction. Isolated from the West, the only external support the People's Republic (PRC) could rely on was from the Soviet Union, which

原爆死歿者を祀る供養塔
毎年8月6日に追悼式が行われる
Monument Dedicated To The Atomic Victims
A memorial service is held on Aug. 6 every year. ↓

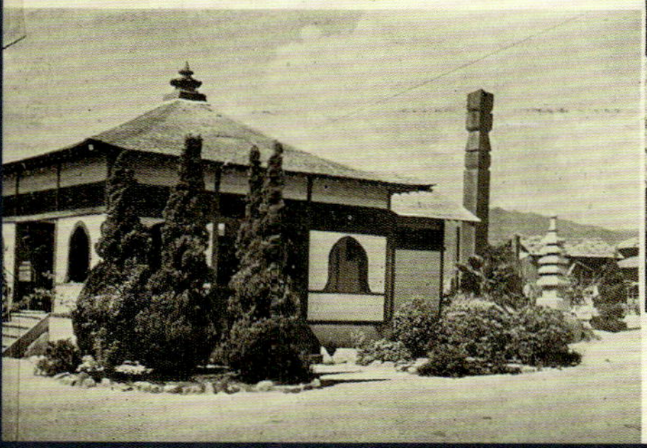

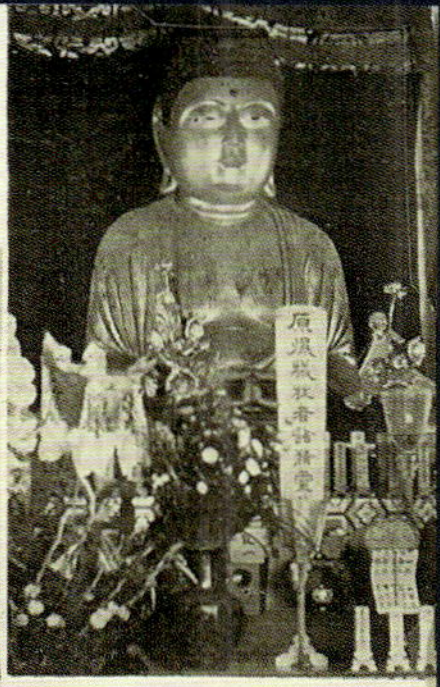

↑原爆犠牲者の供養　廣島大佛
A great image of Buddha dedicated to the dead.

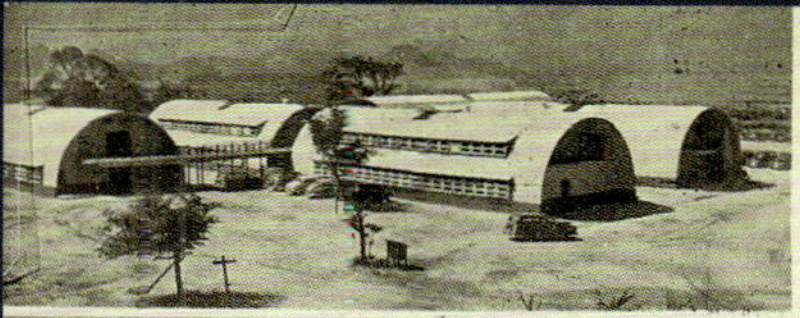

比治山より市街を望む
CITY SEEN FROM HIJIYAMA
右 展 望 台 RIGHT OBSERVATORY
左 百米道路 LEFT 100 METER WIDE HIGHWAY
原爆傷害調査委員會研究所 A B C C
(ATOMIC BOMB CASUALITY COMMISSION)

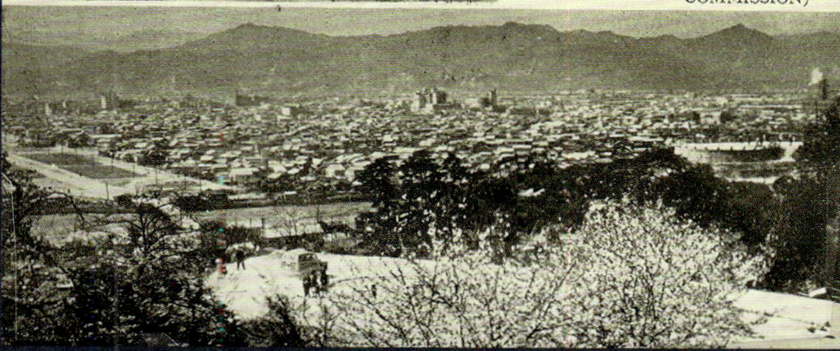

廣島駅夜景 →
Night Scene of HIROSHIMA STATION
復興する本通 (革屋町) ↓
KAWAYA-CHŌ. Main Street on the way of revival.

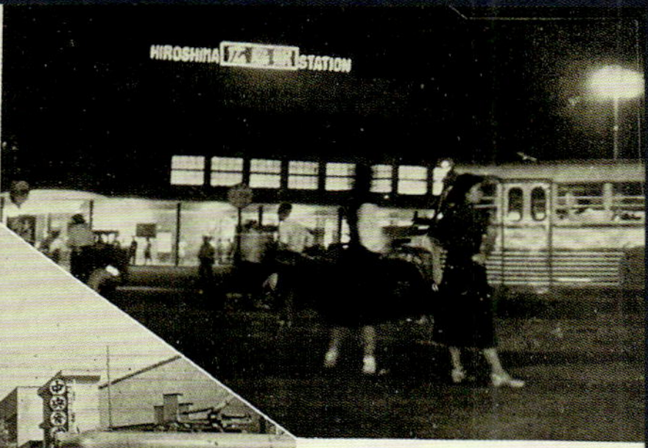

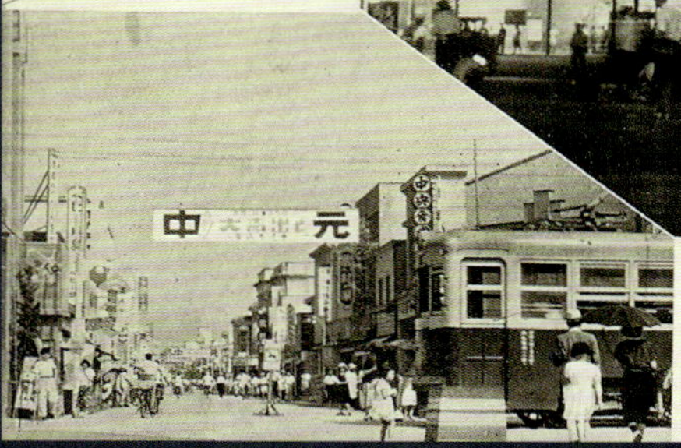

当時の惨状を知るものの誰か今日の復興廣島の姿を予想し得たであろうか.
Of those who witnessed the terrible scene of the atomic disaster, who could have expected HIROSHIMA thus far revived?

繁華街の復興
Busy Quarters Revived
金座街の夜景
↓ Night Scene of the KINZA St.

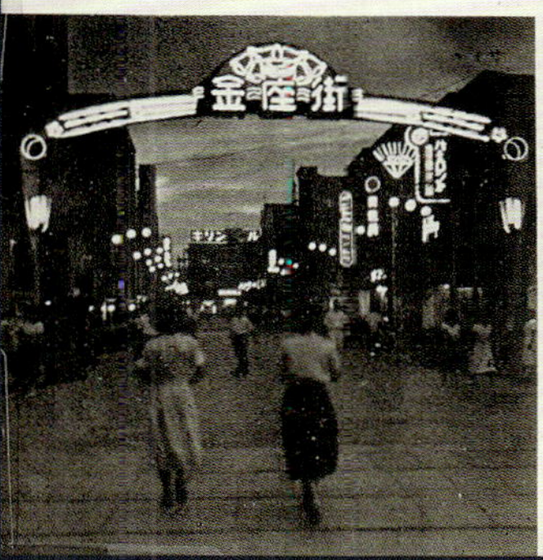

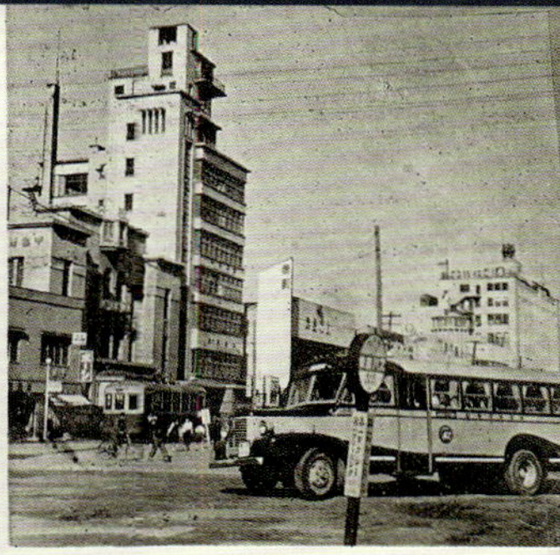

↑ 廣島市中心部　中國ビルと福屋デパート
Business Center of Hiroshima City.
CHUGOKU BUILDING and FUKUYA DEPARTMENT STORE

平和都市「廣島」相生橋 (T字形)
右の袂が記念公園　其の向が産業奨励館
Peace City, HIROSHIMA. AIOI-BASHI BRIDGE, T-shaped.
Peace Memorial Park and the Industrial Exhibition Hall.

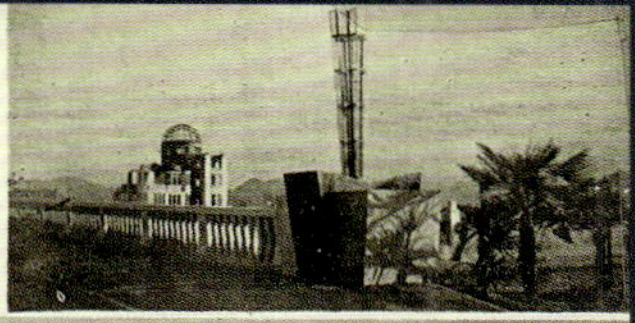

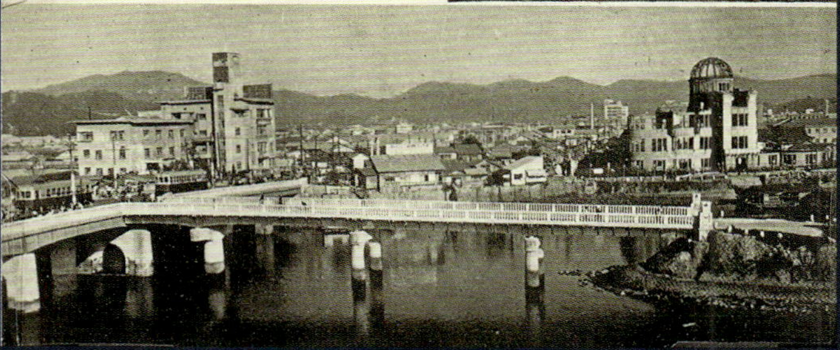

廣島は川の名所イサム野口の平和大橋 ↓
HIROSHIMA, City of Rivers.
Grand Bridge of Peace. Western Grand Bridge of Peace.
Designed by ISAMU NOGUCHI——

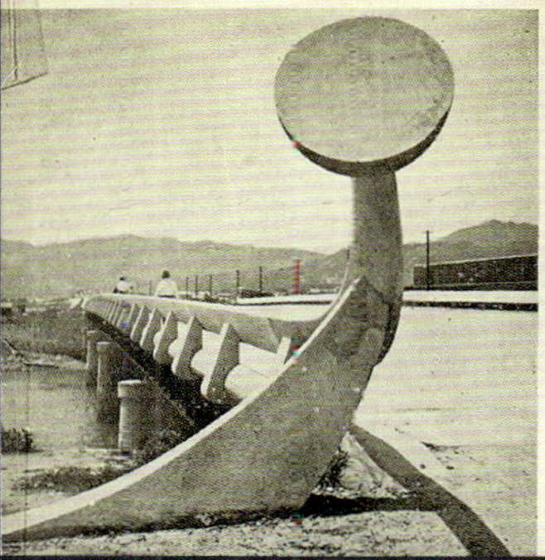

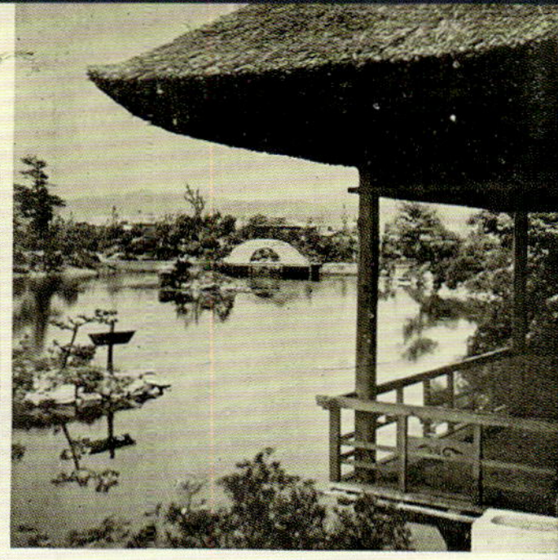

↑ 浅野侯が支那の西湖を模した泉邸 (縮景園)
SENTEI, or SHUKKEI-EN, Garden of Asano, a famous Daimyo.
Miniature of Seiko, China.

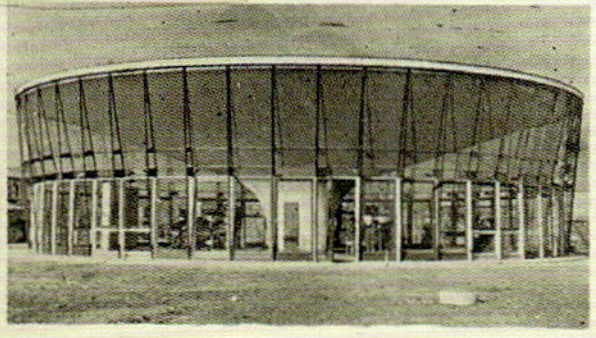

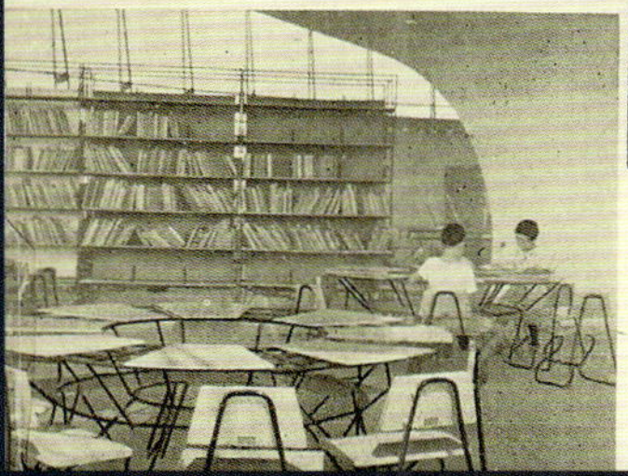

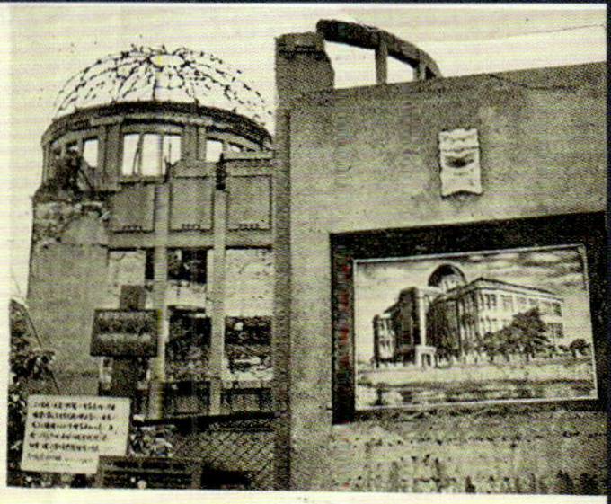

産業奨励館　復興廣島に残る原爆の面影
The INDUSTRIAL EXHIBITION HALL
——The Remnant of the Atomic Explosion in Hiroshima

CHILDREN'S HOME　CHILDREN'S LIBRARY
子 供 の 家 (廣島児童図書館)
上 全 景　WHOLE VIEW
下 内 部　INTERIOR

Fig. 29
Founding the Nation (開國大典), 1990. Reprinted poster from a painting by Dong Xiwen, 1953, subsequently repainted several times. 63 × 106 cm.
British Museum 1992,0416,0.4.3.

contributed advisers, money and modern technology. Mao and Stalin were never happy allies, but by 1950 the world was firmly divided into two camps, and China stood as a loyal partner in the struggle to build world Communism. Sino-Soviet friendship was celebrated in every propaganda format, including magazines for five-year-olds (fig. 30).

Unlike the Soviet Union immediately after the Russian Revolution, the Chinese Communist Party (CCP) had a prepared programme for cultural work.[61] If it was art, it was propaganda. Since 1942, cultural cadres had followed the policies laid out by Chairman Mao Zedong at the Yan'an

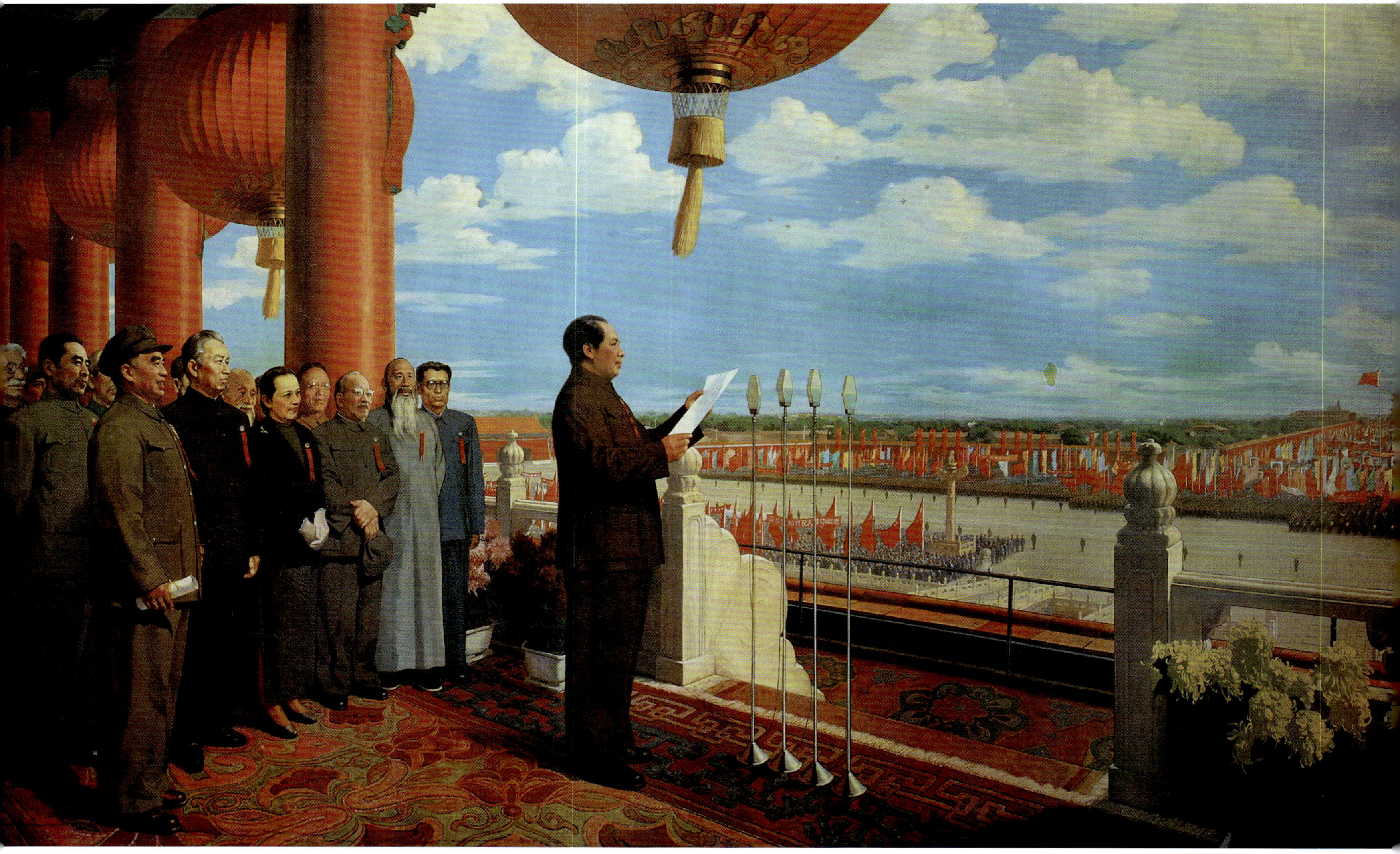

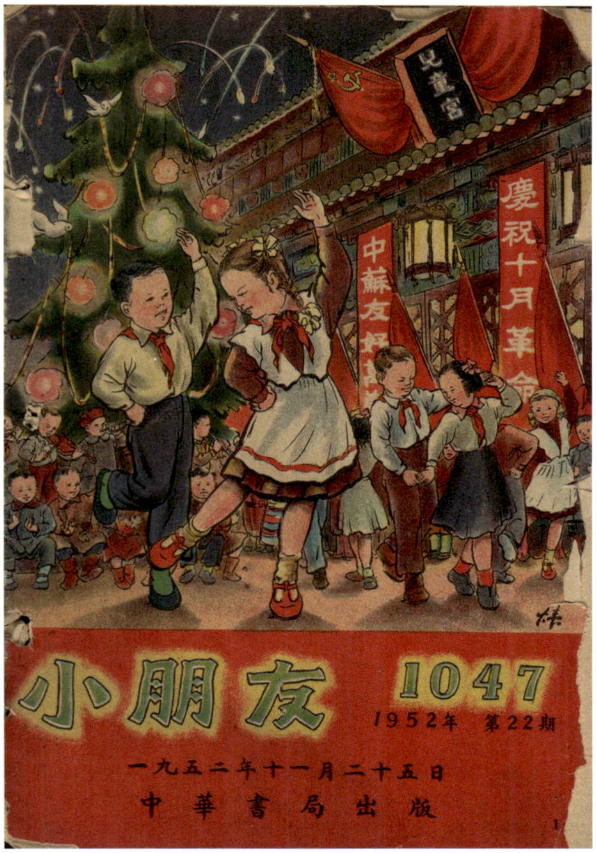

Fig. 30
Xiao Pengyou (小朋友 *Little Friends*), November 1952. The banners say: 'Long live Sino-Soviet friendship' and 'Celebrate the October Revolution'.
Private collection.

Conference on Literature and Art.[62] The same principles were enforced, more or less strictly, until 1976. Organizational channels included reform of the cultural administration, art education institutions, publications and exhibitions.[63] The two strands of propaganda output were folk art (cat. 62) and Socialist Realism (cat. 36).

The first several decades of the PRC were marked by a series of specific propaganda campaigns. In 1950, though still exhausted by its own wars, China mobilized to 'Resist America, Support Korea'. Campaigns for the new marriage and family law (cat. 42) and collectivization followed. By 1956, the economy was stabilized, and propaganda was less intense. During a brief period of liberalization, '100 Flowers' bloomed, but this was followed by the Anti-Rightist Movement in 1957–. The disastrous Great Leap Forward (1958–61) was celebrated at the time in both professionally produced and newly promoted amateur art, much of it related to imaginary abundance (fig. 31).[64] From this time on, posters were the primary format of visual propaganda (cat. 37).[65] In the early 1960s, economic development took priority over politics, but that policy was reversed during the Great Proletarian Cultural Revolution (1966–76). Supported by the People's Liberation Army, Chairman Mao launched this movement to reverse bureaucratization in the CCP and revive the spirit of revolution – and, in fact, to consolidate his power within the CCP.[66]

That tumultuous time was powered by staggering campaigns of visual and performance propaganda, unprecedented even for China. The 'Four Olds'[67] were condemned. The required style was 'red, bright, light' in all media. Its chief message was the glorification of Mao Zedong, in opera and spectacle, poster and painting, badge (cat. 50) and snack wrapper.

Mao, the Great Helmsman, died in 1976. The Gang of Four, perpetrators of the Cultural Revolution's cultural extremes, were quickly imprisoned. China reversed course, pursuing rapid economic development. New propaganda imagery promoted technological progress, while celebrating the glories of the nation's history.

After the Japanese departure in 1945, Korea was divided by the Allies at the 38th parallel (without consulting the Koreans, who felt that after decades of foreign occupation, they should be in charge of their own nation). A right-wing regime was elected in the Republic of Korea (ROK) and was supported by the United States. The Communist northern half (the Democratic People's Republic of Korea, or DPRK), sustained by the

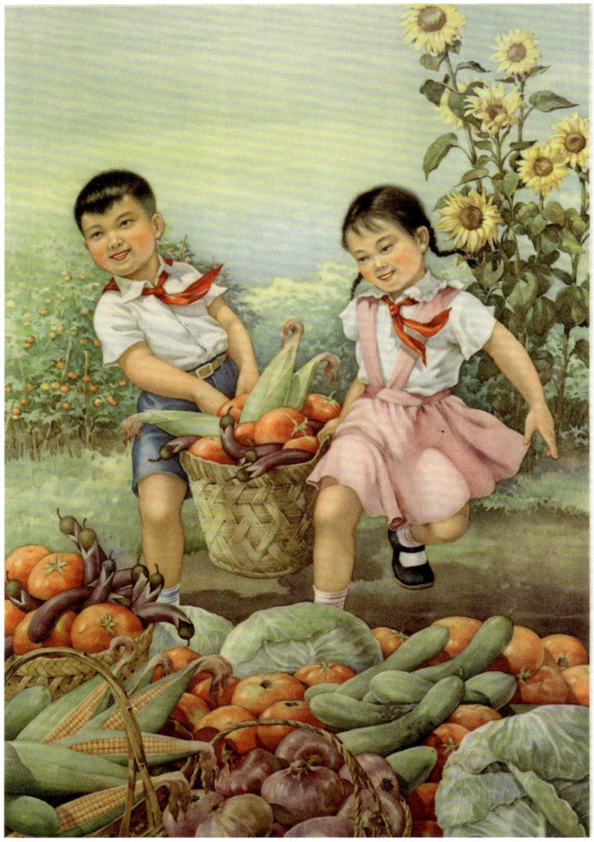

Fig. 31
Schoolchildren Plant a Vegetable Garden (小学生种菜园), Wu Zhefu, 1962.
76.5 × 53 cm.
British Museum 2006,0501,0.14.

Soviet Union and China, was led by Kim Il-sung (1912–94). The North attacked in July 1950, briefly capturing Seoul, South Korea's capital (fig. 32). A United Nations force was mobilized, composed mostly of Americans. The Soviet Union did not send troops, but supplied North Korea with money and materiel. China sent a 'volunteer' force, repaying North Korea's help to the Communist side during the recent Chinese civil war.

The propaganda output was extraordinary. United States PSYOP (psychological operations) units in Japan and Korea produced and disseminated many thousands of different leaflets. At the peak of the conflict, UN forces were dropping twenty million leaflets a week from aircraft (cat. 23).[68] The leaflet in fig. 33 (numbered 1031) offers 'a symbol of hope for a unified Korea'. The text on the reverse promises North Koreans imminent liberation, elections and economic revival.

In fact, combat continued until 1953, while endless negotiations failed to achieve a resolution. An armistice was finally signed, but no treaty has formally ended hostilities. Reunification remains a distant goal.

The close of the Second World War signalled the end of European colonialism in Asia, although it took years to resolve the liberation campaigns in many countries. The Dutch sought to retake the East Indies, but Indonesia finally gained independence in 1949, with Sukarno (former collaborator and freedom fighter) proclaimed as its first president.

The British returned to Malaya and in 1946 established the Malayan Union, unifying the administration of the various pre-war federated and Straits territories.[69] They found that anti-British feeling had been fuelled by the Japanese occupiers under the slogan 'Asia for the Asians'. The social and political situation was further complicated by the varied ethnic population.[70]

The post-war insurgency movement was organized by the Malayan Communist Party (MCP) and its military arm, the Malayan National Liberation Army (MNLA). The MCP, whose members were nearly all Chinese and whose strength had been in the urban trade unions, turned its campaign to rural armed revolution. The Malayan Emergency lasted twelve years (1948–60), but the tide had turned by 1952, and the Communist Terrorists (CTs), as the British called them, were defeated by 1954 (cat. 24). The Federation of Malaya achieved independence in 1957.

The provinces of British India gained independence in 1947. The Hindu-majority Union of India and Muslim Dominion of Pakistan were

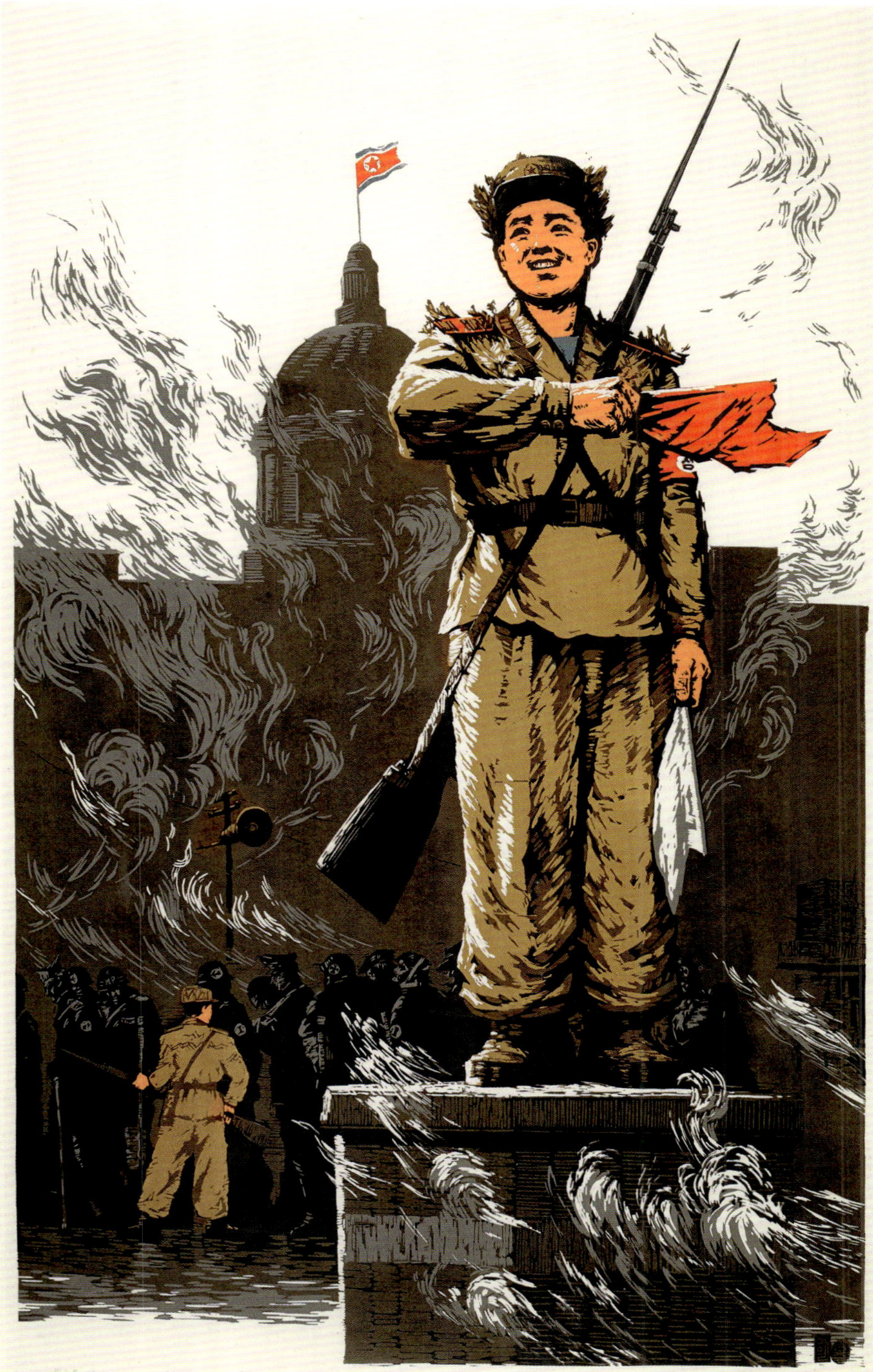

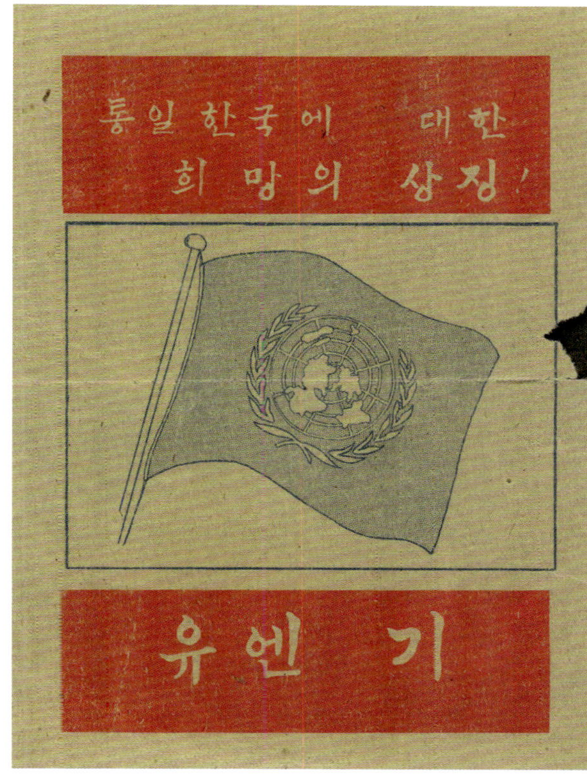

Fig. 32
On the Road to Victory, Park Yong'il, 1998.
Linocut print on paper, 96 x 61 cm.
British Museum 2006,0501,0.14.

Fig. 33
PSYOP leaflet 1031, 1950–3. Ink and colours on paper, 12.5 x 8.75 cm.
Private collection.

partitioned along the Radcliffe Line. Millions of refugees crossed sides in the violence that ensued. Both countries lost their founding leaders the following year: Gandhi was assassinated by a Hindu nationalist, and Muhammad Ali Jinnah (1876–1948), the 'father of Pakistan', died from illness.

Pakistan comprised two regions, East and West, separated by about 1,500 kilometres (900 miles). In 1971, East Pakistan declared independence and, following a nine-month war supported by India, became the nation of Bangladesh, led by freedom fighter Sheikh Mujibur Rahman (1920–75). 'Mujib' was assassinated only a few years later in a military coup. He is shown with Indira Gandhi (1917–84) in fig. 34 on one panel of a vibrantly painted rickshaw.

Wartime Indochina had been occupied by the Japanese, but administered by Vichy France. Immediately after the Japanese departed, Ho Chi Minh declared independence for Vietnam. The French fought to re-establish colonial rule, and the First Indochina War lasted until the Viet Minh's surprising victory at Dien Bien Phu in 1954.[71] A peace negotiated in Geneva split the country into two nations: the Communist Democratic Republic of Vietnam (DRV) in the north, and the non-Communist Republic of Vietnam (RV) in the south.

It was an uneasy peace. The Soviet Union and China shored up the North, providing advisers and material aid. The United States, wary of spreading Communism in Asia, had sustained the French in the early 1950s, then supported the Republic, though not directly engaging in military combat until 1965.[72] Anti-American propaganda was produced in the North at least a decade before then (fig. 35).

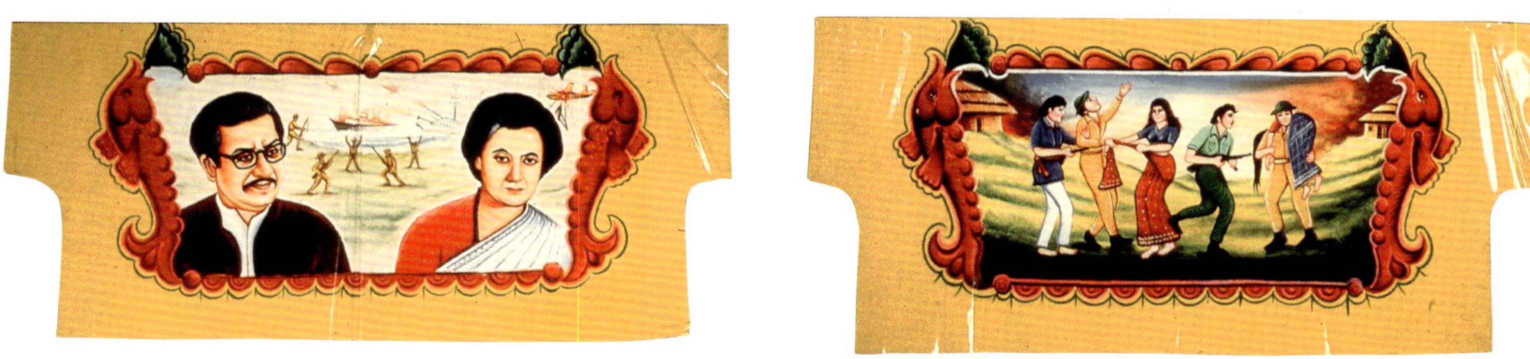

Fig. 34
Rickshaw panel, late 20th century.
Oil paint on plastic, 86 × 41.5 cm.
British Museum 1987.16.76.

Fig. 35
Bullying; Stay Vigilant, Pham Thanh Tam, 1955. Colour poster, 57.5 × 48.5 cm.
Private collection.

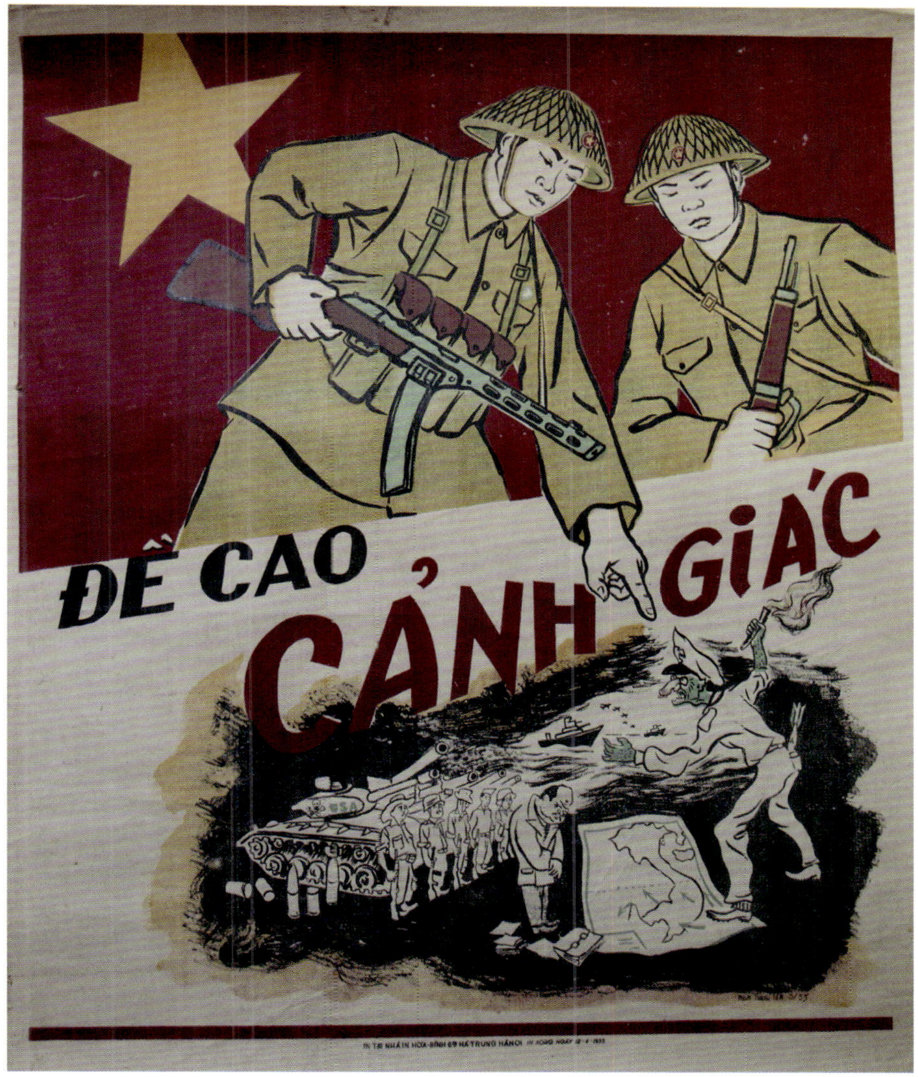

The Viet Minh had a corps of veteran artists from the First Indochina War. The Communist leadership insisted that art was to serve the masses. In 1950 Socialist Realism had become the preferred style, though propaganda still used folk art in posters and traditional woodblock prints (cat. 25). During the American-Vietnam War (1965–73), artists travelled to battlefields and bases, recording the liberation struggle and producing propaganda to boost soldiers' morale (fig. 36).

American involvement continually increased and, by 1968, more than

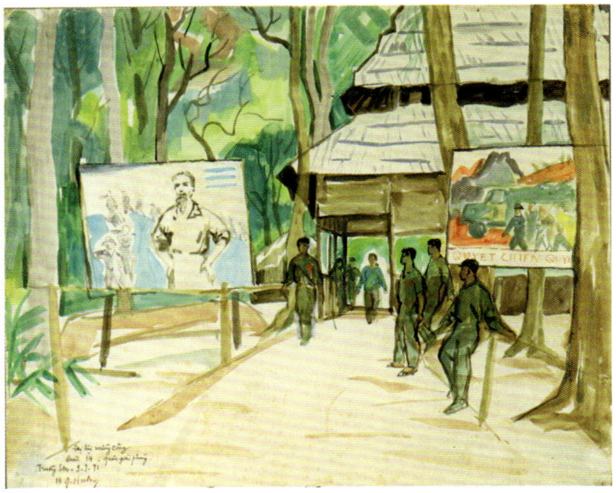

Fig. 36
Political posters on display at an army camp, Vu Giang Huong, July 1971. Watercolour and gouache on paper, 45 × 35.5 cm. A copy of the poster of Ho Chi Minh visible in this painting is in the British Museum (cat. 53).
British Museum 2001,1015,0.9.

half a million American soldiers were in Vietnam. During the Tet Offensive that year, the North Vietnamese attacked urban and military posts all over the South. It was the turning point in the war: the Viet Minh realized they could win, although the American establishment still refused to believe that they could lose.

Although peace negotiations began in 1968, the last Americans did not leave Vietnam until 1975. The North Vietnamese Army and Viet Cong launched a final major offensive, and the South capitulated with little resistance. Saigon fell in April 1975, and the unified Socialist Republic of Vietnam was formally established on 2 July 1976.

For war and revolution, 1968 was a year like no other. While the main sparks were the universally hated war in Vietnam and American global intervention, the issues differed from place to place: the one common thread was the determination to rebel. Popular uprisings of students and workers erupted in the US, Czechoslovakia, Poland, France, West Germany, Italy, Mexico and Japan. Inflammatory imagery was broadcast nightly from around the world, fuelling protest movements everywhere. Was that news or propaganda?

1 Mayo 2001, p. 1.
2 See Jowett and O'Donnell 1999, ch. 2, for a brief history of 'Propaganda through the ages'.
3 Hung 2011, p. 199.
4 At the Yan'an Conference in 1942, Mao Zedong referred to a target audience as the 'receptive object' (接收對象 *jieshou duixiang*). Holm 1984, p. 5.
5 Clark 1997, p. 7.
6 Goebbels 2009, pp. 10, 79, 106–14. Goebbels wrote, 'Only when enemy foreign propaganda had won over the greater part of the neutral states did the German government begin to sense the enormous power of propaganda . . . We lost the war in this area more than any other.' Goebbels 2009, p. 8.
7 Jowett and O'Donnell 1999, p. 6 (their italics).
8 Quoted in Kushner 2006, p. 4.
9 Literally translated as New Year prints, *nianhua* (年畫) is the general term for single-sheet popular prints.
10 Laing 2002, pp. 46–7.
11 Philippe 1982, p. 198.
12 Analysts now grade propaganda from white to grey to black, depending on the degree of truth and transparency of source. Jowett and O'Donnell 1999, pp. 11–18.
13 King 2009, p. 197.
14 Flath 2004, pl. 37. Nearly every home had a print of the Kitchen God. New Year rituals included burning the print and replacing it. This signified sending the Kitchen God up to the Jade Emperor, to whom he would make a report about the family's activities that year.
15 Tony Bennett argues that popular culture forms either support the dominant culture or register opposition to it (Bennett *et al.* 1986, p. xxi).
16 Pinney 2004, p. 117.
17 Edward R. Murrow (1908–65), American journalist, CBS broadcast, 30 November 1954.
18 In fig. 2, the aesthetic qualities of the iconic Admonitions scroll are accepted, but some might see the Zhao Guilan print, with its more obvious political message, only as propaganda rather than art in its own right.
19 Clark 1997, pp. 8–13.
20 Truong Chinh, quoted in Buchanan 2002, p. 15.
21 Barmé 1996, pp. 39–42.
22 Harrison-Hall 2002.
23 Portal 2005.
24 Portal 2000.
25 From the name of their society (義和拳 *yihequan*), the Righteous and Harmonious Fists.
26 £67,500,000, equivalent to about $335,000,000 in 1900, and more than £3 billion ($4.5 billion) today. Preston 2000, p. 310.
27 Laing 2000, pp. 151–2.
28 Kimloan Hill, 'Strangers in a Foreign Land: Vietnamese Workers in France during World War I', in Nhung Tuyet Tran and Anthony J.S. Reid (eds), *Viet Nam: Borderless Histories*, Madison: University of Wisconsin Press 2006, p. 256.
29 Xu 2011.
30 Gerth 2003, pp. 233–5.
31 Quoted in Gerth 2003, p. 246.
32 Pinney 2004, p. 120.
33 Pinney 2004, pp. 120–1.
34 Pinney 2004, pl. 90.
35 Pinney 2004, pp. 120–1. Pinney, an authority on Indian political iconography, remarks that the reason for the alarm raised by the image is 'sometimes hard to discern' (p. 121). In fact, this way of depicting the popular goddess Kali is typical in Bengal, where the print was made (see Blurton 2006, p. 26).
36 Alexandra Green, British Museum Collections Online.
37 Hung 1997, pp. 36–7.
38 In earlier times, Chinese scholar-officials had expressed dissent through painting. For a study of Song dynasty (960–1278) covert dissent, see Alfreda Murck, *Poetry and Painting in the Song Dynasty: The Subtle Art of Dissent*, Cambridge, MA: Harvard University Asia Center 2000. After the fall of the Ming dynasty (1368–1644), symbols such as ruined buildings in paintings expressed quiet opposition to the new Qing dynasty. Paper given by Alfreda Murck, Royal Academy, London 2006, in connection with the exhibition *China: The Three Emperors, 1662–1795*.
39 Hung 1997, pp. 40–1.
40 The Chinese Communist Party (CCP) was founded in 1921. As instructed by the Soviet Communist Party, it accepted the leadership of the Guomindang (GMD). In 1927, following the consolidation of the Northern Expedition, the GMD purged and outlawed the Communist Party. The Communist base was in Jiangxi province until 1934 when, encircled by the GMD, the Communists made the Long March to Yan'an. The second United Front began in 1936, after Chiang Kai-shek's kidnapping by General Zhang Xueliang (1901–2001). With the Japanese attacks of 1937, unified resistance and patriotic fervour prevailed – for a few years. Co-operation effectively ended after the New Fourth Army incident of 1941.
41 *Manhua* (漫畫), from the Japanese *manga*, means more than simply 'cartoon'. It refers to graphic panels, serial cartoons and sketches. See Crespi 2011.
42 Hung 1994, pp. 94–6.
43 Paul Bevan, 'Manhua Artists in Shanghai 1926–1938: From Art-for-art's-sake to Wartime Propaganda', unpublished PhD dissertation 2012, p. 390.
44 Chongqing is now a directly controlled municipality, rather than coming under the Sichuan provincial government.
45 This collection, comprising more than 200 wartime prints, was acquired in 1980. Peter Thompson served in the British Embassy in China and was presented with the prints as a farewell gift in 1949.
46 Hung 1997, pp. 56–7; Flath 2004, pp. 138–9.
47 Andrews 1994, p. 18.
48 Kushner 2006, pp. 122–3.
49 Kushner 2006, p. 120.
50 Beevor 2012, pp. 302–3.
51 Beevor 2012, p. 302.
52 Beevor 2012, pp. 465–6.
53 http://www.hindustantimes.com/news/specials/netaji/speech_13.htm.
54 Kushner 2006, p. 6.
55 Kushner 2006, p. 188.
56 Kushner 2006, p. 6.
57 Dower 1999, p. 45.
58 The Republic of Korea, or ROK.
59 Kushner 2006, p. 188.
60 For a detailed biography of this image see Andrews 1994, pp. 77–86.
61 Chang 1997, p. 77.
62 For analysis of Mao's 'Talks', see McDougall 1980.
63 Andrews 1994, especially pp. 34–75.
64 Estimates vary, but more than thirty-five million people died in the famine resulting from the policies and execution of the Great Leap Forward. Two comprehensive accounts are Dikötter 2010 and Yang 2012
65 Galikowski 1998, pp. 97–8.
66 MacFarquhar and Schoenals 2006, pp. 7–13.
67 The 'Four Olds' (四舊 Si jiu): old customs, old culture, old habits and old ideas. This campaign began in August 1966, shortly after the Cultural Revolution was launched.
68 See www.psywarrior.com/KoreaPSYOPHist.html.
69 This was further reorganized as the Federation of Malaya in 1948.
70 The population was roughly 49 per cent Malayan, 39 per cent Chinese, and the remainder Indian and others. Friedman (Malaya).
71 Short for *Việt Nam Độc Lập Đồng Minh Hội* (League for the Independence of Vietnam), the Communist-nationalist independence movement formed in 1941.
72 Mark Kurlansky notes that by 1954 the US was financing about 80 per cent of France's war effort. Kurlansky 2004, p. 9.

Revolutionary Inspirations

The French Revolution (1789–99) began as a popular movement against royal absolutism and aristocratic privilege, under terrible economic conditions for the poor. The ideals of liberty, equality and fraternity gave way before long to the Reign of Terror and the implementation of dictatorship, as all who opposed the Revolution were silenced – or executed. In the long run, however, the French Revolution established the principles of human rights and fostered the development of nationalism, which have profoundly changed the world order.

Marxist revolutionaries were influenced by the French Revolution and the short-lived Paris Commune of 1871. Concepts such as 'dictatorship of the proletariat' came to fruition under Lenin, and the Bolshevik Revolution of 1917 was the first lasting, regime-changing uprising by the urban working class. Its lessons inspired revolutionaries everywhere, even in countries with overwhelmingly agricultural economies. Political leaders have adapted the tenets of Marxism-Leninism to the specific circumstances of their own societies.

This section presents responses to the French and Soviet revolutions, which figure in all media and formats of twentieth-century propaganda. Over two hundred years later, artists are still asking whether we have learned the lessons of the French Revolution: can violence ever be justified (cat. 1)?

The iconography of the Soviet Revolution was widely adopted and stylized for propaganda featuring banners, the five-pointed star, hammer-and-sickle and raised fist (cats 4, 6). The call for proletarian revolution still resonates: International Workers' Day (May Day) is a national holiday in over eighty countries and celebrated unofficially in many others (cat. 7).

In Pursuit of Light (detail).
Li Hua. 1936–44. China.
See cat. 3

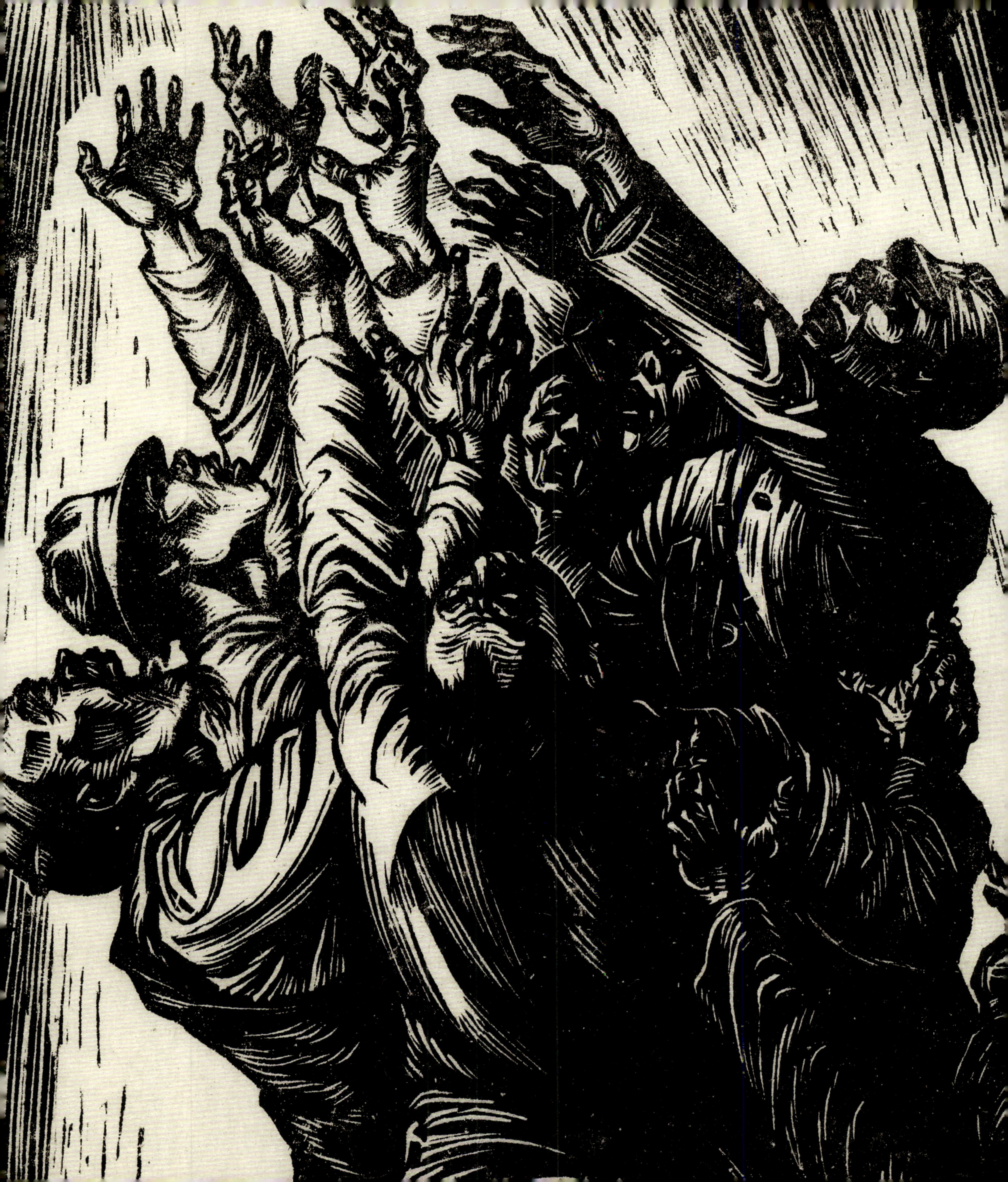

1

Robespierre

Nam June Paik (백남준)

United States

1989

Colour lithograph on paper

75.5 × 56.5 cm

British Museum 2001,0315,0.2

Purchase funded by Brooke Sewell Permanent Fund

Nam June Paik (1931–2006) was a musician, innovative installation artist and pioneer of video art. He was born when Korea was still under Japanese rule, then fled in 1949 before the formal outbreak of the Korean War. He lived in Hong Kong, Japan and Germany before settling in the US. Nam June Paik constantly engaged with the development of telecommunications and the growing influence of television on popular culture. A great many of his works are large installations, particularly robots, made from televisions.

On the two hundredth anniversary of the French Revolution, he made a graphic series of television-robots entitled *Evolution, Revolution, Resolution*. They represent eight leading figures of the Revolution: Georges Danton, Jacques-Louis David, Denis Diderot, Olympe de Gouges, Jean-Paul Marat, Maximilien de Robespierre, Jean-Jacques Rousseau and Voltaire. Each figure is addressed individually, in various notations on the televisions comprising the robot.

Robespierre (1758–94) stood against the monarchy and was considered a champion of justice. Although a popular hero early in the French Revolution, he was later associated with the Reign of Terror and condemned for supporting violence for revolutionary ends. The inscription around Nam June Paik's robot reads, 'Does the revolution justify the violence?'

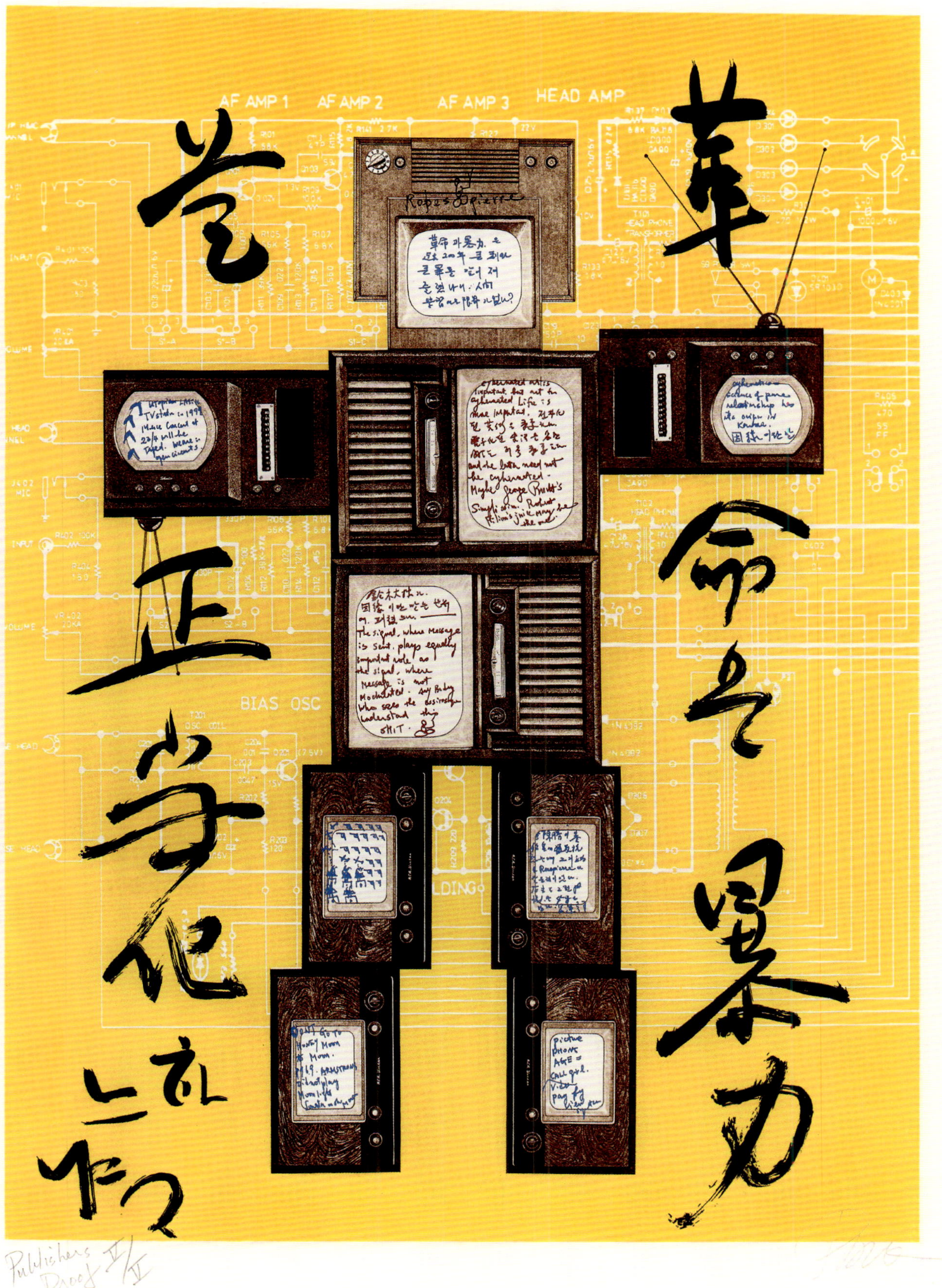

AF AMP 1
AF AMP 2
AF AMP 3
HEAD AMP
BIAS OSC

2

The Carmagnole (Die Carmagnole)

Käthe Kollwitz

China

1901, printed in Lu Xun, *Selected Prints of Käthe Kollwitz* (Shanghai 1936)

Etching and aquatint on paper (photocopied here)

28.5 × 18.7 cm

British Museum Library Collections

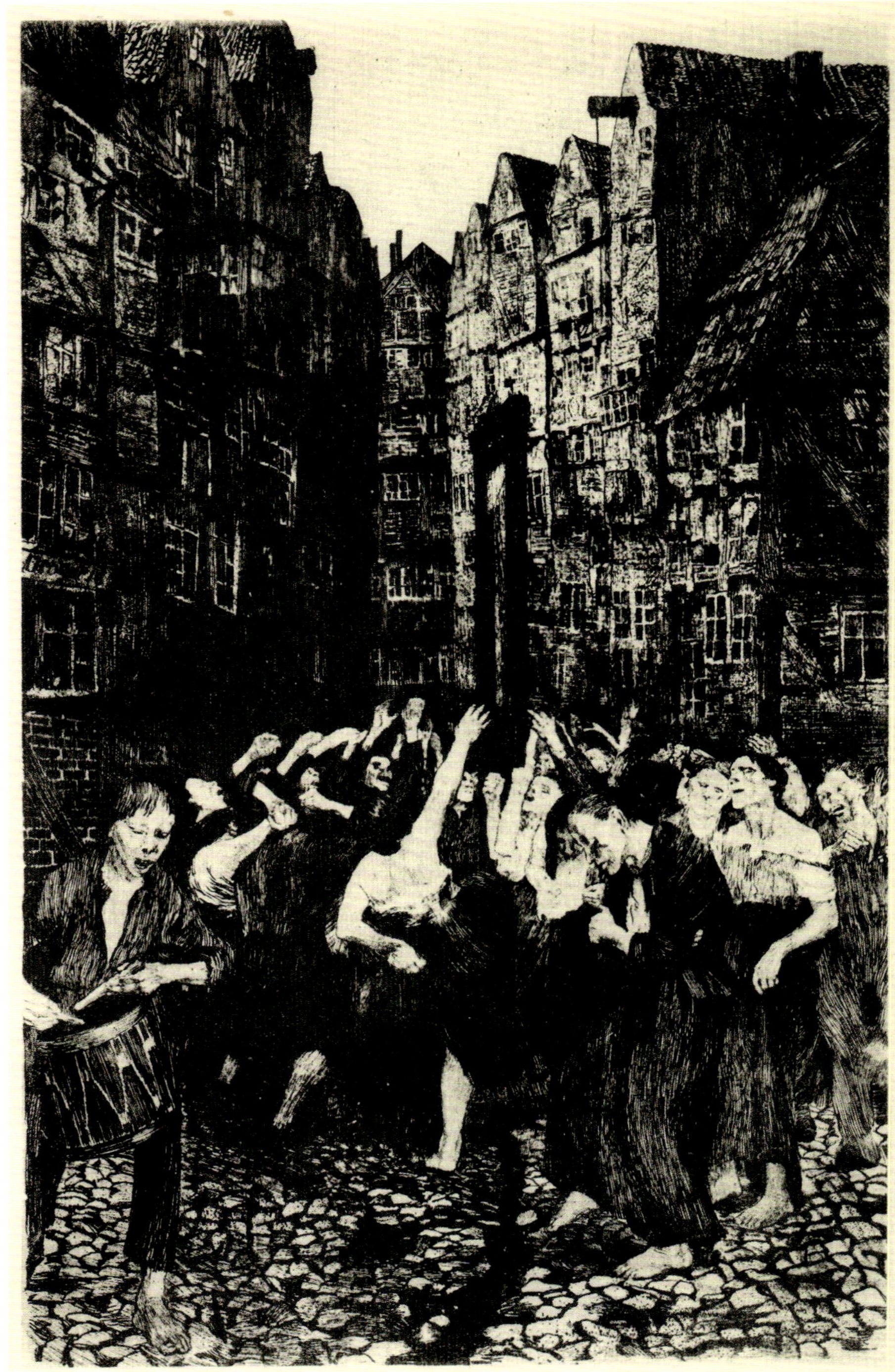

3

In Pursuit of Light (光明的追求 *Guangming de zhuiqiu*)

Li Hua (李樺)

1936–44

China

Woodcut, printed in ink on paper

15 × 15.2 cm

British Museum 1980,0630,0.66

Purchase funded by Brooke Sewell Permanent Fund

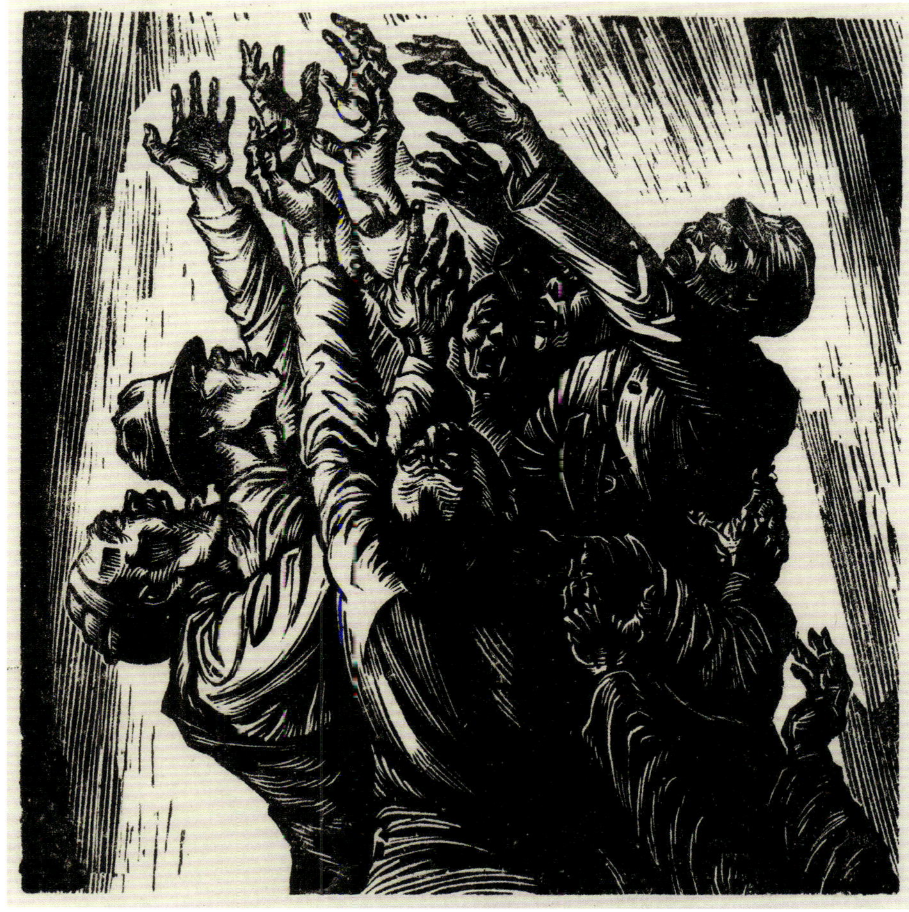

The Carmagnole is number nine in the book of Kollwitz prints that Lu Xun published in Shanghai in 1936. A group of peasant women dance frenziedly around a guillotine, their eyes and hands raised to the sky. Käthe Kollwitz used this theme to depict the French Revolution. The Carmagnole was a popular song of the French Revolution ('O let us dance the Carmagnole, Long live the sound of the cannon').[1]

Li Hua (1907–94) worked closely with Lu Xun, who considered him one of the most promising of the creative printmakers.[2] His themes were both nationalistic and socialist.[3] Li Hua, too, admired Käthe Kollwitz's work and studied her techniques for facial and bodily expression.[4] He adapted some of her prints for his revolutionary woodcuts. Li Hua's *Struggle* (1947), from the *Raging Tide* series, was surely inspired by a 1902 print in Kollwitz's *Peasant War* series.[5] An earlier rendering of that subject, the *Human Plough*, appears in this selection, by Lu Xun, of her work.

In Pursuit of Light was quite possibly inspired by *The Carmagnole*. The faces and hands are particularly expressive and powerful. The figures can neither grasp what they are reaching for nor get out into the light.

1 Martha Kearns, *Käthe Kollwitz: Woman and Artist*, New York: Feminist Press of CUNY 1976, p. 84.
2 Hung 1997, p. 38.
3 Li Hua did not join the Communist Party until 1953, but he worked with left-wing organizations throughout his career.
4 Hung 1997, p. 39.
5 See von Spee 2010, cat. 67 and fig. 25.

4

Plate

Blank produced by State Porcelain Factory; designed by Veniamin Pavlovich Belkin (1884–1961)

Designed 1919; decorated 1920

Russia

Porcelain, polychrome overglaze painting

Diameter: 23.5 cm

British Museum 1981,1208.2

Published: Rudoe 1994, no. 18; Ginsberg 2008, fig. 1

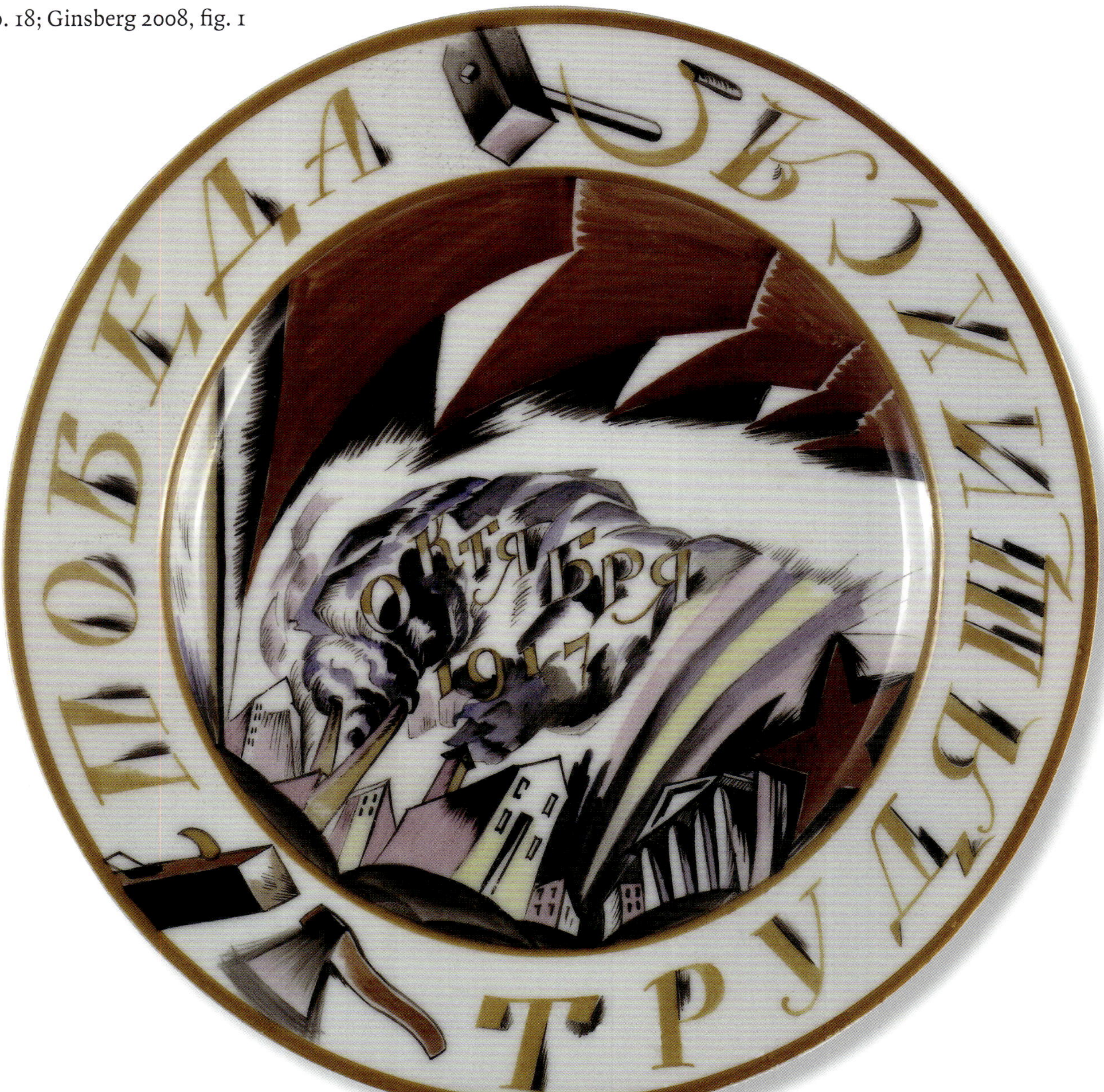

5

Plate

Blank produced by Imperial Porcelain Factory; designed and decorated by Maria Vasilievna Lebedeva (1895–1942)

1914 (blank); designed and decorated 1923

Russia

Porcelain, polychrome overglaze painting

Diameter: 36.6 cm

British Museum 1990,0506.4

Purchased with contribution from the Art Fund (as NACF)

Published: Rudoe 1994, no. 345

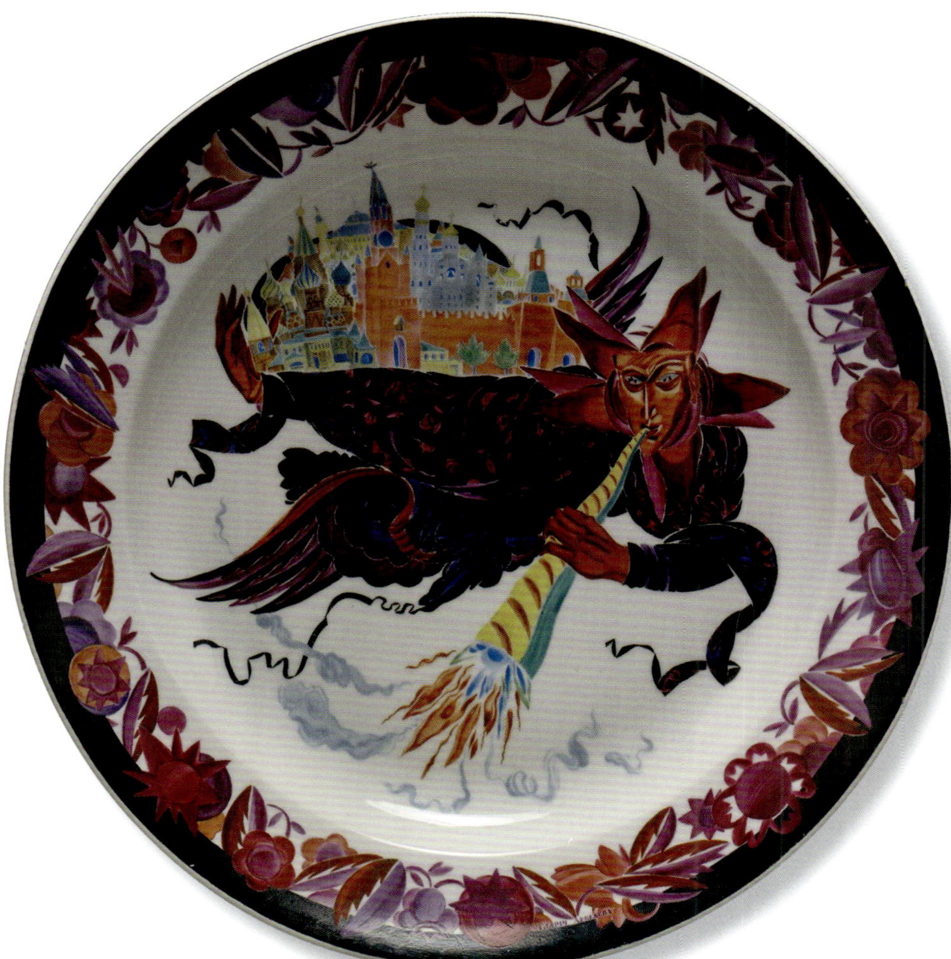

The period immediately following the 1917 Bolshevik Revolution saw great experimentation in the graphic and decorative arts. The Imperial Porcelain Factory in St Petersburg became the State Porcelain Factory (in renamed Petrograd) and came under the control of the People's Commissariat for Education. The factory's production was a propaganda tool from the outset, decorated with slogans and symbols of revolution and the new society.[1]

The first dish displays a new graphic style and iconography: a Futurist scene of factories, with revolutionary red star and ribbon banners. All these motifs feature on various media of the early 1920s, particularly posters, which were the vanguard of political art. Made to commemorate the second anniversary of the Bolshevik Revolution, it is inscribed 'October 1917' in smoke billowing from the factories and 'Victory of the Workers' around the rim.

Other artists reworked traditional styles and motifs. The decoration on the second plate is just like that on old lacquer miniatures. The genie or witch is a type from folk stories, blowing away the old order – recognizably the Kremlin. Folk art was employed on various media, especially textiles and posters derived from *lubki*.[2]

Revolutionary art ceramics were not used for eating. While they employed a visual vocabulary familiar to all, only an elite few could afford them. Many of the revolutionary designs were decorated on blanks left over from pre-Revolution production. Some dishes still bear the mark of the Imperial Porcelain Factory, along with the mark of the State Porcelain Factory. While politically inconsistent to retain it, the imperial mark made the dish more valuable for export.[3] The regime made many such compromises, selling the national heritage to earn badly needed foreign currency.[4]

1 Kudryavtseva 2004, pp. 25–7.
2 *Lubki* are folk art – illustrated woodcuts, made from the early seventeenth century onwards. The origin of the term is uncertain. White 1988, p. 1.
3 MacGregor 2010, pp. 632–3.
4 Odom and Salmond 2009, pp. xix–xx.

6

Three-chuan banknote

Issued by the Sichuan-Shaanxi Soviet Government Workers and Farmers Bank

1933

China

Textile

15.9 × 8.6 cm

British Museum 1949,1101.12

Given by Dr Soothill

The Sichuan-Shaanxi (Chuan-Shaan) Soviet base area was established by the Red Fourth Army in the winter of 1932 and was the second-largest territory of the Chinese Soviet Republic (CSR).[1] The administration instituted land reform and redistribution and maintained military and Party training schools, primary schools, factories, printing facilities, an arsenal and a mint. The base area Workers and Farmers Bank issued a range of banknotes and coins.

This banknote, worth three strings (*chuan*) of cash, bears numerous Communist motifs. On the front are a hammer and sickle, which stand for the unity of industrial workers and farmers; a five-pointed star, which signifies the fingers of the worker's hand; and a clenched fist, symbolizing solidarity under oppression. On the reverse is a cogwheel, representing the industrial proletariat. The inscription includes the mantra, 'Workers of the World Unite' (全世界无产阶级联合起来).

1 The CSR was an unrecognized state within China, declared by Mao Zedong in 1931 with encouragement from the Communist Party of the Soviet Union (CPSU). The largest component was the Jiangxi Soviet base area.

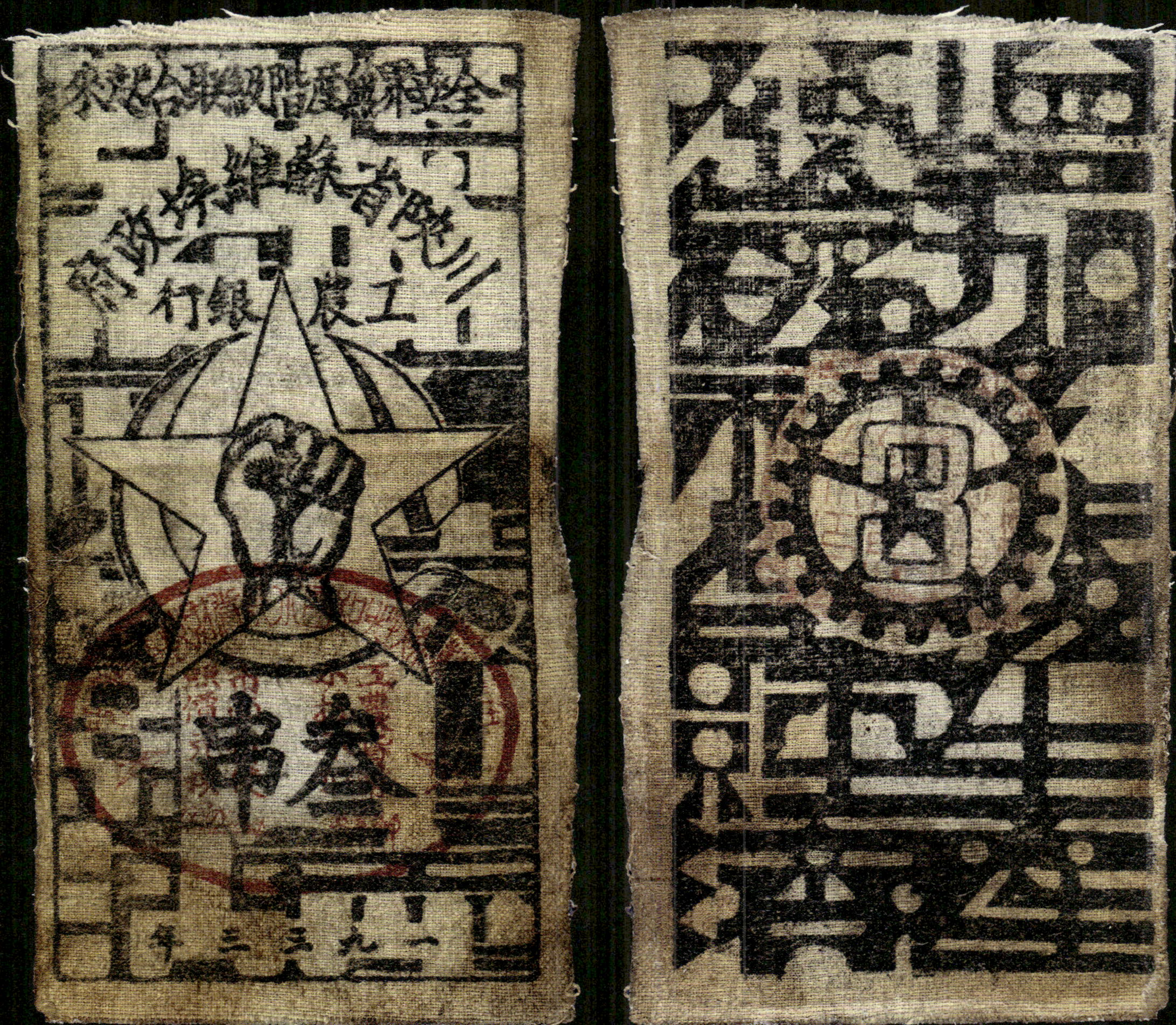
全世界無產階級聯合起來
川陝省蘇維埃政府
工農銀行
叁串
一九三三年

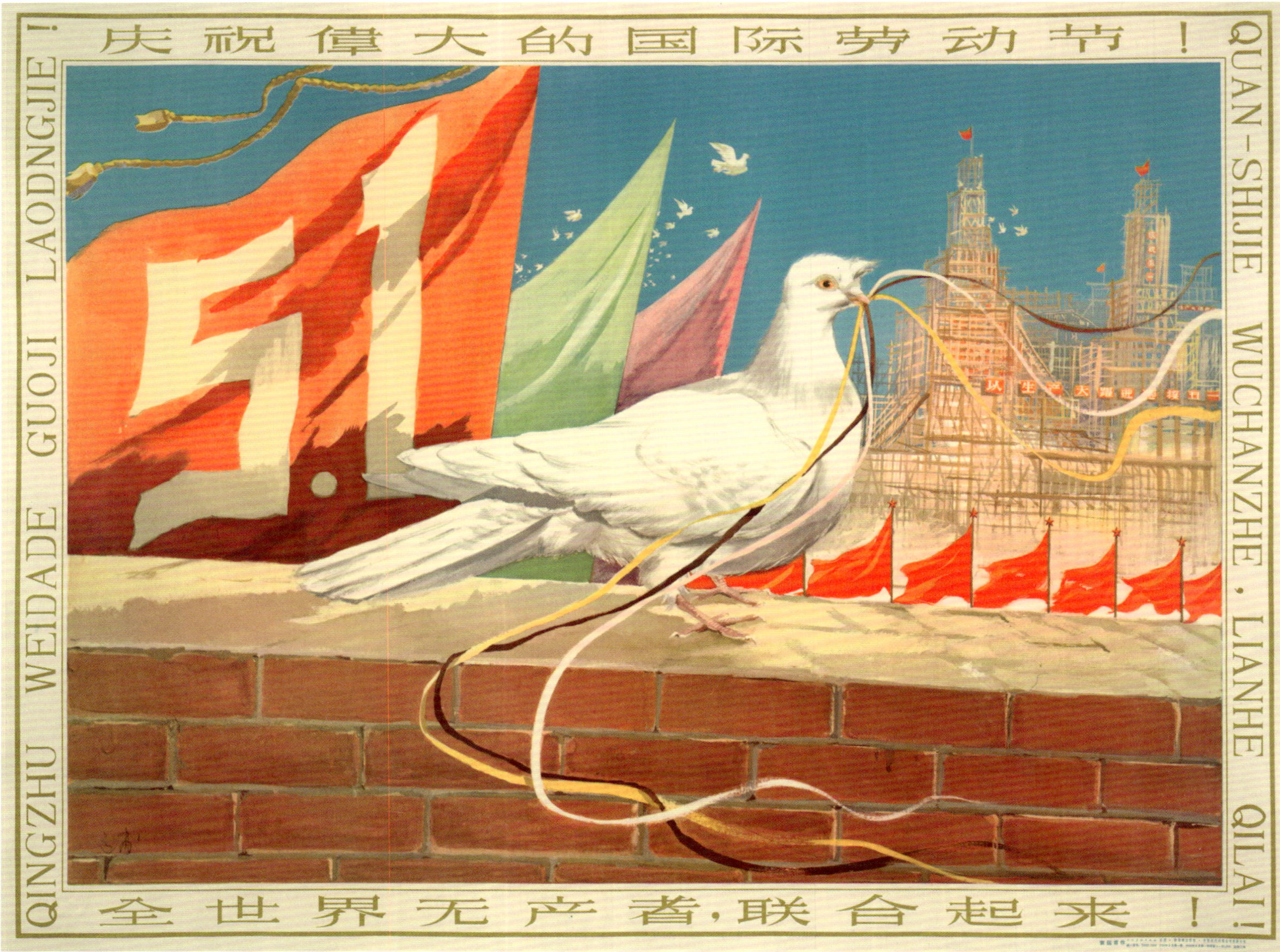

庆祝伟大的国际劳动节！
QINGZHU WEIDADE GUOJI LAODNGJIE!
QUAN-SHIJIE WUCHANZHE, LIANHE QILAI!
全世界无产者，联合起来！

7

Celebrating International Workers' Day, Workers of the World, Unite! (庆祝伟大的国际劳动节全世界无产者联合起来)[1]

Yuan Yunpu

1958

China

Colours on paper

53 × 71.8 cm

Private collection

This poster by Yuan Yunpu (b. 1933) celebrates the first of May (5.1 in China). International Workers' Day is a national holiday in about eighty countries and is particularly associated with Communist and Socialist movements. The slogan 'Workers of all countries, unite!' was the final rallying cry in the Communist Manifesto of 1848 by Karl Marx (1818–83) and Friedrich Engels (1820–95), and was the motto of the USSR.

This is a very decorative call for world revolution, in bright but softer colours than many Chinese posters. The dove is a symbol of world peace, appearing here at front and centre. Banners of varied colours flutter alongside China's red flags. The structures in the back resemble Stalin's 'wedding-cake' buildings: in 1958, China still formally stood in the Soviet camp.

1 Traditional characters: 慶祝偉大的國際的勞動節全世界無產者聯合起來.

A Century of War and Revolution 1900–76

It is impossible to trace the tumultuous events of seventy-six years with just a few objects. This narrative section is divided into four parts: early revolutionary messages; the Asia-Pacific War; post-war reconstruction, civil wars and revolutions; and the new societies which emerged in the 1950s, 1960s and 1970s.

Early revolutionary messages focus on modernity (cats 10, 11) and issues of national self-determination (cat. 12). Education and rapid changes in communication and technology opened opportunities for social and political participation from the start of the twentieth century. New styles and graphic innovations circulated along with progressive ideas. Anti-colonial movements were fuelled by the outcome of the First World War and the Soviet Revolution.

The Asia-Pacific War was perhaps the most significant watershed for many of the countries in Asia, as it resulted in long-term regime changes almost everywhere. The breadth and depth of the British Museum's propaganda collections from this time are exceptional, including material from Nationalist, Communist and Japanese-occupied areas of China, as well as rare survivals of Japanese graphics for the home front (cats 13–21).

Civil war (in China) and proxy wars (in Korea and Vietnam) marked much of the post-war period. Japan underwent rapid systemic change and dynamic economic reconstruction. India and Pakistan adjusted, sometimes painfully, to hard-won independence. New societies emerged in all these places, promoted with pride in economic production, social development and political strength (cats 27–33).

Big tank battle (detail) (坦克大會戰).
1940–5. China. Colour lithograph
on paper, 48.5 × 75.4 cm.
British Museum 1992,0306,0.6
Given by Geoffrey Roome

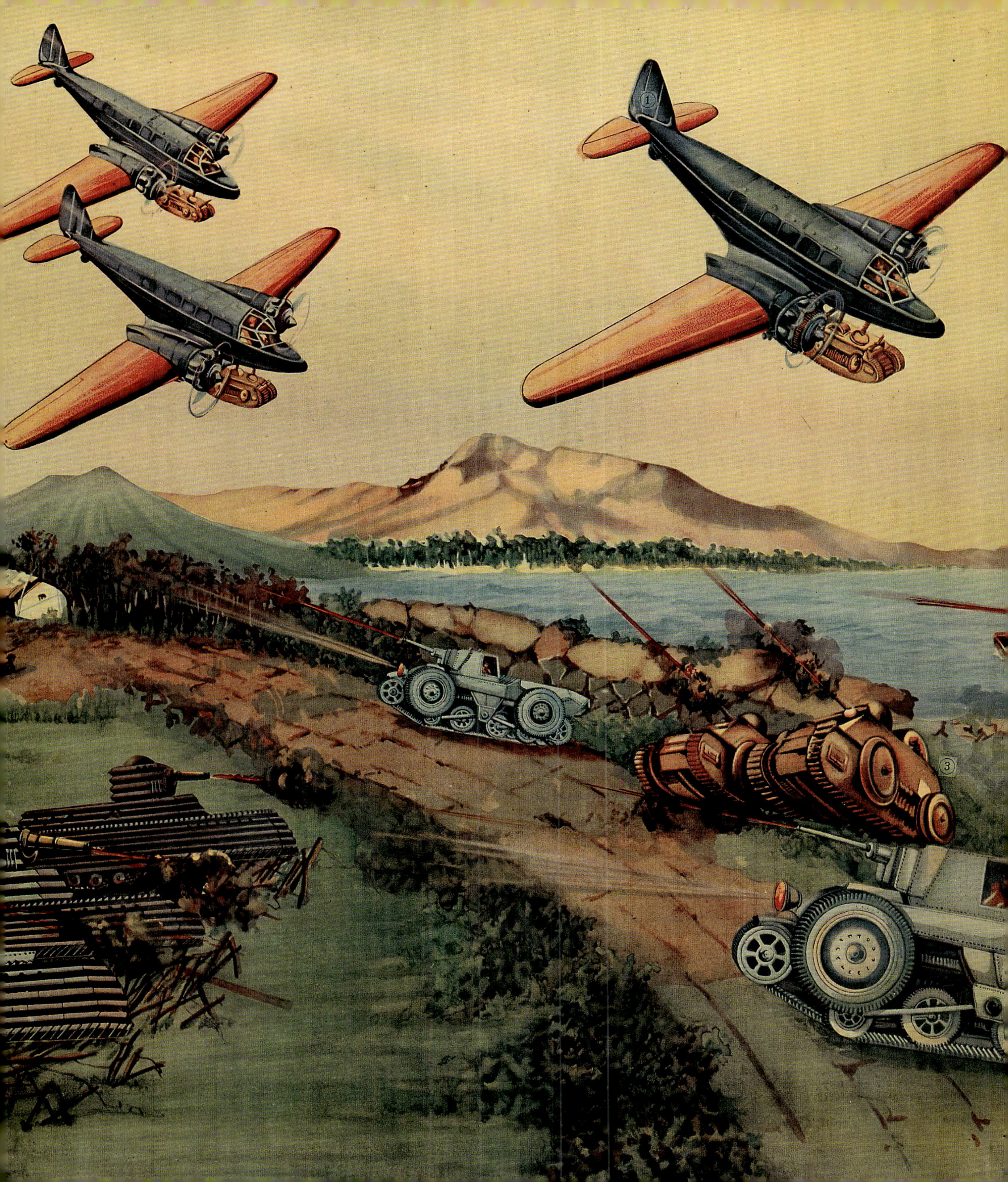
1
3

Early Messages

8

Rout of Foreign Troops by Boxers at Beicang near Tianjin
(天津北倉義和團民打破洋兵)

c. 1900

China

Woodcut, printed in ink and colours on paper

40 × 54 cm

British Museum 1948,0710,0.6

Given by E.B. Howell

9

The Japanese First Army Heads the Allied Bombardment of the Fortress of Tientsin

Fukuda Shuzo

23 July 1900

Japan

Colour lithograph on paper

39.7 × 54 cm

British Museum 1991,0810,0.6

The Boxer Rebellion (1898–1901) was an anti-Christian, anti-foreign movement started by a band who called themselves the *Yihequan* (Righteous and Harmonious Fists). The imperial government under the Dowager Empress Cixi (1835–1908) joined the Boxers, declaring war on the Western powers in China. The critical battle occurred in June 1900, when thousands of Chinese troops attacked foreign settlements in Peking (Beijing) and Tientsin (Tianjin), a major port city. A united force of troops from eight nations ended the sieges. These popular prints show two versions of the battle.

The Chinese woodcut is called a *nianhua*, literally meaning New Year's print, but referring generally to popular prints. Traditionally, *nianhua* displayed protective door gods and other popular deities, but by the end of the nineteenth century some topical prints appeared, featuring scenes from modern life or urging social reforms. This one promotes patriotism, incorrectly showing the Chinese as the victors at Tianjin.

The Japanese print was produced by the more modern technique of colour lithography. It shows a more accurate version of the decisive battle's outcome. The nations of the allied forces imposed a huge bill for reparations on China and demanded major concessions of territory, wealth and trade. This was but one of many sources of anti-imperialism in China in the early twentieth century.

Improvements in technology and transport enabled the production and distribution of these prints almost immediately after the event.

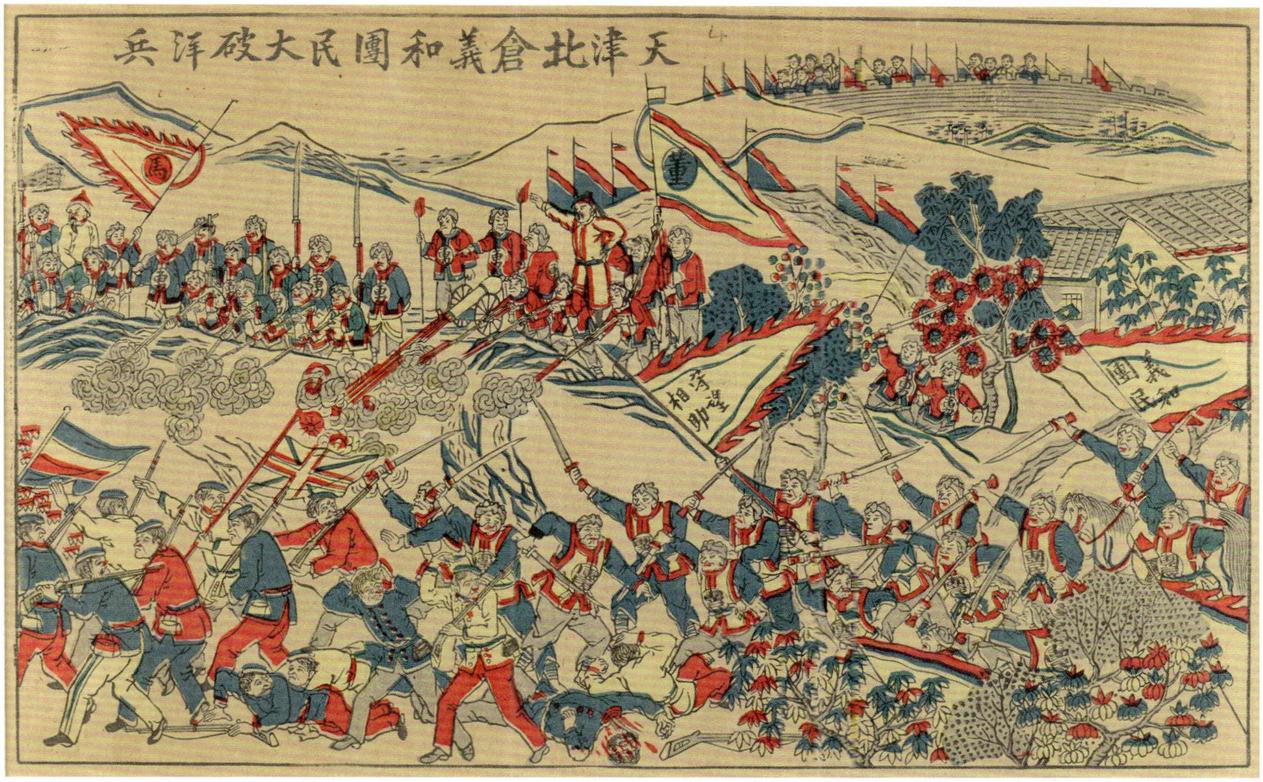
天津北倉義和團民大破洋兵
馬
董
守望相助
義和團民

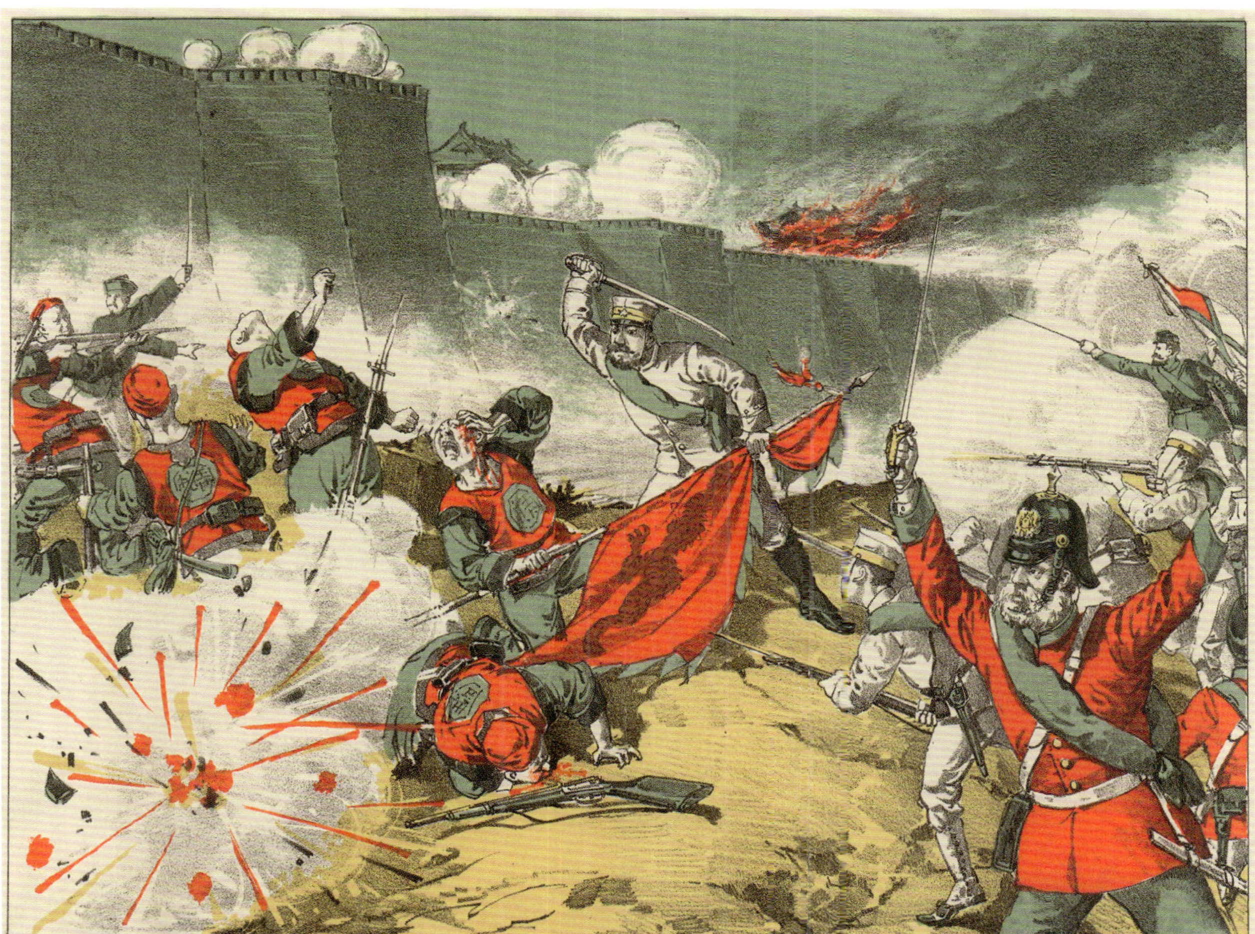

10

Girls' School Catches Monsters (女學堂捉妖)

c. 1920s

China

Woodcut, ink and colour on paper

53 × 95 cm

British Museum 1982,1217,0.286

Published: Flath 2004, pl. 35

The schoolgirls in this vibrant image are battling monsters from the 'Cloudy Mountains' of the Western Ocean. The modern girls are dressed in hats and boots. Fighting alongside them are past heroines with bound feet.

The print has been interpreted in several ways. From the title and text, it may be read as anti-foreign, and the girls are fighting to rid China of Westerners. Or it may be showing that girls are active participants in the new China's political and military affairs. More likely, prints like this are 'objects of fantasy', urging reforms, rather than evidence of rapid social change.

James Flath has traced this and a number of related prints from their production at Yangliuqing, Tianjin, to adaptations in other centres of print capitalism.[1] While their original intent was progressive, these prints were 'altered, exoticized and even sexualized ... for commercial exploitation'.[2] Other versions in the British Museum show similarly dressed schoolgirls lined up for rifle practice in infantry and cavalry units.

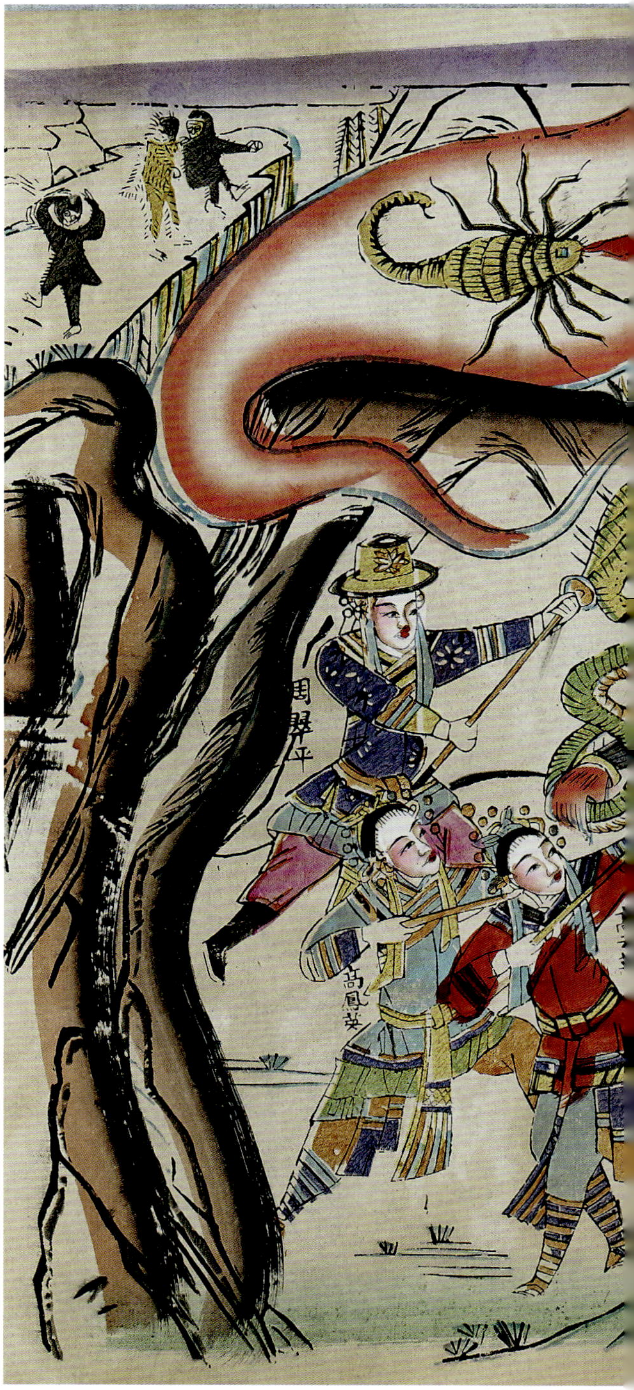

1 See Christopher Reed, *Gutenberg in Shanghai. Chinese Print Capitalism 1876–1937*, Vancouver: UBC Press 2004.
2 See Flath 2004, pp. 128–32, for detailed analysis of this and other 'schoolgirl' reform prints.

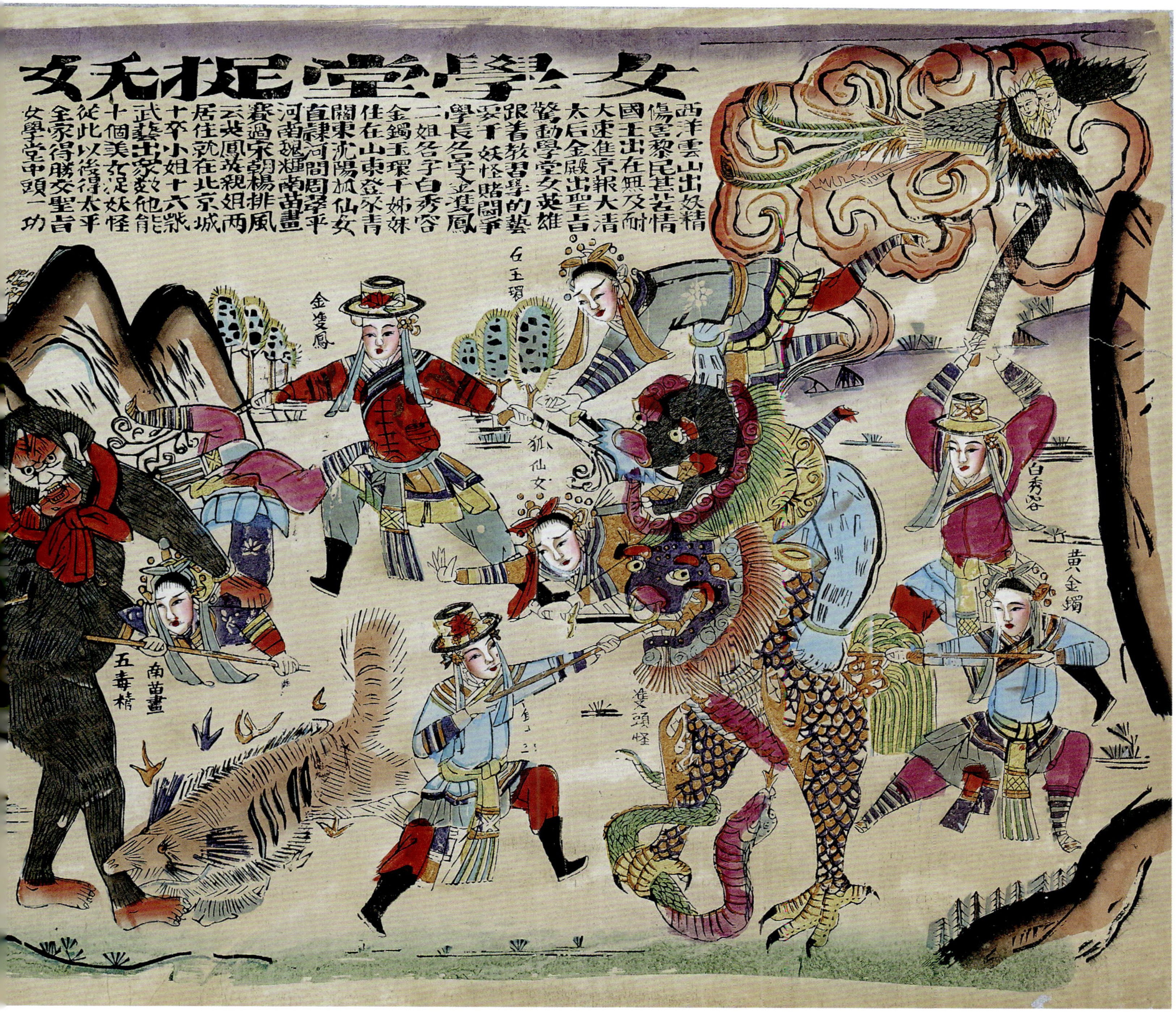
女學堂捉妖
西洋雲山出妖精
傷害黎民甚苦情
國王出在無及耐
大吏進京報大清
太后金殿出聖旨
驚動學堂女英雄
跟着教習學的藝
耍千妖怪賭鬪爭
學長名字叉雙鳳
二姐名字白秀容
金鐲玉環十姊妹
住在山東登萊青
關東沈陽狐仙女
直隸河間周翠平
河南魏耀南苗畫
賽過宋朝楊排風
云共鳳姣親姐兩
居住就在北京城
十卒小姐十六歲
武藝出衆數他能
十個美女捉妖怪
從此以後得太平
全家得勝交聖旨
女學堂中頭一功
金雙鳳
狐仙女
白秀容
黃金鐲
五毒精
南苗畫
雙頭怪

11

Board game (recto) and map (verso)

Board game of new famous places in Tokyo
(東京新名所双六 *Tokyo shin meisho sugoroku*)

Up-to-date Transport Map of Greater Tokyo, with a table of neighbourhood names
(最新大東京交通地図附町名一覧表
Saishin Dai-Tokyo kotsu chizu, tsuke chomei ichiran hyo)

1928 (1 January)

Japan

Colour lithograph

78.7 × 109.1 cm

British Museum 2006,0113,0.5

Purchase funded by Brooke Sewell Bequest

Sugoroku are board games played with dice, following rules very similar to Snakes and Ladders. They became particularly popular in Japan during the eighteenth and nineteenth centuries and were often beautifully produced. They were created around an enormous variety of themes – historical, political, geographic, theatrical, literary – providing 'wholesome and often didactic entertainment for children and the family circle'.[1] *Sugoroku* were often played at the New Year, and newspapers provided them as supplements around this time.

This game board and map on the reverse were issued as a supplement for the New Year edition of *Hō chi Shinbun* (報知新聞 *Hōchi News*). Many of the 'new famous places' were modern buildings and parks that had been constructed – or reconstructed – following the Great Kanto Earthquake of 1923.

The new transport map was another celebration of Tokyo's modernity. Trains and buses already had extensive networks. The subway had been under construction since 1925; on 30 December 1927, Asia's first underground route began operating in Tokyo.[2]

1 Herring 2000, p. viii.
2 http://www.tokyometro.jp/en/corporate/profile/history/index.html.

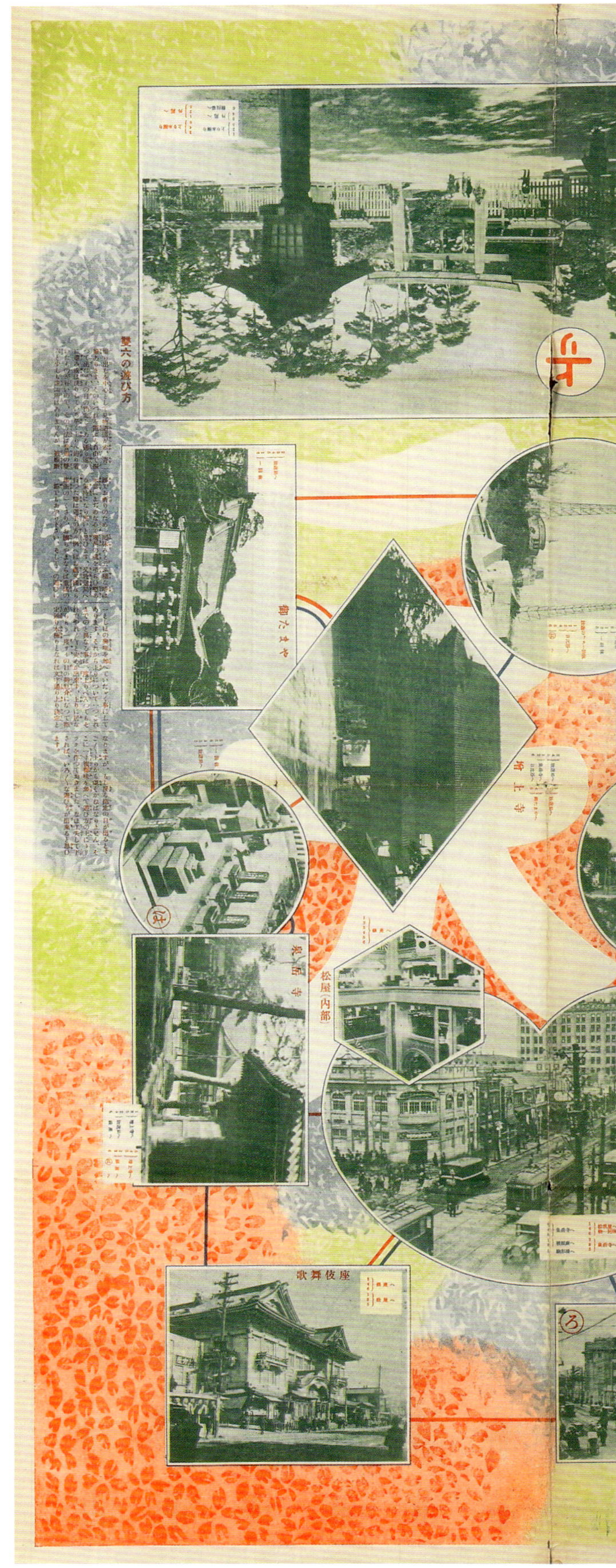

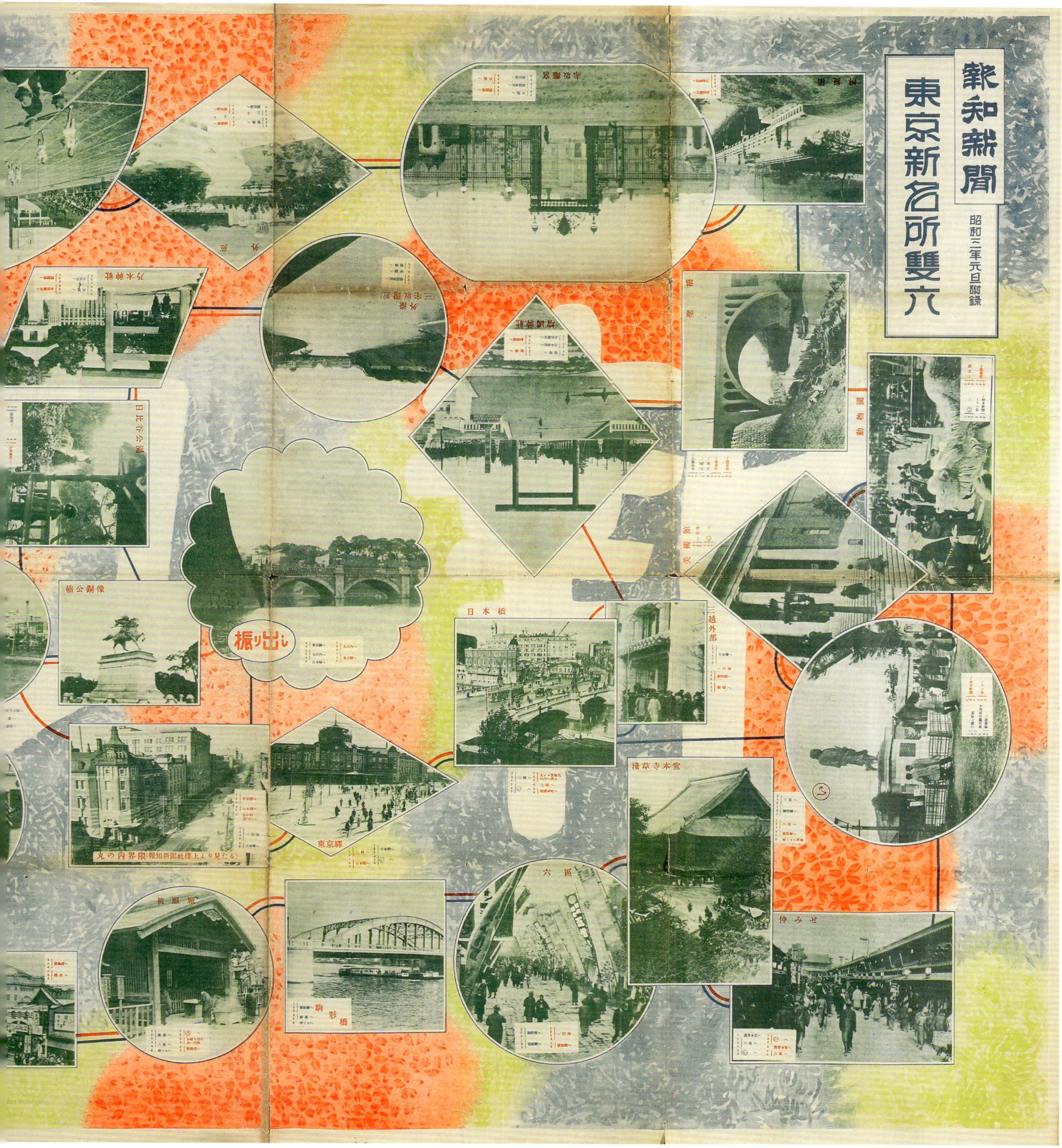

報知新聞
東京新名所雙六
昭和三年元旦附録
振り出し
日本橋
三越外部
淺草寺本堂
仲みせ
六區
駒形橋
東京驛
楠公銅像
日比谷公園
丸の内界隈（報知新聞社樓上より見たる）

12

Plate

1930s (probably)

India

Bamboo, split and coiled, and lacquered

Diameter: 15.2 cm

British Museum 2001,0612.2

Mohandas K. Gandhi (1869–1948), one of the leaders of the Indian independence movement, was committed throughout his life to principles of non-violence (*ahimsa*) and Indian self-sufficiency (*swadeshi*). In the long campaign for self-rule (*swaraj*), Gandhi promoted boycotts of foreign goods (mainly British and Japanese) for both political and economic reasons.

His tool was the spinning wheel (*charkha*), with which he is depicted here. India exported ever-increasing amounts of raw cotton, but would not become a net exporter of cloth piece goods until the 1940s.[1] Gandhi exhorted villagers – especially women – to revive the rural economy by spinning cotton yarn to supplement household agricultural income. The yarn production also supported the carders, weavers and dyers of the cloth. Gandhi's *charkha* became the symbol of *swadeshi* and appeared on the flag adopted by the Indian National Congress in 1931.[2]

This small plate was made in Burma (possibly Pagan) by the laborious and expensive *shwe-zawa* technique using black lacquer and gold leaf. Many Indians settled in Burma in the colonial period.

1 Michael Twomey, 'Cotton Textile Import Substitution. Britain, India, Japan and China: 1790–1930', 1980, pp. 19–25. http://www-personal.umd.umich.edu/ffimtwomey/econhelp/CottonTextiles.pdf.

2 The *dharma chakra* (wheel of the law, an ancient Buddhist device) was considered a more inclusive symbol and was chosen as the central motif of the national flag by the Constituent Assembly in July 1947.

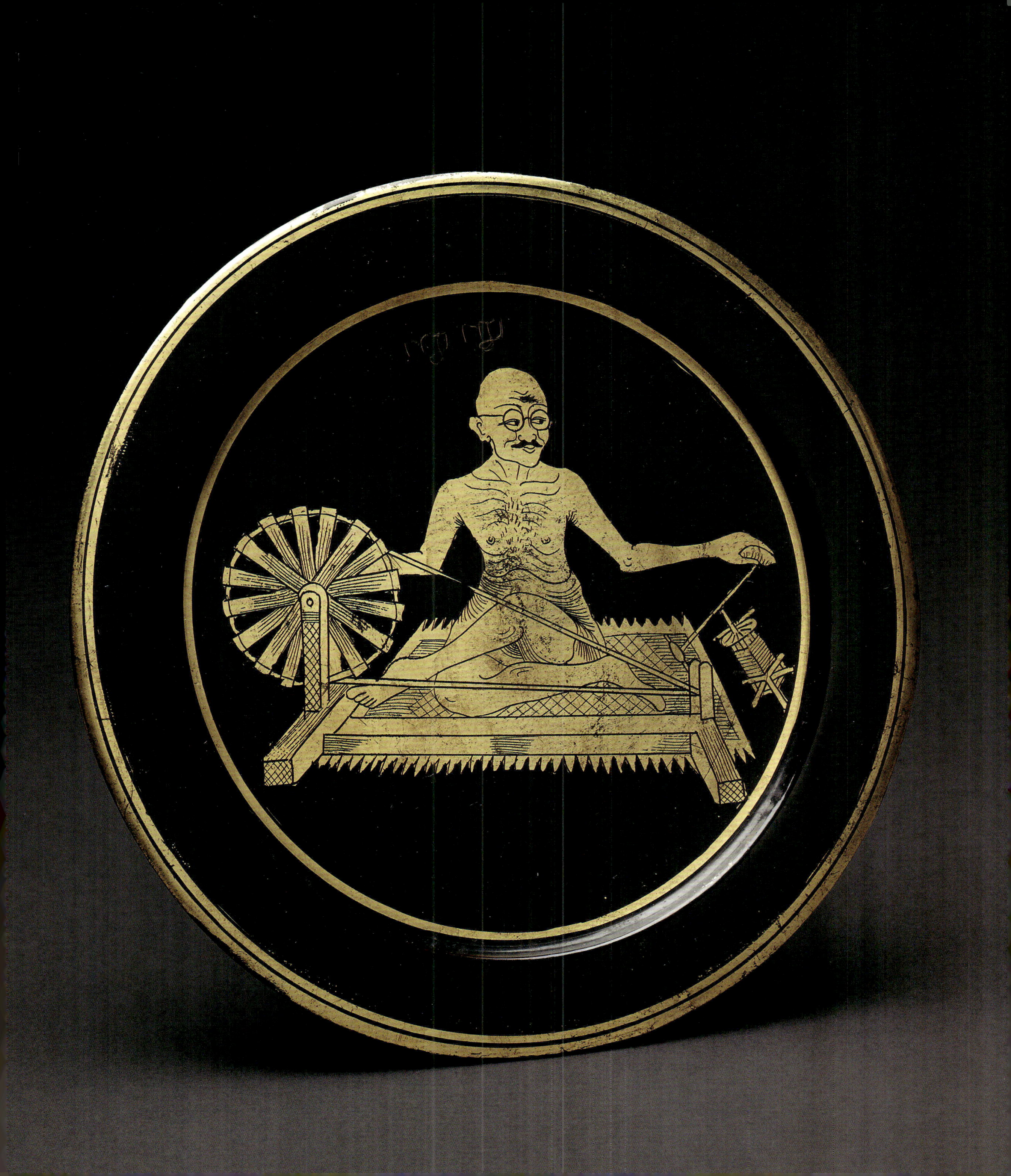

13

Cartoon

Jack Chen (陈依范 Chen Yifan)

1934–6

China

Drawing with ink and slight colours on paper

18.3 × 14.5 cm

British Museum 2009,3022.1

Published: *Moscow Daily News*, 22 January 1936; *Moscow News*, 29 January 1936[1]

In 1931, following the Mukden Incident,[2] Japan seized control of the three north-eastern Chinese provinces comprising Manchuria and the following year proclaimed a new independent entity, Manchukuo. To add legitimacy to the conquest, the Japanese military authorities installed Puyi, the last emperor of China, as head of state. In 1934 they named Puyi as emperor of Manchukuo, under the reign name Kangde. His rule was strictly circumscribed, as all government decisions could be vetoed by Japanese 'vice ministers'.

In this drawing by Jack Chen (1908–95) (see p. 28), Puyi stands by as General Tojo Hideki penetrates further into China. Tojo held various high-ranking positions in the Kwantung Army in Manchuria in the mid-1930s, moving into inner Mongolia and attacking Hebei, before returning to Japan and ultimately serving as prime minister.

Tojo is shown as a centipede, one of the five poisonous creatures (五毒 *wudu*) in Chinese folklore. His tail is the Japanese military flag used throughout the Asia-Pacific War.

1 I am grateful to Paul Bevan for all information about the publication of this drawing.

2 In September 1931 the Japanese staged a small explosion beside the Japanese railway line near Mukden (now Shenyang). Blaming it on Chinese dissidents, Japan used the incident to justify the invasion and later the full occupation of Manchuria.

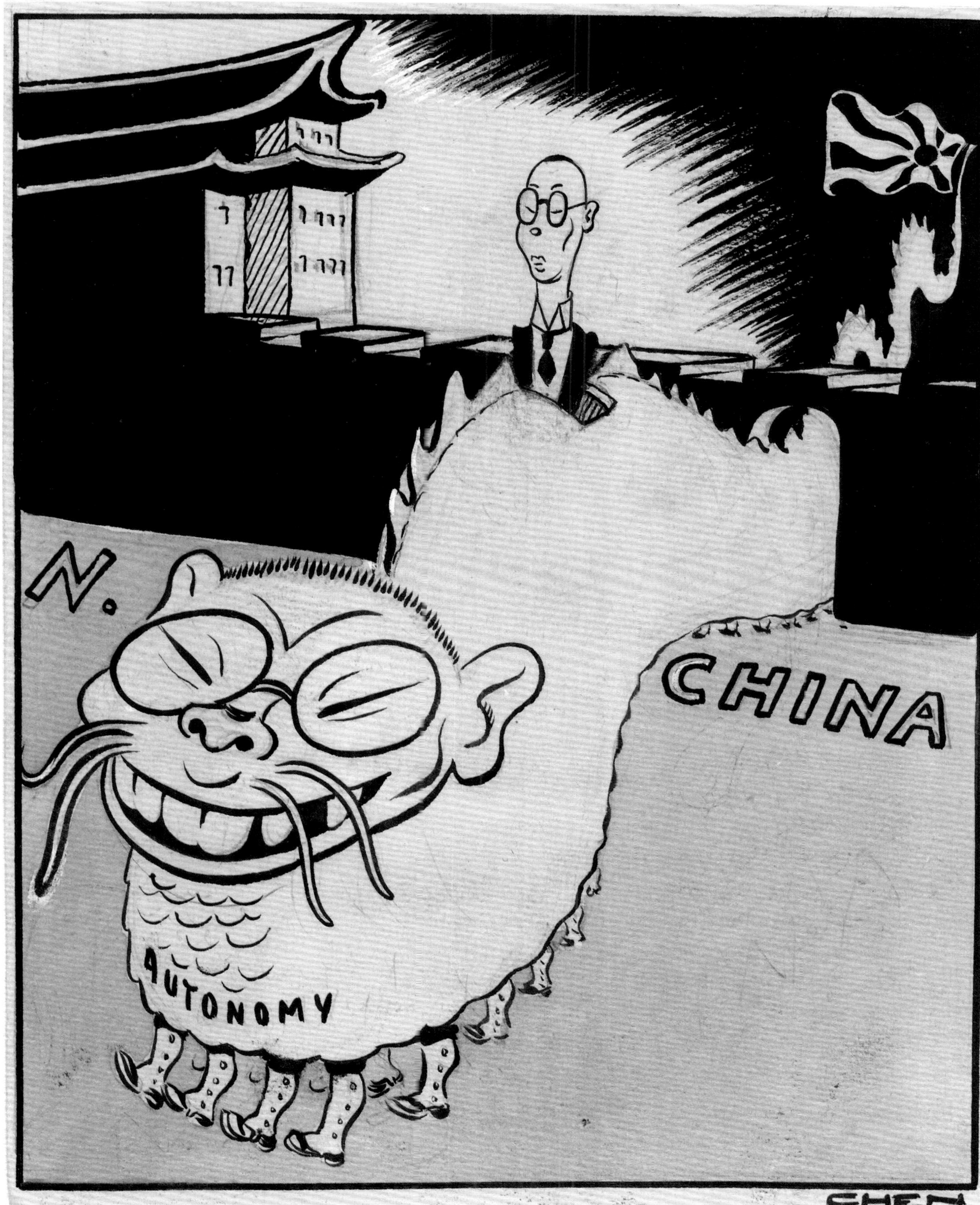
N.
CHINA
AUTONOMY
CHEN

14

The cartoon world climbs the mountains for Double-Ninth [Holiday] (漫畫界重陽登高圖 *Manhuajie Chongyang dengao tu*)

Wang Zimei (汪子美)

1936

China

Ink and colours printed on paper

37.5 × 26 cm

British Museum 2009,3022.74.a

15

All the stars of the cartoon world meet (漫畫界全體明星大會串 *Manhuajie quanti mingxing dahui chuan*)

Yan Zhexi (嚴折西)

1936

Ink and colours printed on paper

18.5 × 26 cm

British Museum 2009,3022.74.b

These two cartoons were included in the exhibition collected and organized by Jack Chen in 1937–8. The exhibition, called *Five Thousand Years Young* in England, travelled through Europe and to the USA. Jack Chen considered the cartoonists – who were young, poor and often self-taught – to be the revolutionary vanguard in art. He wrote: 'En masse they are anti-imperialist, anti-feudalist. Their sympathies are all with the underdog.'[1]

Both cartoons were published in a special edition of *Shanghai Manhua* (上海漫畫 *Shanghai Sketch*) for National Day (10 October) 1936. Wang Zimei's caricature illustrates the most celebrated cartoonists of the day. Twelve of the nineteen are represented in the British Museum's collection. Shown here are (left to right):

Bottom row: Wang Dunqing (王敦慶, 1899–1990), Liang Baibo (梁柏波, 1911?–70), Ye Qianyu (葉淺予, 1907–95), Huang Miaozi (黄苗子, 1913–2012).

Middle row: Wang Zimei (汪子美), Lu Fu (魯夫), Zhu Jinlou (朱金樓), Te Wei (特偉, 1915–2010), Huang Yao (黄堯, 1917–87), Zhang Guangyu (張光宇, 1902–65), Zhang Zhengyu (張正宇, 1903–76), Hu Kao (胡考, 1912–94), Lu Shaofei (魯少飛, 1903–95), Gao Longsheng (高龍生), Zhang Leping (張樂平, 1910–92) .

Top row: Zhang Yingzhao (張英趙), Lu Zhixiang (魯志庠), Ding Cong (丁聰, 1916–2009), Cai Ruohong (蔡若虹, 1910–2002).

The montage by Yan Zhexi (1909–93) illustrates the stars of the cartoon world. Huang Yao's Niubizi (fig. 3) is shown twice, as is Zhang Leping's Sanmao, the three-haired urchin beloved by young and old alike. The ink bottle with pen is Zhang Guangyu's free-speech warrior, which appeared on the cover of the first-ever issue of *Shidai Manhua* (時代漫畫 Modern Sketch) in 1934.[2]

1 Jack Chen, 'China's Militant Cartoons', *Asia Magazine*, May 1938, pp. 308–11 (p. 308).
2 Crespi 2011, p. 1.

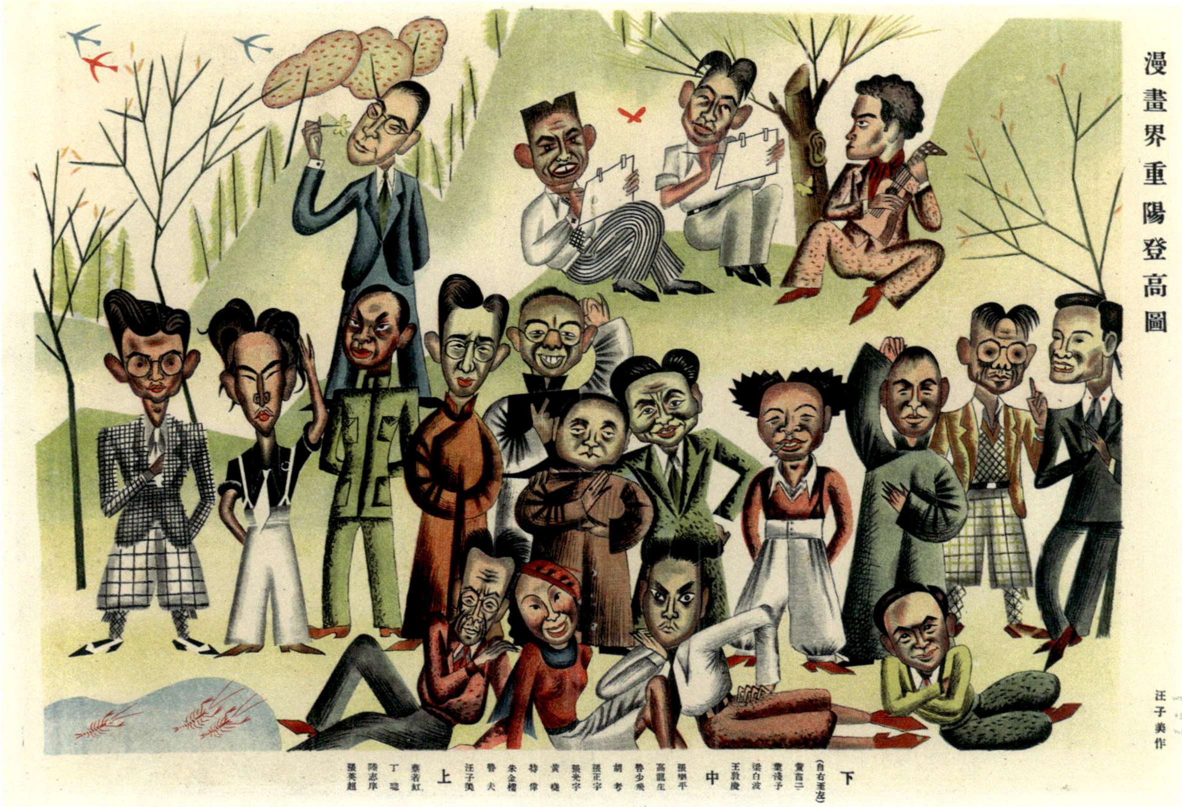
漫畫界重陽登高圖
汪子美作
下（自右至左）
黃苗子 葉淺予 梁白波 王敦慶
中
張樂平 高龍生 魯少飛 胡考 張正宇 張光宇 黃堯 特偉 朱金樓 魯夫 汪子美
上
蔡若虹 丁聰 陸志庠 張英超

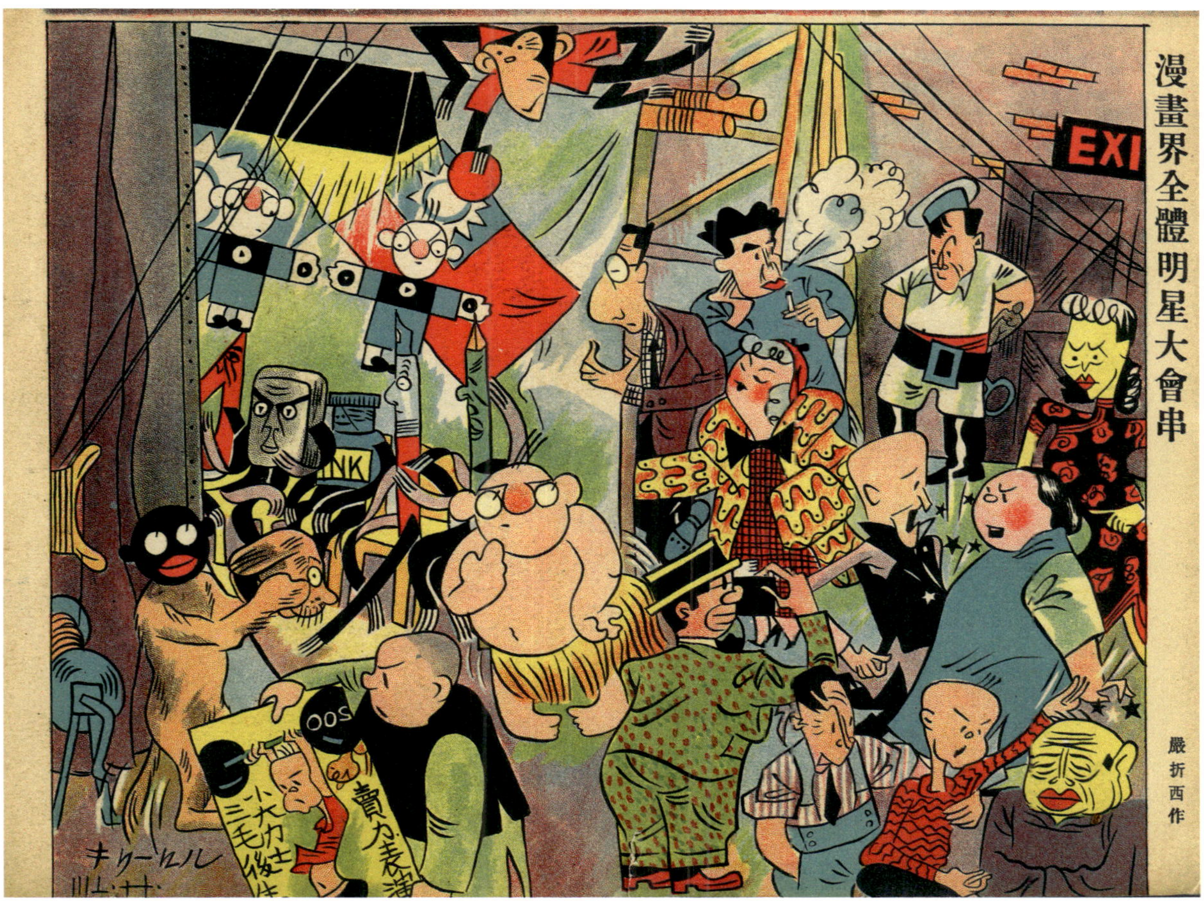
漫畫界全體明星大會串
嚴折西作
EXI
INK

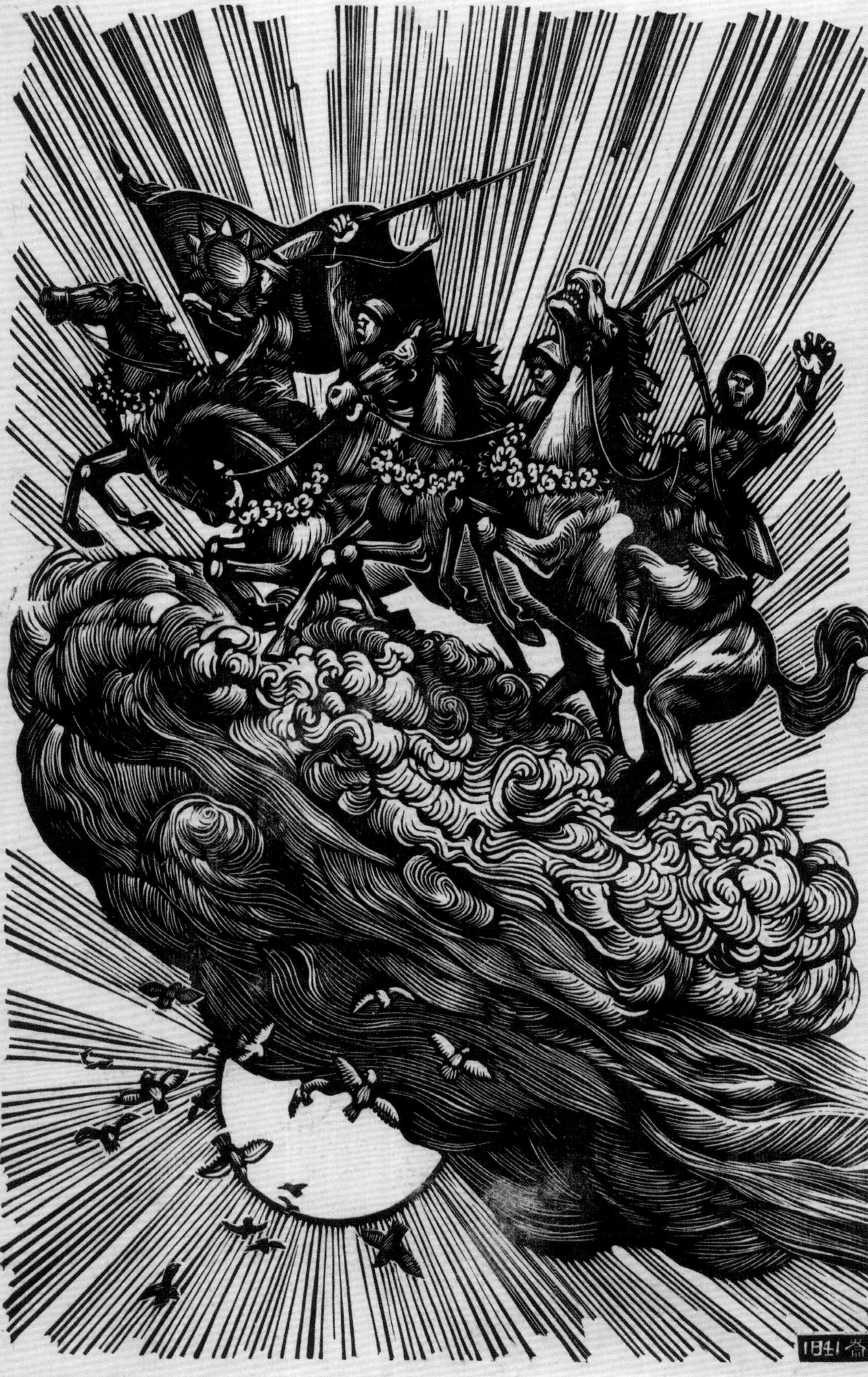
1941

16

Dawn of Victory (勝利的曙光 *Shengli de shuguang*)

Liu Lun (劉崙)

1941

China

Woodcut, ink on paper

24 × 15.5 cm

British Museum 1980,0630,0.86

Purchase funded by Brooke Sewell Permanent Fund

Liu Lun (b. 1913) is a native of Guangdong province, where he trained in printmaking, actively worked in the wartime resistance movement, and taught for many years in higher institutions of art. The British Museum has nine of his works, eight (including this one) from the Thompson collection and one from the international exhibition organized by Jack Chen (Introduction, note 45). Almost all his works are realistic; one print (fig. 16) records the carnage from an actual battle in 1942.

This remarkable patriotic print – heroic cavalrymen charging through the air on a cloud – is unlike any other by Liu Lun. It is rare to know the exact circumstances of a work from this period, but Liu Lun still remembers making it. It was created in 1941, during the second United Front between the Communists and Guomindang. Liu Lun was arts editor of the Creative Committee for the number 4 war district in Guangdong. The Committee published a magazine called *New Construction* (新建設 *Xin jianshe*), and this print was made for its cover, to promote resistance and inspire the public. This was the only wartime print he made in what he calls the romantic style (浪漫主義 *langman zhuyi*), inspired by contemporary Western pictorials.[1]

1 Correspondence with the artist's wife, 楊少娟 Yang Shaojuan, 6 October 2012 (translated by Meixin Wang).

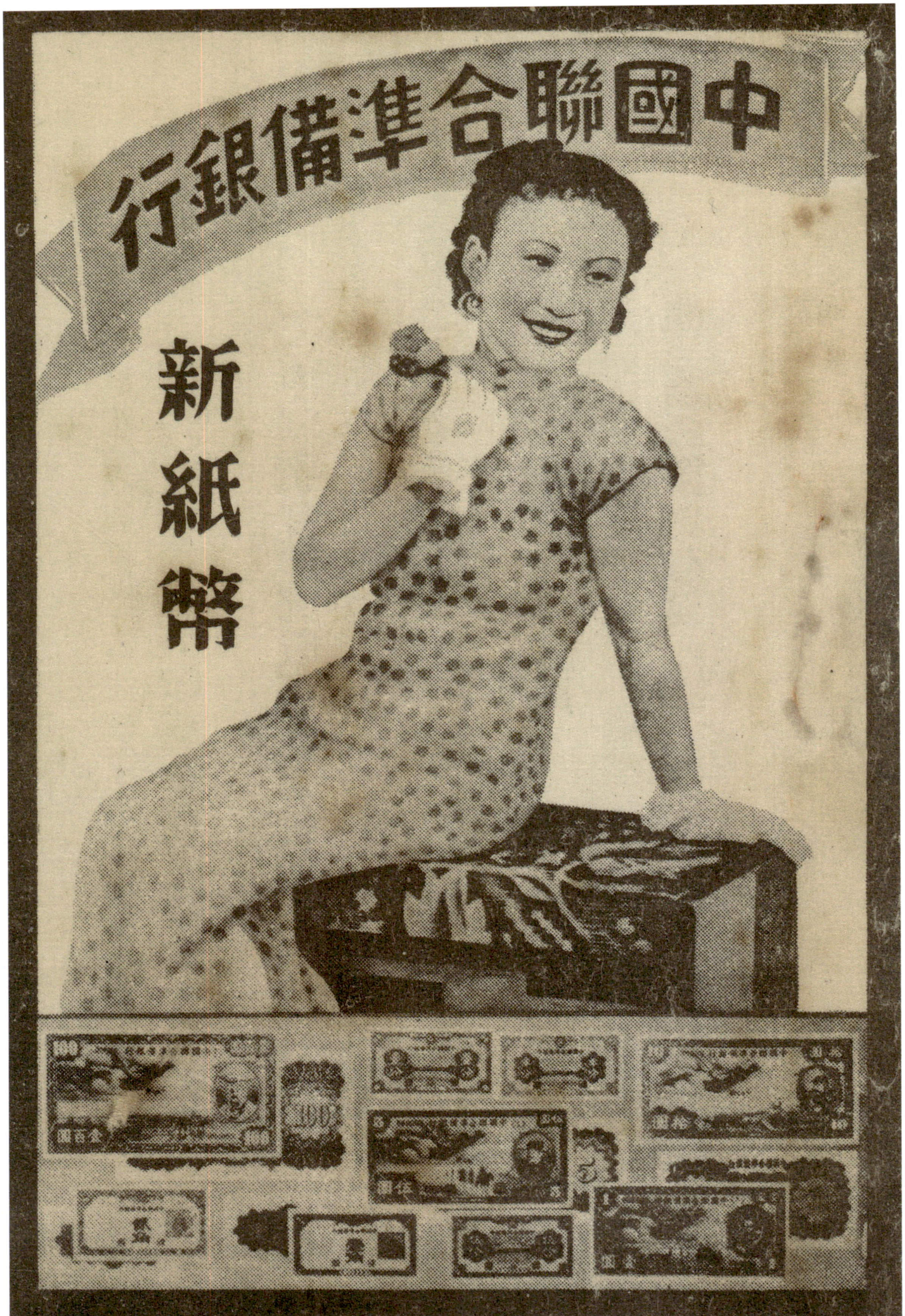
中國聯合準備銀行
新紙幣

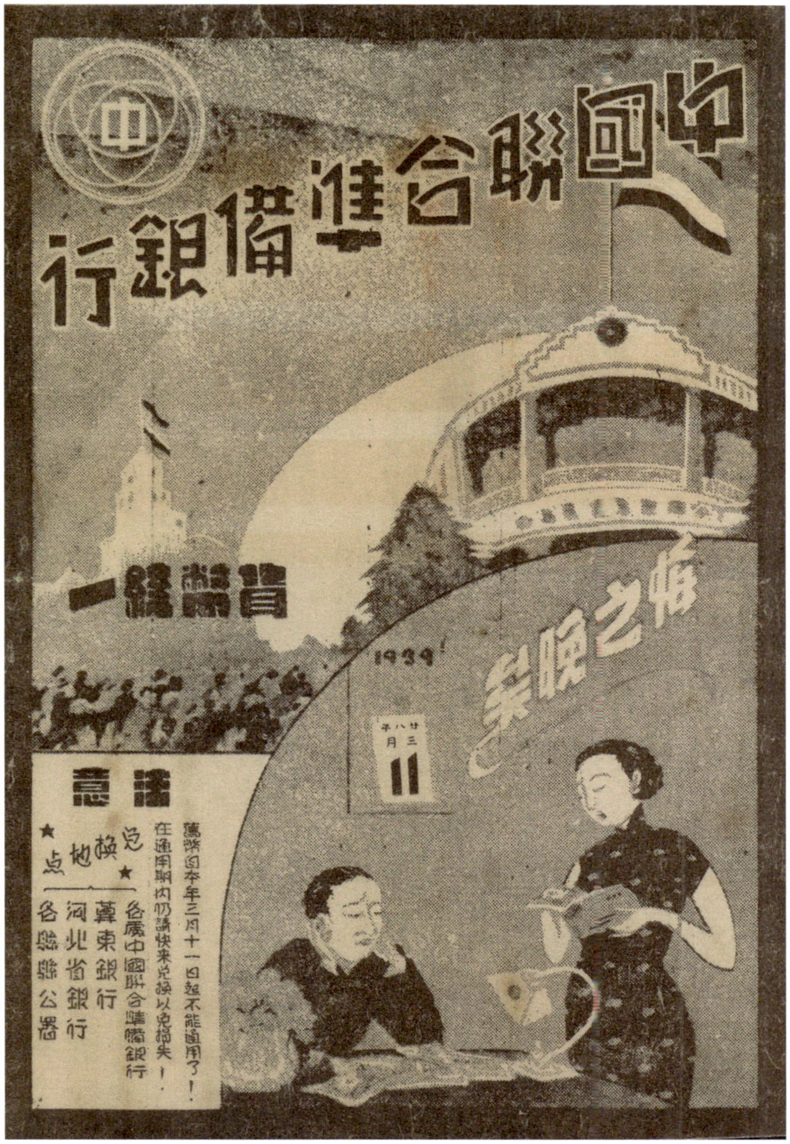

17

Propaganda booklet for occupied north China

1939

China

Photograph and lithograph, black and white on paper

12.8 × 9.5 cm

British Museum 2006,0117,0.51

Purchase funded by Brooke Sewell Bequest

This propaganda booklet was clearly intended for an urban audience. The image on the front is like those on Shanghai advertisement calendar posters, so prevalent in 1930s China.[1] The modern young woman, hair curled, dressed in *cheongsam* and white gloves, promotes the new paper money (新紙幣 *xin zhibi*) issued by the Japanese-established Federal Reserve Bank (中國聯合準備銀行 *Zhongguo lianhe zhunbei yinhang*). In calendar posters, the advertised products were generally arranged across the bottom, just as here are shown the various denominations issued by the new bank.

The Federal Reserve Bank was established in 1938 as the sole money-issuing institution in occupied north China (similar banks were established in other occupied areas, notably the Central Reserve Bank for central and south China).[2]

The back of the booklet gives important information to citizens about the new currency regime. The date shown on the calendar, 11 March 1939, is the deadline to exchange old banknotes for new without loss. The panel on the left lists all the outlets where money can be changed. The crowd of people are running to the bank to make the exchange in time.

1 The most comprehensive study of this commercial art is Laing 2004.
2 Sandrock undated, pp. 25–33.

18

Propaganda cartoon

c. 1939

China

Painted in ink and colours, reproduced as poster on paper

37 × 27 cm

British Museum 2006,0117,0.95

Purchase funded by Brooke Sewell Bequest

This cartoon promoting the use of the puppet Joint Reserve Bank currency is clearly for a less sophisticated audience than the booklet in cat. 17.

A young man walks into a store but is kicked out by the shopkeeper, who shouts, 'I don't want that waste paper!' The young man is in tears, looking at his 'old money' (舊幣 *jiubi*). A Japanese police officer tells him not to cry, there's a solution to the problem: the banknotes issued by the Federal Reserve Bank of China (聯合準備銀行 *Lianhe zhunbei yinhang*) are excellent currency. The young man goes back inside, and the now-friendly shopkeeper tells him that his new notes are the most welcome money.

The Federal Reserve Bank was the only currency-issuing institution in occupied north China. Headquartered in Beijing, it had branches in Tianjin, Qingdao, Jinan, Kaifeng, Tokyo and many other cities. The designs on the banknotes were motifs from Chinese culture, including the Great Wall, Confucius and dragons.[1]

1 Sandrock undated, pp. 22–5.

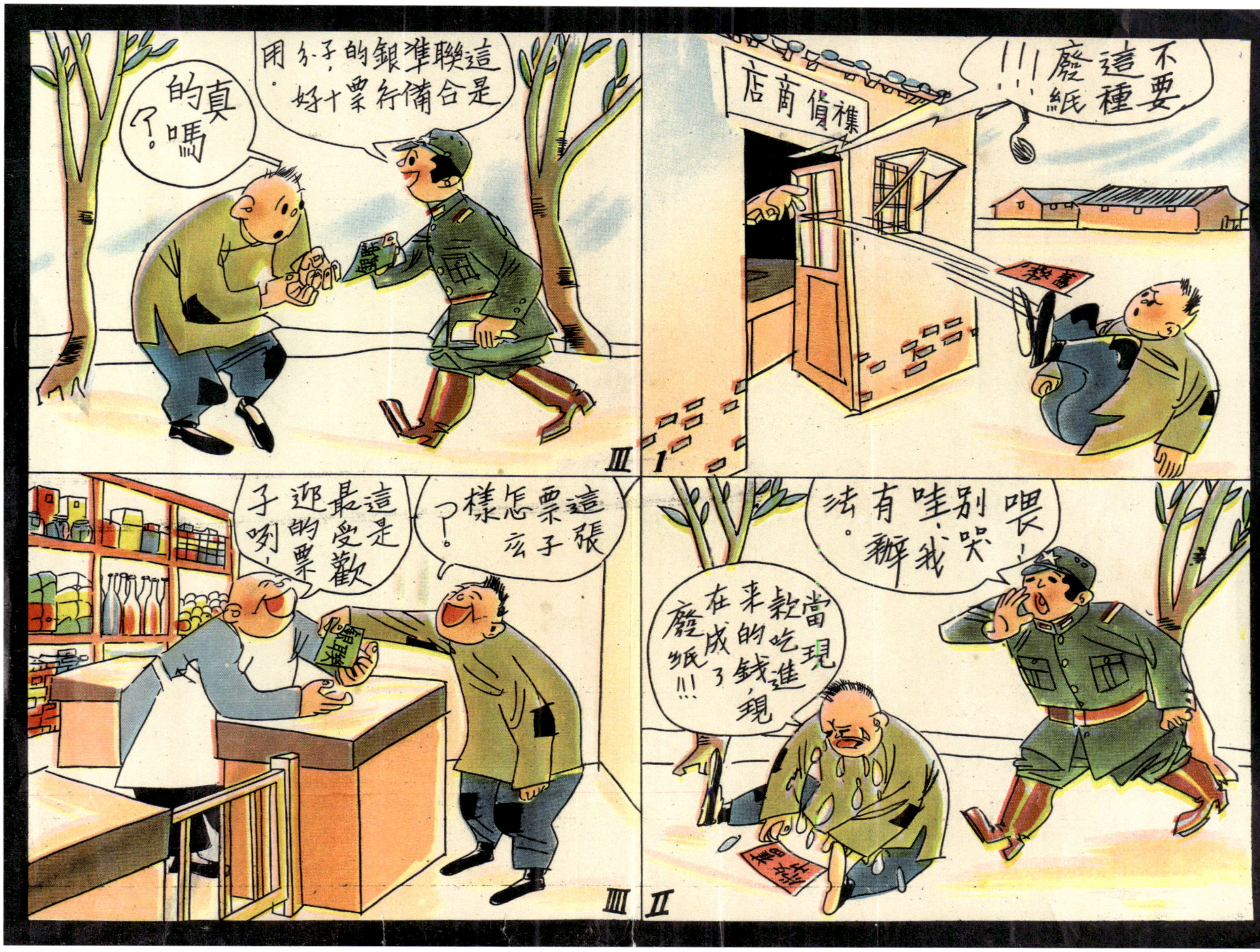
雜貨商店
不要這種廢紙!!!
喂!别哭哇,我有辦法。
當現款吃進来的錢,現在成了廢紙!!!
這是聯合準備銀行的票子,十分好用。
真的嗎?
這張票子怎麼樣?
這是最受歡迎的票子咧!

19

Manchukuo kimono

c. 1937

Japan

Stencil printing on silk

136 × 134 cm

British Museum 2012,3003.1

Purchase funded by American Friends of the British Museum

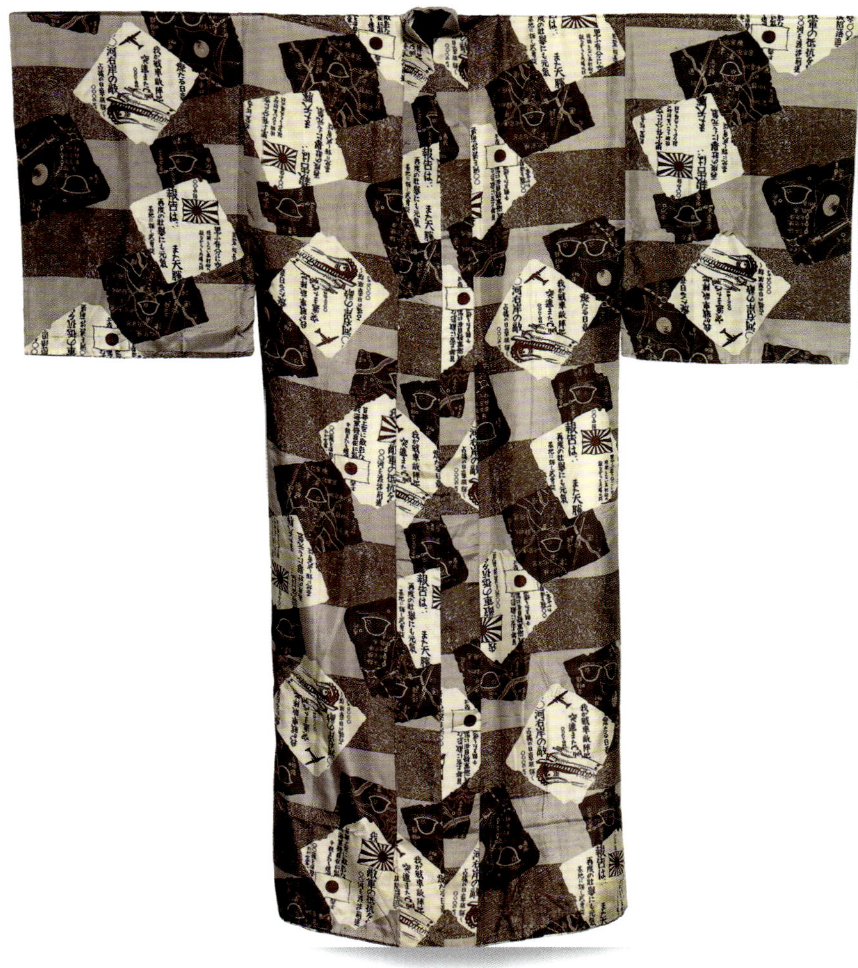

During the Asia-Pacific War, Japanese propaganda saturated 'a society that blended the perfect mixture of home front and battlefront'.[1] An enormous variety of designs, motifs and techniques decorated kimono, wrapping cloths, fans and other textile surfaces. Wearing propaganda was a public expression of commitment to the war effort. Many people also wore such textiles as a private expression of nationalism, with designs in the linings of garments that would not usually be visible.[2]

Propaganda textiles transmitted the spirit of patriotism, militarism and victory. Motifs included armaments, flags, industrial development, Japanese victory celebrations and Manchukuo themes (occupation, development, Japan-Manchukuo friendship and Manchurian railroads).[3]

This Manchukuo kimono is a montage of cartouches. The panels with helmet and soldier motifs are also map fragments. They seem to relate to the Tianjin-Pukou Railway Operation of 1937, where Japanese expansion followed the railway line south. Place names have been 'censored', replaced with blank circles in the propaganda slogans of the other panels.[4] They are interspersed with flags, planes and moving trains.

1 Kushner 2011, p. 9.
2 Taking off a *haori* (jacket over kimono) with a wartime-design lining became a kind of public display: a 'parlor performance'. Kashiwagi 2005, pp. 177–8.
3 Wakakuwa 2005, pp. 191–2. Wakakuwa outlines ten distinct groups of motifs prominent on wartime textiles. Kushner 2011, p. 14, notes the 'overwhelming importance devoted to China and Japan's presence on the mainland' in these textiles.
4 Alfred Haft, British Museum Collections Online.

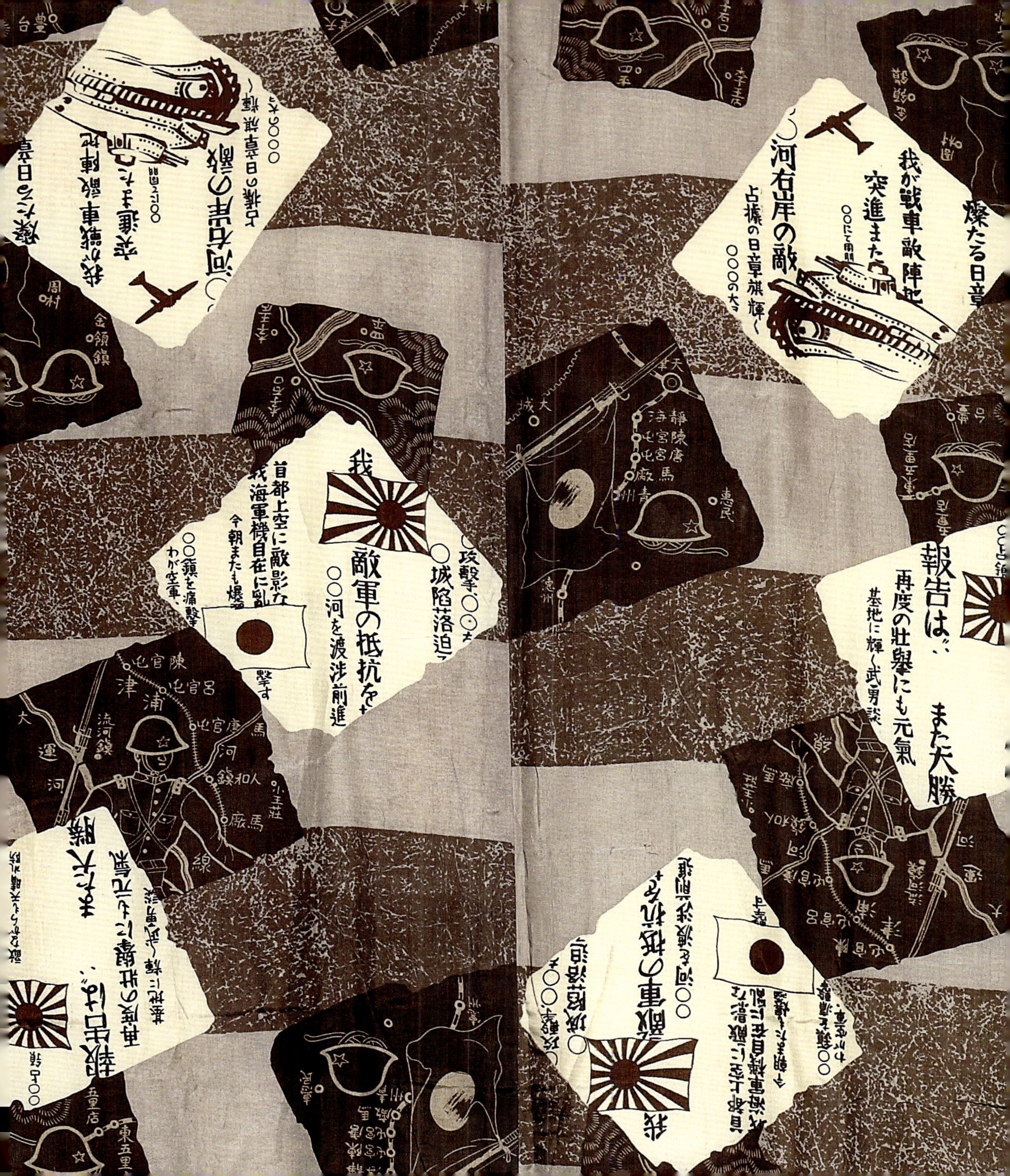

燦たる日章
我が戦車敵陣地
突進また
河右岸の敵
占據の日章旗輝く
我
○攻撃○○
○城陥落迫る
敵軍の抵抗を
○○河を渡渉前進
首都上空に敵影な
我海軍機自在に
今朝また
○○鎮を痛撃
わが空軍
撃す
報告は
再度の壮擧にも元氣
基地に輝く武勇談
また大勝

20

Saké cups

c. 1937–45

Japan

Porcelain with overglaze decoration

Diameter: 5.3–6.8 cm

British Museum 2006,0223.1–7

Given by Dr Nicole Coolidge Rousmaniere

These seven small saké (rice wine) cups were used for drinking toasts on group occasions. They are decorated with patriotic motifs, and each is inscribed with a slogan commemorating an event. They were probably used by Japanese soldiers during the Asia-Pacific War.[1]

One of the porcelain cups is celadon, and the other six are white. They all have overglaze gold and enamel decoration. The designs combine stars, flags and cherry blossoms; other motifs are a helmet, crane and turtle.

The inscriptions celebrate actions by particular Japanese divisions (departing for the Siberian Front, defending the Korean border) and a parade for the conquest of Manchuria. The second from the right, commemorating the Hygiene Department of the Army, is inscribed with the first line of a poem: 'The heart that devotes itself to the land of the Emperor'. Drinking from cups marking specific occasions would have strengthened morale, camaraderie and commitment among the troops.

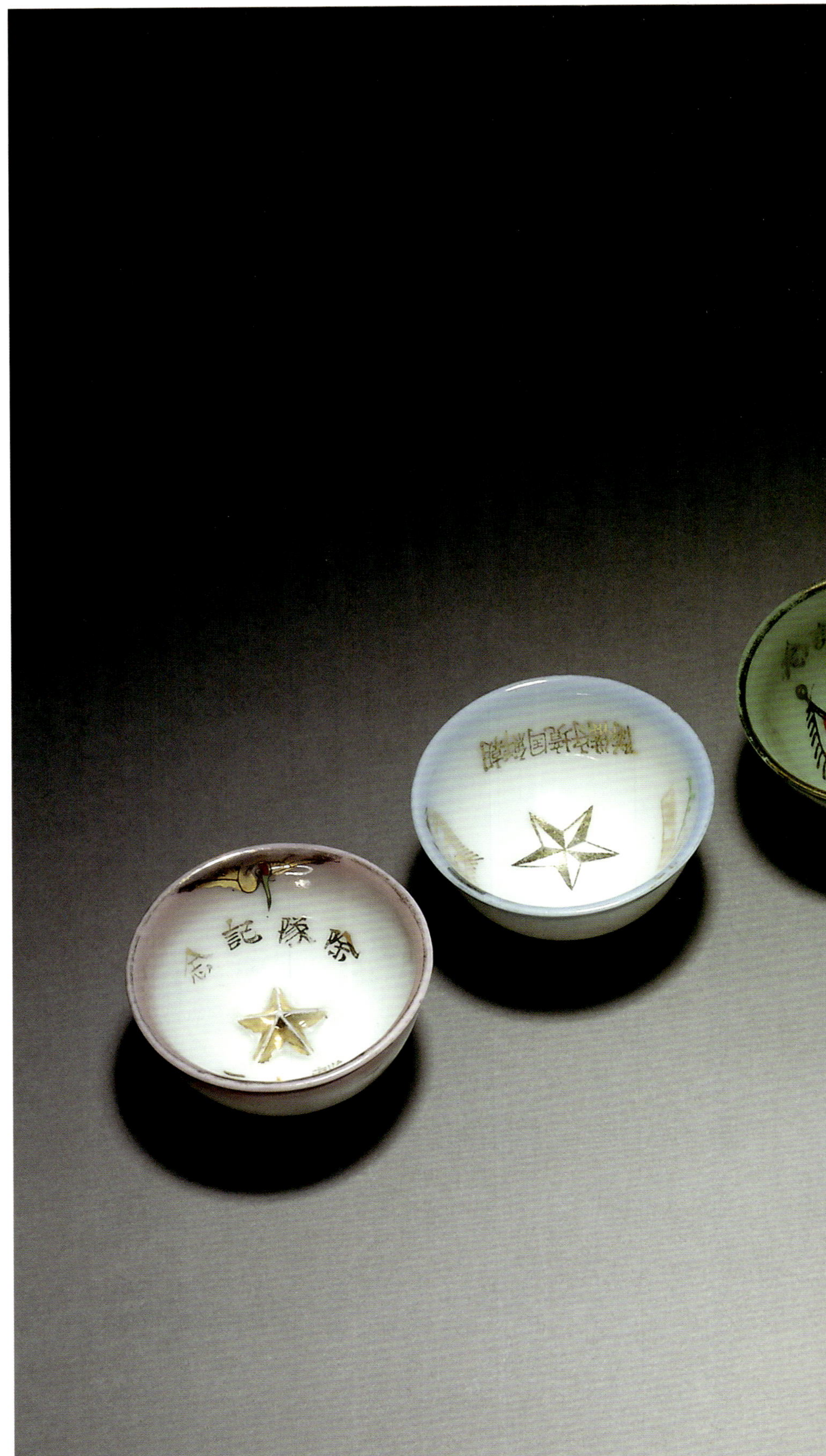

1 Nicole Coolidge Rousmaniere. See British Museum Collections Online for full individual descriptions, transcriptions and translations.

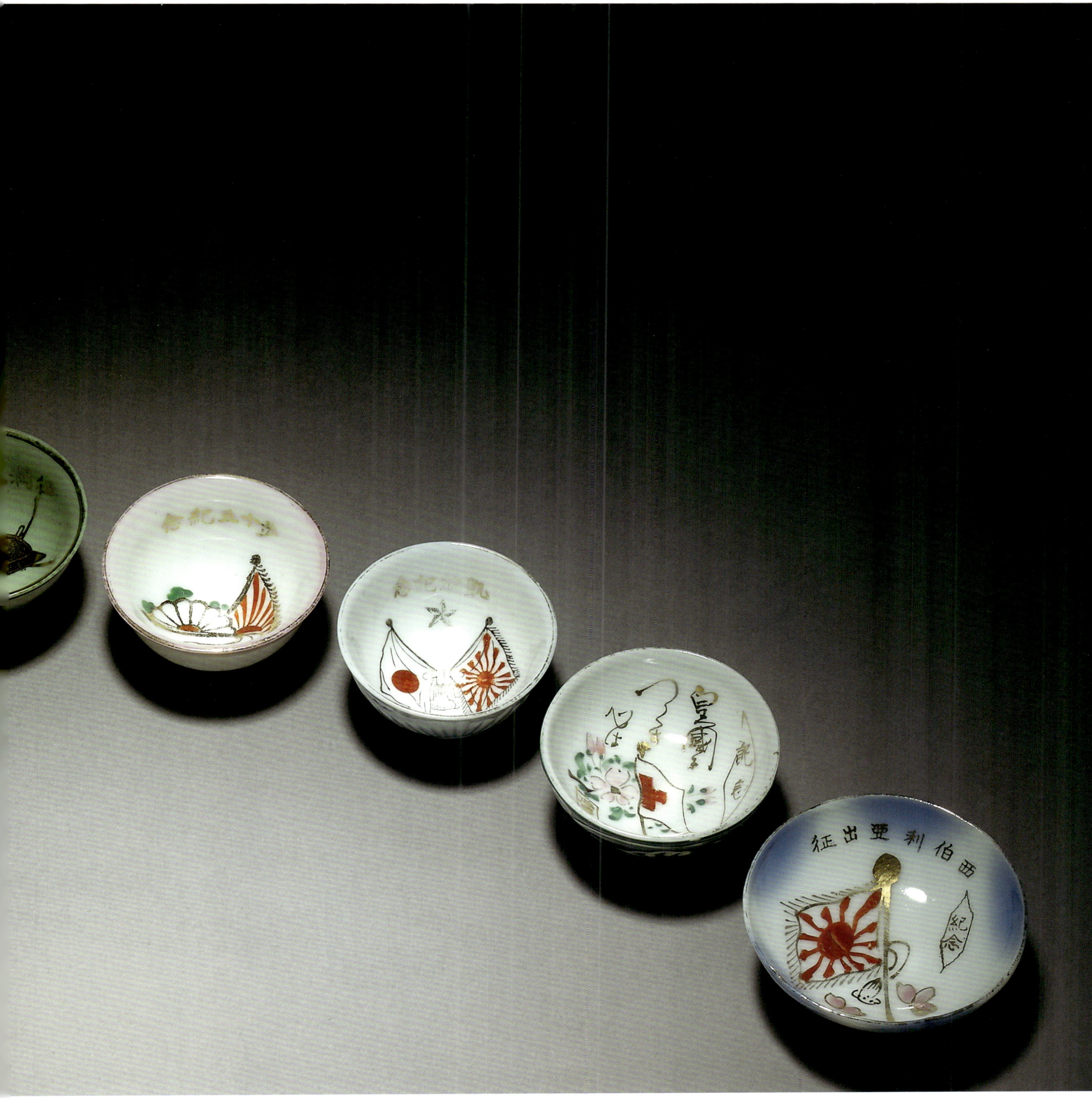
西伯利亜出征
紀念

21

FRONT magazine

1942

Japan

Coloured photographs, printed on paper

41.5 × 19 cm

British Museum 2008,3035.133, PB.390

Purchase funded by Brooke Sewell Bequest

FRONT magazine was published by the Eastern Way Company (Tohosha), a private company established by the Japanese military specifically to produce propaganda for foreign audiences.[1] *FRONT* was modelled on the 1930s publication *USSR in Construction*, which was designed by the avant-garde graphic artist El Lissitzky (1890–1941) with contributions by the photomontage innovator Alexander Rodchenko (1891–1956).[2] Sent to all countries of the Greater East-Asia Co-Prosperity Sphere, *FRONT* was published in fifteen languages.

FRONT portrayed the daily actions of ordinary soldiers, showing the development of the war through dynamic design and the advances of propaganda technology. 'Media technologists' pointed to new ways of working with 'background, foreground, color, layout, font and montage'.[3]

A series of special themed issues of *FRONT* covered branches of the armed services, Manchuria, Tokyo at war and other subjects. The British Museum has three volumes comprising two issues each.[4] The volume dealing with the navy is in French, the air force volume is in English and the Manchuria issues are in Japanese.

1 Kushner 2006, pp. 71–2.
2 Fraser 1996, p. 103. For several covers and double-page spreads, see pp. 103–4.
3 Kushner 2006, p. 74.
4 Ten volumes were produced, but copies of only nine survive. The entire stock of the tenth was destroyed in a 1945 air raid. British Museum Collections Online.

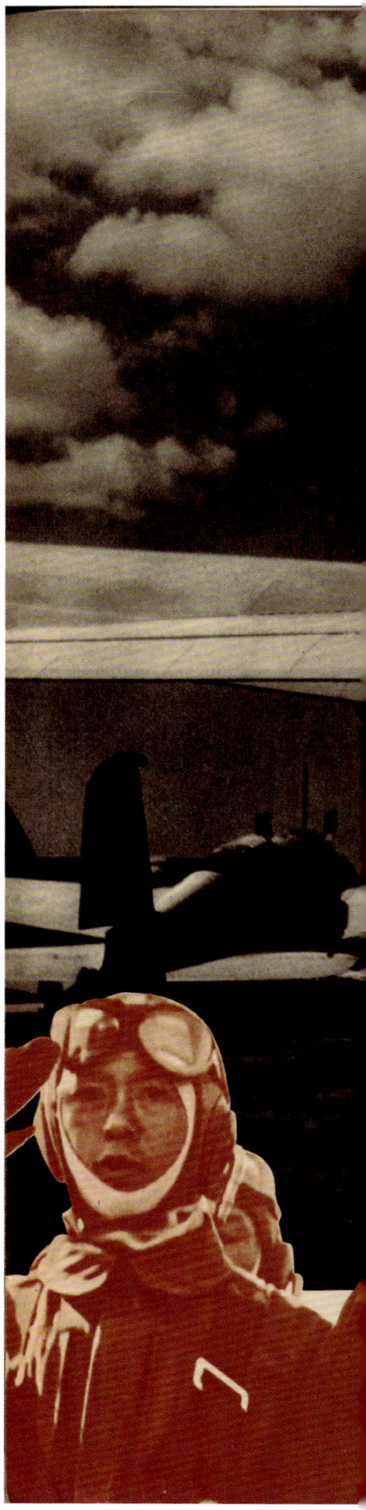

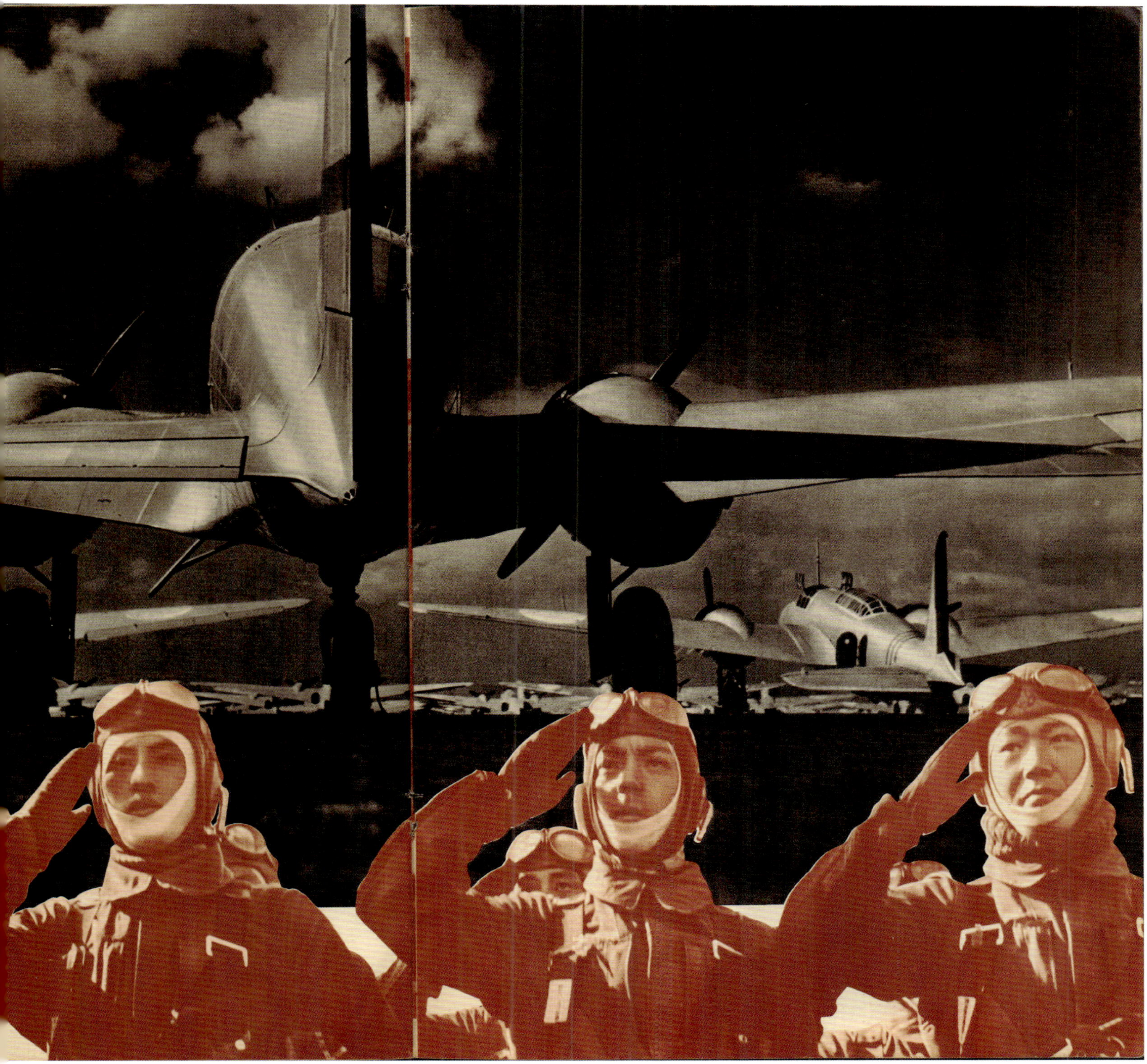

22

Settling Accounts (清算圖)

Mo Pu (莫朴)

China

1949

Woodblock print, ink and colours on paper

20 × 28.5 cm

British Museum 1999,0705,0.13

Land reform was among the Communists' top priorities and key to the Party's relationship with the masses. Land redistribution had direct appeal to the landless: not only for immediate material gain, but to end the practices of unjust and arbitrary exploitation by rich landlords in the villages.[1] A nationwide land reform law was not promulgated until 1950, but various programmes were carried out in the 'liberated areas' after the end of the war against Japan in 1945.

'Settling accounts' struggle sessions were typical in the late 1940s, resulting in the expropriation and division of the landlord's fields, houses and other property.[2] A struggle session is shown here. The peasants are accusing the landlord, literally tearing his house apart brick by brick (perhaps searching for money).

Mo Pu (1915–96), painter and printmaker, taught in the Fourth Route Army from 1940, then at Lu Yi[3] from 1943. He originally painted *Settling Accounts* in oils (1948), but remade it as a coloured woodcut in 1949, for wider circulation. After the establishment of the PRC he served as Vice-Director of the Zhejiang Academy of Fine Arts (ZAFA), until he was condemned as a rightist in 1957 and expelled from the CCP.[4] He returned to ZAFA after the Cultural Revolution (1966–76).

1 Suzanne Pepper, 'The KMT-CCP conflict, 1945–1949', in Eastman et al, 1991, pp. 291–356. During the Civil War (1946–9), Mao was convinced that the peasants stood with the CCP against the GMD where the May Fourth (1946) Land Reform Directive had been carried out; Communist army recruitment also increased directly with land reform (pp. 321–2).

2 Pepper in Eastman et al 1991, p. 322.

3 The Lu Xun Academy for Literature and Art, established in Yan'an in 1938.

4 Andrews 1994, p. 198.

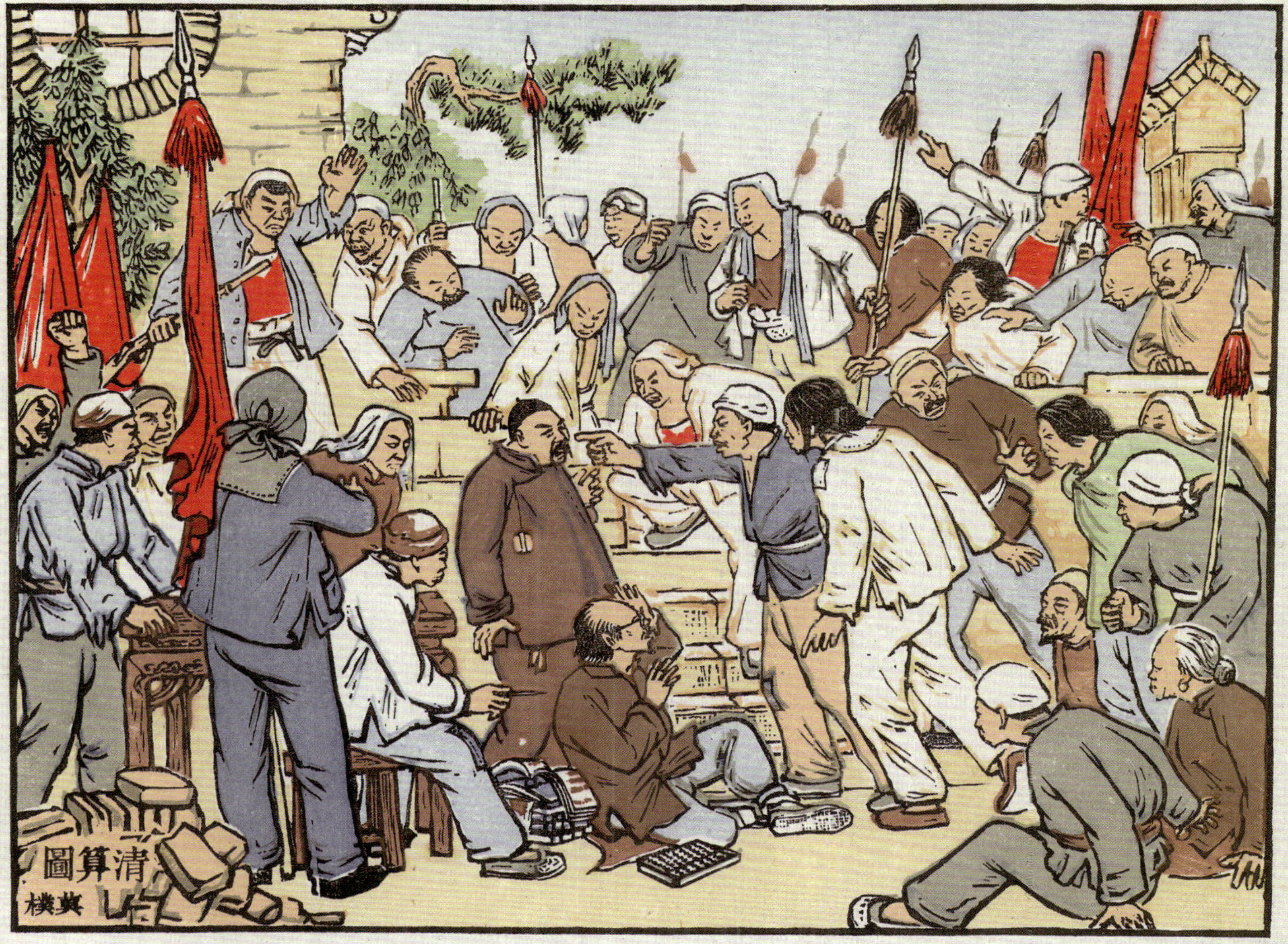
清算圖

23

Korean War Propaganda leaflet number 8729

What is happiness without a wife and children?
(沒有老婆沒有兒女人生還有甚麼幸福 meiyou laopo meiyou ernü rensheng hai you shenma xingfu)

March 1953

Korea

Photograph and text printed on paper

20 × 14 cm

Private collection

Billions of leaflets – the 'workhorse' of United States PSYWAR (psychological warfare) – were dropped from airplanes during the Korean War (1950–3).[1] Some were directed at North Korean Communists, urging them to give up a pointless war. Safe conduct passes promised good treatment to any surrendering fighter. Others encouraged South Korean partisans to support their own countrymen and destroy the Communist enemy. Many carried the theme of Soviet exploitation of China, and also China's exploitation of North Korea. Still others were aimed at the 'volunteer' Chinese forces, asking them why they should die in someone else's war.[2]

This 'pin-up' was aimed at Chinese soldiers. It was a leaflet in 'Plan Divide', intended to stimulate feelings for normal human relationships and to create opposition to the government keeping those men from home. The text is in Chinese characters and the phonetic system known as *bopomofo*. The 'Chinese' woman in traditional dress was in fact a patriotic citizen of the ROK, daughter of a government minister, who never gave permission to use her picture in this way.[3]

1 Friedman's account of US PSYWAR activities says 2.5 billion leaflets. Friedman (Korea) undated, part 1, p. 31. These were produced by three units in Tokyo from 1950 and by the Psychological Warfare Division of the US 8th Army in Korea itself.
2 North Korean propaganda aimed the same question at US servicemen.
3 Friedman (Korea) undated, part 2, p. 21.

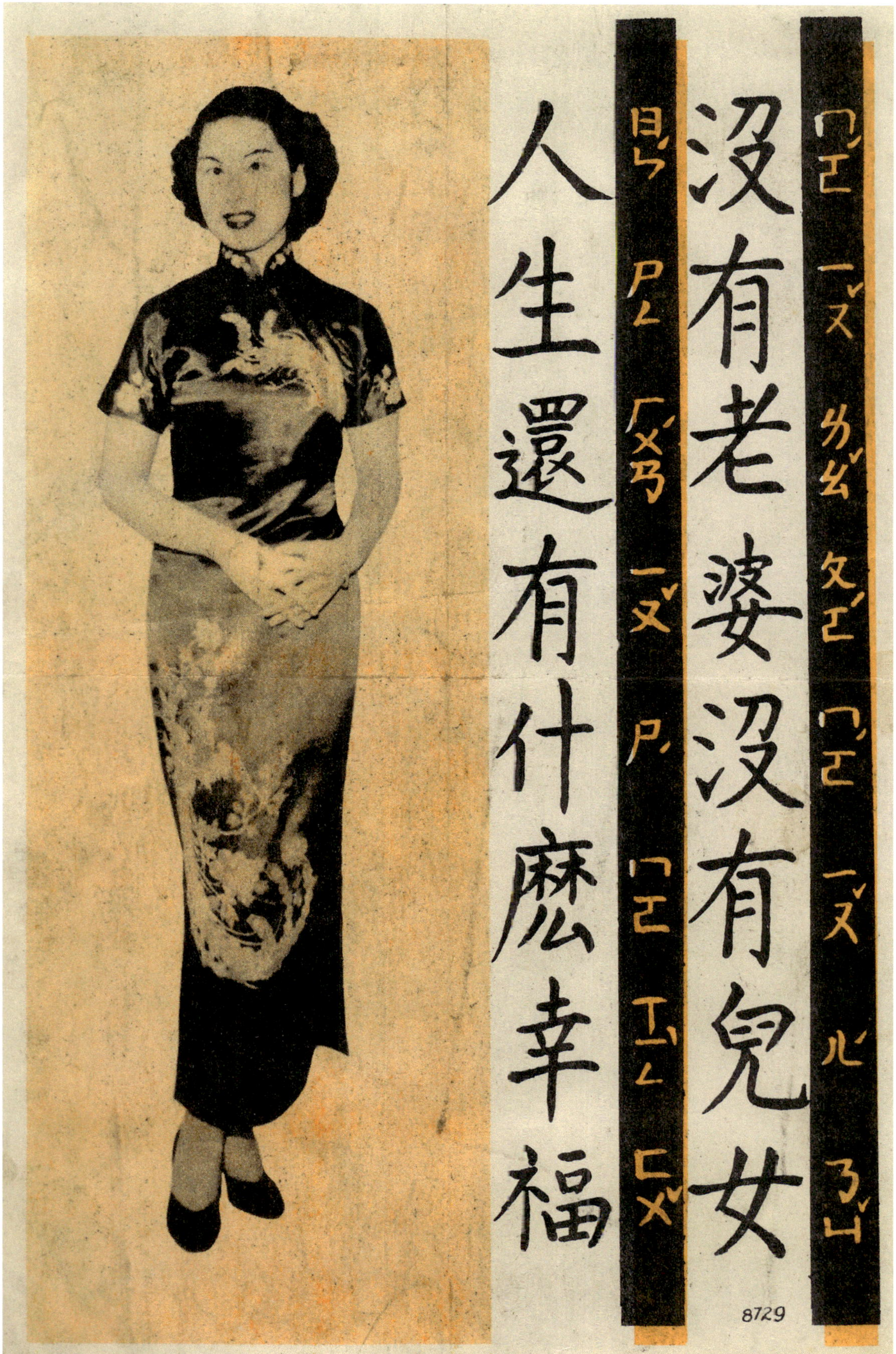
沒有老婆沒有兒女
人生還有什麼幸福
8729

24

Propaganda leaflet no. 3135/HPWS/4

1956–7

Malaya

Photograph and text printed on paper

26 × 16.5 cm

Private collection

The Malayan Emergency is considered a paradigm of successful counter-insurgency and was much studied by the United States military and intelligence authorities during the Vietnam War. The outcome is ascribed to a combination of factors, whose relative importance varied at different points in the drawn-out struggle: 'coercion, "winning hearts and minds", and achieving unified and dynamic control'.[1]

The Communists published numerous newsletters and newspapers to strengthen their ties to the local population. British propaganda activities were more intense and more effective. Propaganda was directed by the head of the Psychological Warfare Section (HPWS). During the twelve years 1948–60, more than 5,000 different leaflets, nearly 500 million in total, were disseminated, mostly dropped from airplanes.[2]

The messages were generally of two types. Leaflets used text and imagery to convince the Communist Terrorists (CTs) that their movement was hopeless and would only lead to misery and death. A common phrase was 'The choice of whether to sacrifice yourself and die is in your hands'.

The second type of message offered incentives to surrender and reminded citizens of official social provision. This leaflet promises that 'You, too, can go to the hospital'. The photograph shows a woman who had been gravely wounded but was well cared for in the modern government hospital. The text which covers the back side offers assurances that the government will look after everyone, including Communists who turn away from the insurgency.

1 Karl Hack, 'The Malayan Emergency as counter-insurgency paradigm', *Journal of Strategic Studies*, 32(3), 2009, pp. 383–414 (p. 383).
2 Friedman (Malaya) undated, pp. 13–14.

你也可以像她一樣得到醫院裡的良好醫藥照顧

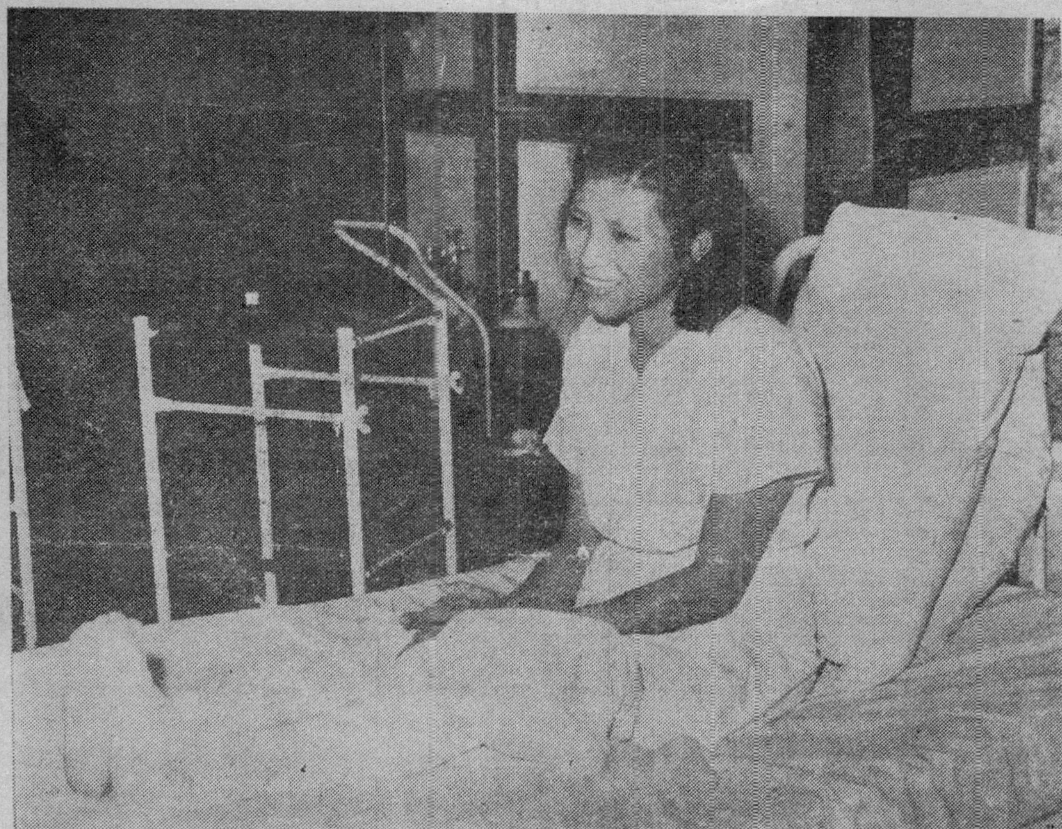

這是三妹(又名亞香)在醫院裡得到優良醫藥照顧的情形，當她於一九五六年七月十三日離開山芭的時候，她是受了重傷·但是現在她得到治療而恢復健康，不必在山芭裡流血致死了·現在她過着自由快樂的新生活，不必憂慮山芭裡的危險了。

3135 / HPWS / 4

25

Inscribed propaganda print

Signed Khu (unidentified artist)

c. 1945–54

Vietnam

Ink and colours on paper

15 × 23 cm

British Museum 1999,0630,0.4

Purchase funded by Brooke Sewell Permanent Fund

Published: Harrison-Hall 2002, cat. 1.9

26

Inscribed propaganda painting

Signed Luong (unidentified artist)

c. 1945–54

Vietnam

Ink, gouache, watercolour and crayon on paper

39 × 31.5 cm

British Museum 1999,0630,0.5

Purchase funded by Brooke Sewell Permanent Fund

Published: Harrison-Hall 2002, cat. 1.10

These two works were probably made during the Franco-Viet War (1946–54). They encourage people to boycott foreign goods and promote domestic self-sufficiency, delivering the same message in completely different styles.

The first is folk art in the style of a New Year print, using the shell-coated paper typical of that genre.[1] The young saleswoman's charms cannot induce the customers to buy imported Philip Morris cigarettes. Pointedly gesturing refusal, the pair leave the shop, declaring '*Không mua!*' (I'm not buying!).

The second work is a mixed-material painting, partially reminiscent of the flat graphic style of Soviet revolutionary cartoons. Caricature featured in Vietnamese anti-colonial posters from the 1920s.[2] Here a young street trader pushes his bicycle loaded with locally produced foods, textiles and other goods. His message is clear, and he practises what he preaches: 'Sell home-made goods. Don't sell luxury goods!' (*Buôn hańg nôi hóa. Không buôn xa xì phẩm!*) The Frenchman and American (identified by their flags) are crushed under the weight of the foreign luxuries they are trying to sell, apparently knocked over by the local hero.

1 Harrison-Hall 2002, p. 67.
2 Buchanan and Heather 2009, p. 7.

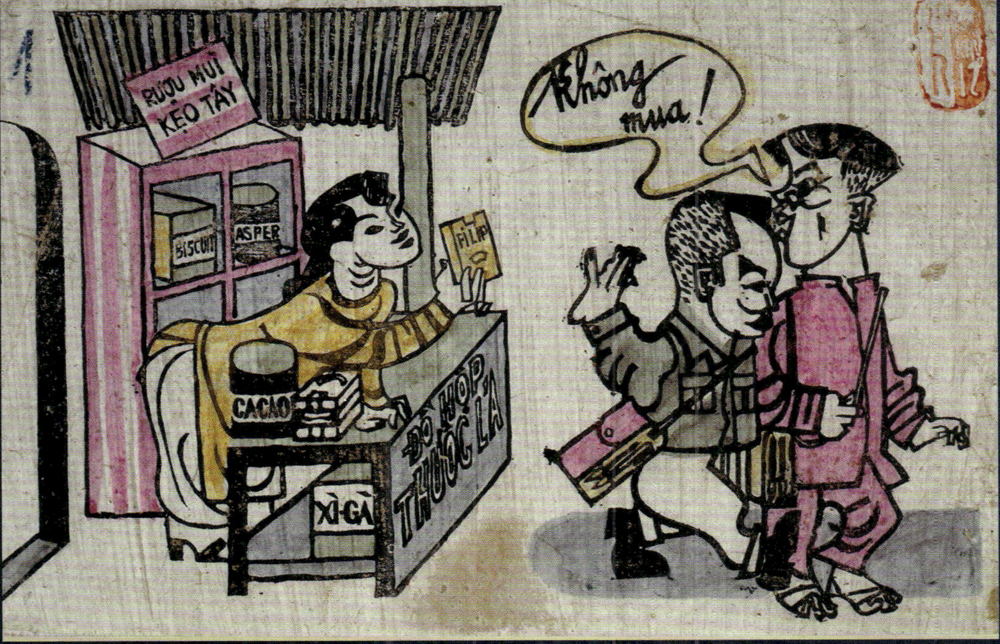
RƯỢU MÙI
KẸO TÂY
BISCUIT
ASPER
PILIP
CACAO
ĐỒ HỘP
THUỐC LÁ
XÌ-GÀ
Không mua!

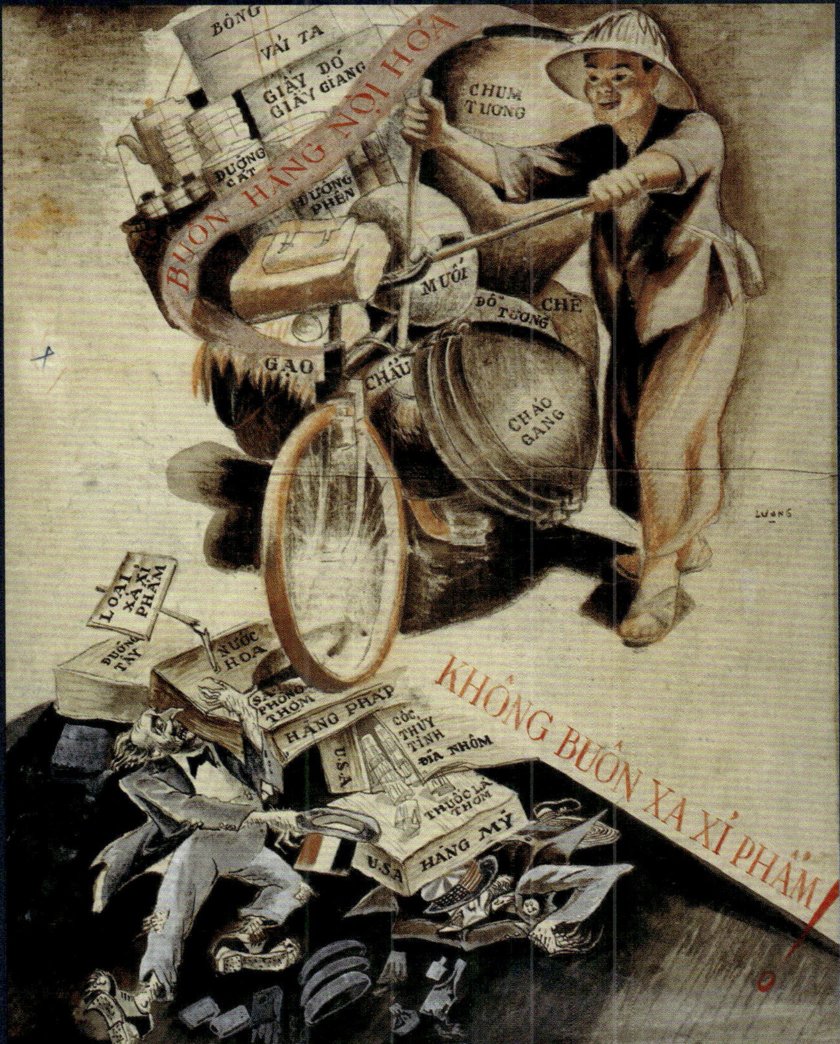
BÔNG
VẢI TA
GIẤY ĐỎ
GIẤY GIANG
CHUM TƯƠNG
ĐƯỜNG CÁT
ĐƯỜNG PHÈN
BUÔN HÀNG NỘI HÓA
MUỐI
ĐỖ TƯƠNG
CHÈ
GẠO
CHẤU
CHẢO GANG
LUONG
LOẠI XA XỈ PHẨM
ĐƯỜNG TÂY
NƯỚC HOA
PHÒNG THƠM
HÀNG PHÁP
CỐC THỦY TINH
ĐĨA NHÔM
U.S.A
THUỐC LÁ THƠM
U.S.A
HÀNG MỸ
KHÔNG BUÔN XA XỈ PHẨM!

27

Popular print of Dr Bhimrao Ramji Ambedkar

Late 20th century

India

Colour print on glossy paper

42.5 × 30 cm

British Museum 2003,0714,0.14

Purchase funded by British Museum Friends, Townley Group

Social mobility has traditionally been highly restricted under the Hindu caste system in India.[1] One of the great early fighters for equality was Dr B.R. Ambedkar (1891–1956), a social and political leader of India's Dalits (Untouchables). Born into a Mahar caste, members of which served in the military under British rule but were treated as Untouchables, he overcame economic and social obstacles to enter higher education, going on to earn doctorates in the US and England. He was a barrister, political economist, prolific author, orator and statesman.

Dr Ambedkar was also the chief architect of India's post-independence constitution. He fought for the annihilation of the caste system and ultimately abandoned Hinduism entirely, as he felt that the caste system was firmly anchored in Hinduism.[2] He also strove for gender equality, resigning from the post-independence government over this issue.

Dr Ambedkar is still honoured across India for his tireless efforts to establish modern social justice. He is always shown in Western clothes, usually a blue suit and tie, marking his rejection of Indian tradition. This is in contrast with Mahatma Gandhi, who always wore a *dhoti*.

1 Himanshu Roy undated, 'Contextualizing Dalit Mobility', http://www.oocities.org/frontierweekly/pdf-files/vol-42-10-13/dalit-42-10-13.pdf, pp. 1–4.

2 A few months before his death in 1956, he publicly and officially converted to Buddhism, as the only hope for achieving class equality. Hundreds of thousands of Dalits converted with him.

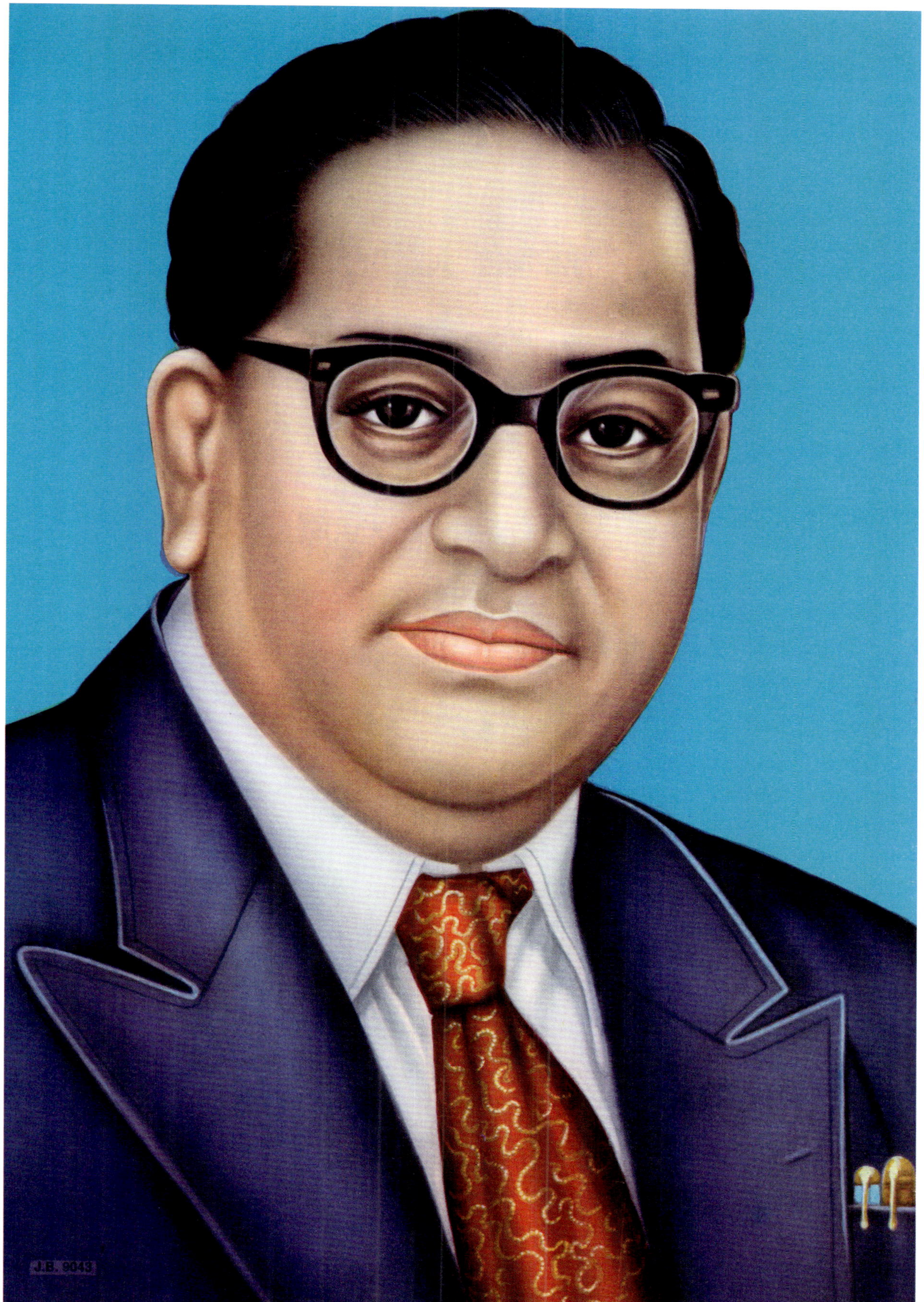
J.B. 9043

28

Mama Comes on a Tractor (妈妈开着拖拉机来了)
(*Mama kaizhe tuolaji laile*)

Zhang Daxin (長大昕)

1960

China

Lithograph, printed in ink and colours on paper

77 × 52 cm

British Museum 2006,0501,0.38

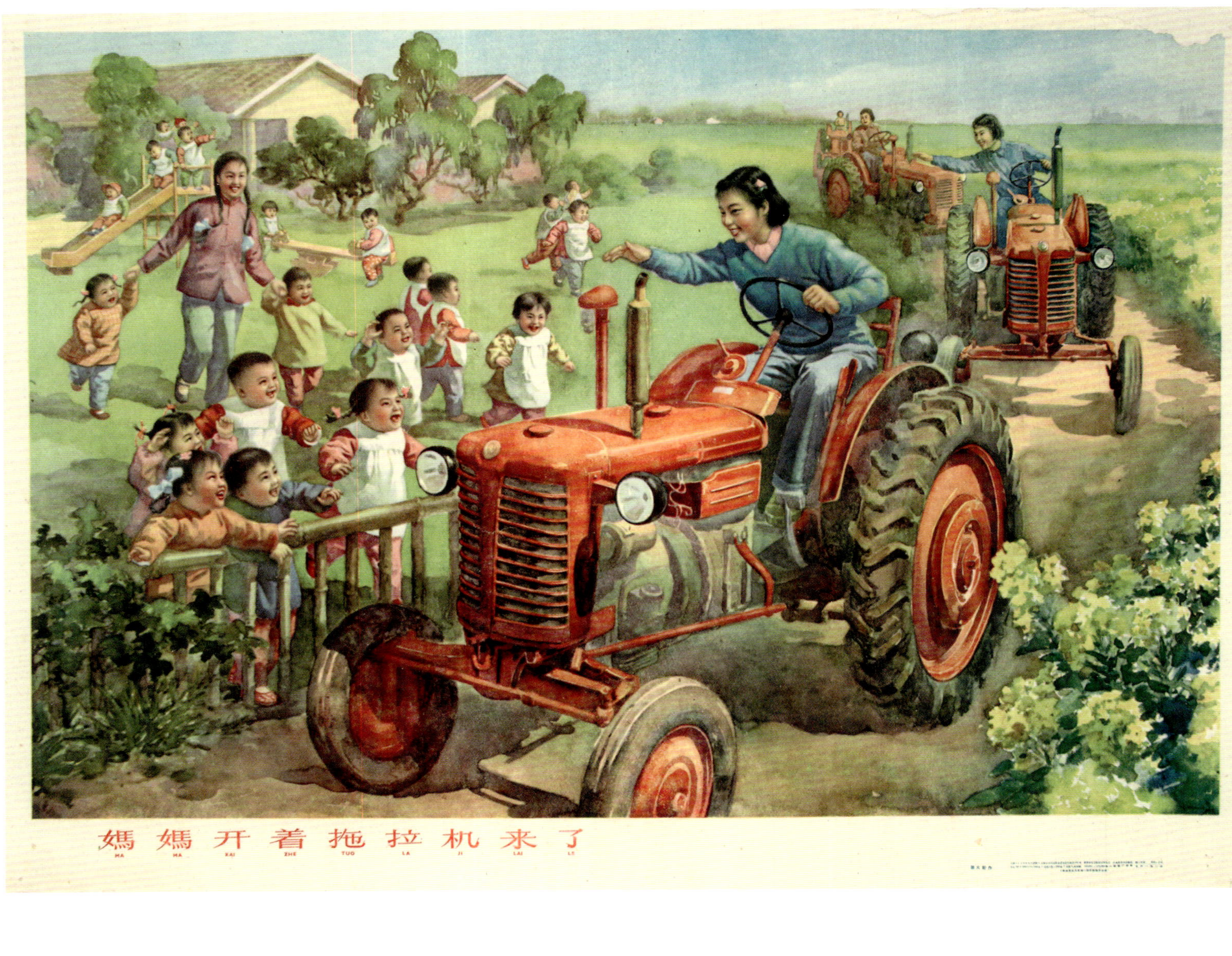

29

Agricultural Mechanization (农业机械化)
(農業機械化 *Nongyye jixiehua*)

1966–76

China

Teapot, polychrome glazed porcelain

24 × 20 cm

Private collection

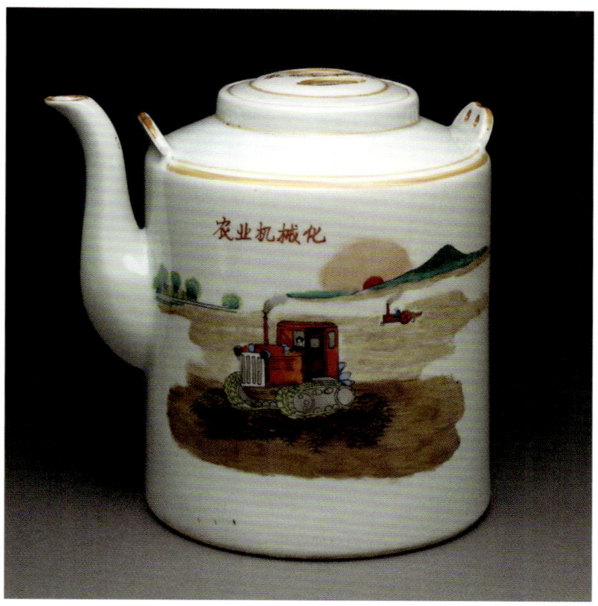

The tractor was a frequently exploited trope in the art of socialist countries (see cat. 32). These were rural societies, ideologically bent on rapid economic development. The tractor, symbol of agricultural mechanization, was the chariot to the future. In these objects, women are the drivers of socialist construction. Female tractor drivers appeared as model workers early and often in the PRC and were known as *nüjie diyi* (女界第一), the 'female-world-first'.

In China, *nianhua* (single-page popular prints), *lianhuanhua* (serial picture books) and other media featured the theme during the optimistic 1950s, as the economy stabilized and grew. The style is of this poster is rather sentimental, with an idealized village setting – the reality was very different. The poster was made during the Great Leap Forward (1958–61), years of disastrous agricultural and industrial policies.

The teapot is part of a seven-piece group made in Jingdezhen, Jiangxi province, consisting of vases, jars and planters. They would have been displayed as a set in an official building, probably associated with agriculture. The painterly style of the decoration is in marked contrast to most porcelain production of the Cultural Revolution. Two tractors are working in the glow of the still-red evening sun (always meaningful). In the background, green smoke billows from local factories.

1 Liang Jun, one of the first, even appeared on the one-yuan banknote issued in 1962. Stefan Landsberger, http://www.chineseposters.net/themes/tractor-girls.php. This website includes many posters of women tractor drivers.

30

Construction Site (工地)

Wang Xuyang (王緒陽), Song Wenzhi (宋文治), Wu Junqi (吳君琪), Cao Fuquan (曹輔荃), Gao Zengxiu (高增修)

June 1961

China

Hanging scroll, ink and colours on paper

58 × 42 cm

Private collection

This painting is a collaborative work by five artists who worked in Jiangsu province in eastern China during the second half of the twentieth century. It shows a large group of enthusiastic workers heading towards a construction site. They carry a double happiness banner (囍), a symbol of celebration most often seen at weddings.

The official painting style in the early 1950s was Socialist Realism, and the prevailing medium was oil painting. Traditional Chinese painting (*guohua*, 國畫) on silk or paper, such as this example, was given much less prominence in the art academies and in state-sponsored exhibitions.

During the Great Leap Forward (1958–61), policies and styles changed. Paintings were meant to combine 'revolutionary realism' and 'revolutionary romanticism'. With the great emphasis on manual labour and rapid industrial development, artists were required to participate in construction projects and to portray the achievements of collective labour. Traditional landscapes were permissible backgrounds, provided they included active agricultural or industrial workers. The colours here are bright, but relatively soft. This painting is also traditional in its hanging scroll format.

Song Wenzhi (1919–99) was one of the leaders of the *guohua* revival. He combined landscapes with politics right through to the end of the Cultural Revolution. In the 1980s he then turned to more traditional scenic imagery, without explicit political content.

1 Laing 1988, p. 30.
2 Sullivan 1996, p. 143.

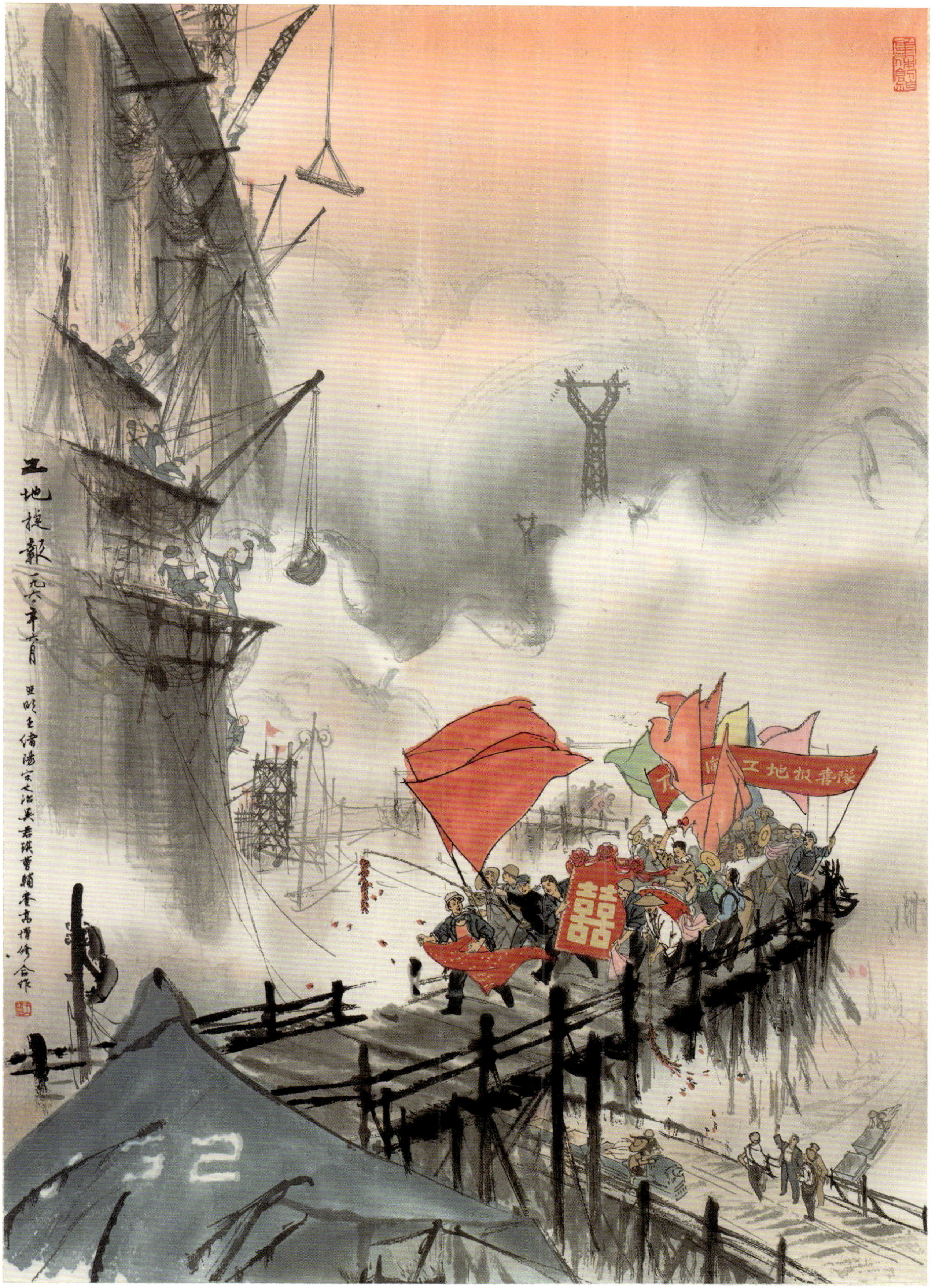
工地捷報
一九六〇年六月
工地報喜隊

31

An Olympic Torch Runner

Photographed by Hayasaki Osamu (早崎治)

Designed by Kamekura Yusaku (亀倉雄策)

Early 1964

Japan

Multicolour photogravure on paper

103.8 × 73 cm

British Museum 2009,3026.4

Purchase funded by Modern Museum Fund

Japan was the planned site for the 1940 Olympics, and Olympic fever had galvanized the nation from the time the announcement was made in 1936. In 1938, however, the financial and material requirements of war forced Japan to cancel the Games.[1] Hosting the 1964 Olympics was thus the realization of a long-held ambition. It showcased Japan's post-war reconstruction and marked the beginning of the country's international rehabilitation, particularly since the summer games had never before been held in Asia. Ninety-three nations participated.

An Olympic Torch Runner was the last in a series of four official posters designed for the Games.[2] Kamekura (1915–97) was one of Japan's most innovative designers. The posters combined graphic motifs of the rising sun and Olympic rings with dynamic photographs of the athletes. It was the first time photography was used to promote the Olympics. The torch bearer in the poster was a track-and-field athlete, Tanaka, at Juntendo University. The final torch-bearer, who lit the Olympic Cauldron, was chosen symbolically: Sakai Yoshinori was born on 6 August 1945, the date of the atomic bombing of Hiroshima.

1 Kushner 2006, pp. 48–9.
2 For discussion of the individual posters, see Tim Clark, British Museum Collections Online.

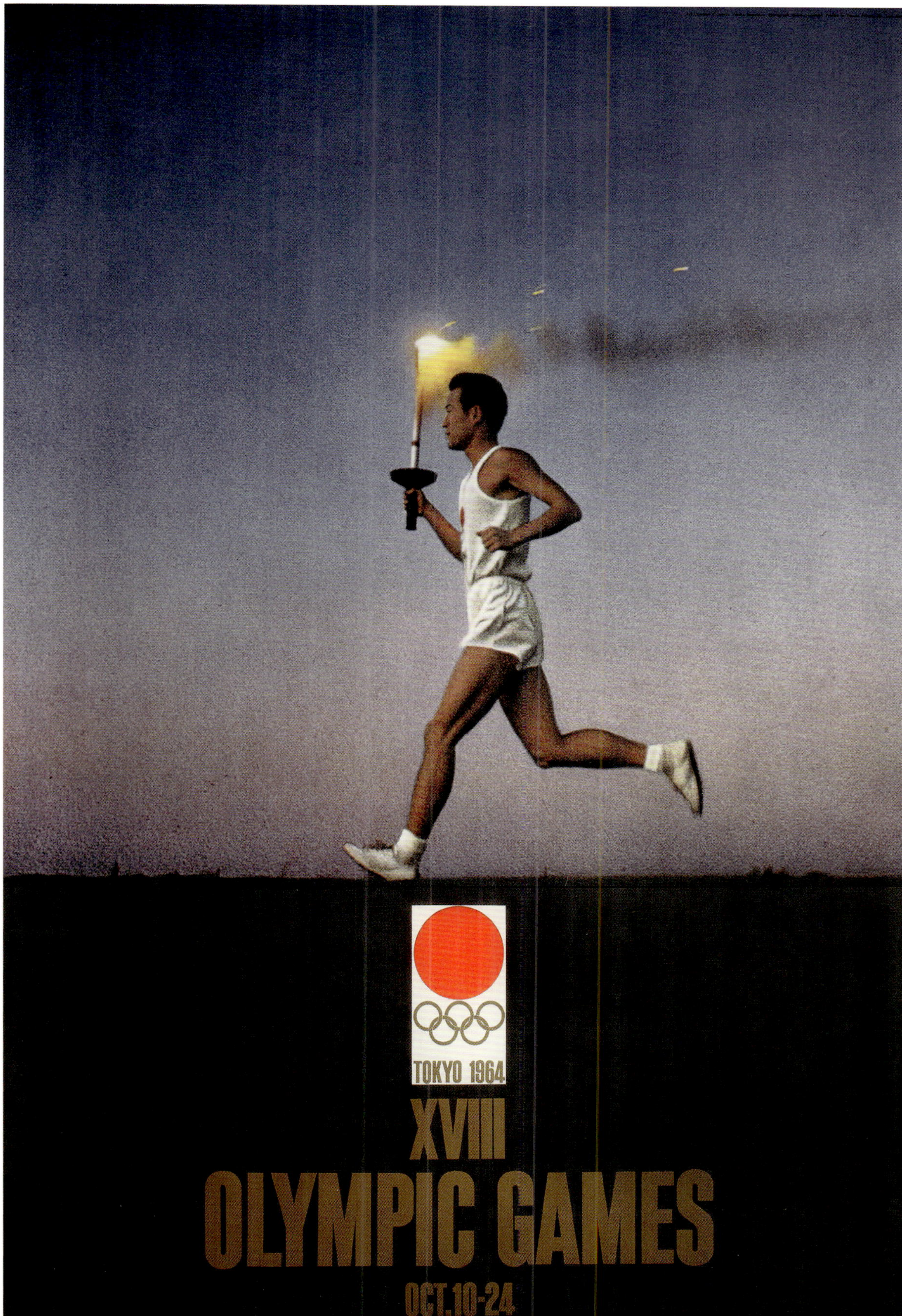
TOKYO 1964
XVIII
OLYMPIC GAMES
OCT.10-24

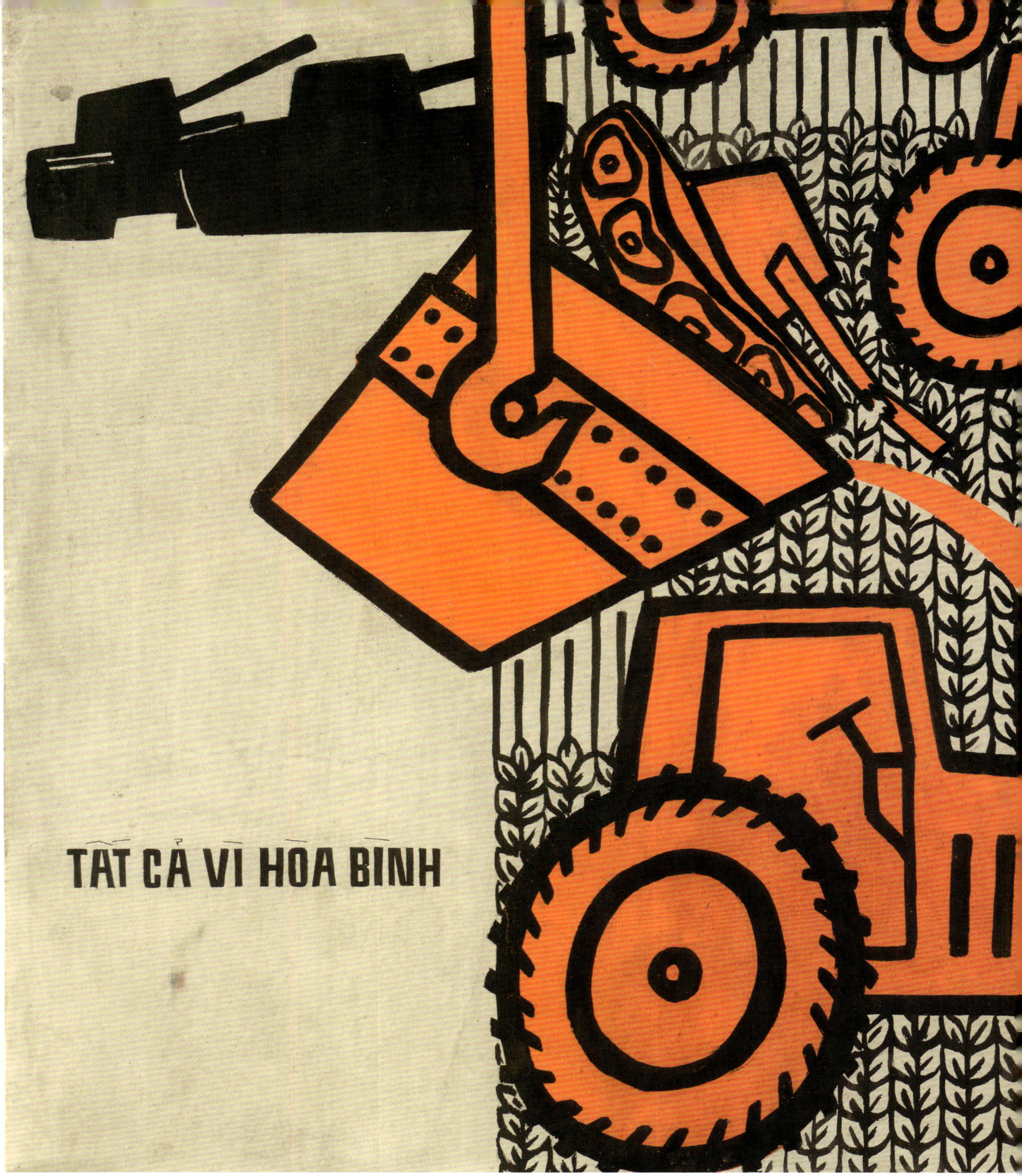
TẤT CẢ VÌ HOÀ BÌNH

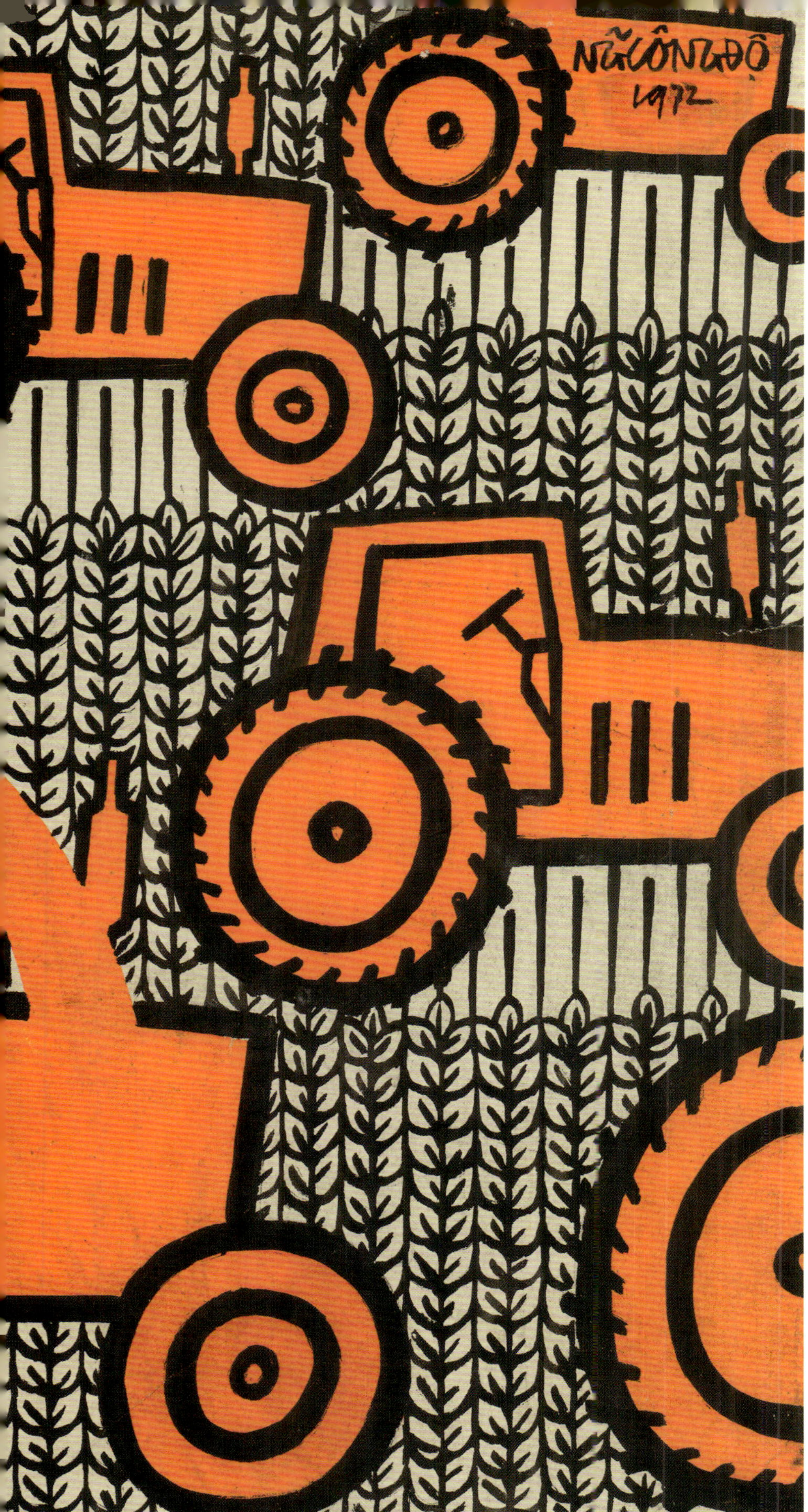

32

All for the sake of Peace (Tất Cả Vì Hòa Bình)

Nguyen Cong Do

1972

Vietnam

Gouache on paper

54.5 × 79 cm

British Museum 1998,1215,0.2

Given by the British Museum Friends

Published: Harrison-Hall 2002, cat. 1.3

Inspired by Ho Chi Minh, Nguyen Cong Do (b. 1930) joined the Army during the Franco-Vietnam War as a journalist and poster artist, and afterwards was a filmmaker for the North. He studied photography and filmmaking in Germany, then at the Fine Arts College in North Vietnam during the 1960s, but returned to the Army in 1970, concentrating on posters.[1]

By 1972 the tide had turned in the American-Vietnam War. This work shows tanks being transformed into tractors: military equipment converted for peaceful production. The flat, geometric graphic design is bold and immediate. Its hopeful message would be perfectly clear without an inscription.

To a Western audience, the poster calls to mind the biblical invocation (Isaiah 2:4): 'They shall beat their swords into ploughshares, and their spears into pruning hooks: nation shall not lift up sword against nation, neither shall they learn war any more.'

1 Stern and Buchanan 2002 p. 87.

33

Applauding February

Song Shi-yop (b. 1934)

2001

Democratic People's Republic of Korea

Painting with ink and colours on paper

163 × 93 cm

British Museum 2002,1001,0.3

Purchase funded by Brooke Sewell Permanent Fund

Published: Portal 2005, pl. 114

The political culture of North Korea has been entirely dominated by the cult of the Kim family. Kim Il-sung (1912–94) is the Great Leader, who ruled the Democratic People's Republic of North Korea (DPRK) from its establishment in 1948 until his death. His son, Kim Jong-il (1942–2011), is referred to as the Dear Leader. In this painting, fireworks over Mt Paektu celebrate the great occasion of Kim Jong-il's birth on 16 February. Officially, the Dear Leader was born on the wartime guerilla base of his father, now known as Jong-il Peak, on Mt Paektu.[1]

Mt Paektu has enormous significance in North Korean propaganda. It is claimed to be not only the birthplace of Kim Jong-il, but also of Tan'gun (Dangun), the legendary founder of Korea (cat. 45). B.R Myers notes that Mt Paektu acquired sacred significance in the 1940s, 'à la Mt. Fuji'. Potent Japanese symbols such as Mt Fuji and the divine founder emperor Jimmu were familiar from the Occupation era (1905–45). Myers argues that Kim Il-sung appropriated and transformed these symbols to recreate North Korean history.[2] He further points to the propaganda message connecting the nation's topographical attributes – lofty peaks, forests and pure lakes – to the virtues of the Korean race, and relates this world-view to Fascist notions.[3]

1 Soviet records indicate that he was born in Khabarovsk on 16 February 1941. Kim Il-sung, the Great Leader, served in anti-Japanese units in both China and Russia, returning to Korea in 1945.
2 Myers 2010, pp. 75–6.
3 Myers 2010, pp. 72–3.

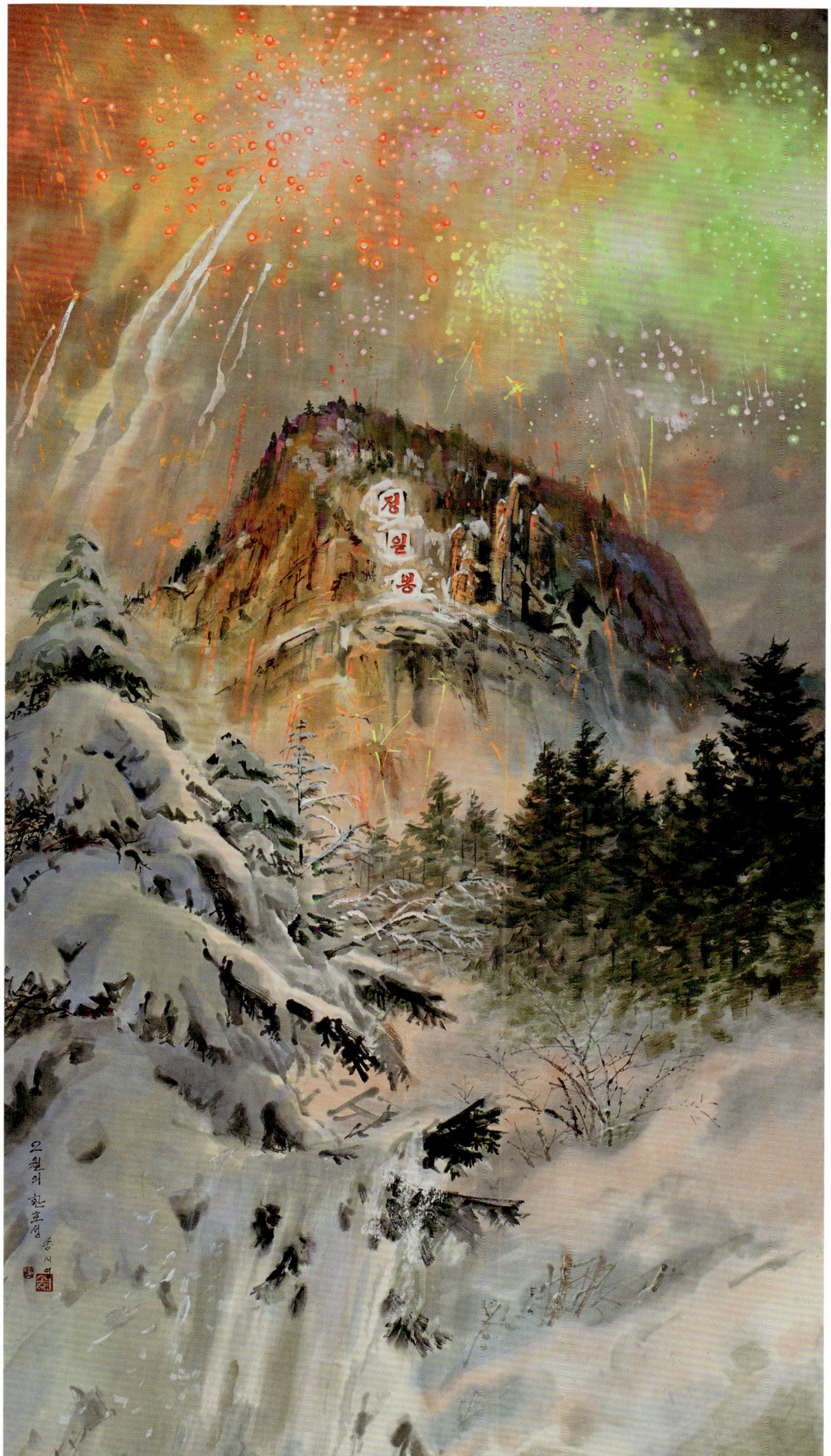
정
일
봉

Propaganda in Daily Life

Defining the techniques of wartime propaganda, Harold Lasswell wrote: 'Not bombs nor bread but words, pictures, songs, parades, and many similar devices are the typical means of making propaganda.'[1] The national anthem and the flag are emotionally charged signs of the state. Other objects, such as coins, banknotes and postage stamps, continually circulate images of authority. Users of these transactional items may or may not be affected by their symbolism in uneventful times. However, national tribulation or celebration can bring special significance to patriotic imagery on money, stamps or ration coupons (cat. 35).

Direct and indirect messages on objects of everyday life surely influence our attitudes and behaviour.[2] The items shown here include some produced by commercial agents as well as official cultural and educational authorities. The textile label was made for the Indian market, with an immediately recognizable image (cat. 34). The ceramic figures similarly represent iconic personages, but would have been objects of honour, not ephemera, as the label was (cat. 39). The cigarette lighter would have been meaningful to a smaller audience (cat. 38). Political posters were vehicles of persuasion, instruction, decoration and social intercourse in 1950s China (cat. 36). The example shown here served as a politically correct wedding gift.

1 Lasswell 1927, p. 206.
2 Elsewhere, Lasswell wrote that: 'the detailed suffering of a little girl and her kitten can motivate our hatred against the Germans, arouse our sympathy for Armenians, make us enthusiastic for the Red Cross, or lead us to give money for a home for cats.' http://www.propagandacritic.com/articles/ww1.demons.html.

Wrapping cloth (detail).
1931–45. Japan.
Printed cotton, 72.5 × 67 cm.
Private collection

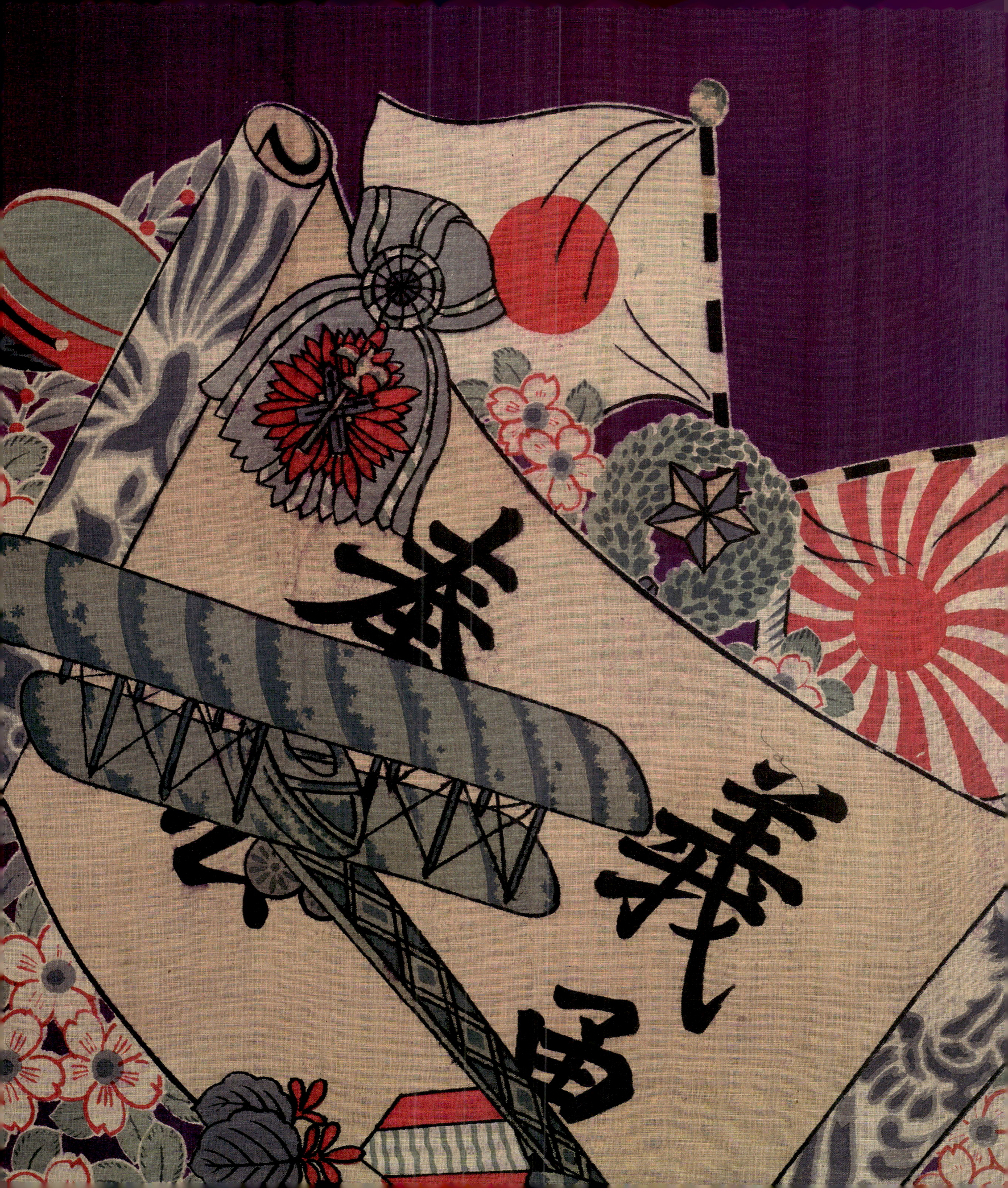

34

Textile label

Early 20th century

India/Great Britain

Chromolithograph on paper

13.7 × 10.3 cm

British Museum 2008,3020.89

This label was produced for Ewing & Co., an important Scottish textile firm. Labels like this were designed in India, printed in Britain and sent back to India, attached as advertisements to export textiles sold in the Indian market. This is one of a group of 112 labels in the British Museum. They are rare, because the labels on the British-made cloth were usually destroyed when the goods were unpacked or sold.

There is a great range of designs and motifs associated with these labels. Among the most common are Hindu gods and goddesses and themes from the great epics, such as the *Ramayana*. This is not propaganda in the usual sense of official sponsorship; it is commercial advertising with a patriotic theme. Queen Victoria was symbolic of the British empire. She is shown here holding a grandchild or great-grandchild, flanked by two loyal attendants, Sheikh Chidda and Ghulam Mustafa.[1] Victoria had a special affection for India and from the time she took the title Empress in 1876, there was usually an Indian member of her personal staff.

1 A very similar image, minus the baby, is a photograph in Shrabani Basu, *Victoria and Abdul: The True Story of the Queen's Closest Confidant*, Stroud: The History Press, 2010, pl. 22. Thanks to T. Richard Blurton for this identification.

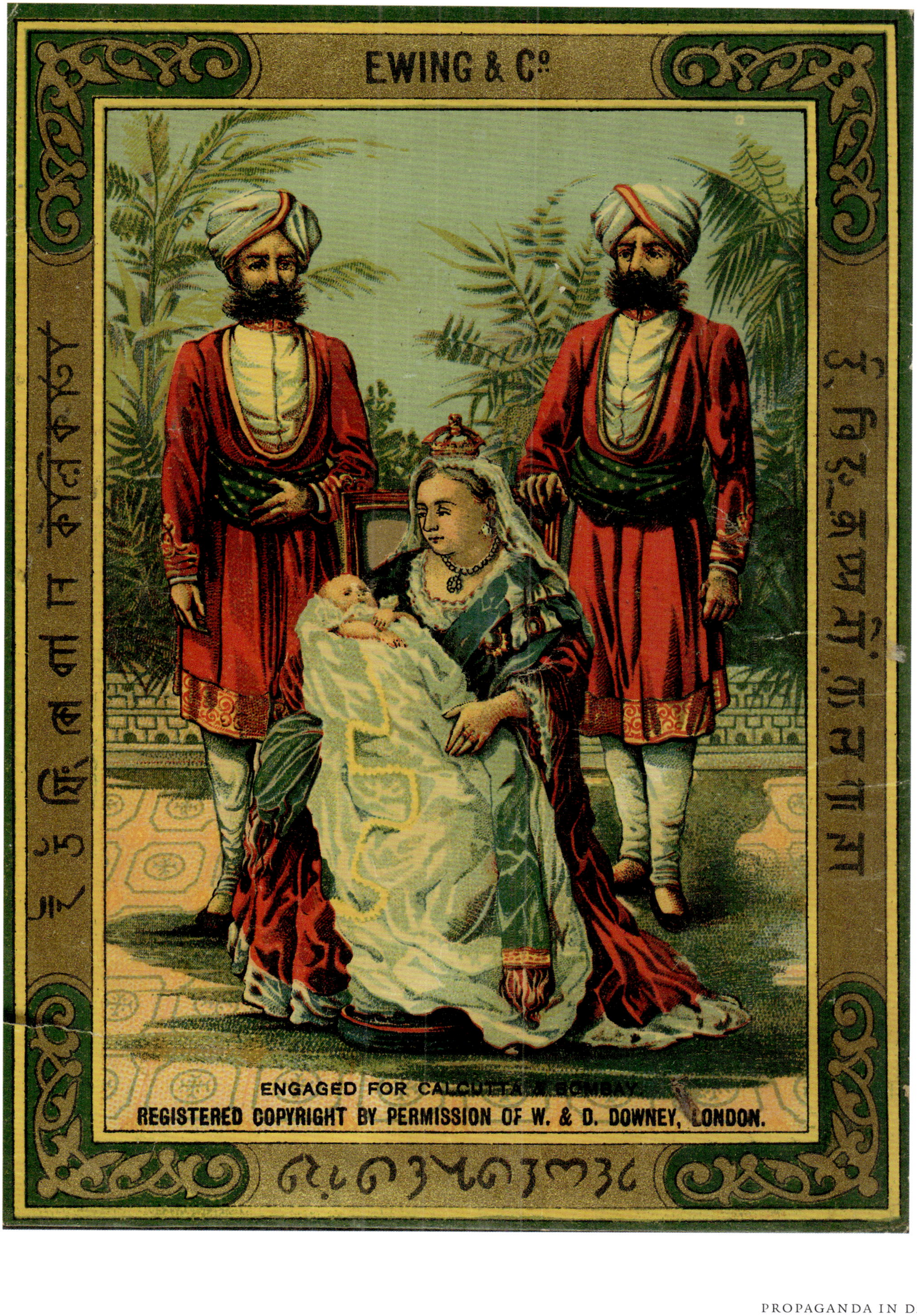
EWING & Co
ENGAGED FOR CALCUTTA & BOMBAY.
REGISTERED COPYRIGHT BY PERMISSION OF W. & D. DOWNEY, LONDON.

35

100-yuan banknote

Issued by the Bank of Taiwan

1947

Taiwan

Printed on paper

8.2 × 15.4 cm

British Museum 1979,1042.76

Japan occupied Formosa (Taiwan) from 1895 until 1945. The banknotes produced after the Asia-Pacific War, when the Japanese had departed, featured portraits of Sun Yat-sen (1866–1925) and other patriotic imagery. On either side of Sun Yat-sen on the front of this banknote are the Bank of Taiwan and a map of the island.

The image on the back portrays the Siege of Fort Zeelandia, an important Chinese victory over European settlers in 1662.[1] When the Ming dynasty (1368–1644) loyalist General Zheng Chenggong (1624–62), also known as Koxinga, was defeated by the Manchus, he retreated to find a new base of operations. In 1661 his forces attacked Fort Zeelandia in southern Taiwan, then controlled by the Dutch East India Company. After a ten-month siege the Dutch governor surrendered, and Koxinga established a new Ming-style administration on the island. He died shortly thereafter and was succeeded by his son. The Dongning (or Tungning) Kingdom lasted until 1683, when Qing dynasty (1644–1911) forces attacked and Taiwan was incorporated into China.

1 Tonio Andrade, 'Lessons from Europe's first war with China', Berfrois, 1 March 2012, http://www.berfrois.com/2012/03/koxingas-war-tonio-andrade.

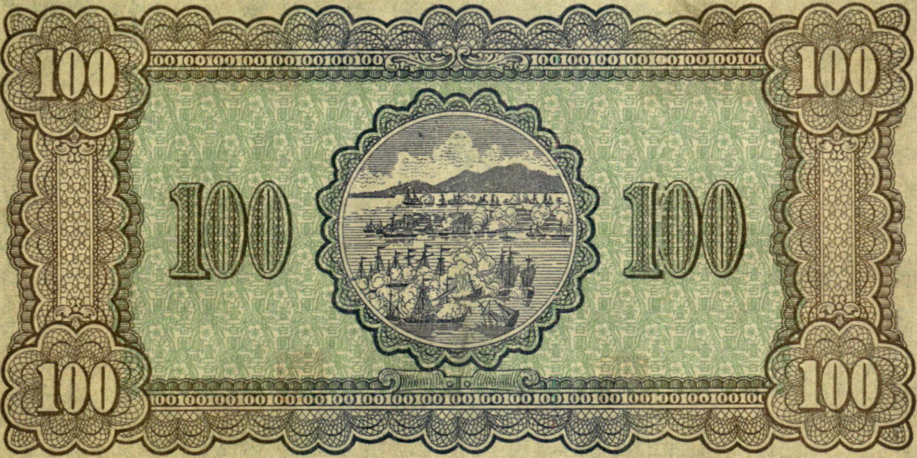
100
100
100
100
100
100

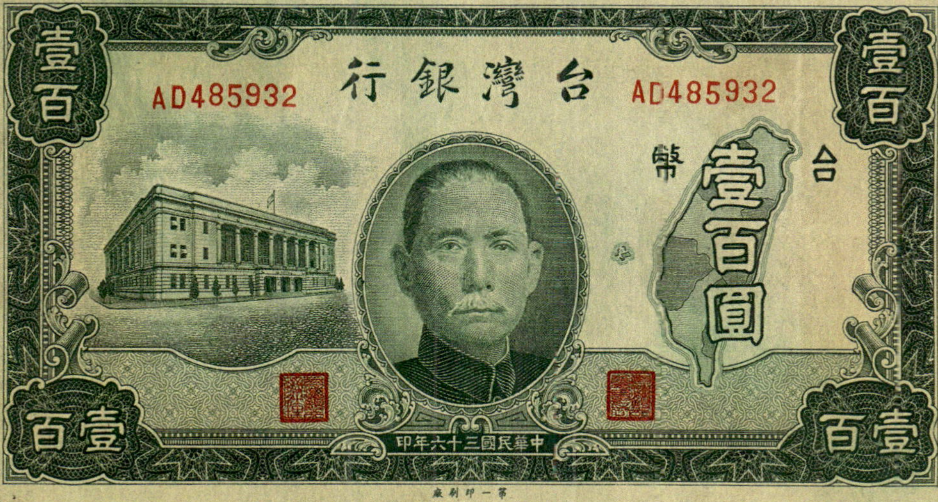
台灣銀行
AD485932
AD485932
壹百
壹百
台幣
壹百圓
壹百
壹百
中華民國三十六年印
第一印刷廠

36

Overcome All Difficulties to Build Socialism
(戰勝一切困難建設社會主義)

Yu Yunjie (俞云階) and Zhao Yannian (趙延年)

1955

China

Colour reproduction of a painting, printed on paper

76.5 × 52.5 cm

British Museum 2006,0501,0.72

Published: Ginsberg 2008, pl. 8; Clunas 2009, pl. 120

This poster was a wedding gift. It was inscribed (top right) to the happy couple, Comrades Peng Jing and Liu Shengjie, and (bottom right) 'from all the comrades in the laboratory [19]56'. It would have served as 'politically correct' gift. Printed in an edition of 35,000, it was likely reproduced from an oil painting (as is fig. 29).

The image is a fine example of Socialist Realism. These works, usually in oil, were highly coloured, very detailed and generally portrayed heroic figures in spotlight.[1] They show 'real' life and labours of workers, peasants and soldiers in ideal form, so 'revolutionary romanticism' is perhaps a better epithet for much of this uplifting art.

Socialist Realism was the official painting style in Stalinist Russia and later in other Socialist/Communist states. Konstantin M. Maksimov (1913–94) arrived in Beijing in 1955 and taught oil painting for two years to a very select group at the Central Academy of Fine Arts (CAFA). Yu Yunjie (1917–92), who designed this poster, was among the twenty officially enrolled artists in Maksimov's class.[2] Zhao Yannian (b. 1924) is universally renowned as a printmaker; this is a most unusual example of his work.

1 Laing 1988, pp. 20–3.
2 Like many of the other participants, Yu was condemned during the Anti-Rightist movement. Andrews 1994, pp. 151–2, 198.

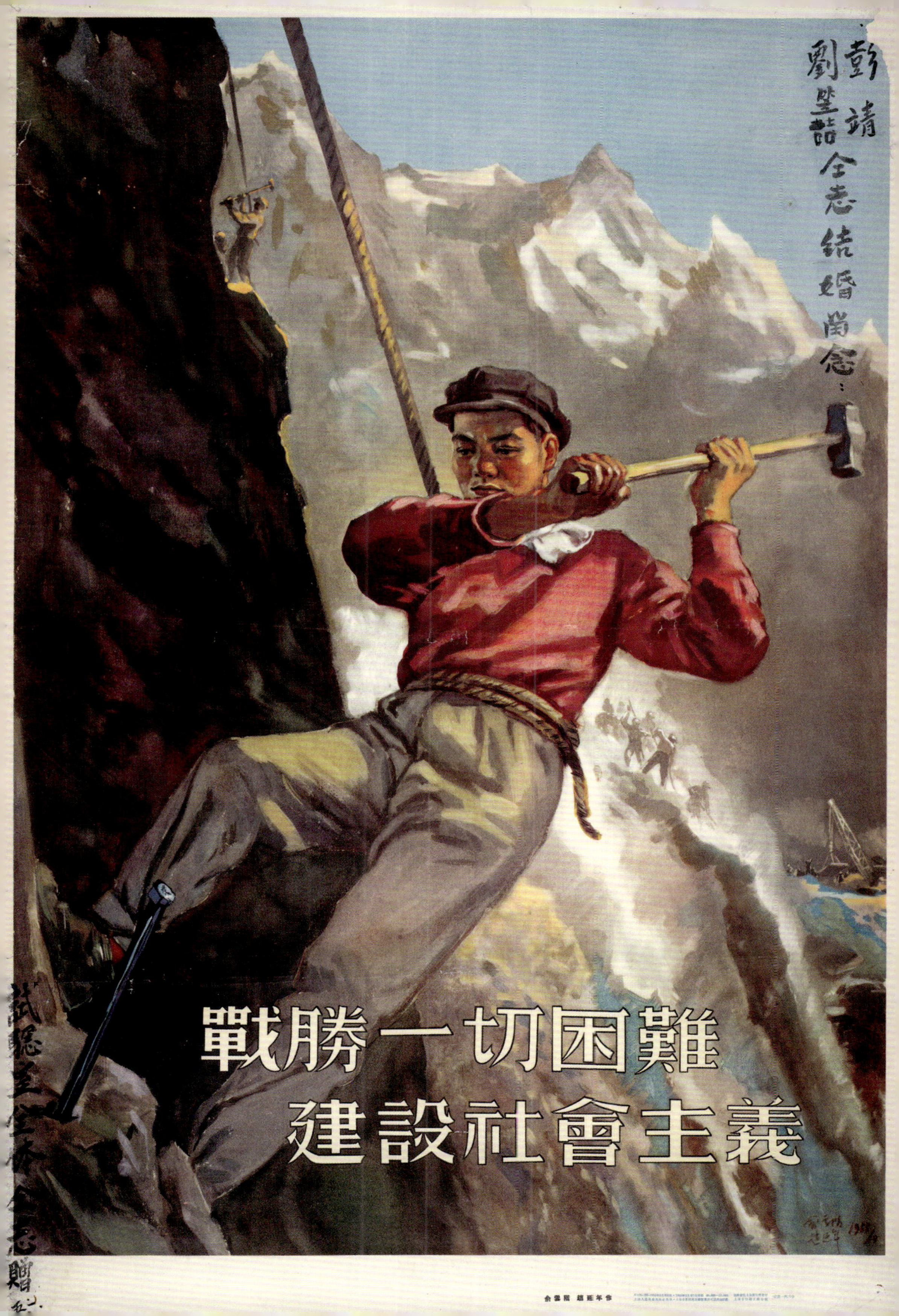
戰勝一切困難
建設社會主義
俞雲階 趙延年 作

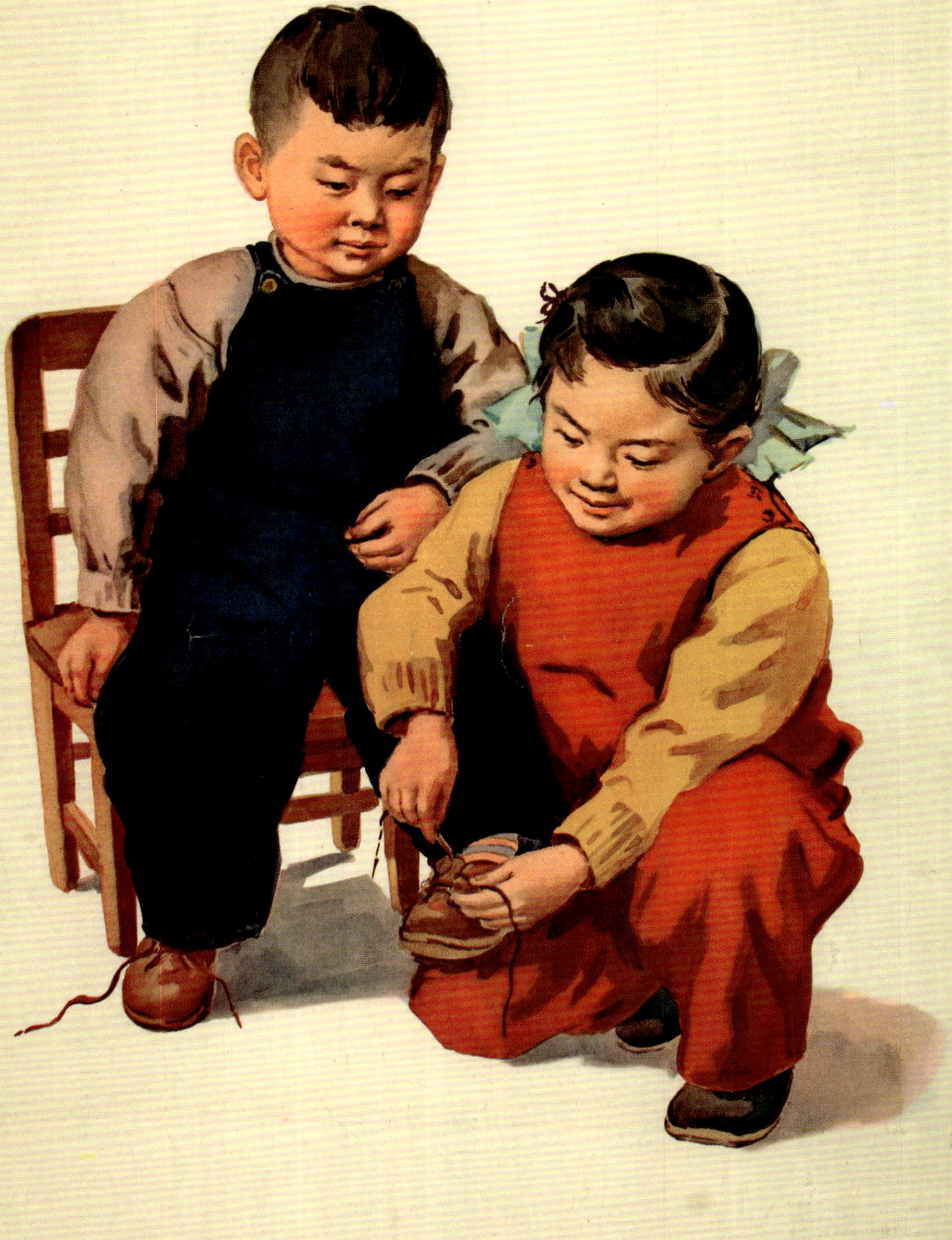

37

Help Others (幫助別人 *Bangzhu bieren*)

Poster

1958 and 1964

China

Painted in ink and colours, printed as poster on paper

76.2 × 52.5 cm

British Museum 2006,0501.11

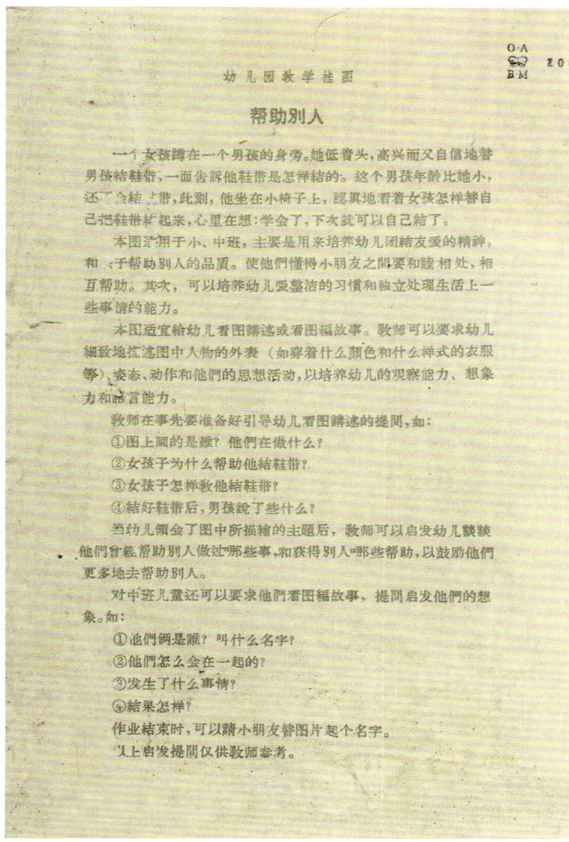

O·A 20

B·M

幼儿园教学挂图

帮助别人

一个女孩蹲在一个男孩的身旁。她低着头，高兴而又自信地替男孩結鞋帶，一面告訴他鞋带是怎样結的。这个男孩年龄比她小，还不会結鞋带，此刻，他坐在小椅子上，認真地看着女孩怎样替自己把鞋带結起来，心里在想：学会了，下次就可以自己結了。

本图适用于小、中班，主要是用来培养幼儿团結友爱的精神，和乐于帮助别人的品质。使他們懂得小朋友之間要和睦相处，相互帮助。其次，可以培养幼儿爱整洁的习惯和独立处理生活上一些事情的能力。

本图适宜給幼儿看图講述或看图編故事。教师可以要求幼儿細致地描述图中人物的外表（如穿着什么颜色和什么样式的衣服等）、姿态、动作和他們的思想活动，以培养幼儿的观察能力、想象力和語言能力。

教师在事先要准备好引导幼儿看图講述的提問，如：

①图上画的是誰？他們在做什么？

②女孩子为什么帮助他結鞋带？

③女孩子怎样教他結鞋带？

④結好鞋带后，男孩說了些什么？

当幼儿領会了图中所描繪的主題后，教师可以启发幼儿談談他們曾經帮助别人做过哪些事，和获得别人哪些帮助，以鼓励他們更多地去帮助别人。

对中班儿童还可以要求他們看图編故事，提問启发他們的想象。如：

①他們俩是誰？叫什么名字？

②他們怎么会在一起的？

③发生了什么事情？

④結果怎样？

作业結束时，可以請小朋友替图片起个名字。

以上启发提問仅供教师参考。

This poster was produced by the Beijing publishing house for educational materials. It is a very straightforward scene of a little girl helping a smaller boy to tie his shoes. The title, *Help Others*, is given in both simplified characters and *pinyin* romanization, making it easier for young children to read. The poster is intended both for language instruction and the teaching of proper behaviour.

On the reverse is a detailed set of instructions for the classroom teacher. First, the children should be asked to describe what they can actually see: what are the children doing? What is the result? What colour clothes are they wearing? After these questions have been covered thoroughly, the children should be allowed to add their own ideas about the story: what are the children's names? What is the relationship between them? How does the girl teach him to tie his shoes? What does the boy say after the shoes are tied? Then the children are asked to give examples of how they have aided others. It is most important that the class come away understanding the happy spirit that comes from helping.

A study of children's early readers from 1963–4 analysed their methodology and thematic content in detail.[1] Behavioural themes featured in at least 25 per cent of lessons in the readers for the first four primary years. Altruism, social and personal responsibility, and achievement were the most frequently occurring central themes.

1 Ridley et al 1971, pp. 136–61. This study also analysed the frequency of informational and political themes in the readers (see pp. 92–135).

38

The sinking of the spy ship
(간첩선 격침 *Gancheopseon gyeokchim*)

1967

Republic of Korea

Cigarette lighter

Brushed steel

6 × 4 × 1.3 cm

Private collection

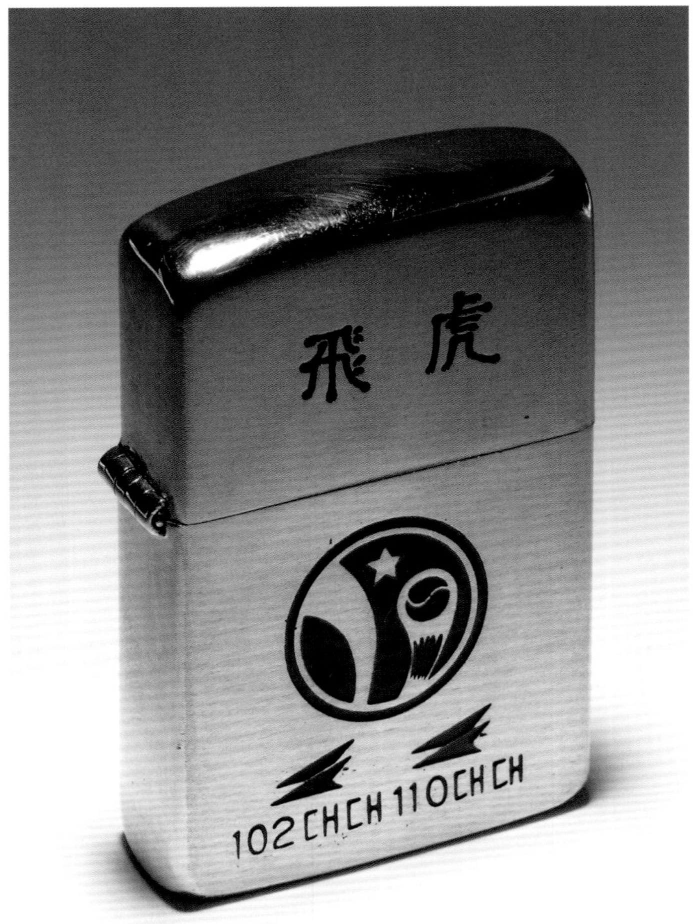

On 17 April 1967, jet fighters of the South Korean Air Force sank a North Korean spy boat.[1] The ship had apparently tried to land several agents in South Korea. This was only one of a long series of military incidents between 1966 and 1969, known as the Korean DMZ (Demilitarized Zone) Conflict, or Second Korean War.

This ABC Sunmy lighter celebrates that event. The picture on the back shows the South Korean planes scoring a direct hit; the spy ship is partly sunk and definitely doomed. The flip top on the front is inscribed (飛虎 *biho*, flying tigers). A logo has been inscribed, possibly that of the successful Air Force unit. ABC Sunmy lighters were often personalized with logos, maps or unit insignia.

ABC lighters strongly resemble Zippos, which have played a part in American military culture. During the Second World War the company ceased manufacturing its regular lines to produce exclusively for the military. In both that war and the Korean War, lighters were made with badges, division insignia and other authorized designs.

Zippos were also ubiquitous during the Vietnam War, but they often served a different propaganda purpose. Soldiers made their lighters personal, having them engraved with slogans, song lyrics and cartoon figures. For many soldiers who were against the war, their lighter was 'the ideal protest vehicle'.[2]

1 'Seoul Reports its Jets Sink North Korean Boat', *New York Times*, 17 April 1967. http://query.nytimes.com/mem/archive/pdf?res=F107 12FB3E5E137A93C5A8178FD85F438685F9.
2 Buchanan 2007, p. 14.

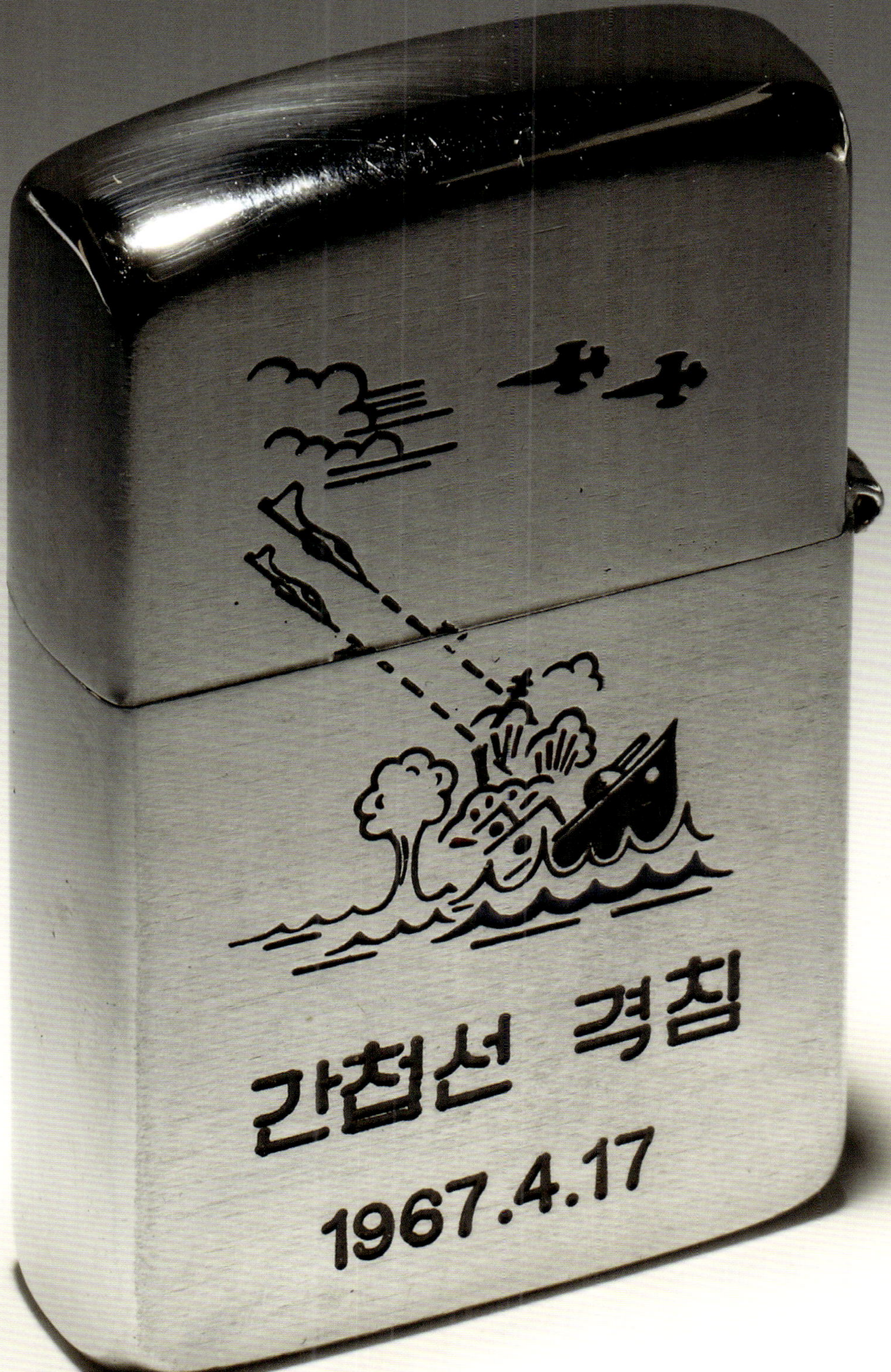
간첩선 격침
1967.4.17

39

Bhagat Singh, Chandra Shekar Azad, Indira Gandhi and Lal Bahadur Shastri

Late 20th century

India

Four painted ceramic figures

Height: 7.5 cm (Singh); 7.3 cm (Azad); 8.5 cm (Gandhi); 7.3 cm (Shastri)

British Museum As1991,07.9; As1991,07.10; As1991,07.7; As1991,07.8

These small ceramic figures represent the Indian nationalists Bhagat Singh (1907–31) and Chandra Shekar Azad (1906–31) and Prime Ministers Indira Gandhi (1917–84) and Lal Bahadur Shastri (1904–66). They were probably used in a domestic setting as figures of honour to be placed on a shelf or mantel, rather than toys.[1]

Bhagat Singh and Chandra Shekar Azad are immediately recognizable by their usual iconography (see cat. 51): the hat, in Bhagat Singh's case, and the Brahmin thread and twirling moustache in Azad's (though here he is twirling with his left hand, unlike in graphic representations). Mrs Gandhi is considerably bigger than the other figures, so may have been made for a different set.

Lal Bahadur Shastri joined the Indian independence movement in the 1920s and was a loyal follower of Mahatma Gandhi and Jawaharlal Nehru, whom he succeeded as Prime Minister (1964–6), leading the nation through the India-Pakistan War of 1965. He signed the Tashkent Agreement ending that war and died the next day under circumstances still contested.

1 T. Richard Blurton, personal correspondence, January 2013.

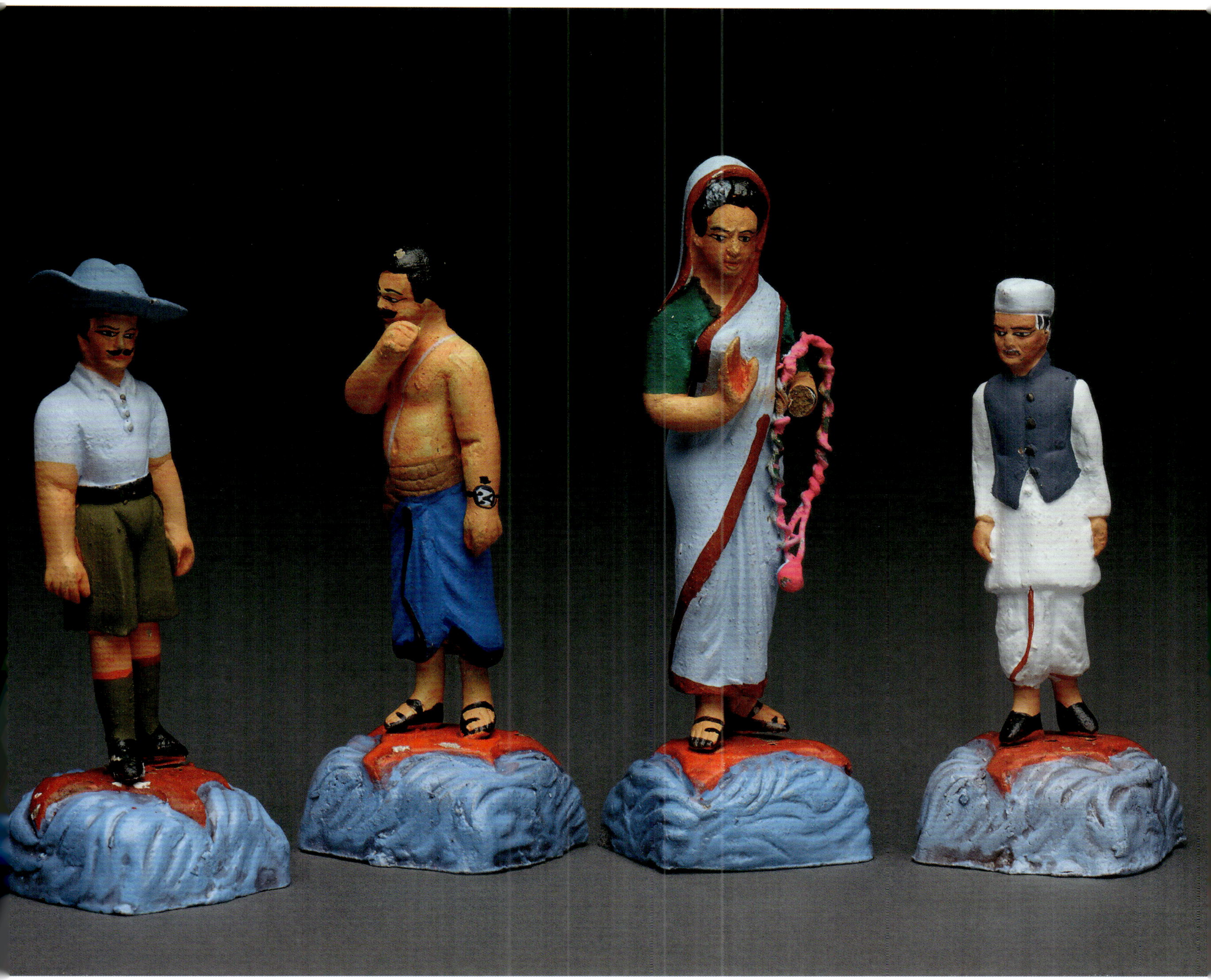

Tradition and Propaganda

Tradition and history are powerful weapons. Mao Zedong famously said, 'Use the past to serve the present' (古爲今用), but he was neither the first nor the last leader to do so, and the dictum has been applied in many varied ways.

The objects in this section illustrate how familiar visual formats and themes can be changed to celebrate new heroes or enforce new attitudes. A traditional Indian story scroll recounts contemporary events (cat. 44). A *kami-shibai* (paper-theatre format) adapts a well-known story for wartime mobilization (cat. 40). The new marriage calendar print would have looked familiar, but its function was, in fact, to discourage old ideas about marriage – using tradition to overthrow tradition (cat. 42). Auspicious papercuts heralded every new year with motifs of wealth and plenty; here they promote Marxism-Leninism-Mao Zedong Thought (cat. 43). Things have symbolic power, as do rituals, giving a sense of order to rapid change and connecting the present to the future.[1]

History is essential to political socialization. A nation's past glories forge the will to fight today's wars. The sacrifices of yesterday must be redeemed to build the future. Legend may be presented authoritatively as history, although it may be pure fabrication (cat. 45). Even in systems where political communication is relatively less one-sided, the official version of historical events is often filtered. And sometimes traditions are invented specifically to instil values and promote a sense of belonging.[2]

1 Csikszentmihalyi 1991, p. 163.
2 Hobsbawm 1983, pp. 1–13.

The Rats' Wedding (detail).
Author Kawamura Aiko.
Print artist Sano Hiroshi.
Japan. 5 August 1943. See cat. 40

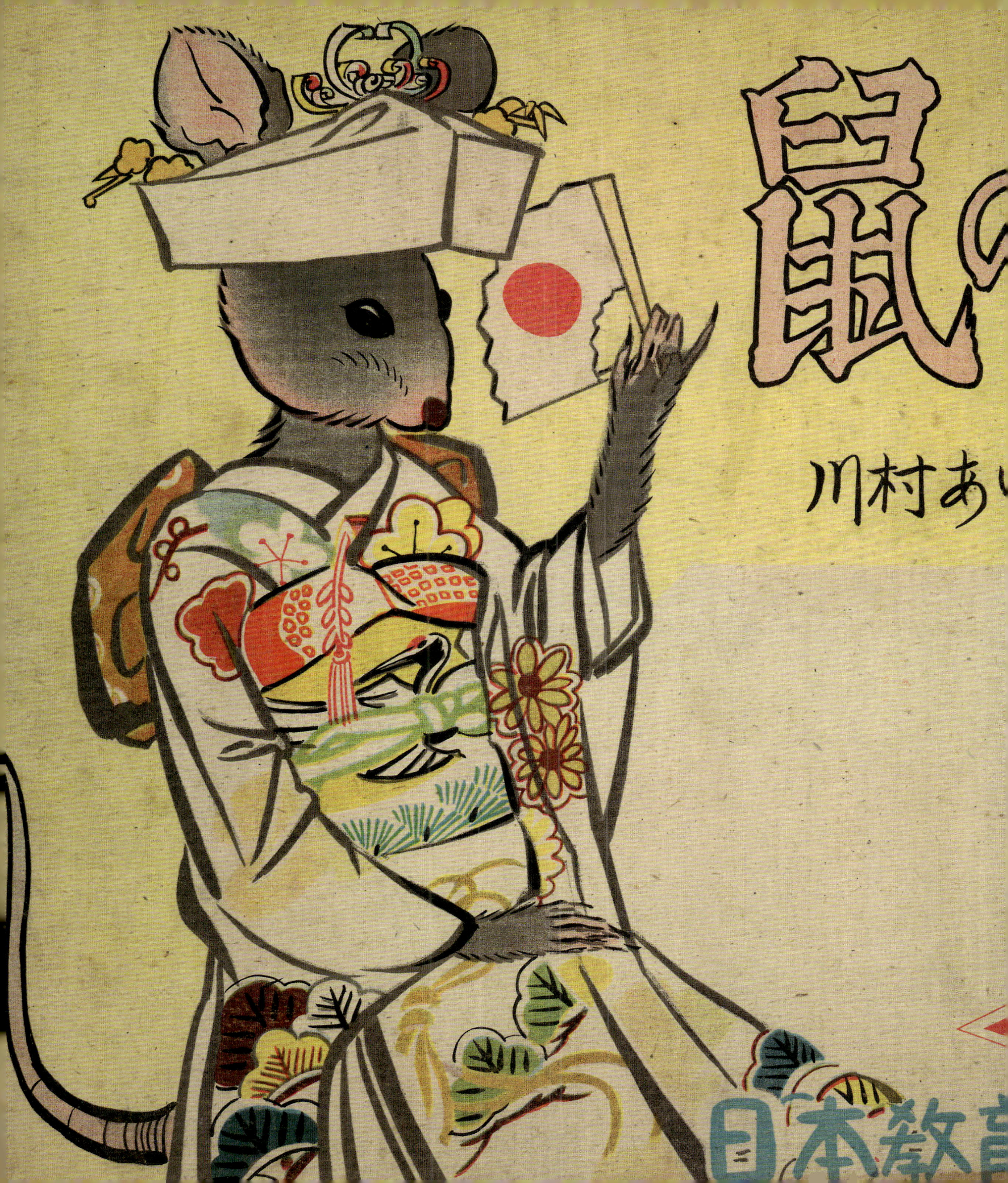
鼠の
川村あい
日本教

40

The Rats' Wedding (鼠の嫁入り, Nezumi no yomeiri)

Author Kawamura Aiko (川村あい子)

Print artist Sano Hiroshi (佐野浩)

5 August 1943

Japan

Colour lithographs on cardboard

26.8 × 38.5 cm

British Museum 2006,0113,03.1–17

Purchase funded by Brooke Sewell Bequest

Children's literature in Japan mixed entertainment with moral lessons and guides to correct behaviour. Starting in the 1910s and 1920s and right through the Asia-Pacific War, children's games and stories promoted glory and empire in forms that Barak Kushner terms 'sweet propaganda'. One favourite format was *kami-shibai* (紙芝居, paper theatre), a centuries-old form of visual storytelling by street performers.

This *kami-shibai* illustrates a traditional folktale, 'The Rats' Wedding'. A beautiful rat's parents seek the world's most powerful bridegroom for their daughter, and they consider the sun, a cloud, the wind and a wall before realizing that a rat is really the most suitable match. The marriage is then celebrated with great happiness.

The scene shown here is the wedding itself. Traditional Japanese wedding attire was elaborate and extravagant. In this wartime version of the tale, the rats wear patriotically simple clothes – the groom in uniform, the bride in patterned cotton garments. Sartorial restraint was encouraged and, in 1940, strictly regulated. Materials and labour were needed for military production, so the manufacture and sale of extravagant goods were prohibited.

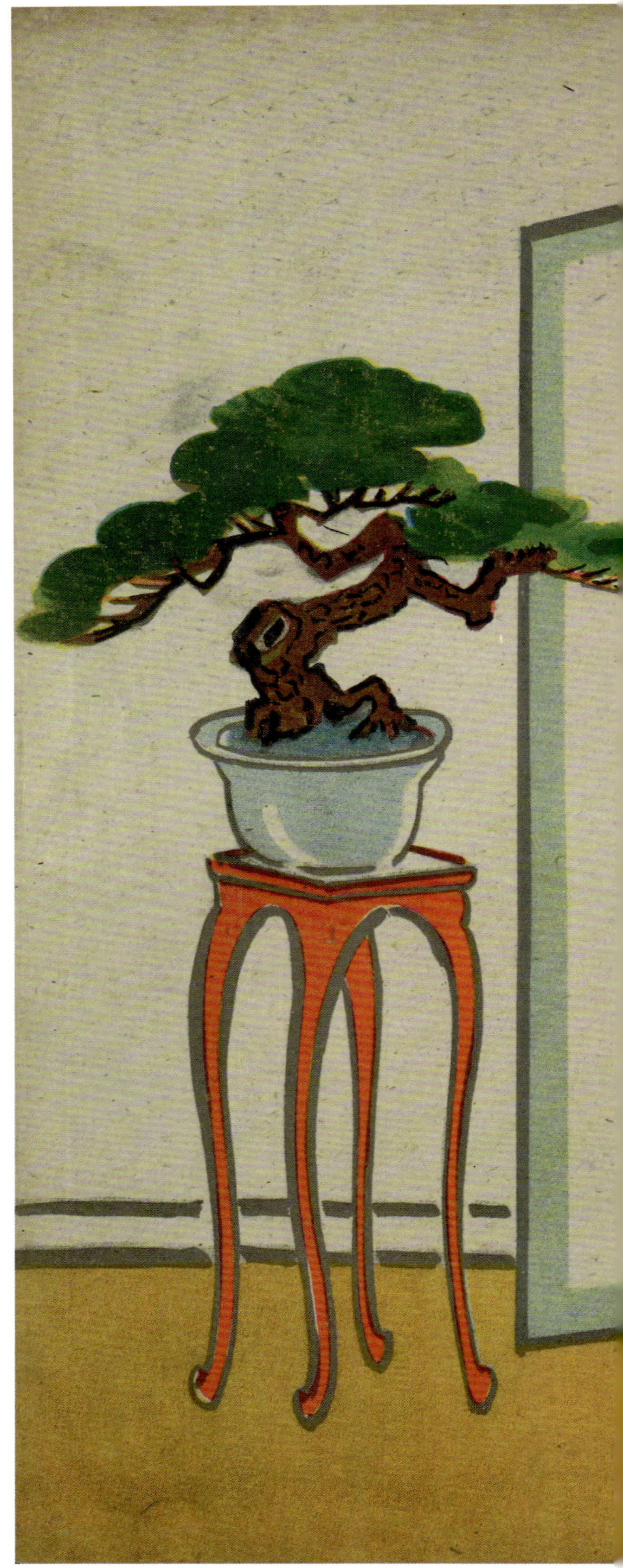

1 Kushner 2009, p. 246.
2 Atkins 2005c, p. 163.

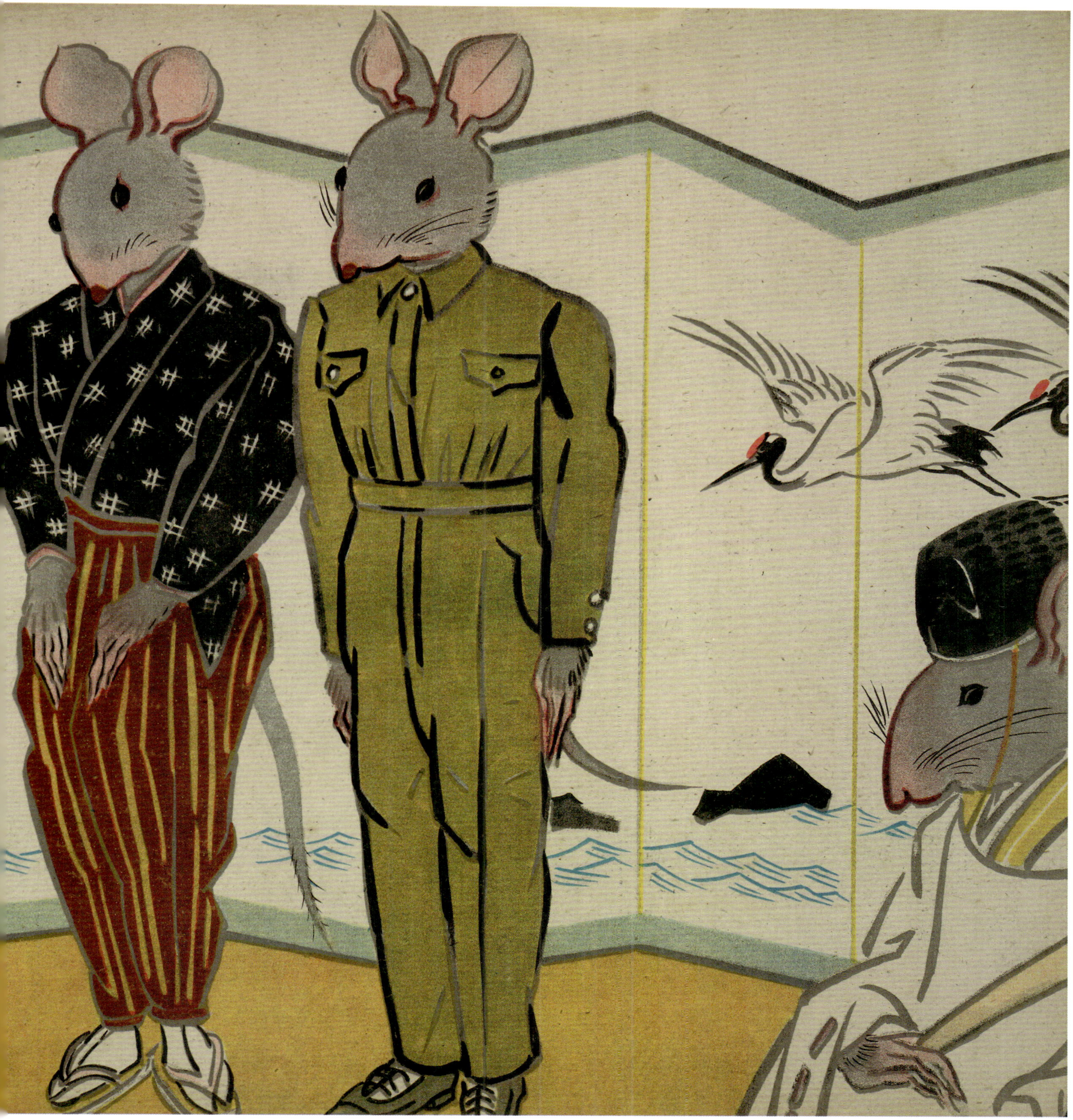

41

Kitchen God calendar print

1931–2

China

Woodcut, ink and colours on paper

35 × 21 cm

British Museum 1982,1217,0.43

42

New Marriage Ceremony (新結婚典禮)

Liu Baixiang (劉百祥)

1951

China

Coloured lithograph on paper

43.5 × 32.8 cm

Private collection

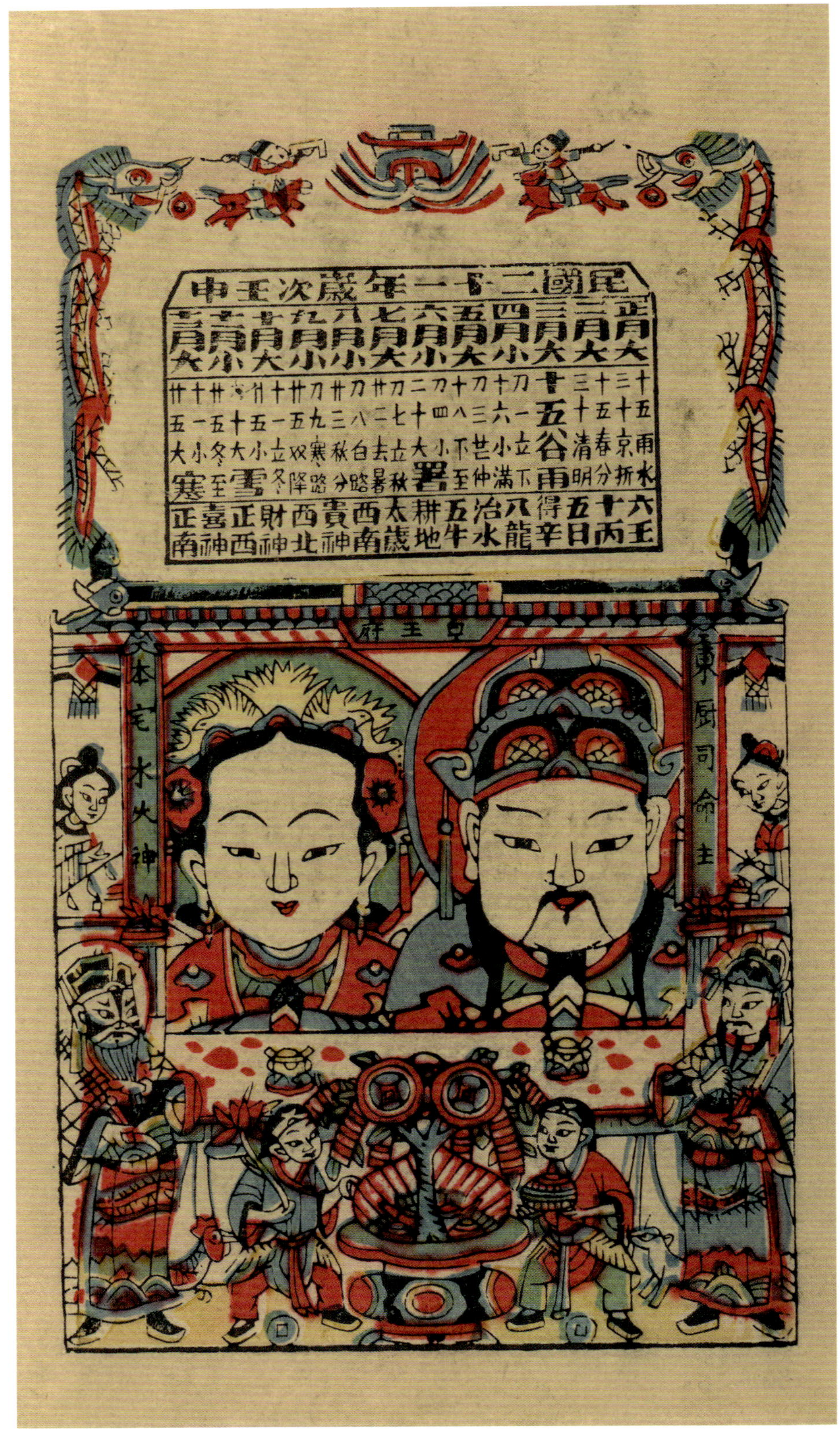

Every household kept an image of the Kitchen God (or Stove God), who observed the family's activities and made a report to the Jade Emperor at the end of every year. A lunar calendar dividing the year into twenty-four seasonal periods appears on most prints of the Stove God. This calendar was for 1932 (Minguo 21: the twenty-first year of the Republic).

After the establishment of the PRC, traditional calendar prints carried new imagery. The second example, with calendars for the three years 1952–4, shows the new type of wedding ceremony under socialism. The banner held by the workers says 'Labour partner' (勞動伴侶 *Laodong banlü*). The accoutrements are simple and few: the bride and groom wear rosettes, and there are flowers and a bowl of fruit. Behind the traditional 'double happiness' (喜喜) lanterns is a banner with hammer and sickle and the five stars of China's flag. Watching over all is Chairman Mao Zedong.

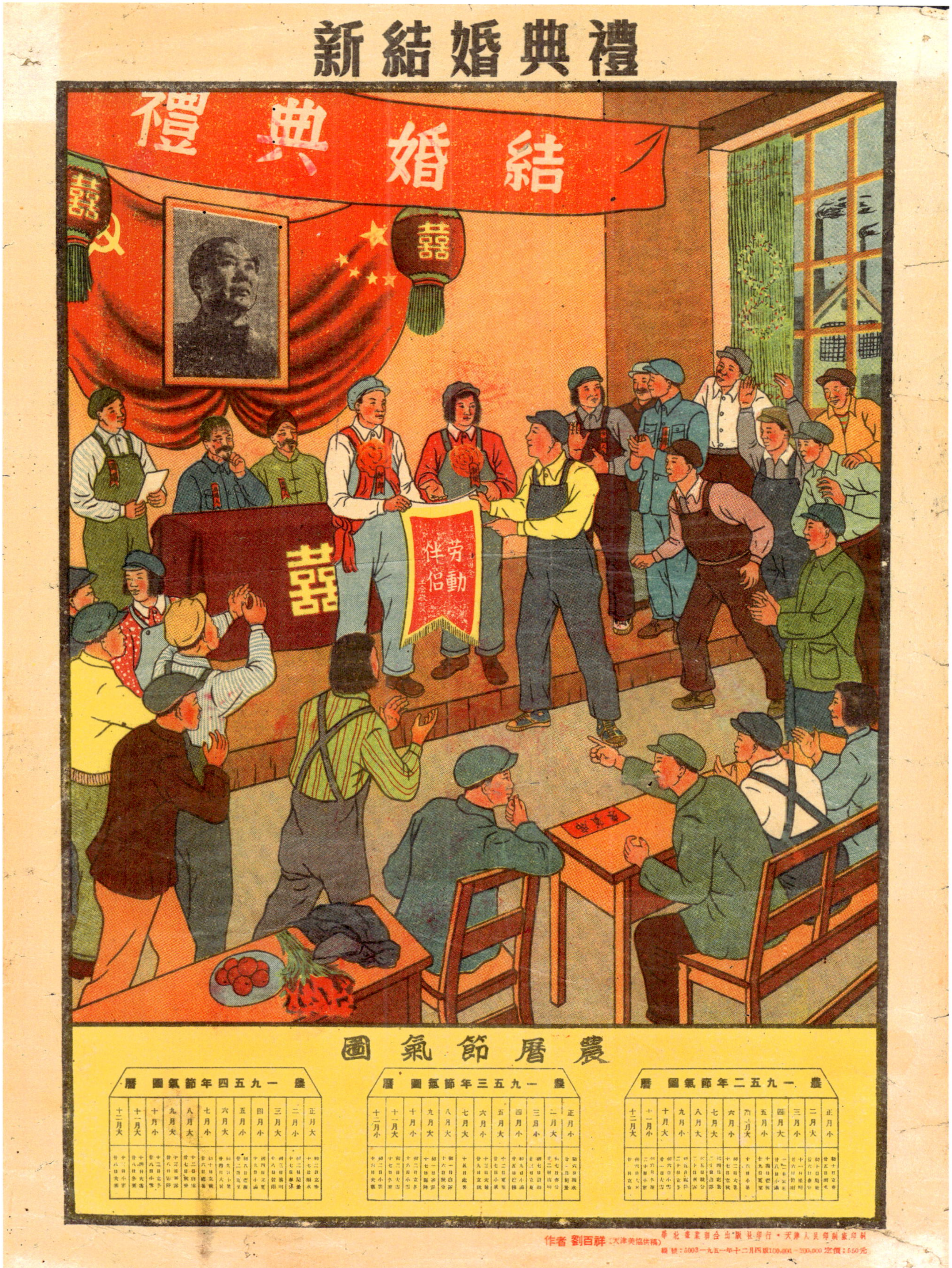

新結婚典禮
結婚典禮
劳動伴侶
農曆節氣圖
農曆一九五四年節氣圖
農曆一九五三年節氣圖
農曆一九五二年節氣圖
作者 劉百祥（天津美協供稿）
華北書業聯合出版社印行・天津人民印刷廠印刷
編號：5003 一九五一年十二月四版100,001－200,000 定價：550元

43

Long live Marxism, Leninism, Mao Zedong Thought
(马克思列宁主义毛泽东思想万岁)

Late 20th century

China

Papercut

16.3 × 27.6 cm

British Museum 2005,0128,0.1

Given by Andrew Bolton

Papercuts were traditionally made in China as decorations for festivals and rituals.[1] This was an art of the common people, for holidays, weddings and marking the seasonal activities of village life. Particularly at the time of Spring Festival (New Year), farmers and craftsmen made 'window flowers' to invoke blessings for the coming year. Among the earliest surviving examples are the ninth–tenth-century flowers found in the so-called Library Cave (Cave 17) at Dunhuang, now in the British Museum.

Communist arts policy transformed this centuries-old folk art into a progressive tool. Decoration for its own sake was anti-revolutionary, but traditional crafts were to be encouraged, their content altered in the service of politics. Gu Yuan and other trained artists at Yan'an produced papercuts during the Resistance War.[2] They were an attractive, comprehensible vehicle to promote production, literacy and support for the army. Propaganda papercuts are still made today.

Papercuts are made with scissors or with knives. Knife-cutting is used for production in large quantities, and professional artists execute topical sets for domestic and foreign consumption. There is nothing left of the bold, colourful folk style in this group portrait of Marx, Engels, Lenin, Stalin and Mao – where Mao is nearest to the viewer, and just a bit larger than the others.

1 Nancy Zeng Berliner, *Chinese Folk Art: The Small Skills of Carving Insects*, Boston: Little Brown, 1986, pp. 97–9.
2 Jiang Feng (ed.), *Yan'an Jian Zhi* (延安剪紙 Yan'an Papercuts), Beijing: Renmin meishu chubanshe, 1986, pp. 160–90.

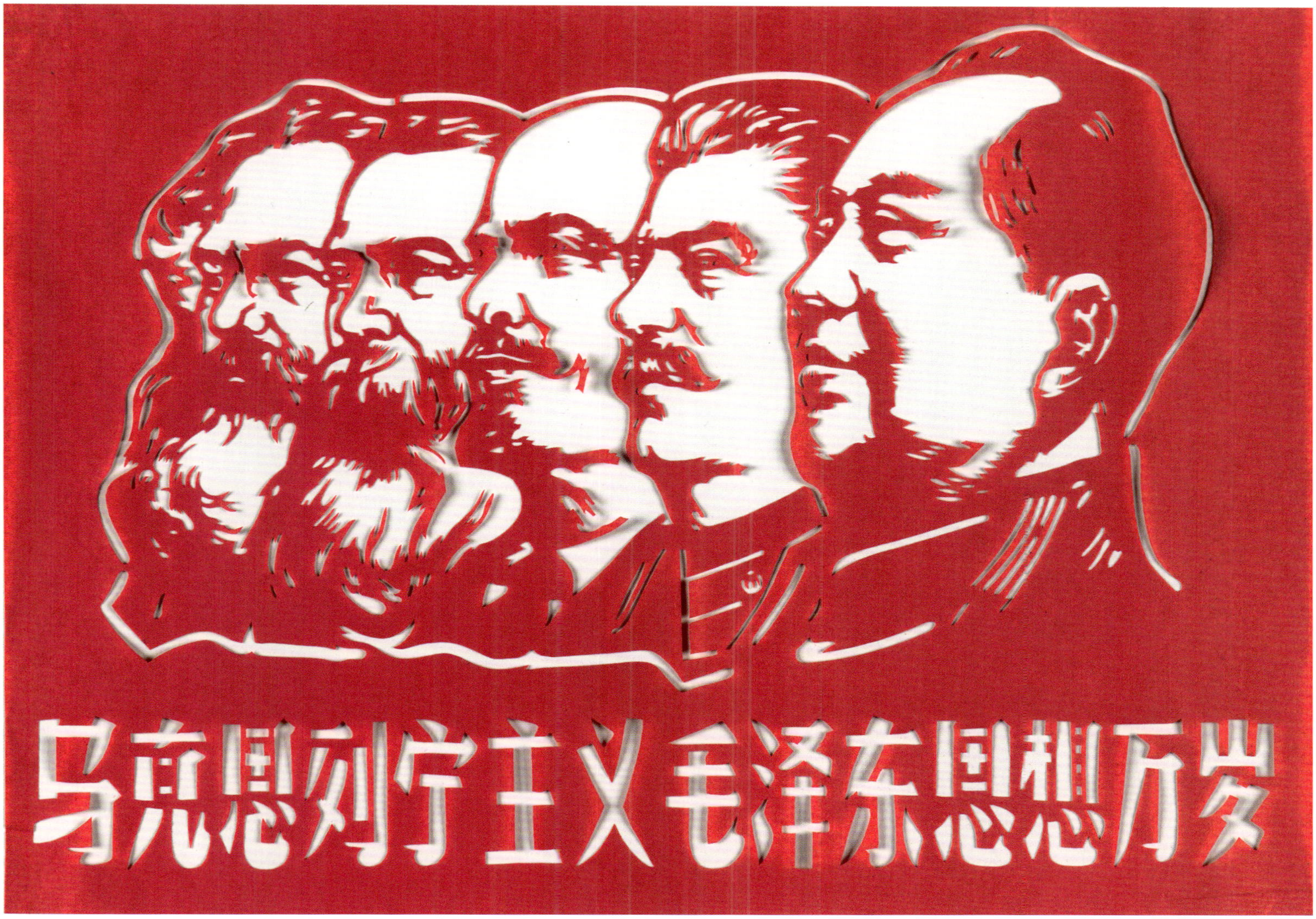
马克思列宁主义毛泽东思想万岁

44

Indira Gandhi story scroll

Ajit Chitrakar

c. 1985

India

Scroll painting, ink and colours on paper

440 × 37.5 cm

British Museum As1986,10.1

Published: Blurton 1989, pp. 425–51, pls 167–71; Blurton 2006, p. 78

For centuries, itinerant storytellers in India narrated the great epics and other tales in conjunction with painted story scrolls. Although this form of travelling entertainment is fast being superseded by electronic media, even in remote villages, some new stories with political and historical subjects have appeared in recent years, 'especially in that uncomfortable region where politics and religion coincide'.[1]

One such story scroll illustrates the life of Indira Gandhi (1917–84), India's third prime minister. In the scroll's first register, she appears as Bharat Mata (Mother India; cat. 46), emerging from a map of India. The three registers shown here depict her birth; reading to Mahatma Gandhi during one of his fasts; and her time at Oxford University.

The long scroll continues through the eventful path of her life and death. She was killed in 1984 by two of her Sikh bodyguards in retaliation for the attack she initiated on the temple complex at Amritsar that year. The last register of the painting shows her being taken into heaven by Vishnu. The scroll thus shows her transformation from her historical to her 'mythic existence ... she is becoming a goddess'.[2]

1 Blurton 2006, p. 77.
2 Blurton 2006, p. 77.

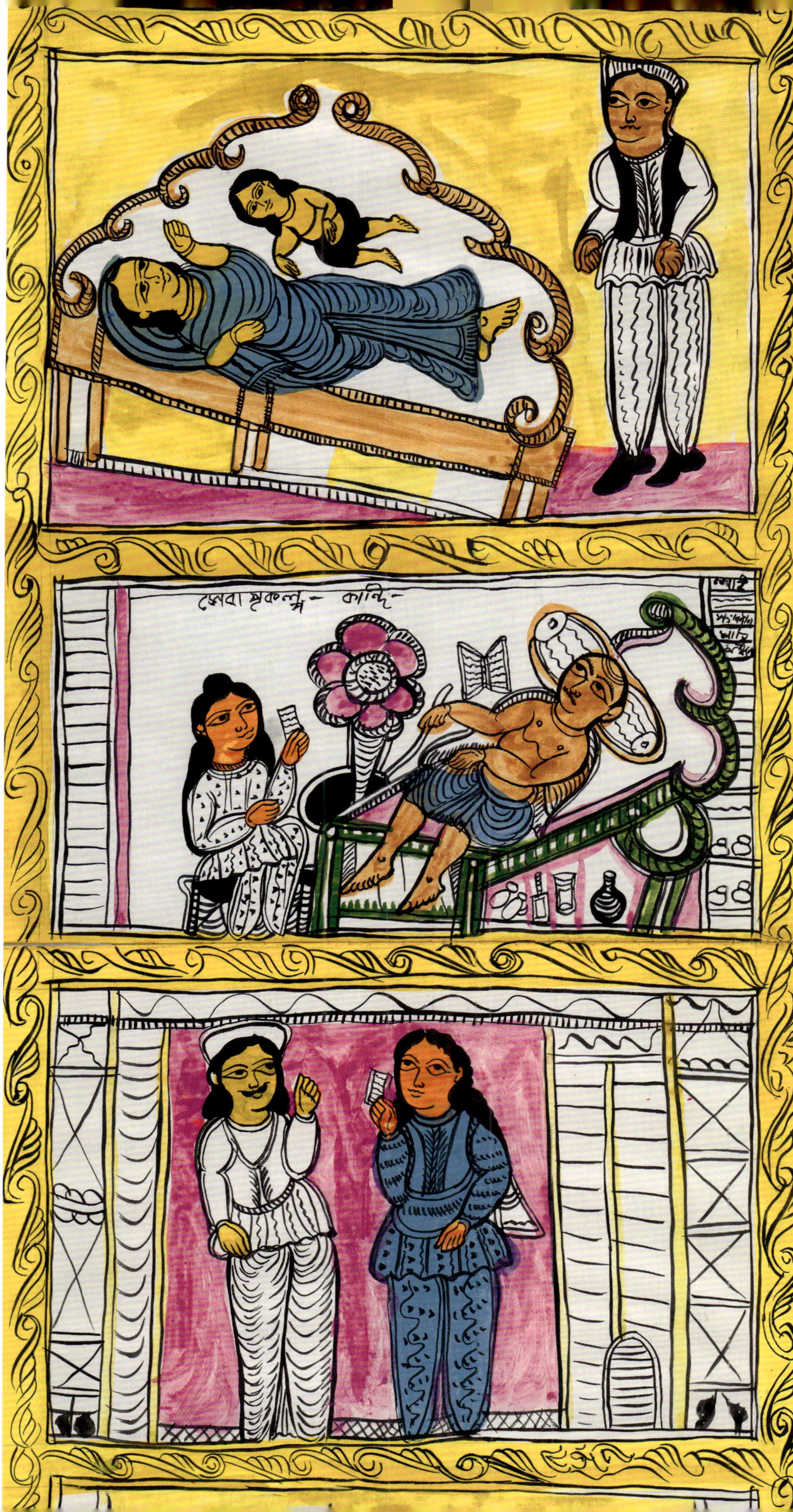

45

Tan'gun's Mausoleum

Song Shi-yop

1995

Democratic People's Republic of Korea

Painting with ink and colours on paper

168 × 91 cm

British Museum 2002,1001,0.2

Purchase funded by Brooke Sewell Permanent Fund

Published: Portal 2005, p. 153

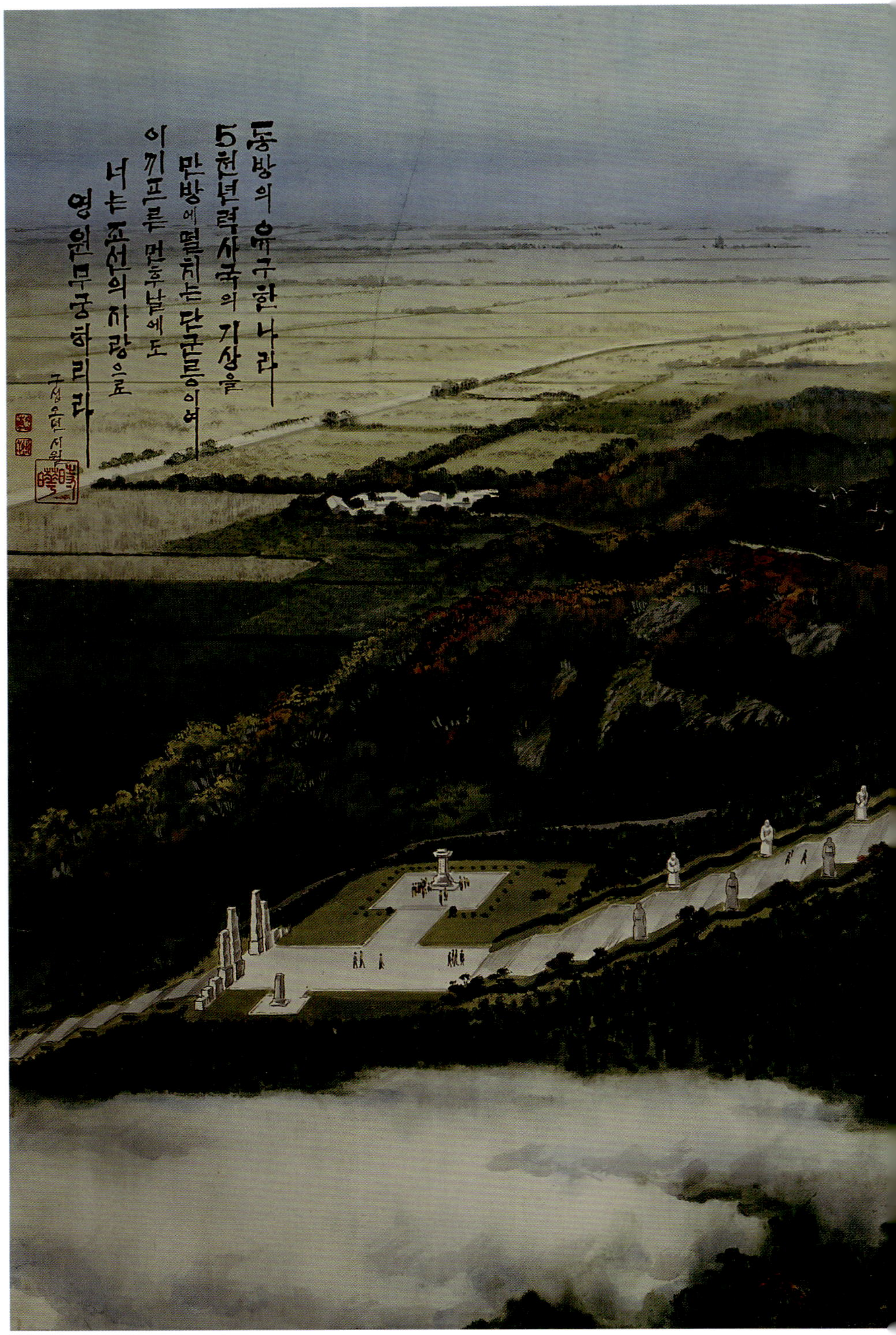

Song Shi-yop (b. 1934) is a leading painter in North Korea. His works show real places – buildings and landscapes – which stake historical claims to unity, legitimacy and national greatness.

Tan'gun (or Dangun) was the legendary founder of the first Korean kingdom, KoChoson (or Gojoseon), in 2333 BC. North Korean archaeologists once agreed that the territory of KoChoson was in present-day Liaoning, China, but in recent years they discovered that, in fact, it was situated right where Pyongyang is today, and it was established much earlier, around 3000 BC. This has obvious implications for North Korean claims of legitimacy relative to South Korea.

In 1993 archaeologists discovered the tomb of Tan'gun, with his bones and those of his wife. His burial place was reconstructed as a huge, near-white, pyramid-shaped mausoleum on the outskirts of Pyongyang. White represents purity and is the dominant colour of Pyongyang monuments and plazas, and of official culture generally.[1]

The inscription on the painting reads: 'Tan'gun's Mausoleum, which brings fame to the power of an eternal Eastern country, a country with 5000 years of history! We will be everlastingly proud of Korea, even in the moss-covered future!'[2]

1 Myers 2010, p. 78.
2 Translation by Jane Portal, Portal 2005, p. 151.

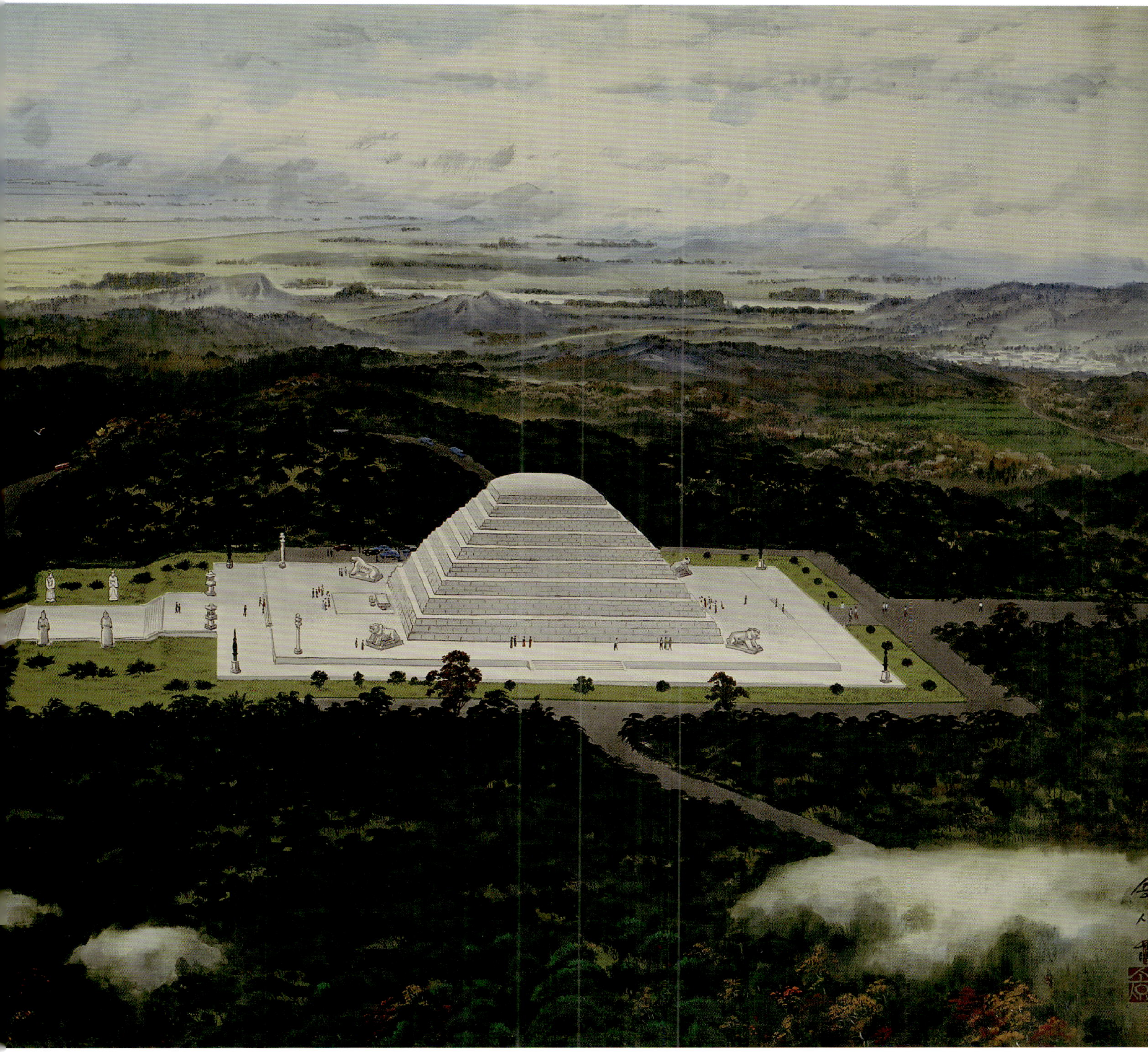
송시

Symbolism

Symbolism is a powerful tool in propaganda, but only if the meaning is understood by the intended audience. Within every country, certain political symbols are taught to children and recognized from an early age: the flag, national monuments and portraits of founding leaders (cat. 50).

Some symbolic images achieve near-universal recognition, even if designed in various distinct ways or presented in stylized forms. The hammer-and-sickle, for example, representing the unity of workers and farmers under Communism, had different variants in China and North Korea, but both would be understood by a general audience.[1] The American flag is another symbol familiar almost everywhere. It is employed for patriotic purposes at home, but can be used to express hostility by America's adversaries (cat. 33).

Other symbols are specific to a particular time and place. A spinning wheel means Mahatma Gandhi to an Indian audience (cat. 12); in China, however, it evokes life in the Communist base areas during the Asia-Pacific War. Of course, symbols may lose their impact over time. In 1930s India, a poster of a Western-style hat – just the hat – stood for the freedom fighter Bhagat Singh (cat. 51). Today's Indian students might not understand the reference.

The symbols shown in some of the images in this section are relatively obscure (cats 47, 49), but their message becomes relevant when the iconography is explained.

Chairman Mao badge.
1969. China.
See cat. 50

1 North Korea's version includes a brush, representing intellectuals.

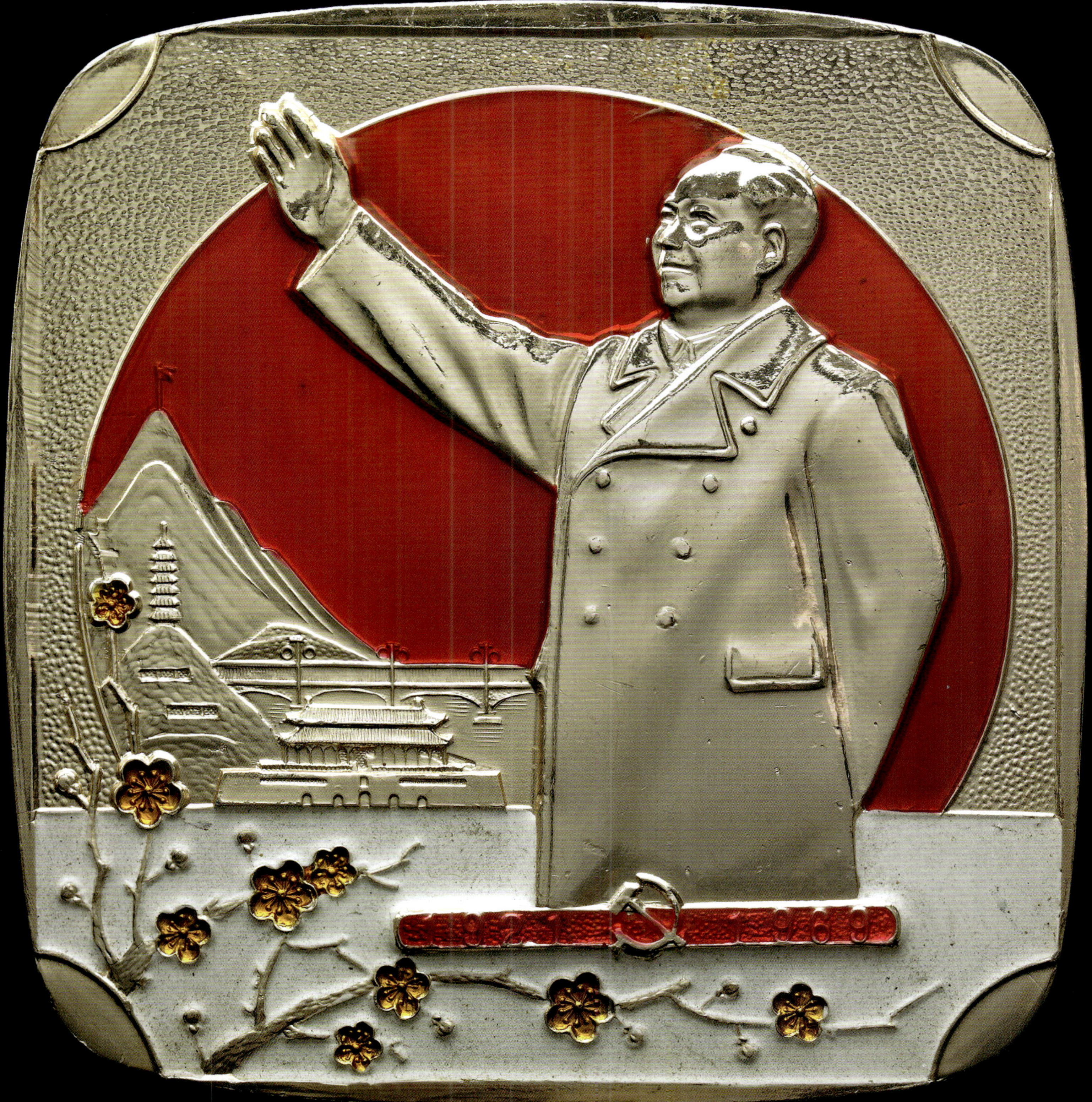
1921 1969

46

Popular print of Bharat Mata

c. 1980–90

India

Chromolithograph on paper

45.5 × 33 cm

British Museum 1990,0707,0.78.1

Bharat Mata is the personification of India as a mother goddess. The symbol first appeared in the 1870s, based on the character from a play, and acquired increasing political significance as the independence movement developed.[1] Prints of the 1930s and 40s show Bhagat Singh (cat. 51) and other martyred nationalists offering their severed heads to Bharat Mata.[2]

In this popular print, Bharat Mata is shown on a lion adorned with a Hindu *tilak*.[3] The lion is the vehicle (*vahana*) for several fierce goddesses. Sometimes Bharat Mata carries a flag of India, but here she holds a banner with the word 'Aum' (or Om).[4]

The shape of the goddess blends into the map of India. This is how Bharat Mata is differentiated from other goddesses. At the Mahatma Gandhi Kashi University in Varanasi (Benares), a temple is dedicated solely to Bharat Mata. Inaugurated by Mahatma Gandhi in 1936, the temple houses an enormous marble relief map of unified India, which is the principal object of veneration.

1 Helsinki Art Museum, *India Express: Sacred and Popular*, Helsinki: Helsinki Art Museum, 2006, p. 26.
2 Pinney 2004, pls 94–5.
3 A mark worn for religious reasons, or to honour a person or event.
4 *Aum* is an auspicious sound, pronounced at the beginning of any undertaking or written at the head of a letter. In popular culture, it is also a sign of Hinduism.

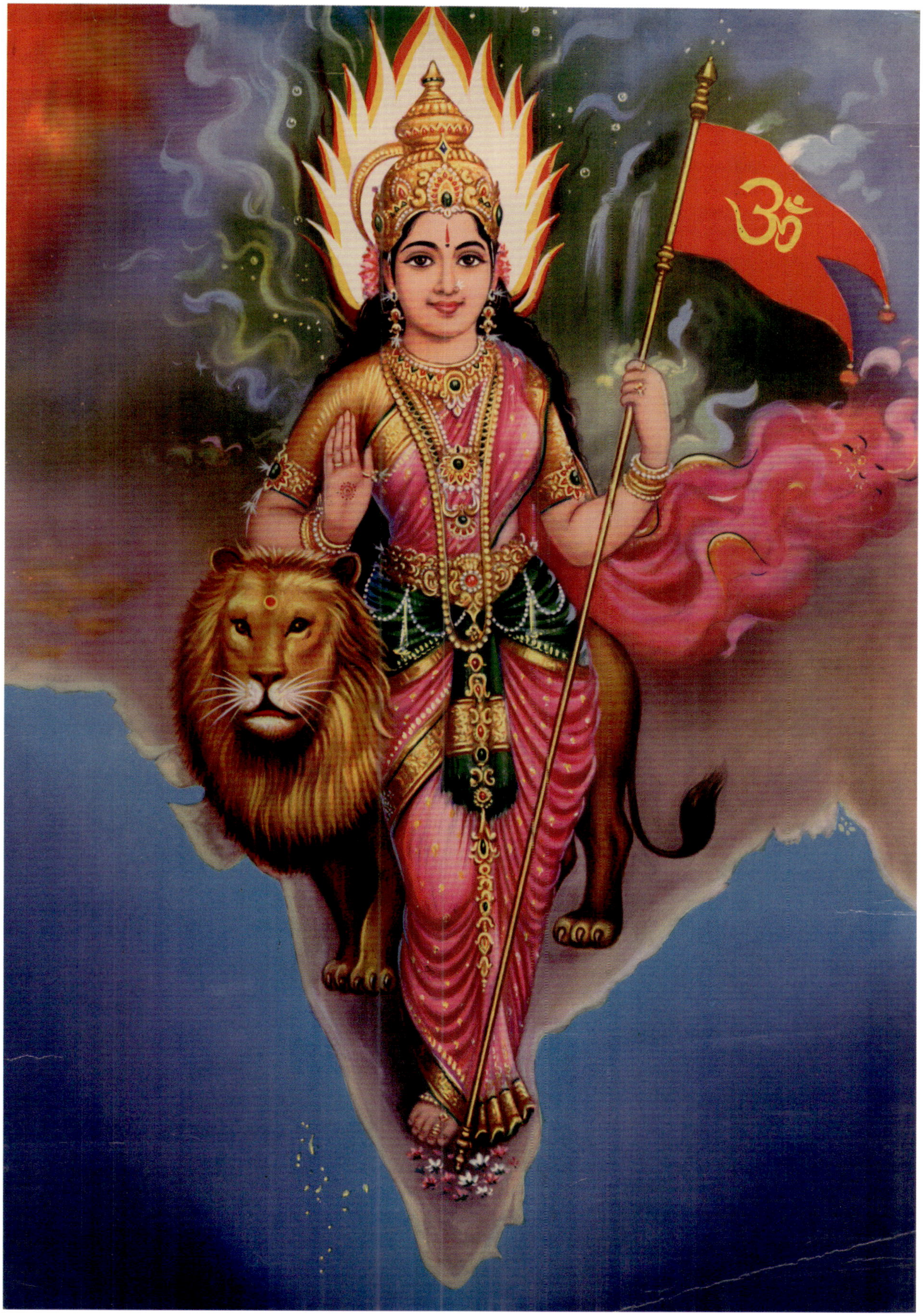

47

In Front of the White Apricot

Kang Chong-nim (강정님)

Probably 1990s

Democratic People's Republic of Korea

Ink and colours on nylon

109 × 64.5 cm

British Museum 2001,0607,0.10

Purchase funded by Brooke Sewell Permanent Fund

Published: Portal 2005, pl. 118

Kang Chong-nim (b. 1926) paints women and children in traditional style. This very sweet portrayal carries political significance which is not immediately obvious: the white apricot was the favourite flower of Kim Il-sung's mother.[1]

Kang Pan-sŏk (1892–1932) is honoured as the mother of the revolution, activist and ardent resistance fighter. She was a staunch helpmate to her heroic husband Kim Hyŏng-jik (1884–1926) and the guiding inspiration for Kim Il-sung. She worked tirelessly in the anti-Japanese struggle. A pioneer of the women's movement in Korea, Kang Pan-sŏk is credited with mobilizing women of all classes for resistance activities.[2]

She is usually portrayed in traditional dress, even when she is at her most revolutionary. In one painting, for example, she is feminine and demure as she hands Kim Il-sung the gun with which he starts the war of liberation.[3]

1 Portal 2005, p. 153.
2 http://www.kcna.co.jp/item/2012/201211/news13/20121113-19ee.html.
3 Myers 2010, p. 98.

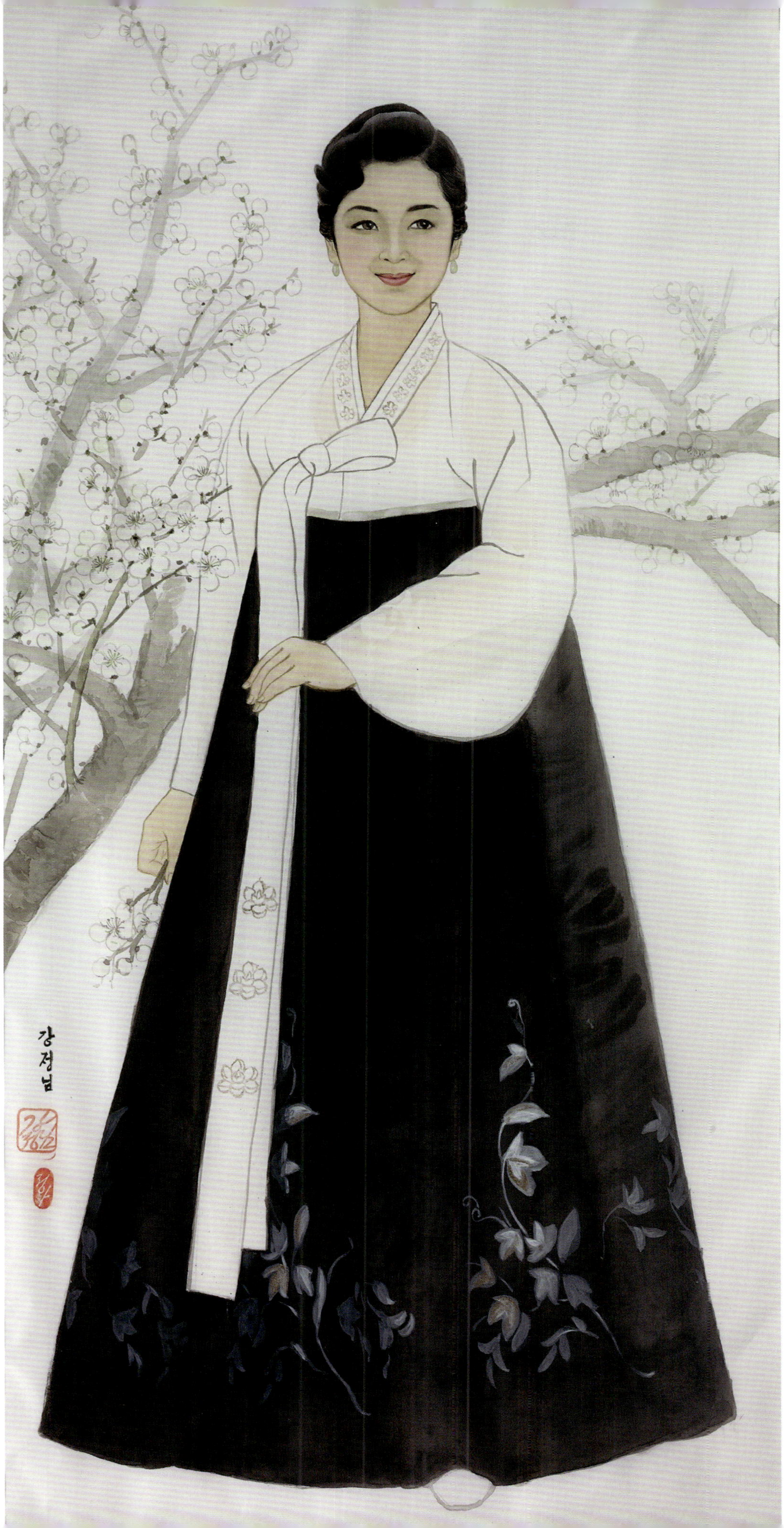
강정님

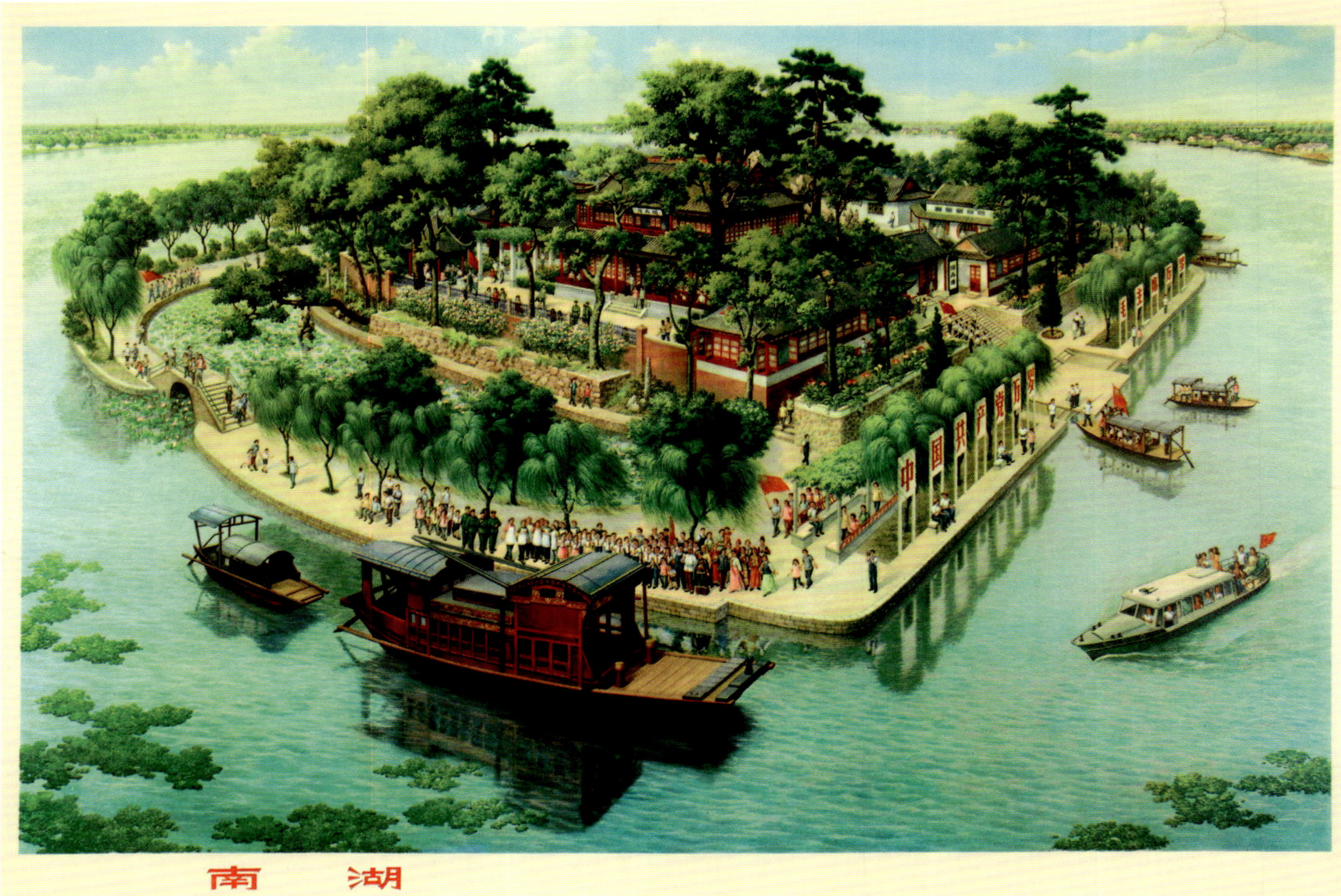
南　湖

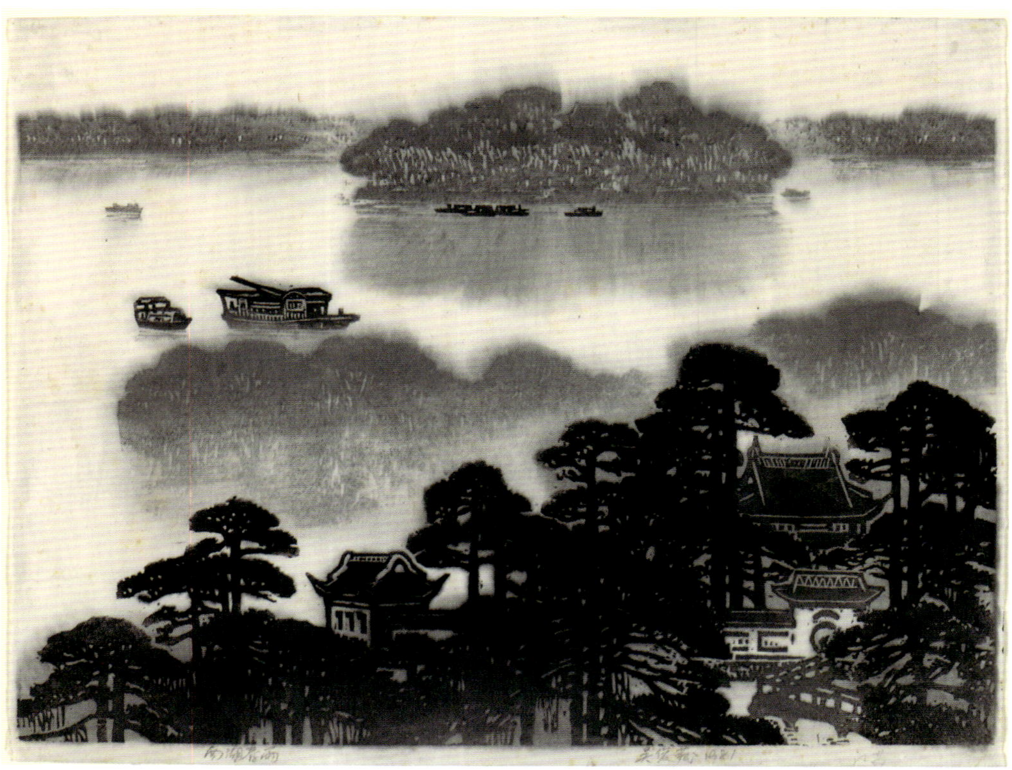

48

Nanhu (南湖 *South Lake*)

Zhang Yuqing (章育青)

1974

China

Coloured poster, printed on paper

53 × 77 cm

British Museum 2006,0501,0.15

49

South Lake Spring Rain (南湖春雨)

Wu Junfa (吳俊發)

1981

China

Woodblock print, ink and colour on paper

30.5 × 45 cm

British Museum 1992,0716,0.100

Published: Ginsberg 2008, pl. 12

The lively, coloured poster is clearly a work of propaganda.[1] Zhang Yuqing (1909–93) was a highly prolific poster designer in the 1950s and 1960s, known for his meticulously detailed depictions of real places and events.[2] The black-and-white print by Wu Junfa (b. 1927) looks like a misty landscape. In fact, the two images represent the same occasion. Its significance is recognizable from the iconography.

In 1921, the first Congress of the CCP met secretly in Shanghai. It was discovered by the police, so the participants had to disband and later reconvened on this distinctive boat on South Lake, just outside the city. A visiting Chinese scholar explained: 'If a Westerner sees a man and a woman riding a donkey under a star, he immediately thinks the image is about the birth of Jesus. When a Chinese sees this boat, it's about the birth of the Communist Party.'[3]

1 Virtually all art produced during the Cultural Revolution was propaganda.
2 Stefan Landsberger, http://chineseposters.net.
3 Huang Xiaofeng, private correspondence, 2008.

50

Chairman Mao badge

1969

China

Stamped aluminium

6 × 6 cm

British Museum 1987,0326.1, DH 1242

Given by Simmons and Simmons

Published: Attwood 2004; Wang 2008a, no. 300; Wang 2008b, fig. 2

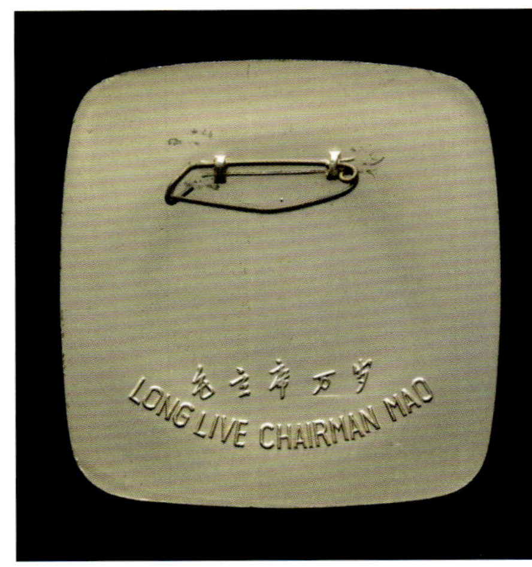

During the Cultural Revolution (1966–76), Chairman Mao badges were iconic markers of loyalty and political correctness. They were also a sign of belonging: the only people who didn't wear them were those who were excluded for political reasons.[1] From 1966 to 1971 about five billion such badges were produced, and the British Museum holds more than 350, the vast majority of which are made of stamped aluminium and decorated with the bust of Chairman Mao.

The imagery on this badge is complex and replete with familiar symbols of Chinese Communism. It was made in 1969, to mark the Ninth National Congress of the CCP. The inscription 1921–1969, on the bar with hammer and sickle, reminds us that the founding Congress was in 1921 (cats 48–9). Three important places are shown on the badge: Jinggangshan, birthplace of the Chinese Red Army; the Baota Pagoda, signifying Yan'an; and Tiananmen, the political heart of new China. Chairman Mao stands, one arm raised, before a glowing red sun.

Yellow and gold plum blossoms also decorate the badge. A traditional symbol of endurance as well as spring and renewal, plum blossoms carry revolutionary meanings. They feature often on visual propaganda and in Chairman Mao's poetry.[2]

1 Wang 2008a, p. ix.
2 Wang 2008a, p. 137

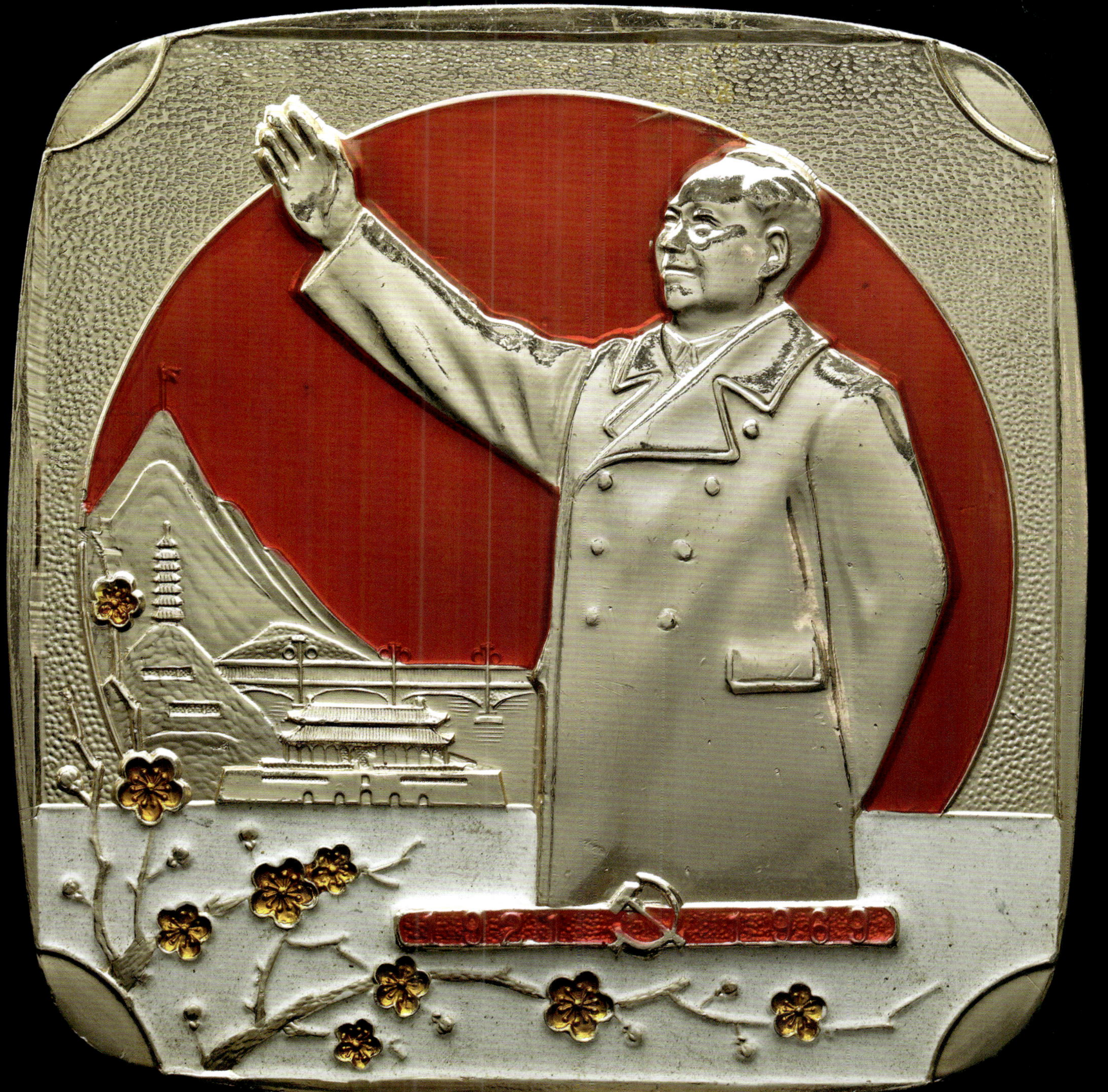
1921
1969

Heroes and Villains

Every country needs heroes for propaganda. They boost morale in times of war and rapid change (cat. 53). Freedom fighters, who may be outlaws under a colonial or occupying authority, serve as national symbols long after the struggle is over and a new regime is in place (cat. 51). Some heroes saturate the political culture, as in the perpetual personality cult of North Korea's Kim Il-sung (the Great Leader) and that of China's Chairman Mao Zedong during the Cultural Revolution. Occasionally a hero is claimed by several nations, each for a different purpose (cat. 54).

Heroes are hailed as models to emulate, personifying patriotic values. 'Learn from Lei Feng' (學習雷鋒) has been a slogan for fifty years in China (cat. 55). The legendary soldier appears in propaganda campaigns – sometimes years apart – as an exemplar of selfless service to the Communist Party and the nation.

Every state also needs its villains. An enemy – real or imagined, domestic or foreign – pulls the citizenry together, reminding them what they stand for (and against). Certain devices are common in this type of imagery. Enemies are often portrayed as animals or as devils (fig. 22). They are caricatured to make them look evil or ridiculous (cat. 60). Demonizing or simply dehumanizing the enemy makes him less threatening, and also makes it easier to justify killing him.

He says himself, he's already got a new appearance!
Lu Shaofei. 1931–8. China.
See cat. 56

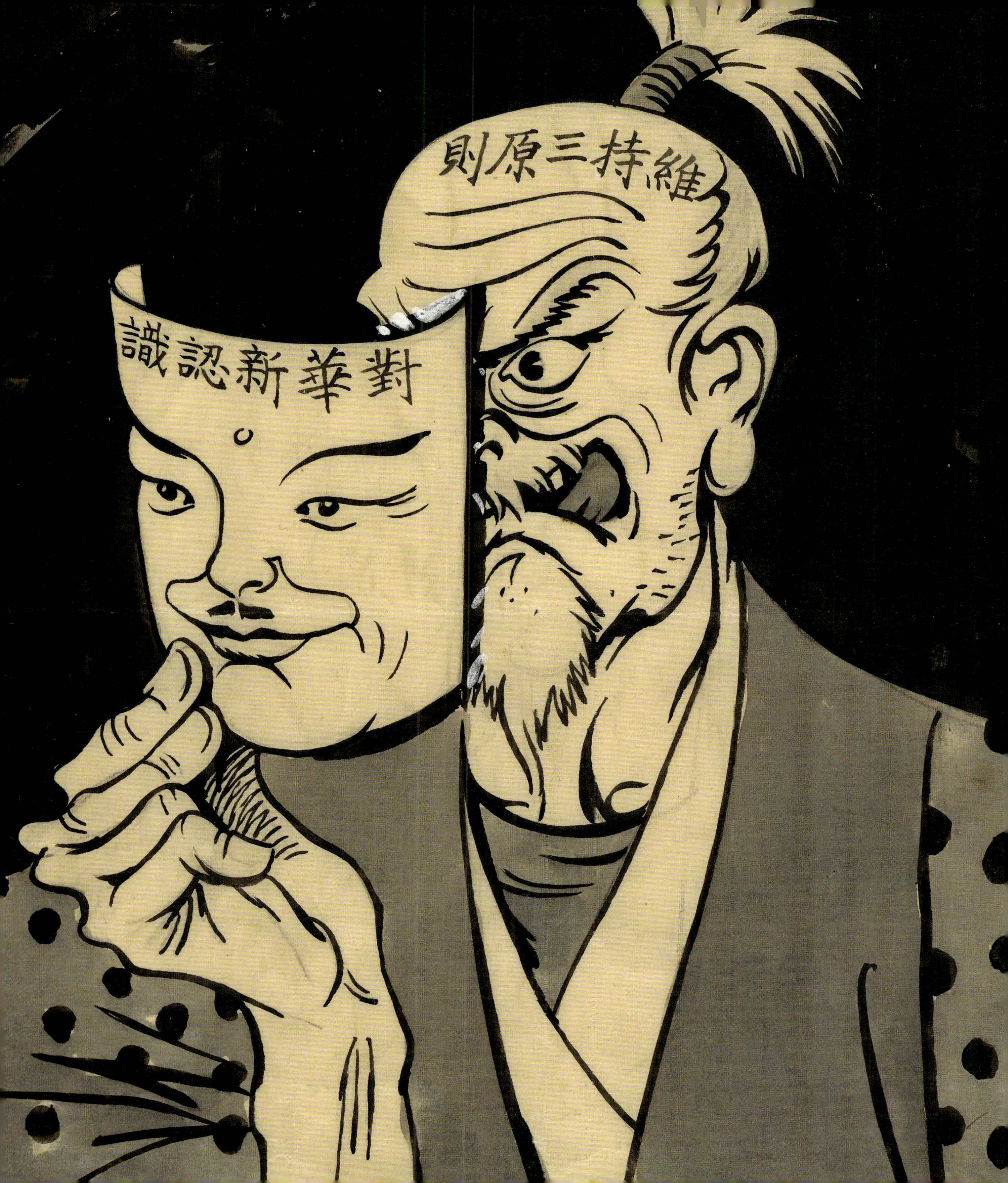
維持三原則
對華新認識

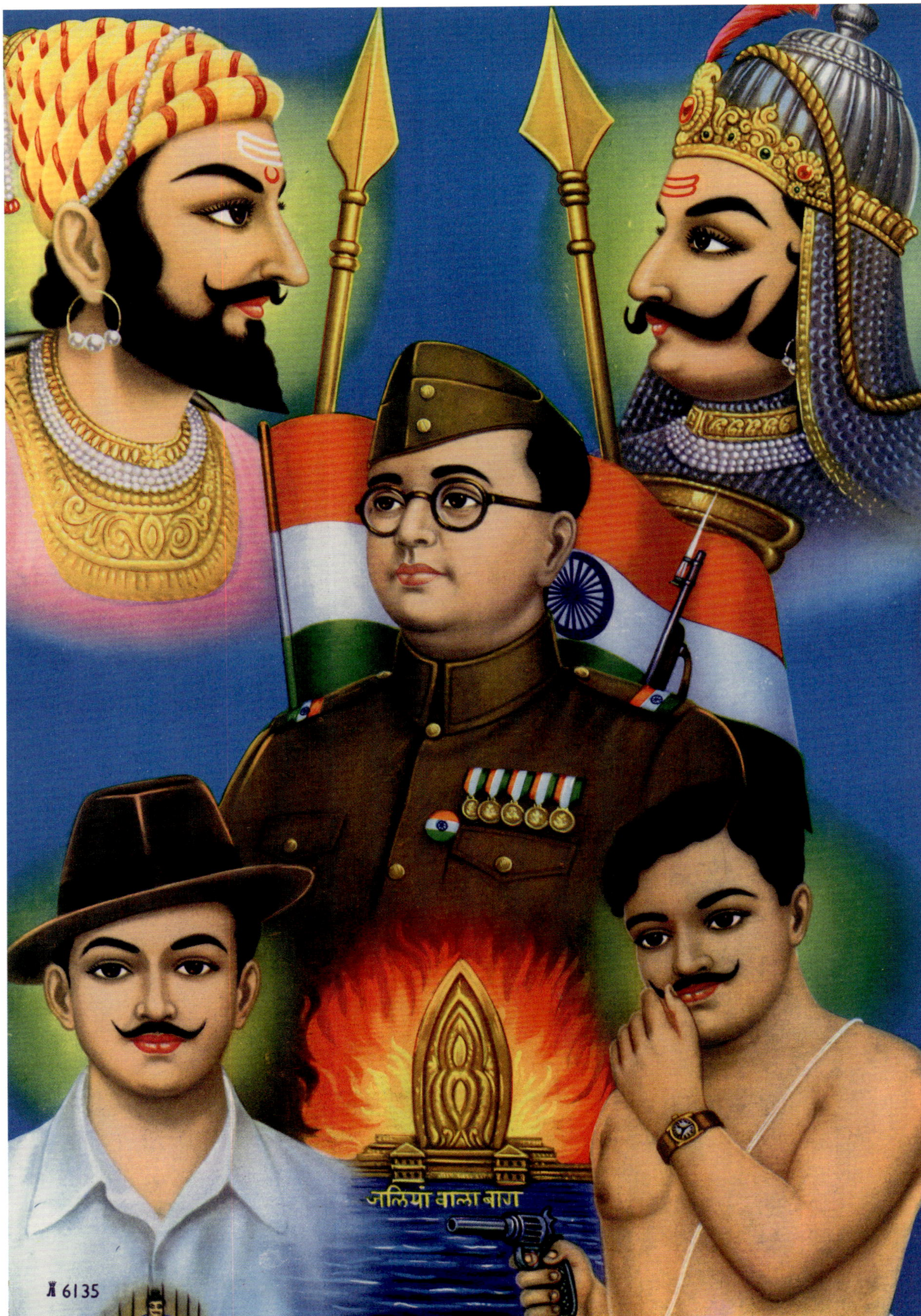
जलियां वाला बाग
6135

51

Untitled poster of Indian nationalists

c. 1980–9

India

Popular print, colour inks on glossy paper

46.5 × 32.2 cm

British Museum 2003,0714,0.9

Purchase funded by British Museum Friends, Townley Group

This popular print features five Indian nationalists. At the top are are Shivaji Bhosale (1627–80) and Maharana Pratap (1540–97), Hindu resistance leaders against the Mughal empire. In the middle is Subhas Chandra Bose, known as Netaji (fig. 26). At the bottom are Bhagat Singh (1907–31) and Chandra Shekar Azad (1906–31), freedom fighters who died martyrs to their cause. The monument between them is the Jallianwala Bagh Memorial, commemorating the massacre of a crowd in the public gardens of Amritsar in 1919. These revolutionary subjects are universally recognized by their specific iconography.

Shaheed ('martyr') Bhagat Singh and Chandra Shekar Azad ('liberated')[1] were organizers of the radical Hindustan Socialist Republican Association. They were both involved in the shooting of a policeman in Lahore in 1928.[2] Following this event, Baghat Singh cut his hair, put on Western clothes and made it to Calcutta by train, though the station was being carefully watched by police. The hat became a well-known symbol of his escape, his later trial and hanging, and above all of imperial injustice. The image first circulated as a photograph, then as poster and calendar art.[3] The hat immediately identified Bhagat Singh, in whatever context it appeared.

Chandra Shekar Azad managed to escape arrest for longer than Bhagat Singh. He was betrayed in Allahabad in 1931 and surrounded by police. He killed three of them, but when he ran out of ammunition he shot himself rather than be captured. He was born into a Brahmin family and is invariably shown with the sacred Brahmin thread clearly seen over his left shoulder. In graphics, Azad is always depicted twirling the right side of his moustache with his left hand, on which he wears a watch.

1 He was born Chandra Shekar Tiwari. When asked his name by a colonial magistrate, he defiantly named himself Azad. He was publicly punished for it, and the name stuck.
2 The target was Lahore's Police Superintendent Scott, in retaliation for the death of a non-violent protester, Lala Rajpat Rai. Misidentified as Scott, J.P. Saunders was shot and killed.
3 For the original photograph, see Maclean 2011, fig. 1. For other versions of the Bhagat Singh image in contemporary and later contexts, see Maclean 2011, pp. 1072–5, and Pinney 2004, pp. 124–9, 176–9.

52

Two-piso (peso) banknote

Issued by the Central Bank of the Philippines

c. 1970

Philippines

Paper

6.1 × 16.2 cm

British Museum 2008,4196.16

Given by Elizabeth Sandor

The Philippine Islands were colonized by Spain from 1565 to 1898, then by the United States until 1946.[1] It is not surprising that the Republic's currency bears portraits of heroes who fought for Filipino independence.

The front of this banknote shows José P. Rizal (1861–96), founder of La Liga Filipina and one of the earliest Asian proponents of non-violent national liberation. Convicted of sedition and conspiracy by association with leaders of the Katipunan rebellion of 1896, he was executed by the Spanish administration. Monuments, statues, ships and parks have been named in his honour around the world.

Another nationalist leader, Emilio Aguinaldo (1869–1964), appears on the reverse of the note. He is shown declaring Philippine independence, following Spain's defeat in the Spanish-American War of 1898. The First Republic did not last long, though, as the Americans settled into territorial administration. Standing against the US authorities until 1946, Aguinaldo co-operated with the Japanese occupation. He served in the post-independence Council of State.

1 The British ruled for a short period (1762–4), and the Japanese occupation lasted from 1942 until the end of the Second World War.

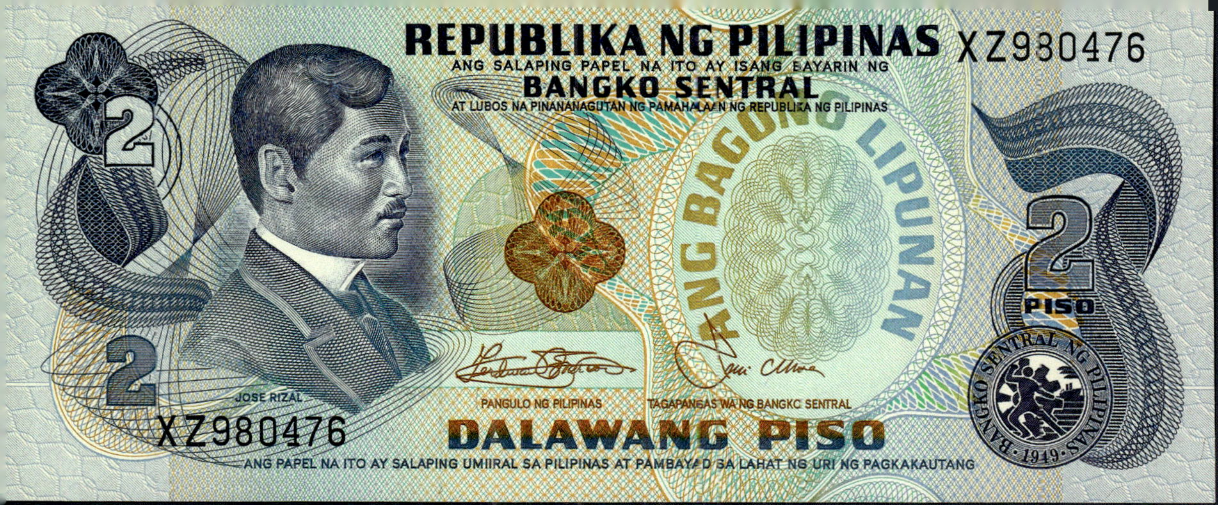
REPUBLIKA NG PILIPINAS
XZ980476
ANG SALAPING PAPEL NA ITO AY ISANG BAYARIN NG
BANGKO SENTRAL
AT LUBOS NA PINANANAGUTAN NG PAMAHALAAN NG REPUBLIKA NG PILIPINAS
ANG BAGONG LIPUNAN
2
2 PISO
JOSE RIZAL
PANGULO NG PILIPINAS
TAGAPANGASIWA NG BANGKO SENTRAL
BANGKO SENTRAL NG PILIPINAS 1949
XZ980476
DALAWANG PISO
ANG PAPEL NA ITO AY SALAPING UMIIRAL SA PILIPINAS AT PAMBAYAD SA LAHAT NG URI NG PAGKAKAUTANG
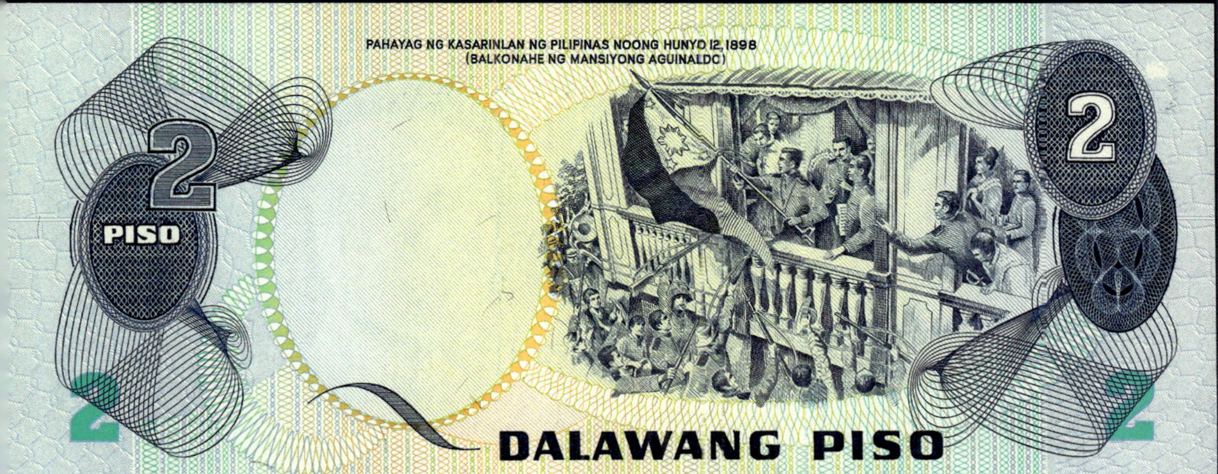
PAHAYAG NG KASARINLAN NG PILIPINAS NOONG HUNYO 12, 1898
(BALKONAHE NG MANSIYONG AGUINALDO)
2 PISO
2
2
DALAWANG PISO

53

Uncle Ho is Still Fighting in our Military Operations
(*Bác vẫn cũng chúng cháu hành quân*)

Nguyen Thu

Poster

1970

Vietnam

Poster paint, graphite and ink on paper

62 × 83 cm

British Museum 1999,0630,0.2

Purchase funded by Brooke Sewell Permanent Fund

Published: Harrison-Hall 2002, cat. 1.6

Ho Chi Minh (1890–1969), the charismatic leader also known as 'Uncle Ho', led the independence movement in Vietnam from 1941. He declared the Democratic Republic of Vietnam (DRV) in 1945, serving as prime minister until 1955 and president until his death in 1969. Although the outcome of the American War was still unclear when he died, Ho Chi Minh remained the inspiration for the cause of a united Communist Vietnam. He is portrayed here in black and white, while the platoon he still leads in spirit is shown in colour.

This poster was painted in 1970 by Nguyen Thu (b. 1930), soldier and prize-winning artist for the National Resistance (against the French) from the age of sixteen. After leaving the army, he spent his career as a teacher and cultural official.[1] This well-known work was painted into the 1971 watercolour by Vu Giang Huong showing posters on display at an army camp (fig. 36).

1 Harrison-Hall 2002, p. 88.

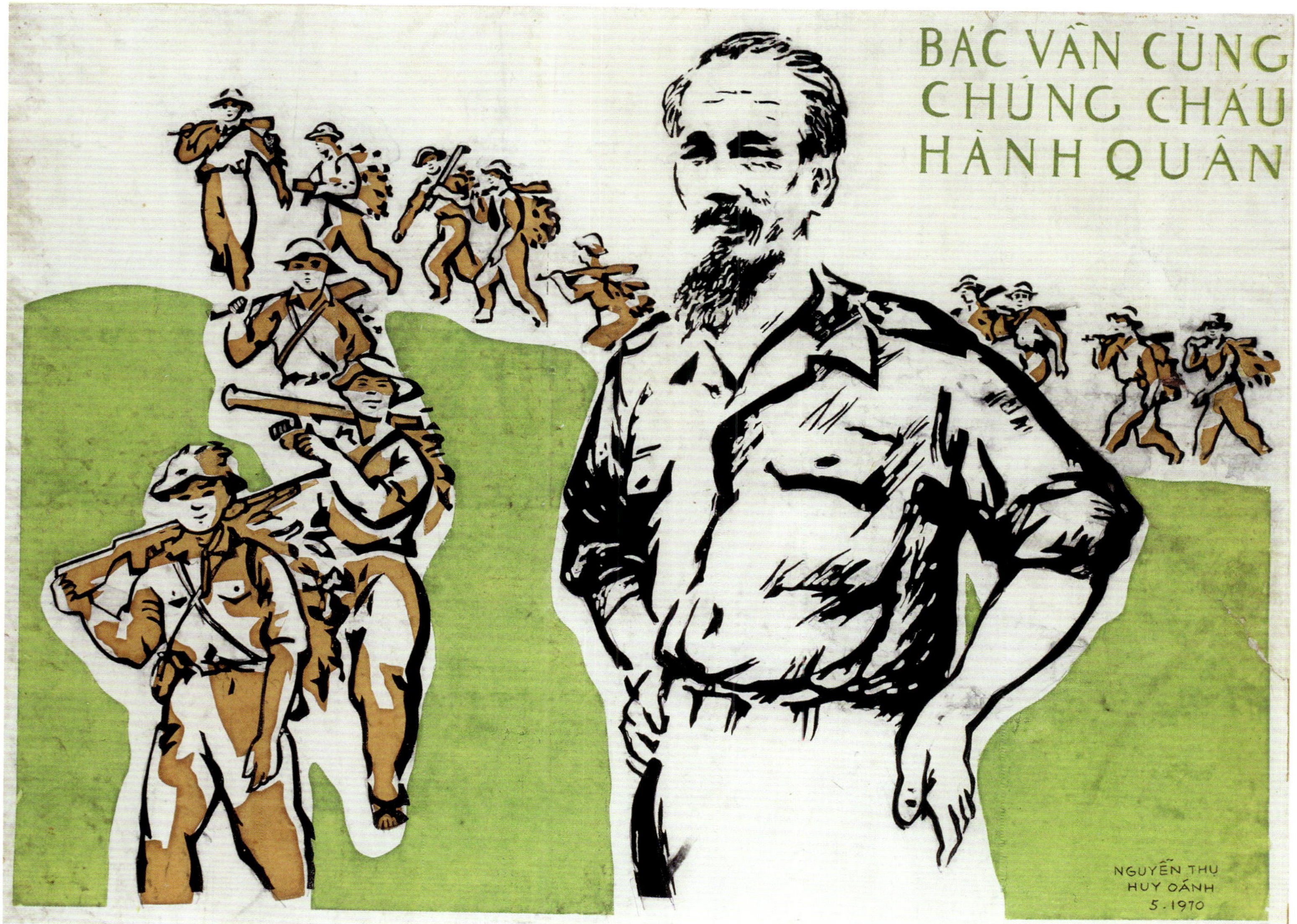
BÁC VẪN CÙNG
CHÚNG CHÁU
HÀNH QUÂN
NGUYỄN THU
HUY OÁNH
5.1970

54

Kazi in Noman's Land

Naeem Mohaiemen

2008

New York, USA

Paper sculpture with postage stamps

India: 2.8 × 4 cm; Pakistan: 3.4 × 4.2 cm; Bangladesh: 3.8 × 4.5 cm

British Museum 2012,3050.1.1

Purchase funded by Brooke Sewell Permanent Fund

This work by Naeem Mohaiemen – visual artist, journalist, filmmaker – explores the partition of India and the co-opting of a cultural and political hero by three nations for their own purposes.[1]

Kazi Nazrul Islam (1899–1976) is celebrated as the national poet of Bangladesh, but he has also been claimed by both India and Pakistan. Born into a Muslim family in India (in what is now West Bengal), he served in the British Indian Army, where his political ideas were forged. He became an inspiring leader of the Indian independence movement, his poetry of revolution frequently landing him in trouble. His best-known poem, *Bidrohi* (*The Rebel*), published in 1922, profoundly changed Bengali literature.

From 1942 Kazi Nazrul Islam suffered from a degenerative illness, which worsened until he was practically unable to move without help. Kazi strongly opposed partition and stayed in India after independence was attained in 1947. His decision was trumpeted at the time as an example of Muslims finding a home in the new nation. In 1989 the government of India issued a commemorative stamp.

Pakistan also claimed Kazi Nazrul Islam, as a Muslim counterpoint to the dominance of the Hindu literary giant, Rabindranath Tagore (1861–1941). Of the 328 stamps issued by Pakistan between independence and the formal establishment of a separate Bangladesh in 1971, only one honoured a Bengali figure: Kazi Nazrul Islam, in 1968.

The newly independent state of Bangladesh then claimed Kazi Nazrul Islam as a cultural icon, celebrating him with stamps, international conferences and other commemorations.

1 This account is based on the artist's article: Naeem Mohaiemen, 'Kazi in Nomansland', http://www.departmag.com/archive/6th_issue/kazi_in_nomansland.html.

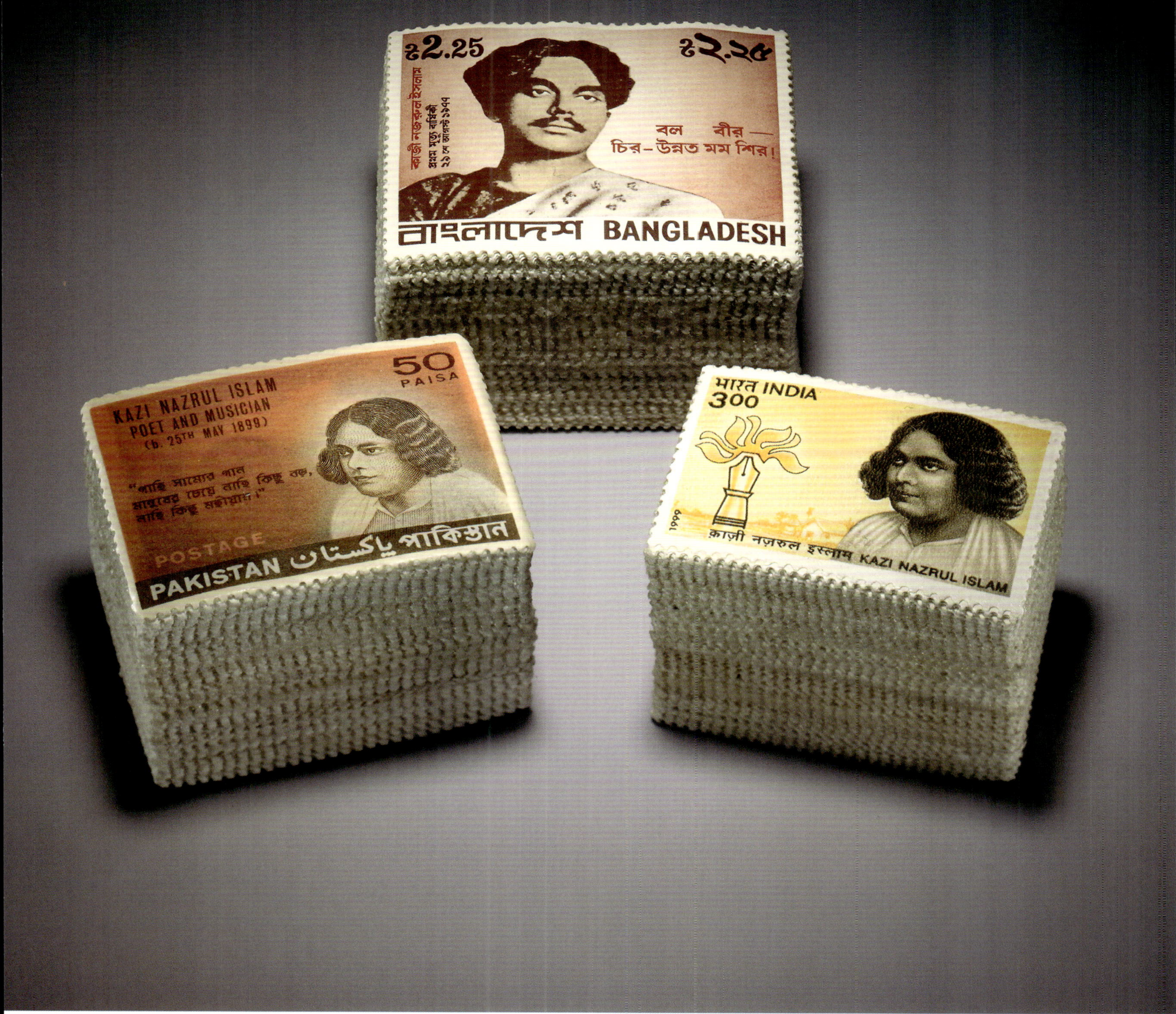
৳2.25
BANGLADESH
50
PAISA
KAZI NAZRUL ISLAM
POET AND MUSICIAN
(b. 25TH MAY 1899)
POSTAGE
PAKISTAN
INDIA
3.00
1999
KAZI NAZRUL ISLAM

55

Chairman Mao's Good Soldier – Lei Feng
(毛主席的好战士–雷锋)

Chen Ziyun (陳子云)

1963 (1965 reprint)

China

Coloured poster on paper

76 × 53 cm

British Museum 2006,0501,0.26

Lei Feng is a cultural icon in China. Born in 1940 to a farming family in Hunan province, his father was killed by Japanese invaders and his mother was driven to suicide by her rapacious landlord's family. The orphaned Lei Feng was brought up by the Communist Party, and he joined the People's Liberation Army to serve the country. His goal was to be 'a revolutionary screw that never rusts'.[1] He gave his little money to the poor, treated sick comrades and taught children to read. In short, Lei Feng modestly and selflessly served the revolution and the new society.

Lei Feng died in an accident in 1962, while on active service. A soldier-comrade, backing up a truck, knocked over a pole and killed him. A campaign was launched in March the following year to 'Learn from Lei Feng'. The diary he had kept, recording his daily good deeds, was published and became a bestseller. Every year on 5 March the spirit of Lei Feng is invoked to encourage voluntary service. As China has become more consumer-orientated and less ideologically driven, Lei Feng represents the revolutionary values of a bygone era.

In this poster, a rather sweet-looking Lei Feng holds his bayonet in one hand and the works of Mao Zedong in the other. He is surrounded by sunflowers, a symbol of loyalty to Chairman Mao ('We are all Chairman Mao's sunflowers' was a familiar slogan). It is evident from Lei Feng's rank stars on his collar that the poster was designed before the Cultural Revolution, when rank designations disappeared on posters and other propaganda images.

1 Stefan Landsberger, http://chineseposters.net/themes/leifeng.php.

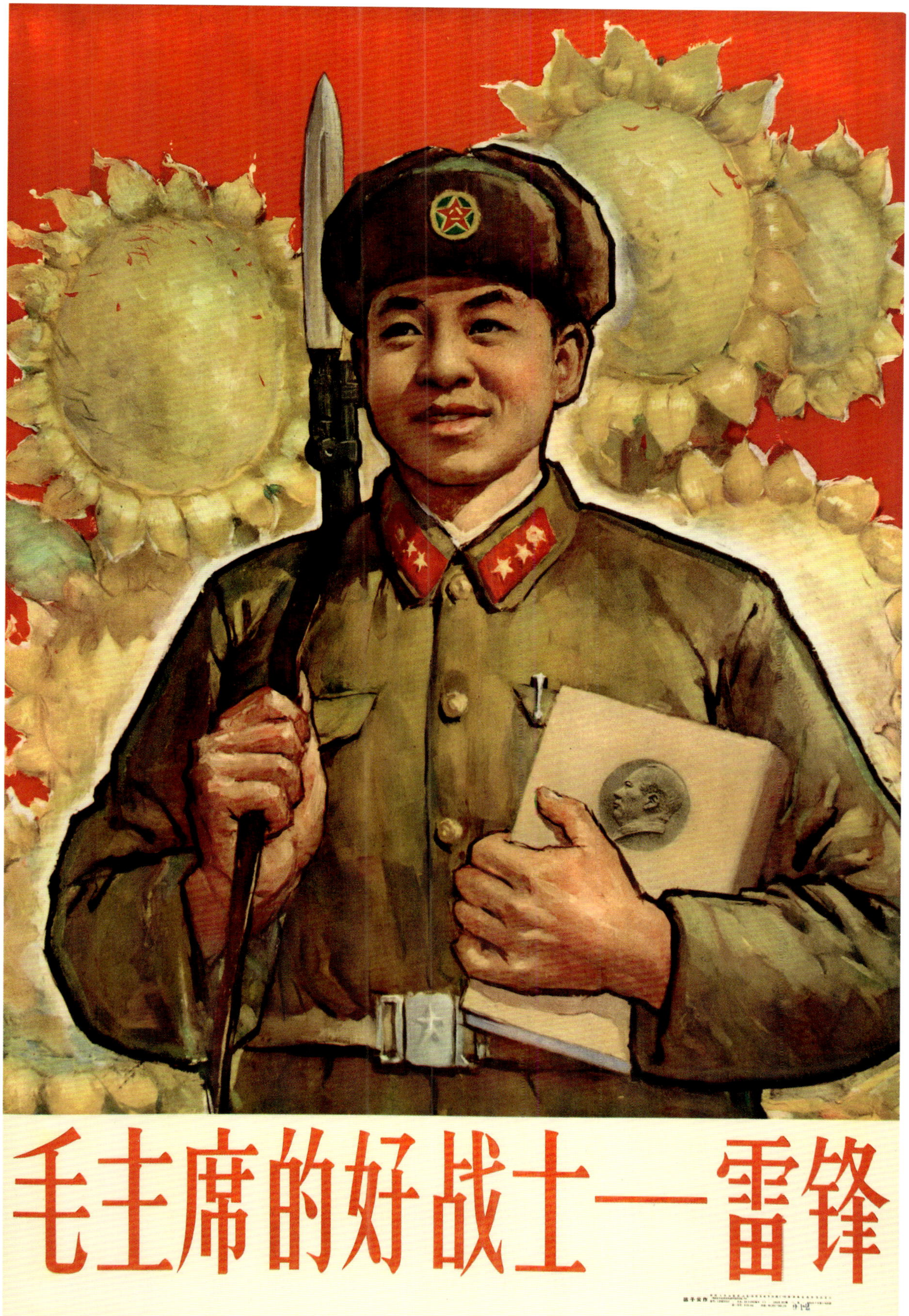
毛主席的好战士—雷锋

56

He says himself, he's already got a new appearance!
(自謂己 - 新面目！)

Lu Shaofei (鲁少飛)

1931–8

China

Drawing, ink and slight colours on paper

25.5 × 19.5 cm

British Museum 2009,3022.4

Lu Shaofei (1903–95) was a leader among the resistance cartoonists during the Asia-Pacific War. A sharp, witty critic of the modern social and cultural scene, he designed lurid magazine covers for *Shanghai Manhua* (上海漫畫 *Shanghai Sketch*), a pictorial published 1928–30.[1] He was the founding editor of *Shidai manhua* (時代漫畫 *Modern Sketch*), the most influential of the many humour magazines in China's 'golden age of cartoon art'.[2] When Japan attacked Shanghai in August 1937, Lu Shaofei, along with Ye Qianyu (葉淺予, 1907–95) and Ding Cong (丁聰, 1916–2009), founded the artists' association which published *National Salvation Cartoons* (救亡漫畫 *Jiuwang manhua*), the first resistance cartoon magazine of national significance.[3]

This drawing was in the 1938 travelling exhibition organized by Jack Chen (Chen Yifan) (see p. 28). The Japanese man holding a mask represents Japan's aggressive policy towards China, hidden behind a diplomatic front. The inscription on the man's head reads 'Maintain the Three Principles', and on the mask 'A new understanding of China'.

A figure wearing a mask to hide his (or his nation's) true political nature is a well-established propaganda device. Many Soviet revolutionary artists employed it, including Viktor Deni (1893–1946).[4] It also appeared in Japanese anti-Communist propaganda in wartime China.[5]

1 *Shanghai Manhua* was published weekly for 110 issues. Its print run was about 3,000, very high for the time (Laing 2010). The entire series was reproduced in two volumes in 1996 by *Shanghai shudian chubanshe* (上海書店出版社). This was a different publication from the *Shanghai Manhua* (*Modern Sketch*) which appeared during the 1930s (cats 14–15).
2 Crespi 2011, p. 1.
3 Andrews and Shen 2012, p. 118.
4 White 1988, fig 1.19.
5 Landsberger and van der Heijden 2009, p. 31.

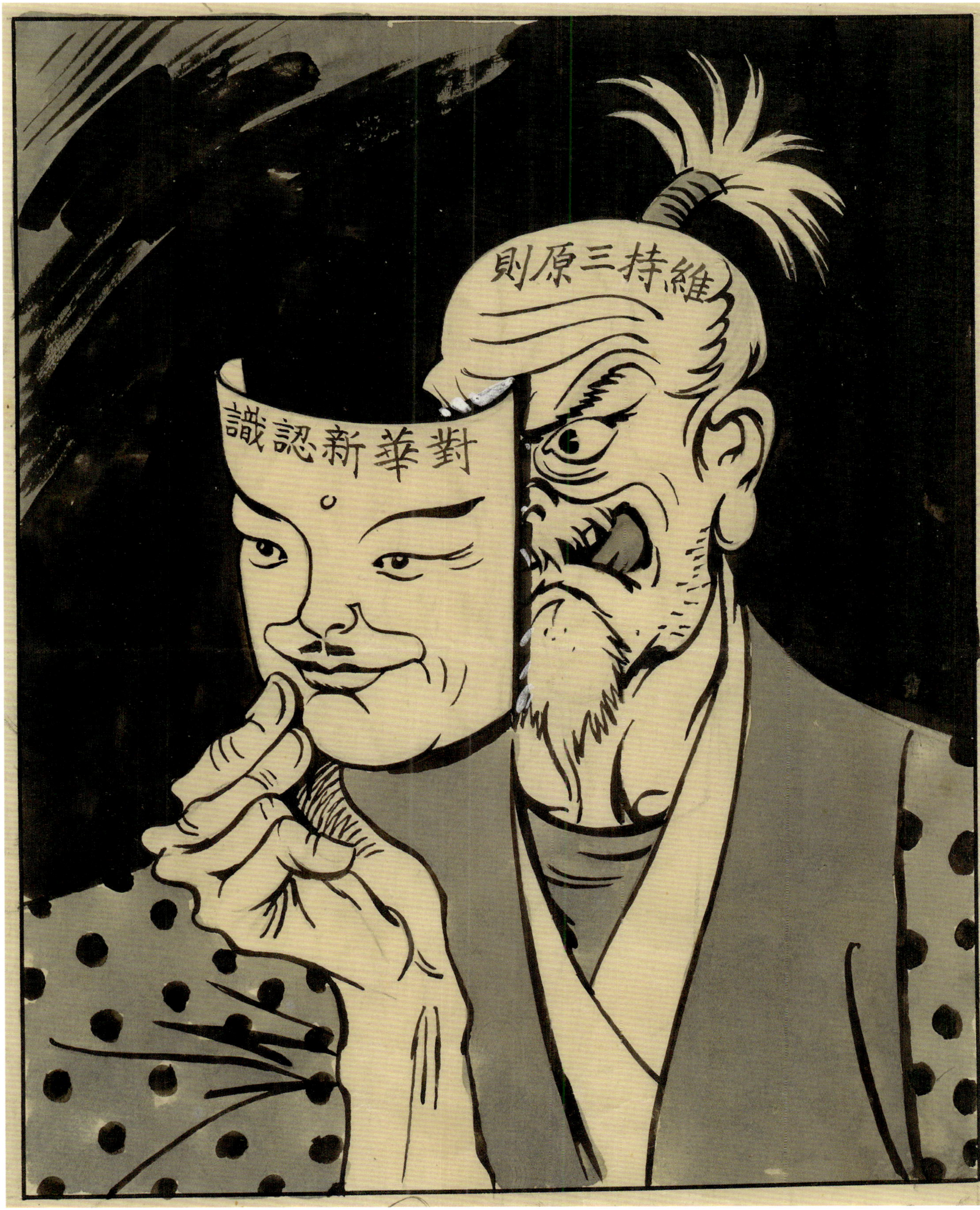
對華新認識
維持三原則

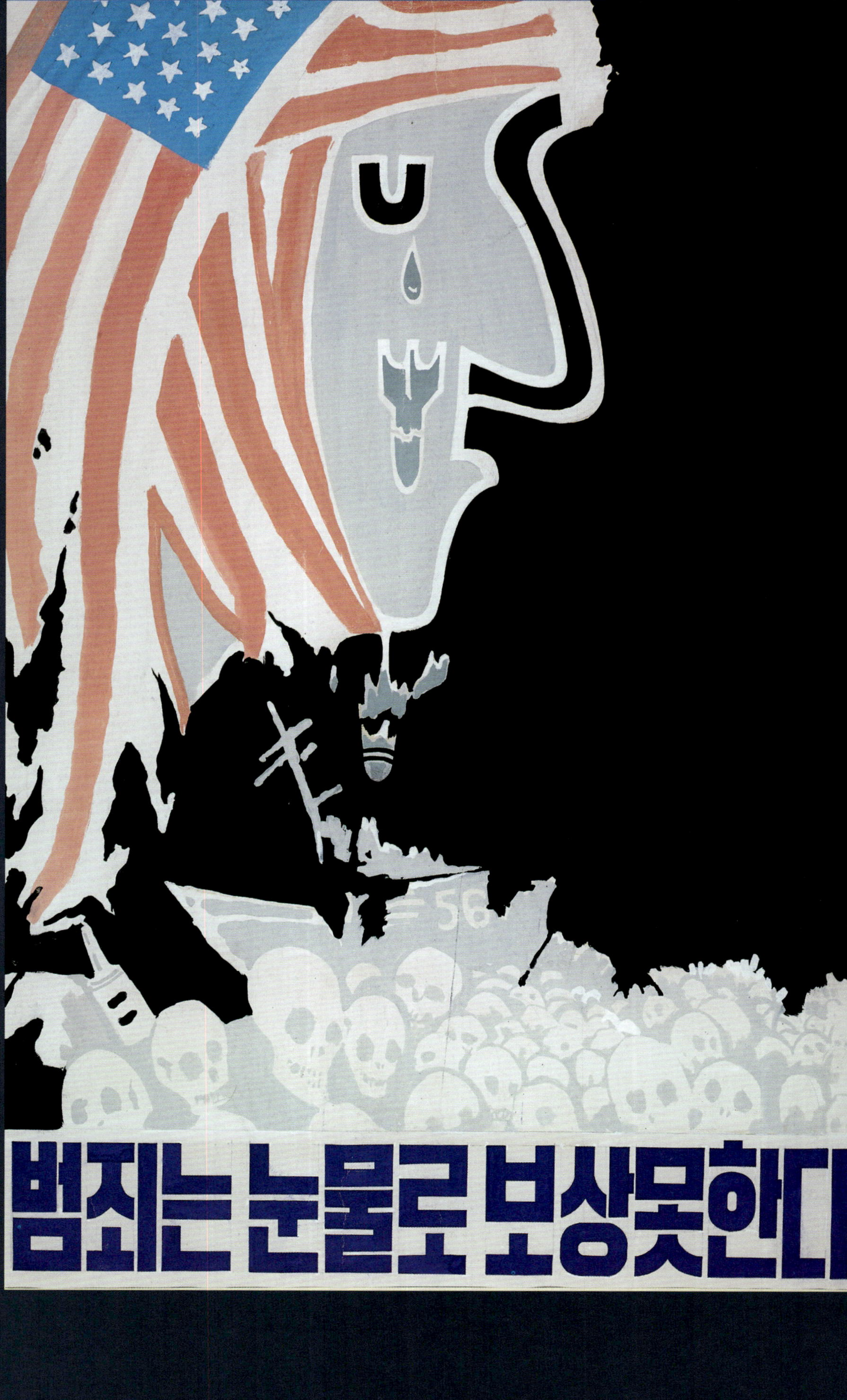
56
범죄는 눈물로 보상못한다

57

Crime cannot be compensated by tears
(범죄는 눈물로 보상못한다)

c. 2000

Democratic People's Republic of Korea

Painting, ink and colours on paper

98 × 67 cm

British Museum 2002,1001,0.9

Purchase funded by Brooke Sewell Permanent Fund

Published: Portal 2005, fig. 128

This painting is the original artwork for a poster. It is a departure from the usual style of Socialist Realism that has prevailed for decades in North Korea (DPRK). It shows America as a head wrapped in a flag. The eye and nose say 'US'. Rockets fall from the eye, sinking a ship, its wreckage blending with a pile of skulls. Piled-up heads have appeared in propaganda since the French Revolution.[1]

North Korean art and literature often condemn the US as a nation which massacres innocents. In children's picture books, the enemy soldiers are portrayed as both brutal and cowardly.[2] In dictionaries and textbooks, Americans have 'paws' and 'snouts'.[3] The US itself is sometimes shown as dog, recognizable by the American flag wrapped around it. On one such poster, a speeding train (representing North Korea) leaves the barking dog in the dust.[4]

1 Schnapp 2005, p. 88.
2 Zur 2011, pp. 289–91.
3 Myers 2010, pp. 135–6.
4 Heather and de Ceuster 2008, p. 261. The caption reads, 'Though the dog barks, the procession moves on.'

Women and Children

During the twentieth century, women and children became political actors in their own right in many Asian societies. Governments gradually expanded provision for girls' education, investing in human capital and nation-building. The world opened up for women, with new opportunities for work and leisure (cat. 58). Obviously this happened more quickly in some countries than others.

Women had achieved the right to vote in only a few Asian countries by the 1930s; in most, suffrage was granted in the wake of the regime changes that followed the Asia-Pacific War. During the war years, women generally held the fort on the home front and provided support services for the troops: few saw military action. In post-war conflicts – including the Civil War in China and the American-Vietnam War – women were active fighters (cats 59, 60). Campaigns for gender equality made great strides. Political leadership became a reality: in the 1960s, Sri Lanka and India elected female prime ministers, long before most Western democracies.

Children were mobilized for the Asia-Pacific War, particularly in Japan, where all aspects of life were marshalled for national glory. In other countries, too – both Asian and Western – magazines and films, games and clothing brought children closer to war. Cartoon characters created for children were enormously popular among citizens of all ages: Sanmao, a Chinese orphan, and Norakuro, a Japanese stray dog, even served in their respective armies (cat. 15). The children of post-1949 China were depicted as active fighters and revolutionaries participating in propaganda activities (cat. 62).

Children of New China.
Zhang Ding. 1950. China.
See cat. 62

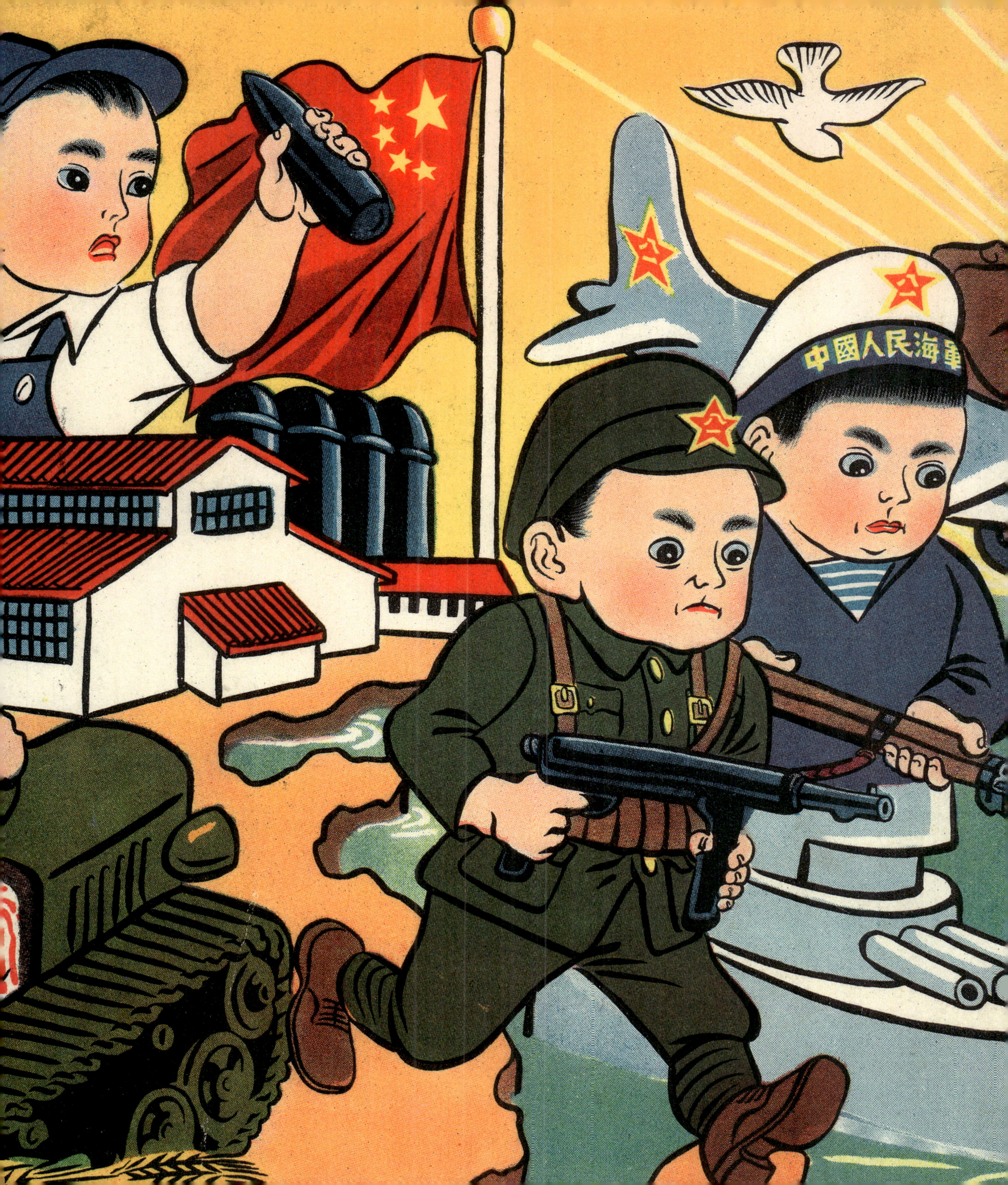
中國人民海軍

58

Manga board game

Okamoto Ippei (岡本一平)

Japan

1 January 1929

Colour lithograph on paper

63.6 × 94.5 cm

British Museum 2006,0119,0.2

Purchase funded by Brooke Sewell Bequest

Sugoroku (a type of board game) were made based on an enormous range of subjects (cat. 11). They were often distributed as supplements by newspapers or magazines, especially around the New Year. This *manga* board game was issued by *Shufu no tomo* (Housewife's Friend), one of the first women's magazines in Japan. It began publishing in 1917 and by 1926 had achieved the highest circulation among magazines.[1]

Shufu no tomo was aimed at middle- and working-class housewives. It dealt with issues of home (and husband) management, and many working women, such as waitresses in the stylish café milieu, also read it. By the late 1920s, women's magazines featured modern international styles of clothing and hairstyles. Consumption and modern lifestyle choices appeared more frequently.[2]

Against a background of newly won rights of political participation, women were far more visible in Japanese public life – particularly after the 1923 Kanto earthquake.[3] This board game shows numerous activities and entertainments for the modern woman – who she spends her time with, how she looks, where she goes and how she gets there.

1 Kaneko 1995, p. 8.
2 Silverberg 2006, p. 28.
3 Kaneko 1995, p. 6.

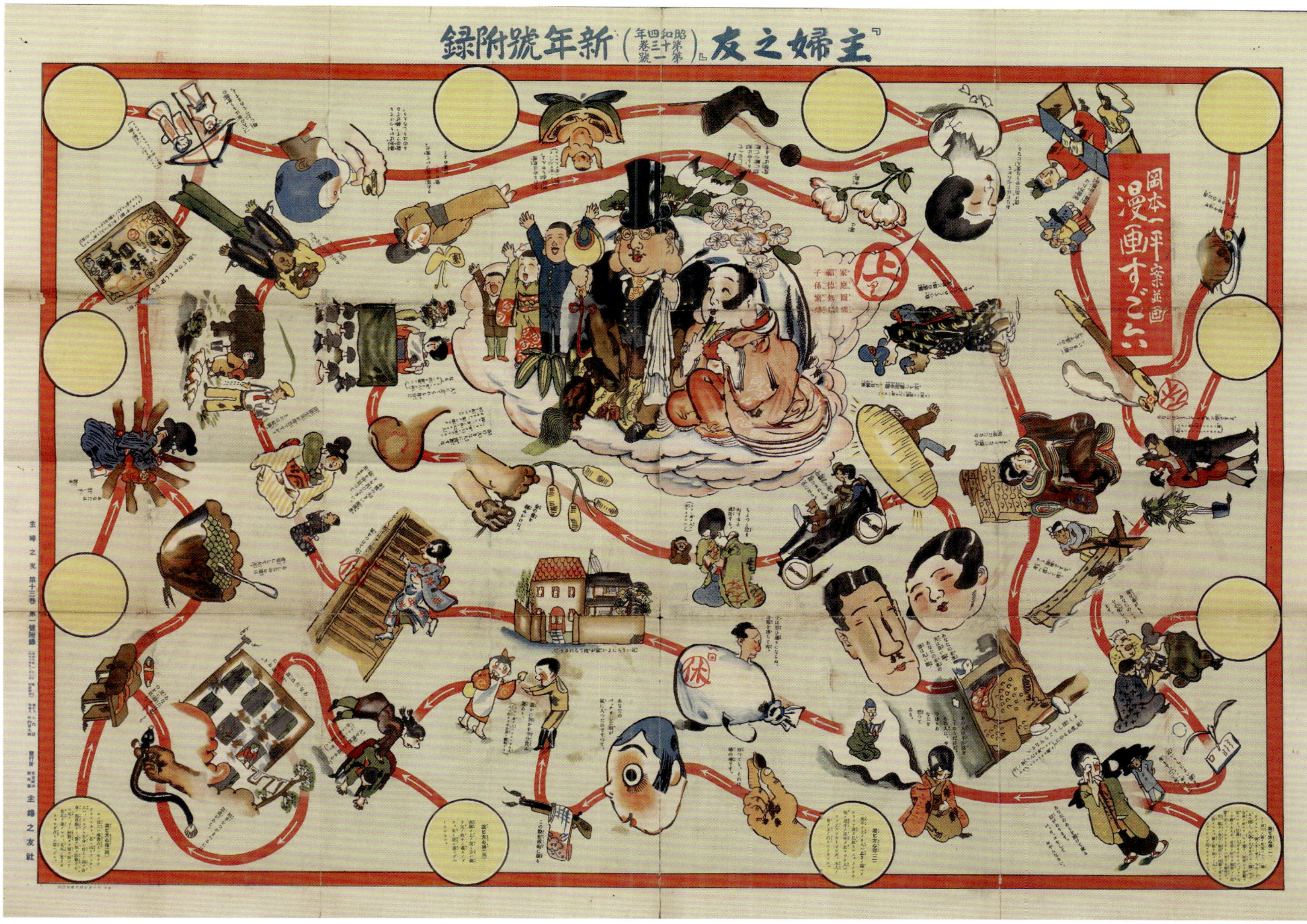

『主婦之友』（昭和四年第十三巻第一號）新年號附録
岡本一平案並画
漫画すごろく

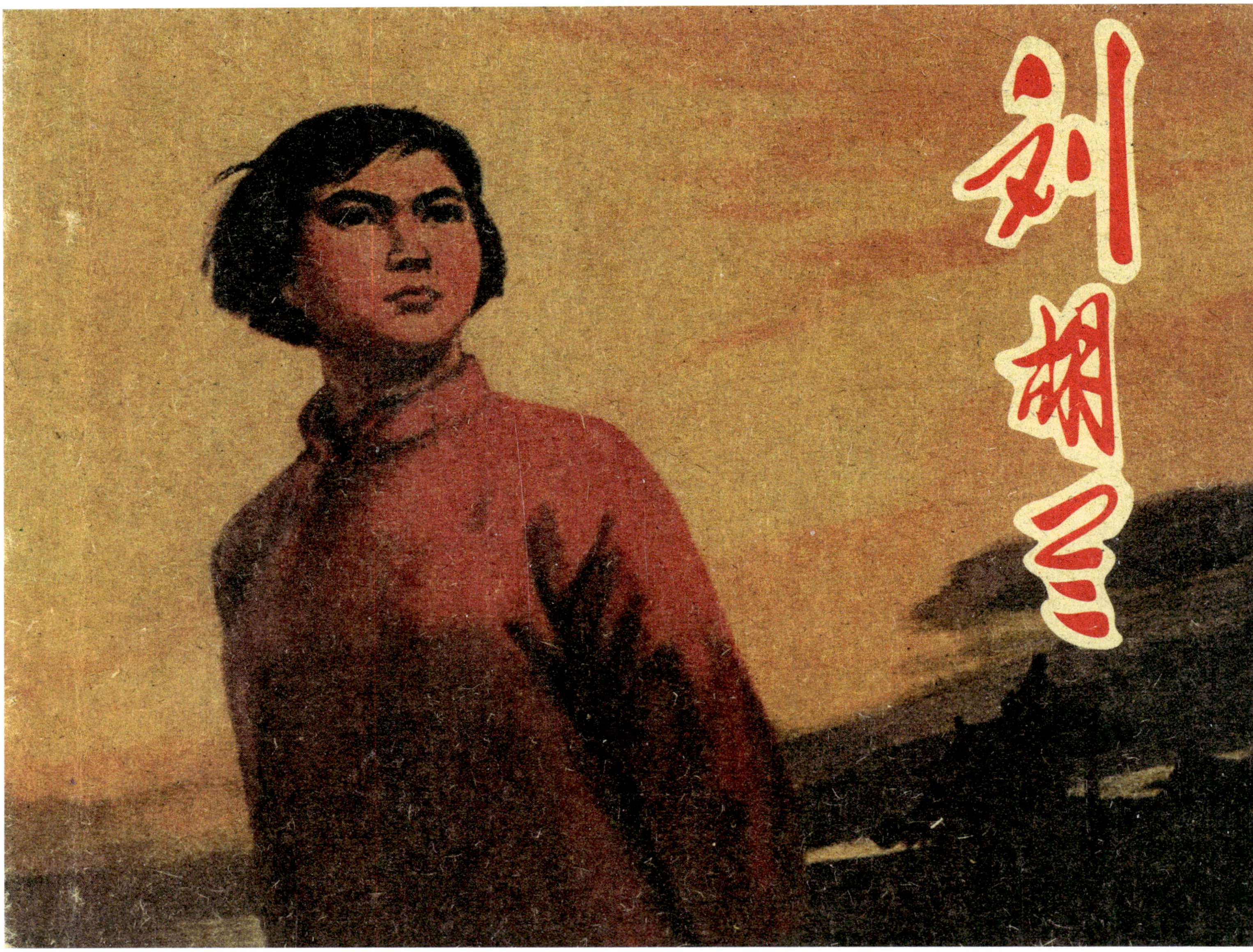
刘胡兰

59

Liu Hulan 刘胡兰 (劉胡蘭)

Lianhuanhua creative group (連環畫創作組編會)

1972

China

Serial picture book (連環畫 *lianhuanhua*)

9 × 12.5 cm

Private collection

Liu Hulan (1932–47) was a Communist recruiter and spy against the Guomindang during the Chinese Civil War (1945–9). She joined the Communist Party in 1946 and organized her local chapter of the Women's Federation. When the GMD surrounded her Shanxi village in 1947 and pillaged the public granary, Liu Hulan led the resistance. The GMD gathered the locals and demanded the names of Communist Party members. Under threat of death, Liu Hulan refused to divulge any names. Because she was so young, the GMD leader offered her a final chance, but she walked bravely forward to the executioner and was decapitated. Liu Hulan served as a model heroine from that time forward. To honour her, Chairman Mao penned the slogan, 'A great life, a glorious death' (生的偉大死的光榮), which appears on the frontispiece of this serial picture book (*lianhuanhua*).

Large single-sheet serial picture stories had appeared at the end of the Qing dynasty, but the later form of little pocket-size books flourished from the time of the May Fourth Movement (1919). They were horizontal in format, usually about the size of this one, with a single picture on a page and text underneath or on the side. The cover was almost always coloured, and the story inside illustrated in black and white. Image techniques included photography, lithography, ink and wash drawing, woodcut and paper cut.

Lianhuanhua were a powerful socialization tool for the CCP. It is estimated that from 1949 to 1963, more than 12,700 different titles were issued and 560 million copies distributed.[1] This enormously popular production was not just for children, as *lianhuanhua* were an important tool in literacy campaigns among adults.

Most cultural forms were curtailed during the Cultural Revolution, and it was not until 1971 that *lianhuanhua* were produced again. From then on, they made an enormous comeback. In 1982, for example, 2,100 different titles were issued, in a total of 860 million copies.[2]

1 John C. Hwang, '*Lian Huan Hua*: Revolutionary Serial Pictures', p. 54, in Chu 1978, pp. 51–72.

2 http://courseweb.lis.illinois.edu/ffimchen6/LIS303A/fluctuation.htm.

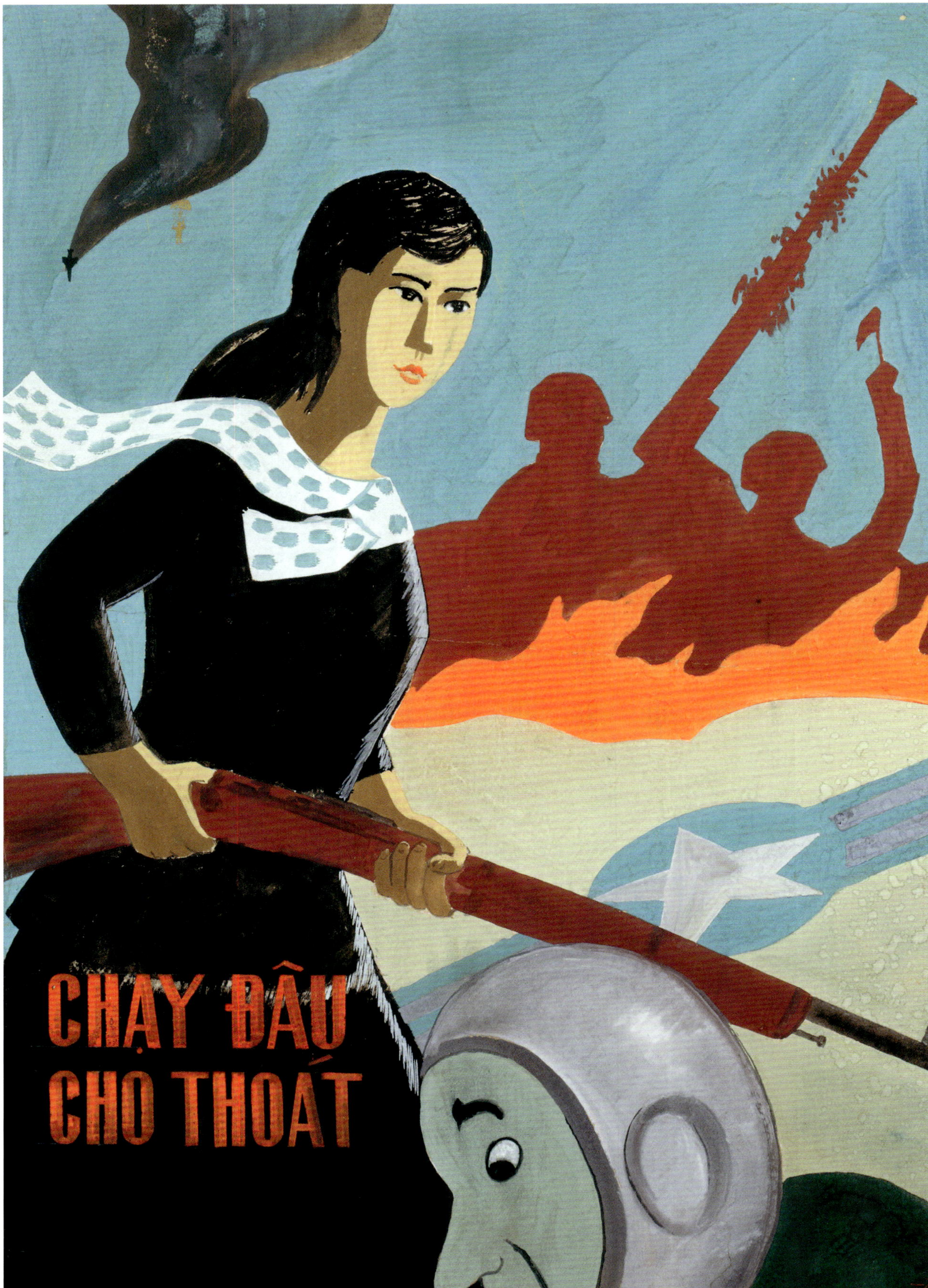
CHẠY ĐÂU
CHO THOÁT

60

Nowhere to run to escape (Chạy đâu cho thoát)

Signed Ta (unidentified artist)

1967

Vietnam

Poster paint, colours on paper

108.1 × 79 cm

British Museum 1999,0630,0.13

Given by the British Museum Friends

Published: Harrison-Hall 2002, cat. 1.4

An American plane has crashed and is burning. Above, another is headed for disaster, one of its personnel escaping by parachute. Also in the background are two Vietnamese soldiers, one holding a weapon, the other a flag. They are clearly in the shadow of their heroic female comrade in the foreground. The young woman pursues the enemy pilot with a rifle. The pilot is shown as a much smaller cartoon figure – a green spaceman, not to be feared. Ridiculing the enemy in this way would boost morale amid the atrocities of war. Caricature was a potent element in poster design throughout the French and American Vietnam wars.[1]

'One need have no beard to be a hero', noted To Huu, national poet of the DRV.[2] The war-ready heroine in this poster, with long hair, flowing scarf and bolt-action rifle, exemplifies the point. Women fought bravely behind enemy lines, built roads, operated radios and printing presses, and engaged fully in political struggle. One Vietnamese military historian and veteran estimates that nearly a million women served in the North in local guerilla and militia units.[3]

1 Buchanan and Heather 2005, p. 7.
2 Quoted in Harrison-Hall 2002, p. 40.
3 Professor Nguyen Quoc Dung, cited in Buchanan 2002, p. 20, n. 9.

61

Little Friends (小朋友 *Xiao Pengyou*)

January 1949, February 1950, August 1951

China

Children's magazine, printed on paper

18.2 × 12.8 cm

Private collection

Children's magazines are a hybrid of official and popular literature. They offer a variety of imagery and activities, and their features require the active participation of their readers. They are also up-to-the-minute transmitters of policy and programmes, as they are published every two weeks or monthly and can highlight current campaigns.

Xiao Pengyou (*Little Friends*) has been published almost continually since 1922, for children aged about five to seven.[1] Examining the format, covers and content of several issues illustrates the changing function and ideological practices of China's revolutionary children's literature. For example, in the early years, *Xiao Pengyou* included translations of many Western children's stories. These mostly disappeared after the establishment of the PRC. The proportion of text to imagery was greatly reduced post-1949, and the language simplified, as part of the campaign for universal literacy.

The issue of January 1949 (dated Minguo 38: the thirty-eighth year of the Republic) features stories and drawing activities; there is little political content. The cover of the February 1950 magazine already shows a new focus. The border design at the top shows children playing as workers, peasants and soldiers; the bottom border shows various aspects of industry and agriculture. The text at the bottom reads, 'Little friends, have you bought government bonds? Have you encouraged your family to buy government bonds?' Finally, the August 1951 issue is far simpler in design and more explicit in content: children are themselves engaged in propaganda activities, hanging posters urging increased agricultural production.

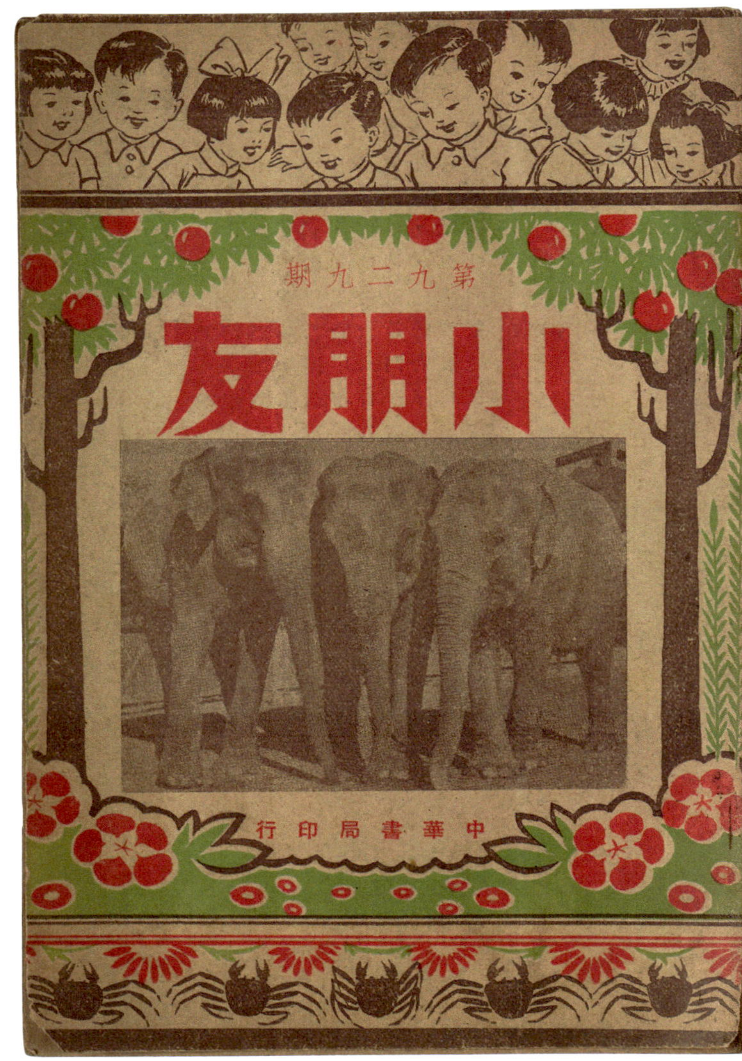

1 The only breaks were during the Asia-Pacific War years and the Cultural Revolution.

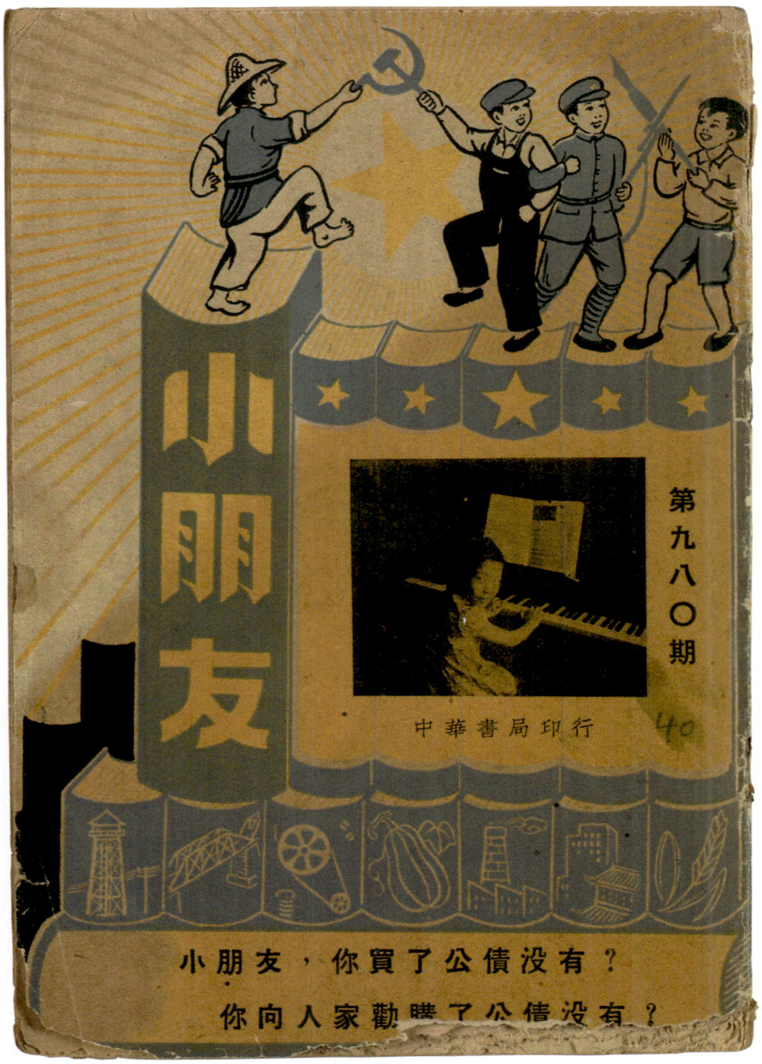
小朋友
第九八〇期
中華書局印行
40
小朋友，你買了公債没有？
你向人家勸購了公債没有？

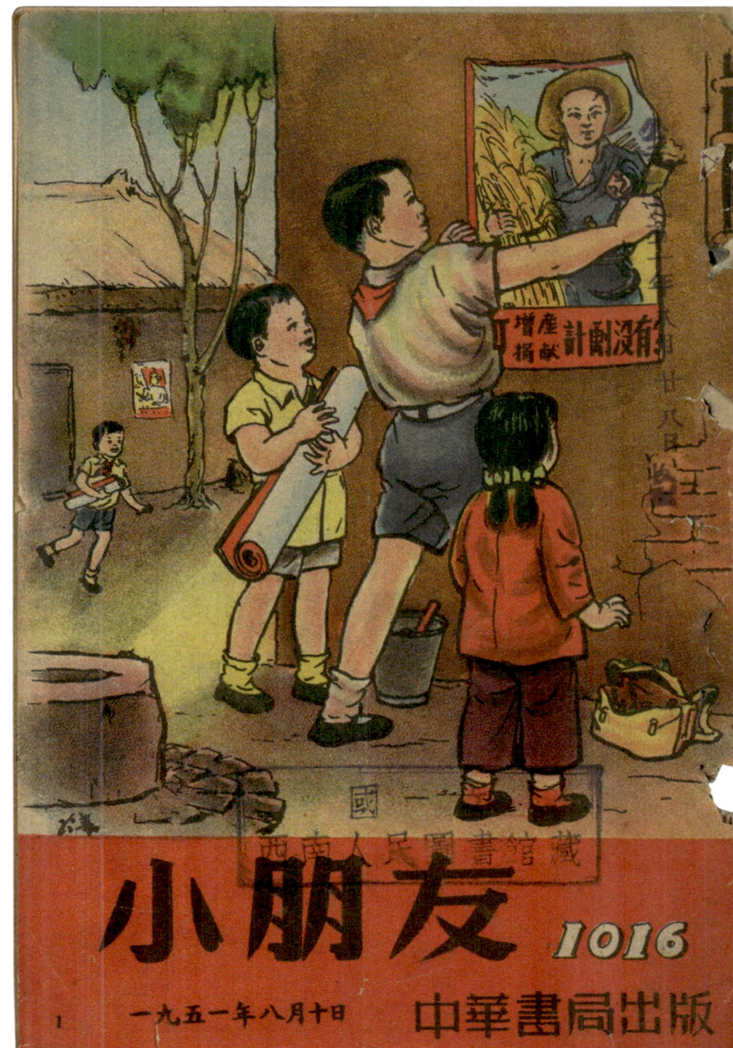
增產捐獻計劃没有
西南人民圖書館藏
小朋友
1016
一九五一年八月十日
中華書局出版

62

Children of New China (新中國的兒童 *Xin Zhongguo de ertong*)

Zhang Ding (張仃)

1950

China

Woodblock print, ink and colours on paper

14.5 × 21.5 cm

Private collection

This prize-winning *nianhua* (single-page popular print) is full of propaganda imagery for the newly established PRC. The children represent all spheres of the revolutionary society. The girl drives a tractor (see cats 28–9), bringing in a bountiful harvest. The boy representing industrial production brandishes a torpedo. The army, navy and air force are advancing, crossing the Straits to take back Taiwan from Chiang Kai-shek, who clings desperately to the sinking American General MacArthur. The new national flag flutters, the sun is rising, and the dove signifies China's hope for peace.

Zhang Ding (1917–2010) was a prolific printmaker, cartoonist and painter. He went to Yan'an in 1938 and taught at Lu Yi during the War of Resistance. After the establishment of the PRC, he taught at the Central Academy of Fine Arts in Beijing. He was purged during the Anti-Rightist Movement in the late 1950s and again in the Cultural Revolution. He was rehabilitated in 1978 and went on to serve as President of the Chinese Artists Association.

In later life Zhang Ding painted mostly landscapes, but he is better known outside China for his 1950s propaganda prints, many of which feature children, sometimes recognizably his own.[1]

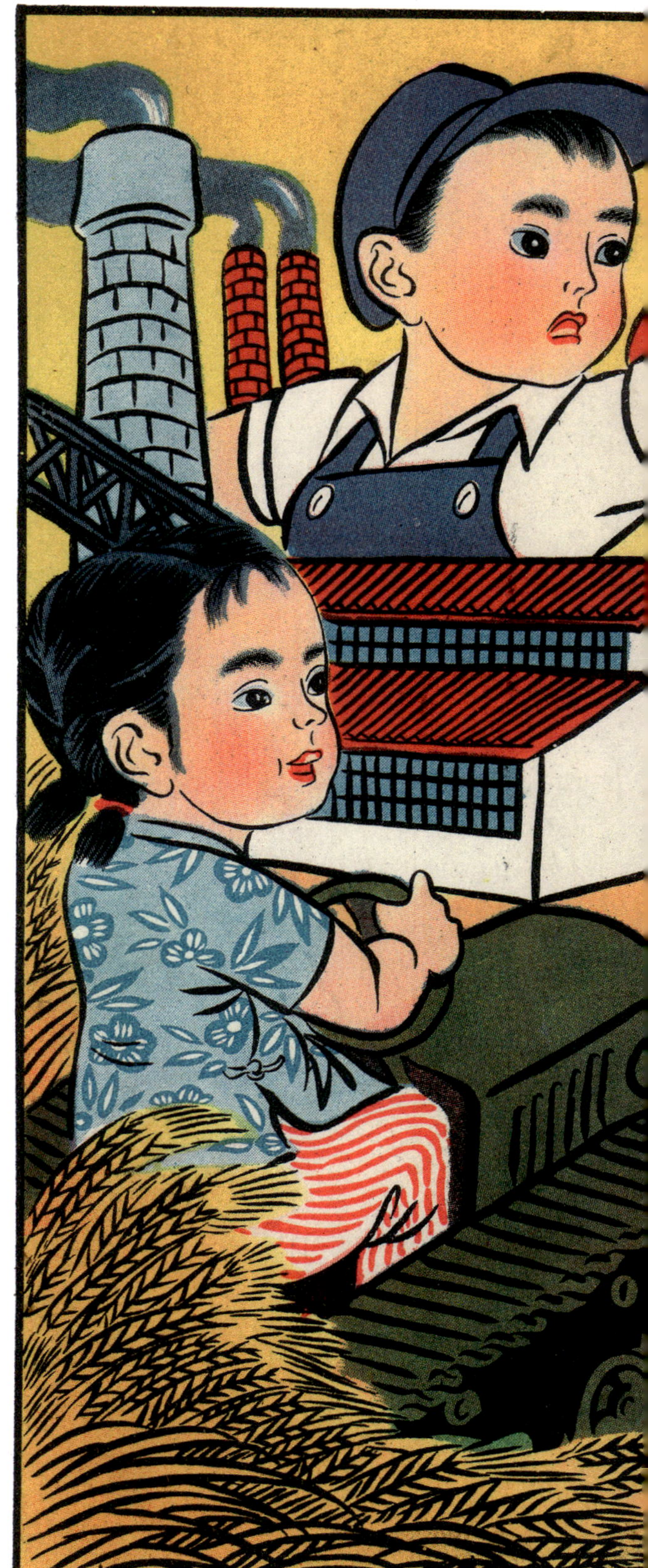

1 For example, von Spee 2010, cat. 71. Stephanie Mitchell, private correspondence 2011.

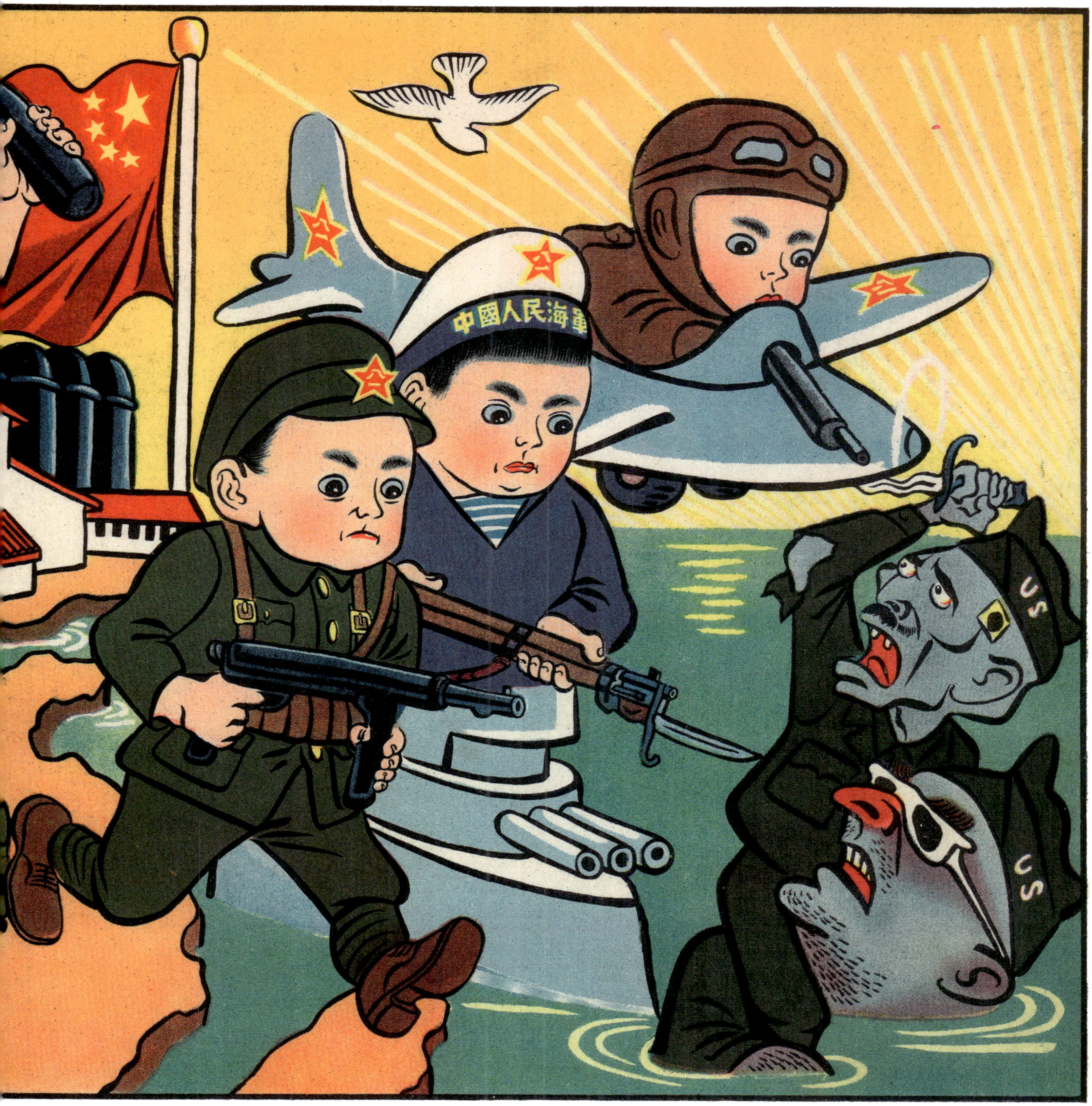
中國人民海軍
US
US

Protest

States use varying degrees of pressure to influence attitudes and behaviour. Coercion and suppression may be the flip side of propaganda. It is important to distinguish between societies where communication is one-sided – only top-down – and those where alternative sources of information foster open debate. What are the personal and political consequences of ignoring these messages, or of actively flouting them?

This catalogue includes many examples of resistance to colonial overlords and wartime occupation. This section shows how artists both participate in and document protest, when governments fail to act in times of trouble (cat. 63) or enforce decisions without regard to those affected.

Oppositional propaganda may be expressed through the words or images of a symbolic figure such as Qu Yuan (cats 64–5). Symbols of opposition can either be easily recognizable or intended to be understood by only a few. Indeed, opposition is sometimes assumed where none has been expressed, which may have dire consequences for the artist.[1]

The American-Vietnam War galvanized global dissent. Prints and drawings showed the terror and devastation of that prolonged conflict (cats 67, 68). Powerful graphics, radical journals and the immediacy of broadcast news were all employed as effective protest weapons and surely helped bring the war to a close.

1 During the Cultural Revolution in China, Huang Yongyu was condemned for a winking owl, and Chen Dayu for a rooster's eyes. Laing 1988, pp. 85–6.

Vietnam with Helicopters and Kids, from the series *Gift of America*. Sigmund Abeles. 1967. See cat. 68

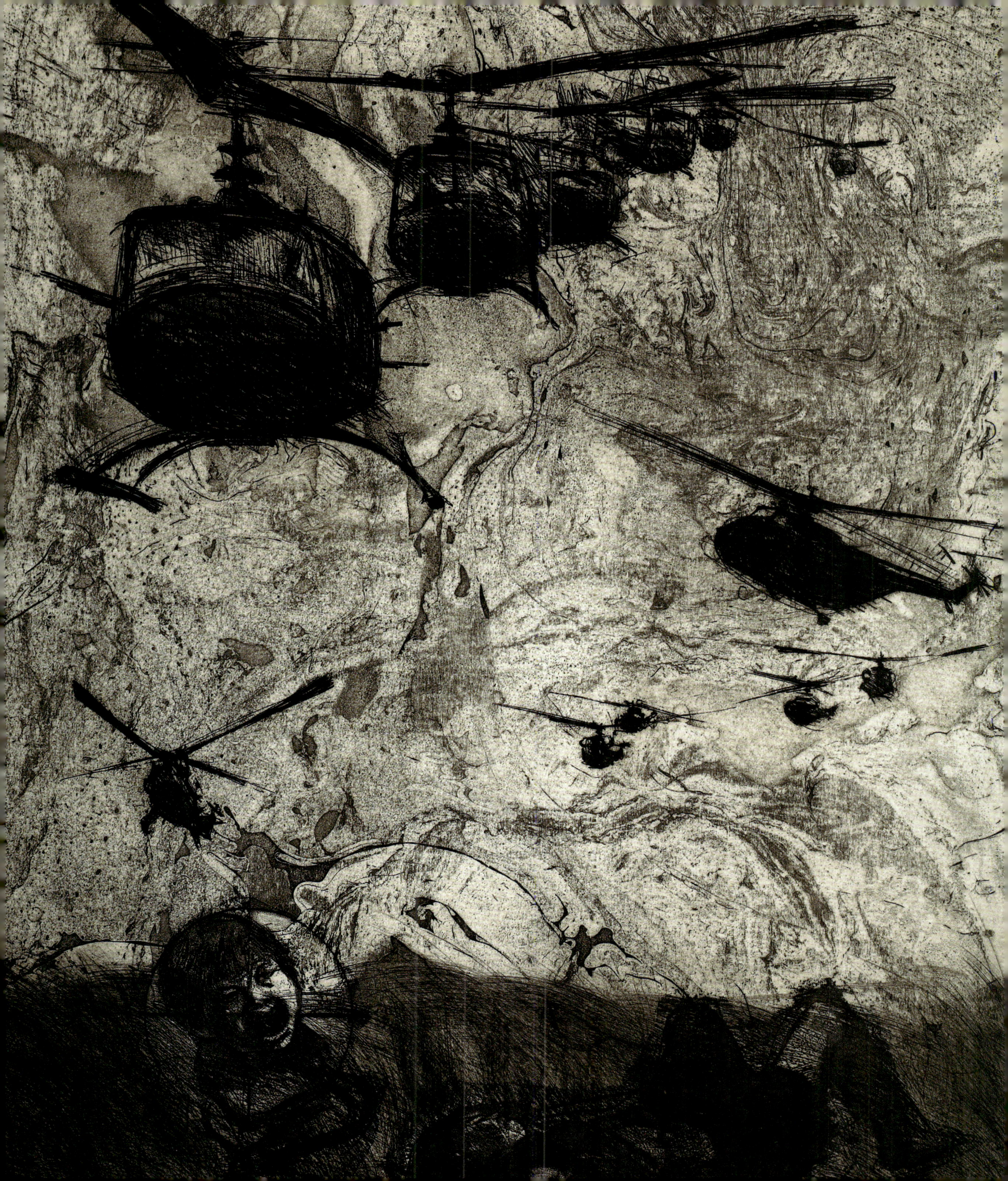

63

Famine

Zoinul Abedin

1943

Bangladesh

Drawing, Chinese ink on paper

45 × 29 cm

British Museum 2012,3027.1

Funded by Modern Museum Fund

This powerful drawing shows human suffering: a family caught up in the man-made Bengal Famine of 1943. Two to three million people died during this catastrophe,[1] brought about by British colonial policy and administrative inaction during a poor crop harvest in wartime.

Abedin (1914–76) was trained in Calcutta and became a pioneer of Bengali modern art. He is best known for the iconic series *Famine Sketches*. The drawings, done in Chinese ink on cheap packing paper, express social protest through realism and show the influence of German Expressionists such as Käthe Kollwitz. This drawing was the cover illustration of Ela Sen's scathing account, *Darkening Days, Being a Narrative of Famine-stricken Bengal*, published in Calcutta in 1944 and banned by the British authorities.

After the partition of 1947, Abedin settled in Dhaka, capital of East Pakistan. He was the principal founder of the Government Institute of Arts and Crafts (now Institute of Fine Arts). In the early 1950s he trained for two years in London, returning home with a new 'Bengali' style.

Abedin was heavily involved in the Liberation Movement, which saw the emancipation of East Pakistan into the sovereign nation of Bangladesh in 1971 after a bloody war. He was at the forefront of the movement to re-establish Bengali identity, which had been marginalized by the Pakistan government

1 Mukerjee 2010, p. ix.

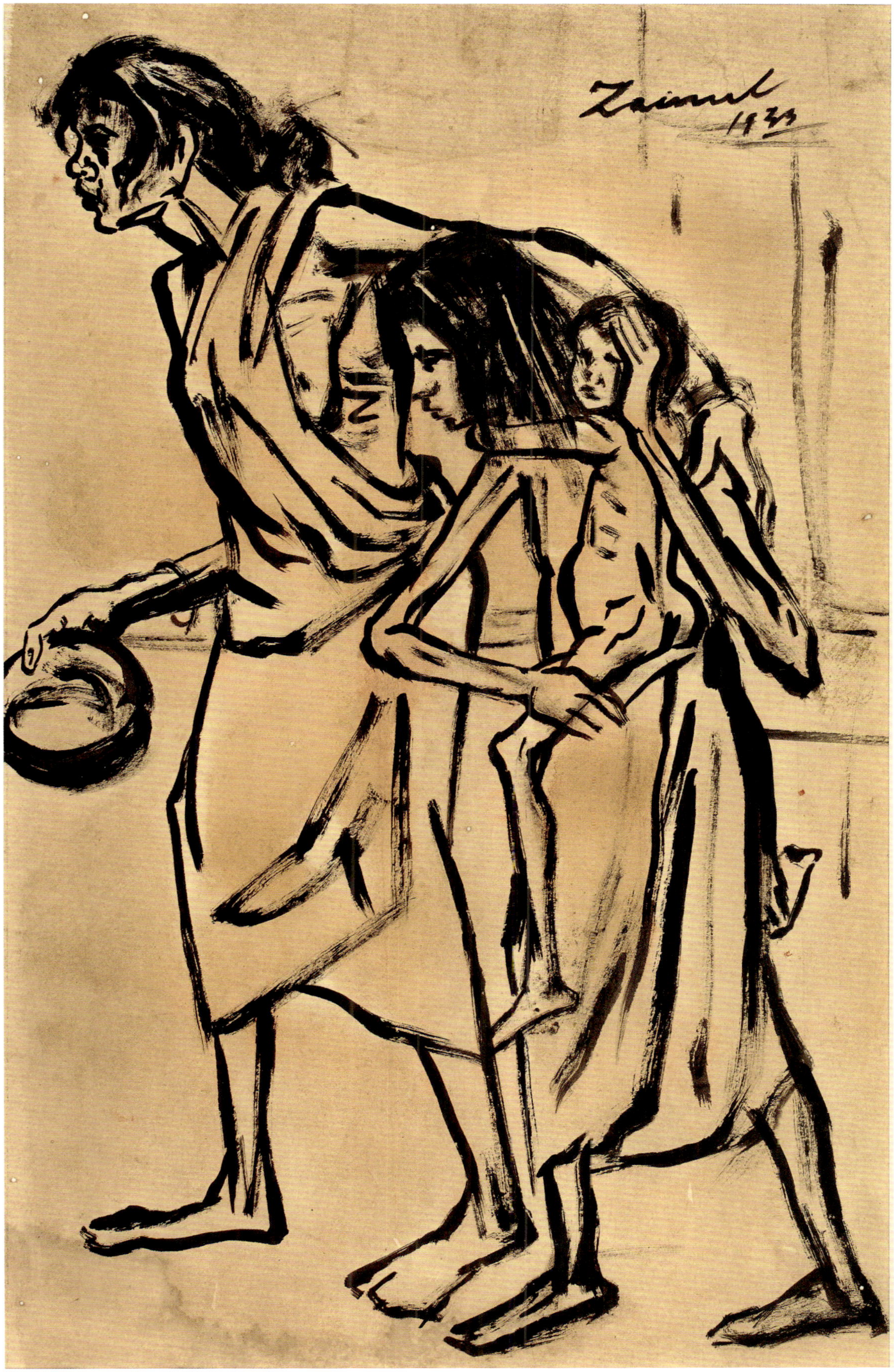

64

The Poet-Statesman Qu Yuan (屈原)

Yang Newei
(楊訥維, also known as Yang Nawei 楊納維)

1942

China

Colour woodcut on paper

16.4 × 13 cm

British Museum 1980,0630,0.163

Purchased funded by Brooke Sewell Permanent Fund

Published: von Spee 2010, cat. 60

65

Premonition

Zhang Zhengyu (張正宇)

1966

China

Pair of hanging scrolls, ink on paper

136.8 × 33.8 cm (right); 136.6 × 33.8 cm (left)

British Museum 1996,0614,0.20.1-2; Ch.Ptg.Add.654

Given by Yang Xianyi, through Gordon Barrass

Published: Barrass 2002, fig. 83

These very different Chinese artworks are related acts of protest.

During the Warring States period (475–221 BC), Qu Yuan (c. 340–278 BC) – scholar, poet, minister of state – was slandered by his colleagues and banished by King Huai of Chu (r. 329–299 BC). He wandered in sadness and dignified exile for years until, when Chu was conquered, he drowned himself in the Miluo River, loyal to the end of a lost cause. In the millennia since, Qu Yuan has become a symbol of loyalty, intellectual autonomy and integrity in the face of corruption,[1] and has been portrayed as a figure of dissent by many artists.[2]

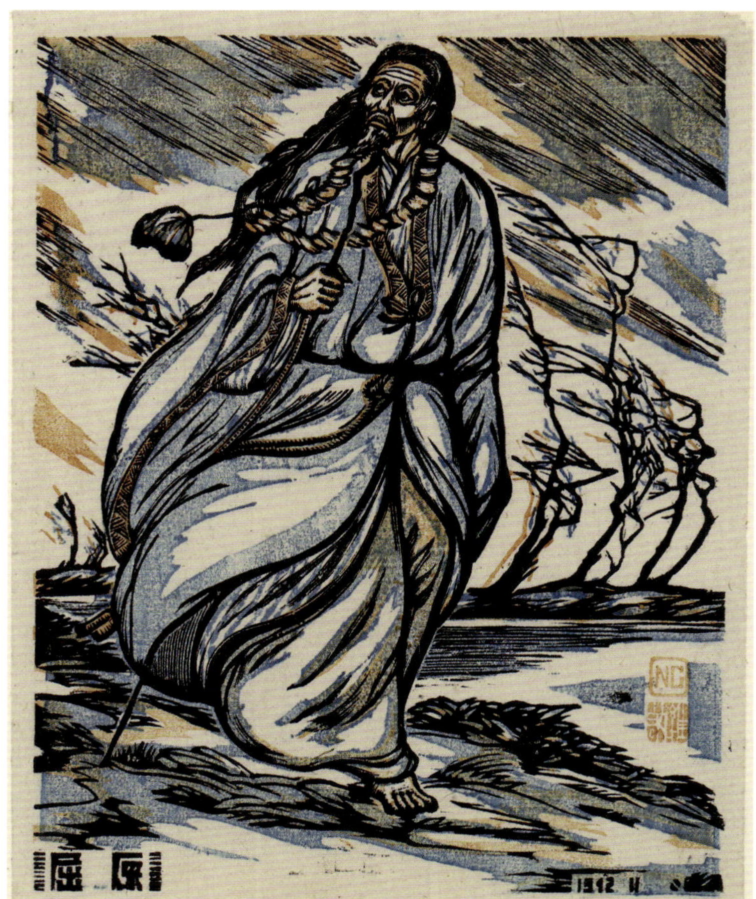

Yang Newei (1912–82) spent the second Sino-Japanese War (1937–45) in his native Guangxi, active in the All-China Woodcut Artist Association for Resistance (中華全國木刻界抗敵協會). Many of his works show human tragedies caused by government failings in wartime (fig. 17). This print is probably a protest against the government of Chiang Kai-shek. It was made in the same year as Guo Moruo's drama *Qu Yuan*, in which the Generalissimo was substituted for King Huai.[3]

The couplet in bold calligraphy by Zhang Zhengyu (1904–76) was taken from the two separate lines of Qu Yuan's most famous poem, the *Li Sao* (離騷, Encountering Sorrow). He wrote the couplet in 1966, as the political atmosphere grew increasingly tense. Having been a victim of the Anti-Rightist campaign in the late 1950s, he feared the gathering storm that became the horrific Cultural Revolution. His premonition was correct: condemned as a 'ghost and monster', he was banished to the countryside and did five years of hard labour. He died just days after the Gang of Four were arrested in 1976.

The couplet reads as follows:

望崦嵫而勿迫	*Wang Yanzi er wu po*
恐鵜鴂之先鳴	*Kong tizhu zhi xian ming*

I look West towards Mount Yanzi, but do not proceed,

Afraid that the shrike will sing before the equinox.[4]

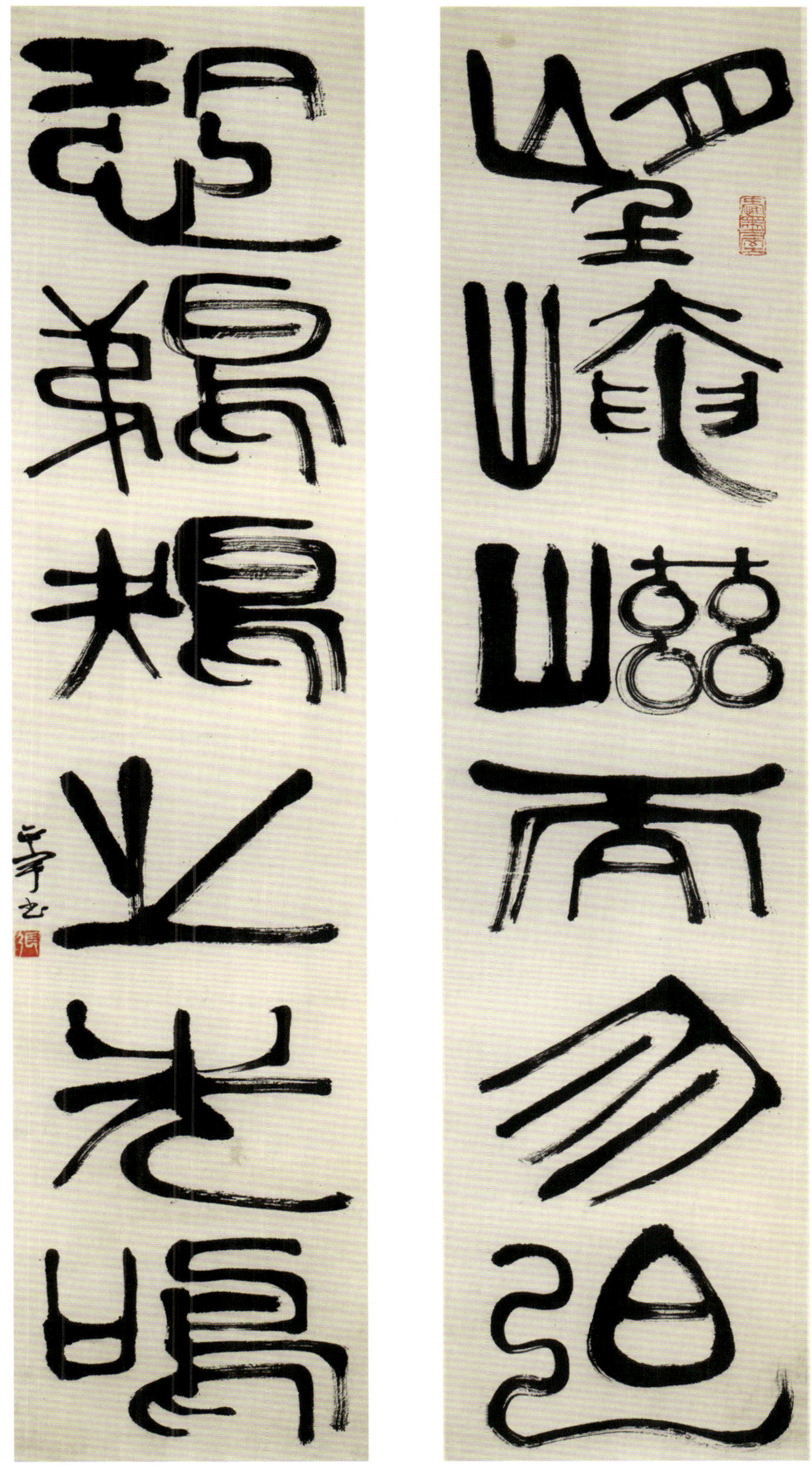

1 He is considered the father of Chinese poetry (attributed author of the *Chu Ci* 楚辭, *Songs of Chu*, better known in English as *Songs of the South*). In popular culture, his sacrifice is commemorated in the annual Dragon Boat festival.

2 Croizier 1990 recounts the twists and turns of Qu Yuan's posthumous career.

3 Croizier 1990, p. 30.

4 Translated in Barrass 2002, p. 121.

66

Propaganda leaflet

Signed Sarohandojo (unidentified artist)

Indonesia

1958

Drawing in ink on paper

29.5 × 21 cm

Private collection

This Indonesian leaflet was made for an organized week of protest against atomic (fission) and even more powerful hydrogen (fusion) bombs. The slogan reads, 'Save our children from the danger of A + H bombs'. The drawing is crude but powerful. Mothers flee with their children from burning villages. A ring of skulls emerges through the nuclear gas cloud.

Beginning in 1956, the British government conducted a series of hydrogen bomb tests high in the atmosphere over the central Pacific. Christmas Island, the base for this exercise, is less than 500 km (about 300 miles) from Jakarta, capital of Indonesia. This leaflet was probably made on Java, where Jakarta is located.[1] The United States also conducted numerous tests over Christmas Island, including the first test of a live nuclear warhead in 1962.

The international anti-nuclear movement developed in two phases. The first was in opposition to nuclear weapons, the second against nuclear power stations. Early public activism was fuelled by the death of a Japanese sailor following a 1954 nuclear test over the Pacific.[2] By the late 1950s, organizations in Asia, Europe and North America were pressing for the end of nuclear testing.

1 Sarohandojo (the artist) is a Javanese name. Private correspondence, Dany Waugh, February 2013.

2 http://deregulatetheatom.com/reference/history-of-the-antinuclear-movement-part-1/

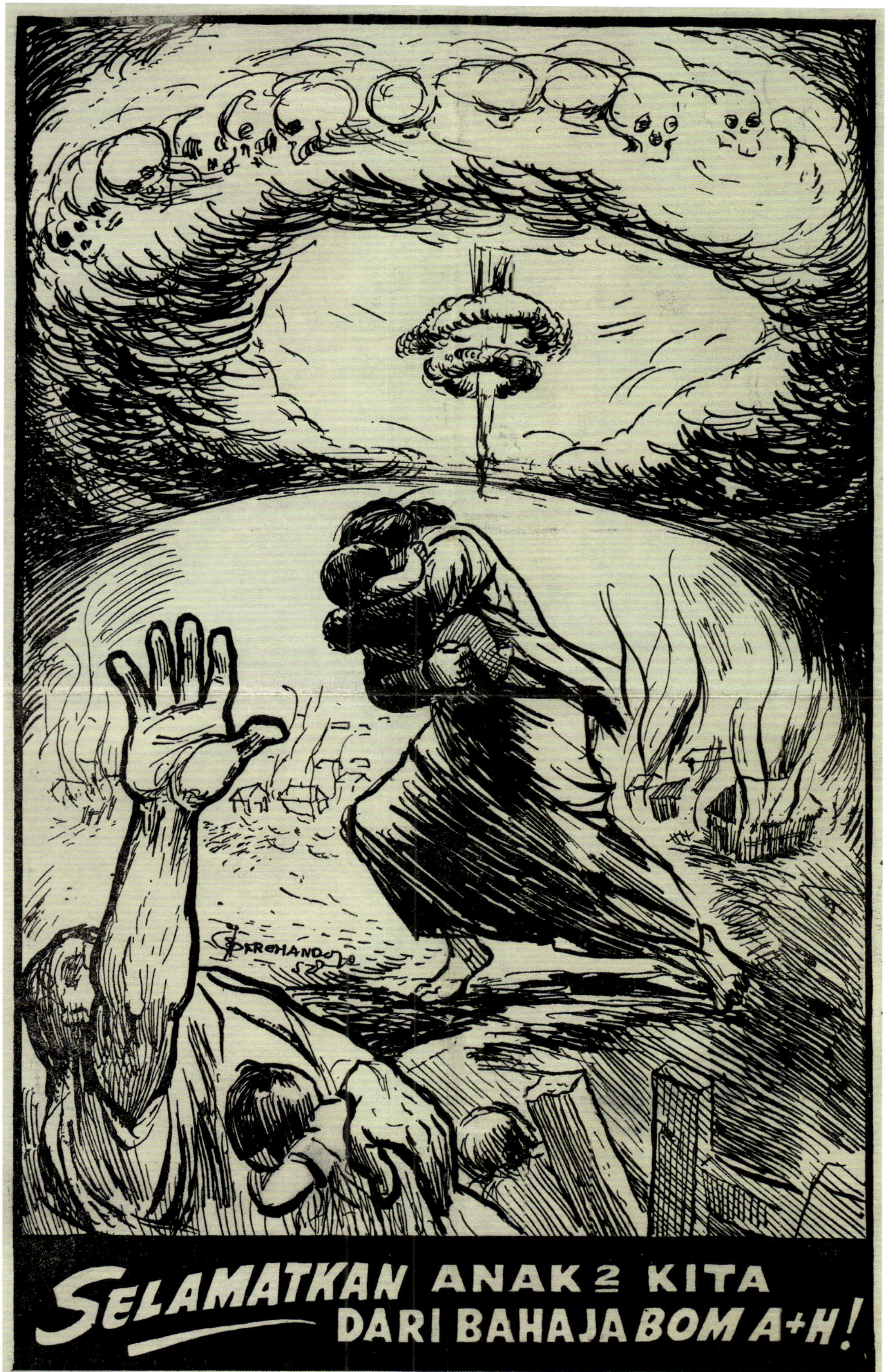
SELAMATKAN ANAK2 KITA
DARI BAHAJA BOM A+H!

67

Drawing

Van Da and Nguyen Thu

1965

Vietnam

Charcoal on paper

27.5 × 39 cm

British Museum 1999,0630,0.12

Given by the British Museum Friends

Published: Harrison-Hall 2002, cat. 2.11

Van Da (Nguyen Van Da, b. 1928) served forty-three years in the North Vietnamese Army, recording the lives and sacrifices of ordinary soldiers.[1] Professor Nguyen Thu (b. 1930) joined the resistance against France in 1946 and served in various art production and teaching positions his entire career. During the American-Vietnam War he took students to the countryside to record not only military action but also everyday activities in agriculture and industry.

This powerful, stark drawing shows two soldiers walking through a landscape destroyed by chemical weapons. Agent Orange, Napalm B and other chemicals were employed by the US military in Vietnam to defoliate forests, which gave cover to guerilla fighters, and also to destroy agricultural crops.[2] Hundreds of thousands of soldiers and civilians were killed or disabled by these burning agents. The Vietnamese author Bao Ninh (Hoàng Ấu Phương, b. 1952), who served in the Glorious 27th Youth Brigade, described the horror of napalm sprayed through the forest: 'a sea of fire enveloped them, spreading like the fires of hell'.[3]

1 Stern and Buchanan 2002, p. 90.
2 The term 'napalm' is used to refer both to an incendiary gelling agent, mixed with petroleum, and to the resulting mixture. Napalm B is a different chemical mixture, used in both the Korean and Vietnam Wars.
3 Harrison-Hall 2002, p. 70.

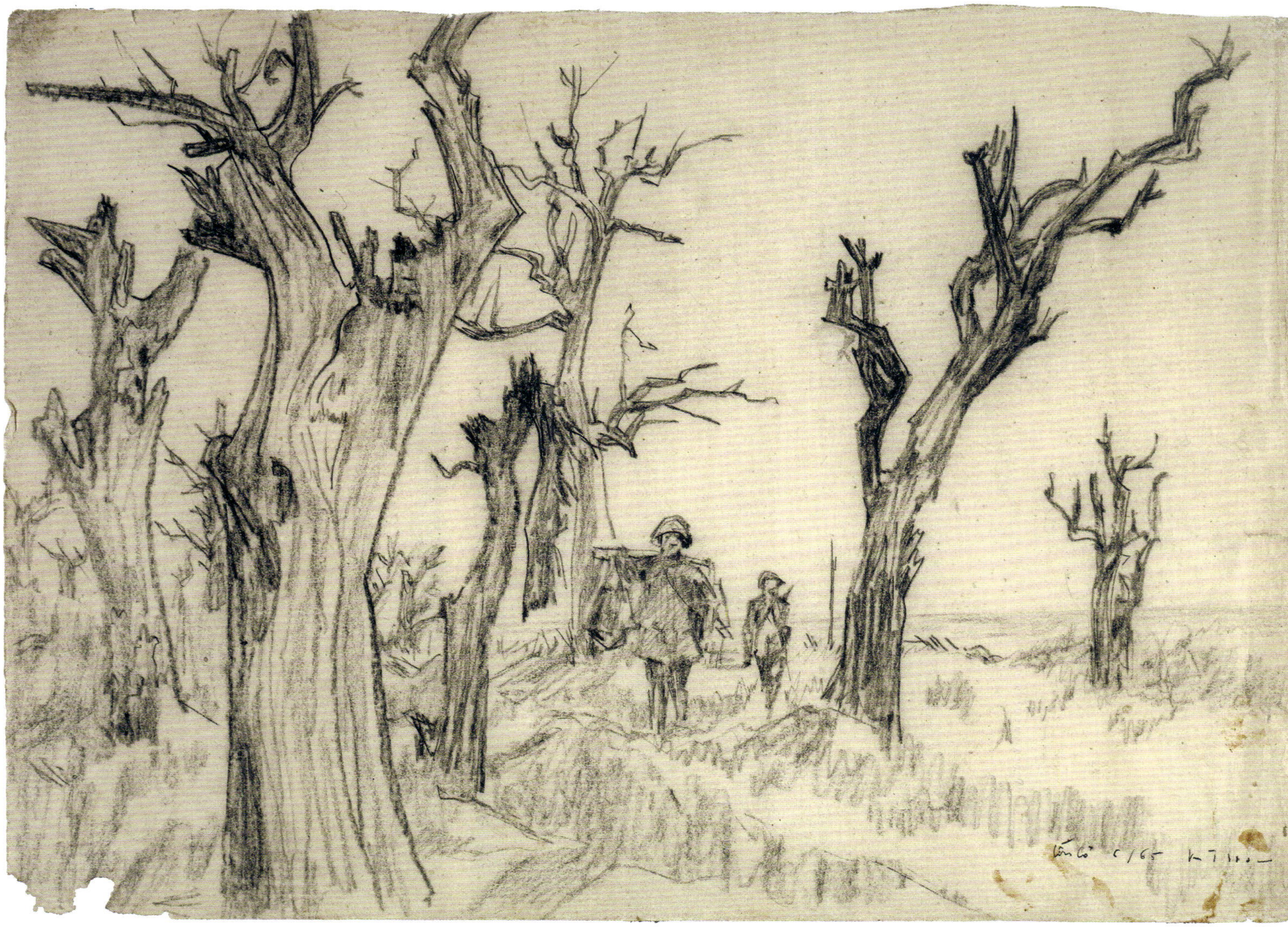

68

Vietnam with Helicopters and Kids, no. 3 from the series *Gift of America*

Sigmund Abeles

1967

United States

Sepia etching and aquatint on paper

58.8 × 38.8 cm

British Museum 1995,0507.2

Given by the artist

This print is one of a series by Sigmund Abeles (b. 1934) protesting against the Vietnam War. It powerfully expresses war's impact on innocent masses. Two children watch terrified as a fleet of helicopters approaches. One lies on the ground, the other is screaming.

Abeles joined a politically active group in Boston called Artists Against Racism and War. The group issued a series of works protesting against the use of napalm in Vietnam. *Helicopters* was number three in the series, known as *Gift of America*.[1]

Napalm was a galvanizing force in the American anti-war movement. Dow Chemical, which produced it,[2] was the 'evil-corporation poster child of the 1960s'.[3] Robert Kennedy, running for President largely on a platform against the Vietnam War, said that the Gross National Product 'grows with the production of napalm and nuclear missiles ... It can tell us everything about America, except whether we are proud to be Americans.'[4]

1 The series plays on the word 'gift', which in German means 'poison'. Correspondence from the artist, 21 February 2013.
2 Dow Chemical produced Napalm B for the US military until 1969, and also Agent Orange.
3 Kurlansky 2004, p. 9. Kurlansky cites a National Student Association report that, of 71 student demonstrations on 62 university campuses in October-November 1967, twenty-seven of them were against Dow Chemical.
4 Kurlansky 2004, pp. 140–1.

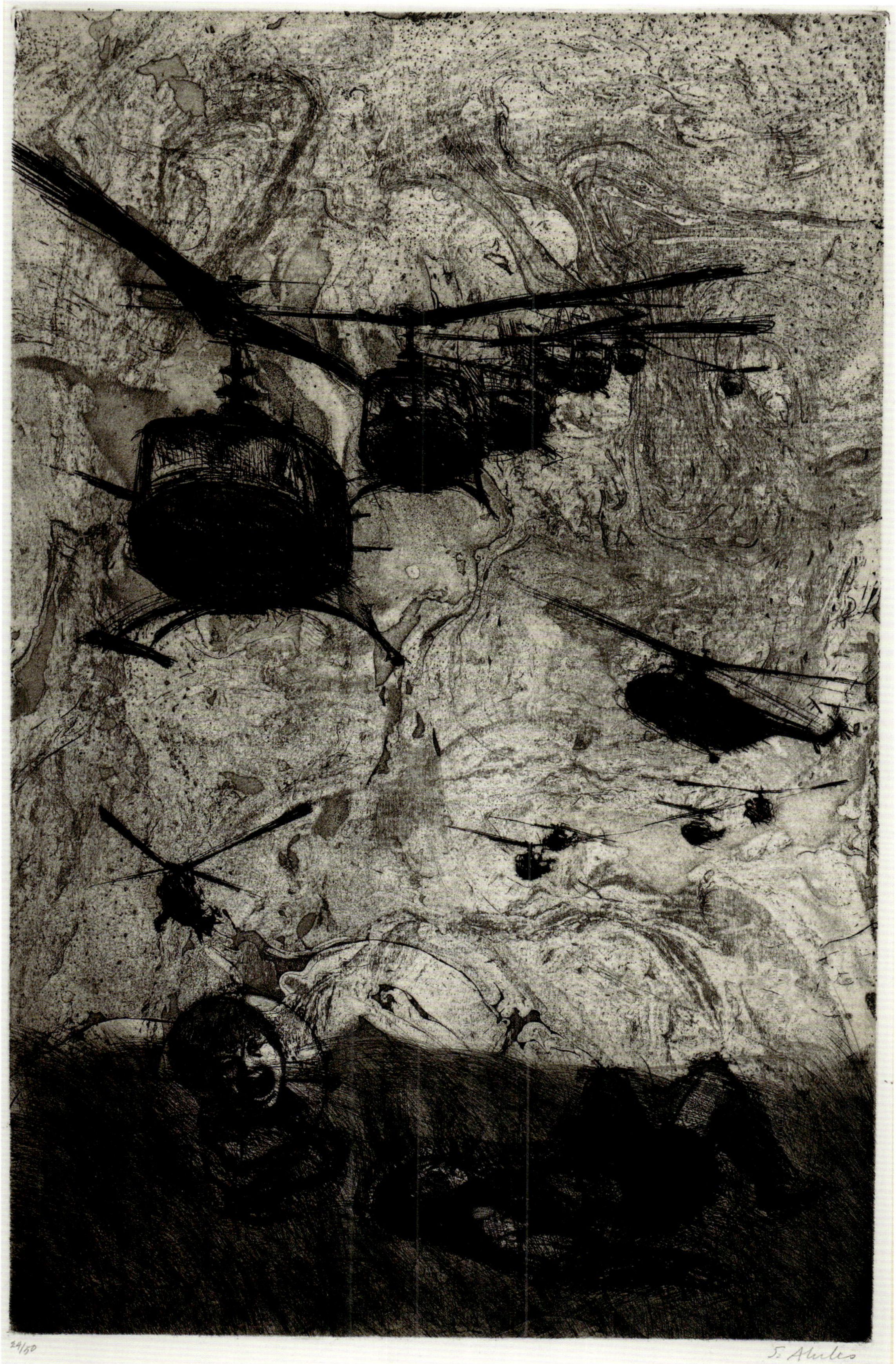

Chronology

	CHINA	INDIA/PAKISTAN	JAPAN	KOREA	VIETNAM	OTHER
1890–1900						
1894				Donghak Rebellion		
1894–5	First Sino-Japanese War		First Sino-Japanese War			
1900–1910						
1898–1901	Boxer Rebellion					
1904–5			Russo-Japanese War			
1905				Protectorate of Japan		
1905–8		*Swadeshi* Movement				
1910–1920						
1910				Annexed by Japan		
1911–12	Fall of Qing dynasty Republic established					
1914–18	World War I	World War I	World War I		World War I	World War I
1917						Bolshevik Revolution
1919	May Fourth Movement			Independence movement		Paris Peace Conference
1920–30						
1920–5	Communist Party founded (1921)	Communist Party founded (1920)	Communist Party founded (1922)	Communist Party founded (1925)	Communist Party founded (1925)	
1923			Kanto earthquake			
1926–8	Northern Expedition					Indonesian National Party (1927)
1928		Civil Disobedience Movement				
1930–45						
1931–45	Asia-Pacific War/WWII	Asia-Pacific War/WWII	Asia-Pacific War/WWII	Asia-Pacific War/WWII	Asia-Pacific War/WWII	Asia-Pacific War/WWII

	CHINA	INDIA/PAKISTAN	JAPAN	KOREA	VIETNAM	OTHER
1945–55						
1945			Atomic bombs/surrender	Divided at 38th parallel		
1945–9	Civil War					Indonesian War of of Independence
1945–52			Occupied by USA			
1945–53						Start of Cold War
1946–54					Franco-Viet War	
1947		Indpendence/Partition				
1948		Ghandi/Ali Jinnah die				
1948–60						Malay Emergency
1949	PRC established					Indonesia independence
1950–3	Korean War			Korean War		
1954					Dien Bien Phu; divided north/south	
1955–65						
1955						Bandung Conference
1956	Hundred Flowers Movement					
1957–8	Anti-Rightist Movement					
1958–61	Great Leap Forward					
1960			US Treaty protests	April Revolution (ROK)		Malaysian Federation
1964			Tokyo Olympics			
1965		Indo-Pakistani War				
1965–76						
1965–75					American-Vietnam War; anti-War movement	American-Vietnam War anti-War movement
1966–71			Narita Airport protests, first stage	DMZ Conflict		
1966–76	Cultural Revolution					
1969					Ho Chi Minh dies	
1971		Indo-Pakistani War; Bangladesh established				
1976	Mao Zedong dies Cultural Revolution ends				Formal unification	

Bibliography

Andrews 1994, Julia F. Andrews, *Painters and Politics in the People's Republic of China 1949–1979*, Berkeley: University of California Press 1994

Andrews and Shen 2012, Julia F. Andrews and Kuiyi Shen, *The Art of Modern China*, Berkeley: University of California Press 2012

Apter and Sawa 1984, David E. Apter and Nagayo Sawa, *Against the State: Politics and Social Protest in Japan*, Cambridge, MA: Harvard University Press 1984

Atkins 2005a, Jacqueline M. Atkins (ed.), *Wearing Propaganda: Textiles on the Home Front in Japan, Britain, and the United States, 1931–1945*, New Haven: Yale University Press 2005

Atkins 2005b, Jacqueline Atkins, 'An Arsenal of Design: Themes, Motifs, and Metaphors in Propaganda Textiles', in Atkins 2005a, pp. 258–363

Atkins 2005c, Jacqueline Atkins, '"Extravagance is the Enemy": Fashion and Textiles in Wartime Japan', in Atkins 2005a, pp. 157–69

Aulich 2007, James Aulich, *War Posters: Weapons of Mass Communication*, London: Thames & Hudson 2007

Barmé 1996, Geremie R. Barmé, *Shades of Mao: The Posthumous Cult of the Great Leader*, Armonk, NY: M.E. Sharpe 1996

Barrass 2002, Gordon S. Barrass, *The Art of Calligraphy in Modern China*, London: British Museum Press 2002

Beevor 2012, Antony Beevor, *The Second World War*, London: Weidenfeld & Nicolson 2012

Bennett *et al.* 1986, Tony Bennett, Colin Mercer and Janet Woollacott (eds), *Popular Culture and Social Relations*, Milton Keynes: Open University Press 1986

Blurton 1989, T. Richard Blurton, 'Continuity and Change in the Tradition of Bengali *Pata*-painting', in Anna Libera Dallapiccola (ed.), *Shastric Traditions in Indian Arts*, Stuttgart: Steiner 1989, vol. 1, pp. 425–51

Blurton 2006, T. Richard Blurton, *Bengali Myths*, London: British Museum Press 2006

BM Satires, Frederic George Stephens and M. Dorothy George (eds), *Catalogue of Political and Personal Satires Preserved in the Department of Prints and Drawings in the British Museum*, 11 vols, London: British Museum, 1870–1954

Brokaw and Reed 2010, Cynthia Brokaw and Christopher A. Reed (eds), *From Woodblocks to the Internet: Chinese Publishing and Print Culture in Transition, circa 1800 to 2008*, Leiden and Boston: Brill 2010

Buchanan 2002, Sherry Buchanan, 'Artists and the Role of Propaganda', in Harrison-Hall 2002, pp. 15–20

Buchanan 2007, Sherry Buchanan, *Vietnam Zippos*, London: Thames & Hudson 2007

Buchanan and Heather 2009, Sherry Buchanan and David Heather, *Vietnam Posters: The David Heather Collection*, Munich: Prestel 2009

Buttinger 1958, Joseph Buttinger, *The Smaller Dragon: A Political History of Vietnam*, New York: Frederick A. Praeger 1958

Chang 1997, Julian Chang, 'The Mechanics of State Propaganda: The People's Republic of China and the Soviet Union in the 1950s', in Timothy Cheek and Tony Saich (eds), *New Perspectives on State Socialism in China*, Armonk, NY and London: M.E. Sharpe 1997, pp. 76–124

Chu 1978, Godwin C. Chu (ed.), *Popular Media in China: Shaping New Cultural Patterns*, Honolulu: University Press of Hawaii 1978

Clark 1997, Toby Clark, *Art and Propaganda in the Twentieth Century: The Political Image in the Age of Mass Culture*, London: Weidenfeld & Nicolson 1997

Clunas 2009, Craig Clunas, *Art in China*, 2nd edn, Oxford: Oxford University Press 2009

Cohn 2000, Don J. Cohn, *Virtue by Design: Illustrated Chinese Children's Books from the Cotsen Children's Library*, Los Angeles, Cotsen Occasional Press 2000

Collins 2011, Ross F. Collins, *Children, War and Propaganda*, New York: Peter Lang 2011

Crespi 2011, John A. Crespi, 'China's *Modern Sketch*: The Golden Era of Cartoon Art, 1934–1937', MIT Visualizing Cultures website, http://ocw.mit.edu/ans7870/21f/21f.027/modern_sketch/index.html

Croizier 1990, Ralph Crozier, 'Qu Yuan and the Artists: Ancient Symbols and Modern Politics in the Post-Mao Era', *Australian Journal of Chinese Affairs*, no. 24 (July 1990), pp. 25–50

Csikszentmihalyi 1991, Mihaly Csikszentmihalyi, 'Design and Order in Everyday Life' [1991], in Ben Highmore (ed.), *The Design Culture Reader*, London: Routledge 2009, pp. 158–64

Dikötter 2010, Frank Dikötter, *Mao's Great Famine: The History of China's Most Devastating Catastrophe, 1958–62*, London: Bloomsbury 2010

Dower 1999, John W. Dower, *Embracing Defeat: Japan in the Wake of World War II*, New York: W.W. Norton 1999

Eastman *et al.* 1991, Lloyd E. Eastman, Jerome Ch'en, Suzanne Pepper and Lyman P. Van Slyke, *The Nationalist Era in China, 1927–1949*, Cambridge: Cambridge University Press 1991

Ellul 1965, Jacques Ellul, *Propaganda: The Formation of Men's Attitudes*, New York: Alfred A. Knopf 1965

Farquhar 1995, Mary Ann Farquhar, 'Sanmao: Classic Cartoons and Chinese Popular Culture', in John A. Lent, *Asian Popular Culture*, Boulder: Westview Press 1995, pp. 139–58

Farquhar 1999, Mary Ann Farquhar, *Children's Literature in China: From Lu Xun to Mao Zedong*, Armonk, NY: M.E. Sharpe 1999

Flath 2004, James A. Flath, *The Cult of Happiness: Nianhua, Art, and History in Rural North China*, Vancouver and Seattle: UBC Press and University of Washington Press 2004

Frank 2011, Rüdiger Frank (ed.), *Exploring North Korean Arts*, Nuremberg: Verlag für moderne Kunst 2011

Fraser 1996, James Fraser, *Japanese Modern: Graphic Design Between the Wars*, San Francisco: Chronicle Books 1996

Friedman (Korea) undated, Herbert A. Friedman, 'The American PSYOP Organization during the Korean War', http://www.psywarrior.com/KoreaPSYOPHist.html; http://www.psywarrior.com/KoreaPSYOPHist2.html

Friedman (Malaya) undated, Herbert A. Friedman, 'Psychological Warfare of the Malayan Emergency, 1948–1960', http://ics-www.leeds.ac.uk/papers/vp01.cfm?outfit=pmt&folder=64&paper=2648

Galikowski 1998, Maria Galikowski, *Art and Politics in China 1949–1984*, Hong Kong: Chinese University Press 1998

Gerth 2003, Karl Gerth, *China Made: Consumer Culture and the Creation of the Nation*, Cambridge, MA: Harvard University Asia Center 2003

Ginsberg 2008, Mary Ginsberg, 'Revolutionary Art at the British Museum', *Transactions of the Oriental Ceramic Society*, vol. 71, 2008 (2006–7), pp. 33–43

Glaser and Ilić 2006, Milton Glaser and Mirko Ilić, *The Design of Dissent*, Gloucester, MA: Rockport Publishers 2006

Goebbels 2009, Joseph Goebbels, *Goebbels on the Power of Propaganda*, digital edn, Shamrock Eden Publishing 2009

Harootunian 2000, Harry D. Harootunian, *Overcome by Modernity: History, Culture, and Community in Interwar Japan*, Princeton: Princeton University Press 2000

Harrison-Hall 2002, Jessica Harrison-Hall, *Vietnam Behind the Lines: Images from the War 1965–1975*, London: British Museum Press 2002

Heather and de Ceuster 2008, David Heather and Koen de Ceuster, *North Korean Posters: The David Heather Collection*, Munich: Prestel 2008

Heller 2008, Steven Heller, *Iron Fists: Branding the 20th-century Totalitarian State*, London: Phaidon 2008

Herring 2000, Ann Herring, *The Dawn of Wisdom: Selections from the Japanese Collection of the Cotsen Children's Library*, Los Angeles: Cotsen Occasional Press 2000

Hobsbawm 1983, Eric Hobsbawm, 'Introduction: Inventing Traditions', in Eric Hobsbawm and Terence Ranger, *The Invention of Tradition*, Cambridge: Cambridge University Press 1983

Holm 1984, David Holm, 'Folk Art as Propaganda: The Yangge Movement in Yan'an', in Bonnie S. McDougall (ed.), *Popular Chinese Literature and Performing Arts in the People's Republic of China 1949–1979*, Berkeley: University of California Press 1984, pp. 3–35

Holm 1991, David Holm, *Art and Ideology in Revolutionary China*, Oxford: Clarendon Press 1991

Hung 1994, Chang-tai Hung, *War and Popular Culture: Resistance in Modern China, 1937–1945*, Berkeley: University of California Press 1994

Hung 1997, Chang-tai Hung, 'Two Images of Socialism: Woodcuts in Chinese Communist Politics', *Comparative Studies in Society and History*, 39-1, January 1997, pp. 34–60

Hung 2011, Chang-tai Hung, *Mao's New World: Political Culture in the Early People's Republic*, Ithaca: Cornell University Press 2011

Jowett and O'Donnell 1999, Garth Jowett and Victoria O'Donnell, *Propaganda and Persuasion*, 3rd edn, Thousand Oaks, CA: Sage Publications 1999

Kaneko 1995, Sachiko Kaneko, 'The Struggle for Legal Rights and Reforms: A Historical View', in Kumiko Fujimura-Fanselow and Atsuko Kameda (eds), *Japanese Women: New Feminist Perspectives on the Past, Present, and Future*, New York: Feminist Press 1995, pp. 3–14

Kashiwagi 2005, Hiroshi Kashiwagi, 'Design and War: Kimono as "Parlor-Performance" Propaganda', in Atkins 2005a, pp. 171–81

King 2009, David King, *Red Star over Russia: A Visual History of the Soviet Union from 1917 to the Death of Stalin*, London: Tate Publishing 2009

Kudryavtseva 2004, Tamara Kudryavtseva, *Circling the Square: Avant-Garde Porcelain from Revolutionary Russia*, London: Fontanka 2004

Kurlansky 2004, Mark Kurlansky, *1968: The Year that Rocked the World*, New York and London: Random House and Jonathan Cape 2004

Kushner 2006, Barak Kushner, *The Thought War: Japanese Imperial Propaganda*, Honolulu: University of Hawai'i Press 2006

Kushner 2009, Barak Kushner, 'Planes, Trains and Games: Selling Japan's War in Asia', in Jennifer Purtle and Hans Bjarne Thomsen (eds), *Looking Modern: East Asian Visual Culture from Treaty Ports to World War II*, Chicago: Center for the Art of East Asia, University of Chicago 2009, pp. 243–94

Kushner 2011, Barak Kushner, *Dreams of Empire: Japanese Propaganda Textiles*, San Francisco: MHJ Collection 2011

Laing 1988, Ellen Johnston Laing, *The Winking Owl: Art in the People's Republic of China*, Berkeley: University of California Press 1988

Laing 2000, Ellen Johnston Laing, 'Reform, Revolutionary, Political and Resistance Themes in Chinese Popular Prints, 1900–1940', *Modern Chinese Literature and Culture*, vol. 12-2, 2000, pp. 123–76

Laing 2002, Ellen Johnston Laing, *Art and Aesthetics in Chinese Popular Prints: Selections from the Muban Foundation Collection*, Ann Arbor and London: Center for Chinese Studies, University of Michigan and Muban Foundation 2002

Laing 2004, Ellen Johnston Laing, *Selling Happiness: Calendar Posters and Visual Culture in Early-Twentieth-Century Shanghai*, Honolulu: University of Hawai'i Press 2004

Landsberger and van der Heijden 2009, Stefan R. Landsberger and Marien van der Heijden. *Chinese Posters: The IISH-Landsberger Collection*, Munich: Prestel 2009

Lary 2007, Diana Lary, *China's Republic*, Cambridge: Cambridge University Press 2007

Lasswell 1927, Harold Lasswell, *Propaganda Technique in the World War*, New York: Alfred A. Knopf 1927

Lasswell 1939, Harold Lasswell, *World Revolutionary Propaganda: A Chicago Study*, New York: Alfred A. Knopf 1939

Lippard 1980, Lucy R. Lippard, 'Some Propaganda for Propaganda', *Heresies* no. 9 (1980), pp. 35–9

MacFarquhar and Schoenhals 2006, Roderick MacFarquhar and Michael Schoenhals, *Mao's Last Revolution*, Cambridge, MA: Belknap Press of Harvard University Press 2006

MacGregor 2010, Neil MacGregor, *A History of the World in 100 Objects*, London: Allen Lane 2010

MacKinnon *et al.* 2007, Stephen R. MacKinnon, Diana Lary and Ezra F. Vogel (eds), *China at War: Regions of China, 1937–45*, Stanford: Stanford University Press 2007

Maclean 2011, Kama Maclean, 'The Portrait's Journey: The Image, Social Communication and Martyr-Making in Colonial India', *Journal of Asian Studies*, vol. 70, no. 4 (November), 2011, pp. 1051–82

Marlin 2002, Randal Marlin, *Propaganda and the Ethics of Persuasion*, Peterborough, Ontario: Broadview Press 2002

Mayo 2001, Marlene J. Mayo, 'Introduction', in Marlene J. Mayo and J. Thomas Rimer (eds), *War, Occupation and Creativity: Japan and East Asia 1920–1960*, Honolulu: University of Hawai'i Press 2001, pp.1–42

McDougall 1980, Bonnie S. McDougall, *Mao Zedong's Talks at the Yan'an Conference on Literature and Art*', Ann Arbor: Center for Chinese Studies, University of Michigan 1980

Mishra 2012, Pankaj Mishra, *From the Ruins of Empire: The Revolt Against the West and the Remaking of Asia*, London: Allen Lane 2012

Mitter 2004, Rana Mitter, *A Bitter Revolution: China's Struggle with the Modern World*, Oxford: Oxford University Press 2004

Mukerjee 2010, Madhusree Mukerjee, *Churchill's Secret War: The British Empire and the Ravaging of India during World War II*, New York: Basic Books 2010

Myers 2010, B.R. Myers, *The Cleanest Race: How North Koreans See Themselves – and Why it Matters*, New York: Melville House 2010

Odom and Salmond 2009, Anne Odom and Wendy R. Salmond (eds), *Treasures into Tractors: The Selling of Russia's Cultural Heritage, 1918–1938*, Seattle and Washington, DC: University of Washington Press 2009

Philippe 1982, Robert Philippe, *Political Graphics: Art as a Weapon*, Oxford: Phaidon 1982

Pinney 2004, Christopher Pinney, *'Photos of the Gods': The Printed Image and Political Struggle in India*, London: Reaktion 2004

Portal 2000, Jane Portal, *Korea: Art and Archaeology*, London: British Museum Press 2000

Portal 2005, Jane Portal, *Art under Control in North Korea*, London: Reaktion 2005

Preston 2000, Diana Preston, *The Boxer Rebellion: The Dramatic Story of China's War on Foreigners that Shook the World in the Summer of 1900*, New York: Berkley 2000

Ramakrishna 2002, Kumar Ramakrishna, *Emergency Propaganda: The Winning of Malayan Hearts and Minds, 1948–1958*, Richmond: Curzon 2002

Reed 2010a, Christopher A. Reed, 'From Woodblocks to the Internet: Chinese Printing, Publishing, and Literary Fields in Transition, Circa 1800 to 2008', Introduction, in Brokaw and Reed 2010, pp. 1–35

Reed 2010b, Christopher A. Reed, 'Advancing the (Gutenberg) Revolution: The Origins and Development of Chinese Print Communism, 1921–1947', in Brokaw and Reed 2010, pp. 275–311

Ridley et al 1971, Charles Price Ridley, Paul H.B. Godwin and Dennis J. Doolin, *The Making of a Model Citizen in Communist China*, Stanford: Hoover Institution Press 1971

Rudoe 1994, Judy Rudoe, *Decorative Arts 1850–1950: A Catalogue of the British Museum Collection*, 2nd edn, London: British Museum Press 1994

Sandler 1997, Mark Sandler (ed.), *The Confusion Era: Art and Culture of Japan during the Allied Occupation, 1945–1952*, Washington, DC: Arthur M. Sackler Gallery, Smithsonian Institution 1997

Sandrock undated, John E. Sandrock, 'Japanese sponsored coin and bank note issues for the occupied regions of China, The Currency Collector, http://www.docstoc.com/docs/95804346/Japanese-Sponsored-Coin-and-Bank-Note, pp. 1–33

Schnapp 2005, Jeffrey T. Schnapp, *Revolutionary Tides: The Art of the Political Poster 1914–1989*, New York: Skira 2005

Silverberg 2006, Miriam Silverberg, *Erotic Grotesque Nonsense: The Mass Culture of Japanese Modern Times*, Berkeley: University of California Press 2006

Smith 2002, Lawrence Smith, *Japanese Prints During the Allied Occupation 1945–1952*, London: British Museum Press 2002

von Spee 2010, Clarissa von Spee (ed.), *The Printed Image in China: From the 8th to the 21st Centuries*. London: British Museum Press 2010

Stern and Buchanan 2002, Thu Stern and Sherry Buchanan, 'Biographies of the Artists', in Harrison-Hall 2002, pp. 87–90

Sullivan 1996, Michael Sullivan, *Art and Artists of Twentieth-Century China*, Berkeley: University of California Press 1996

Tang 2008, Xiaobing Tang, *Origins of the Chinese Avant-Garde: The Modern Woodcut Movement*, Berkeley: University of California Press 2008

Taylor 1990, Philip M. Taylor, *Munitions of the Mind: A History of War Propaganda*, Wellingborough: Patrick Stephens 1990

Timmers 1998, Margaret Timmers (ed.), *The Power of the Poster*, London: V&A Publications 1998

Tipton and Clarke 2000, Elise K.Tipton and John Clark (eds), *Being Modern in Japan: Culture and Society from the 1910s to the 1930s*, Honolulu: University of Hawai'i Press 2000

Wakakuwa 2005, Midori Wakakuwa, 'War-promoting Kimono (1931–45)', in Atkins 2005a, pp. 183–203

Wang 2008a, Helen Wang, *Chairman Mao Badges: Symbols and Slogans of the Cultural Revolution*, London: British Museum 2008

Wang 2008b, Helen Wang, 'Charged Icons', *British Museum Magazine*, vol. 60, Spring/Summer 2008, pp. 34–5

White 1988, Stephen White, *The Bolshevik Poster*, New Haven: Yale University Press 1988

Xu 2011, Xu Gucqi, *Strangers on the Western Front: Chinese Workers in the Great War*, Cambridge, MA: Harvard University Press 2011

Yang 2012, Yang Jisheng, *Tombstone: The Untold Story of Mao's Great Famine*, trans. Stacy Mosher and Guo Jian, London: Allen Lane 2012

Yeh 2011, Wen-hsin Yeh, 'Beyond the Frame: The Camera in Republican China and Wartime Chongqing', in Jeffrey W. Cody and Frances Terpak (eds), *Brush and Shutter: Early Photography in China*, Los Angeles: Getty Research Institute 2011, pp. 111–19

Zur 2011, Dafna Zur, 'The Korean War in Children's Picturebooks of the DPRK', in Frank 2011, pp. 276–97

Author's Acknowledgements

Many people made this collaborative exhibition and catalogue possible. I am indebted above all to Jan Stuart, who has supported and guided every step of the project from its inception. I am grateful to the generous curators and scholars in four departments at the British Museum, who shared their time and knowledge with me. In the Department of Asia, Richard Blurton, Timothy Clark, Sona Datta, Alexandra Green, Alfred Haft, Jessica Harrison-Hall, SooMi Lee, Nicole Rousmaniere, Sascha Priewe, Clarissa von Spee and Meixin Wang advised on objects and research. Hiromi Uchida tirelessly helped with translation and copyright issues. Sushma Jansari designed the complicated China map, the first of its kind. Long-term volunteers Paul Bevan, Hee-jung Lee, Andrea Shen and Keith Southwell contributed greatly with research, translation and technological support. Robert Bracey, Tom Hockenhull and Helen Wang (Coins and Medals), Judy Rudoe (Prehistory and Europe), Stephen Coppel and Sheila O'Connell (Prints and Drawings) shared their expertise.

It is a pleasure to acknowledge all those who worked on the development and production aspects of the project. John Williams and Kevin Lovelock worked photographic magic on difficult objects. The publications team of Coralie Hepburn, Andrew Shoolbred, Nina Shandloff, Katie Anderson and Susan Walby meticulously and creatively designed, edited and managed this catalogue through its various editorial and production stages. Hannah Payne and Sonia D'Orsi designed and executed the exhibition with flair and imagination. Paul Goodhead created the Asia map in record time. Interpretation by David Francis added depth and clarity to the themes of the exhibition. Thanks to Joanna Kosek for creative conservation solutions, and to David Green, Loretta Hogan, Megumi Mizumura, Nicola Newman, Valentina Marabini, Monique Pullan, Jixian Qiu, Keisuke Sugiyama and particularly Carol Peacock, who skilfully conserved and mounted the objects. The Department of Asia's Museum Assistants managed the installation and logistics with care and efficiency, especially Iestyn Jones, who worked on the exhibition from the outset. Thanks also to Amanda Gregory, Jim Peters and Angela Roche for assistance with objects, Alison Hollis for organizing the loans, and David Bone and Christopher Stewart for frequently clearing the administrative path.

Outside the British Museum, I echo Jan Stuart's gratitude to Paul Bevan, Sherry Buchanan, John Cloake, Stephanie Mitchell, Alfreda Murck and Carolyn Wong, not only for material support, but for their academic expertise and encouragement over time. I am also indebted to Angela Chiu, Ed Harris, Mac Jeffery and Frances Wood. For knowledge and new directions, I thank, belatedly, Jeremy Aynsley, Christine Guth and Sarah Teasley at the Royal College of Art.

Finally, my heartfelt thanks to Peggy Grieve, William Knowles and Helen Wang for head-clearing support, text reading and always constructive critique.

Illustration Acknowledgements

The author and publisher would like to thank the copyright holders for granting permission to reproduce the images illustrated. Every attempt has been made to trace accurate ownership of copyrighted images in this book. Errors and omissions will be corrected in subsequent editions provided notification is sent to the publisher.

All photographs of British Museum objects are © The Trustees of the British Museum, courtesy of the Department of Photography and Imaging. Registration numbers are given in the caption or catalogue entry. Further information about objects in the British Museum can be found on the Museum's website at britishmuseum.org.

Maps
p. 9 By Paul Goodhead
p. 29 By Sushma Jansari after John K. Fairbank and Albert Feuerwerker (eds), *The Cambridge History of China, 1912–1949*, Part 2, Cambridge University Press 1986, pp. 549, 645

Introduction
Fig. 1 British Museum 1921,0306.12
Fig. 2 (a) British Museum 1903,0408,0.1
Fig. 2 (b) Private collection
Fig. 3 The Muban Foundation, London. Image © Huang Yao Foundation
Fig. 4 British Museum 1967,1016,0.5.4. Given by E.S.A. Mathie
Fig. 5 British Museum 1967,1016,0.5.3. Given by E.S.A. Mathie
Fig. 6 British Museum 1991,0810,0.5. Purchase funded by Brooke Sewell Bequest
Fig. 7 British Museum 1946,0209,0.103. Bequeathed by Arthur Morrison
Fig. 8 Alfreda Murck Collection # 77/British Museum
Fig. 9 British Museum 1950,1014,0.24
Fig. 10 British Museum 1998,0723.76/Isaacs 76. Given by Ralph and Ruth Isaacs
Fig. 11 © 2013, State Russian Museum, St Petersburg
Fig. 12 British Museum 1992,0716,0.380. © Zhang Wangqing
Fig. 13 British Museum 1999,0705,0.7
Fig. 14 British Museum 2009,3022,0.3
Fig. 15 British Museum 1980,0630,0.170. Purchase funded by Brooke Sewell Permanent Fund
Fig. 16 British Museum 1980,0630,0.85. Purchase funded by Brooke Sewell Permanent Fund
Fig. 17 British Museum 2009, 3022. 64
Fig. 18 British Museum 1980,0630,0.215. Purchase funded by Brooke Sewell Permanent Fund
Fig. 19 British Museum 2006,0117,0.51. Purchase funded by Brooke Sewell Bequest
Fig. 20 British Museum 2006,0117,0.76. Purchase funded by Brooke Sewell Bequest
Fig. 21 British Museum 2006,0117,0.05. Purchase funded by Brooke Sewell Bequest
Fig. 22 British Museum 2006,0117,0.45. Purchase funded by Brooke Sewell Bequest
Fig. 23 British Museum CIB,EA.215. Given by the ifs School of Finance Collection
Fig. 24 British Museum 2005,0610,0.1 Purchase funded by Brooke Sewell Bequest
Fig. 25 Private Collection
Fig. 26 British Museum 1990,0707,0.69.7. Purchase funded by British Museum Friends (Townley Group)
Fig. 27 British Museum 1987,0316,0.9. Purchase funded by Brooke Sewell Bequest
Fig. 28 British Museum 2007, 3018,3.1-7. Purchase funded by Brooke Sewell Bequest
Fig. 29 British Museum 1992,0416,0.4.3. Purchase funded by Brooke Sewell Permanent Fund
Fig. 30 Private collection
Fig. 31 British Museum 2006, 0501, 0.14
Fig. 32 British Museum 2002,1001, 0.24. Purchase funded by Brooke Sewell Permanent Fund
Fig. 33 Private collection
Fig. 34 British Museum 1987.16.76
Fig. 35 Sherry Buchanan and William Spurgin Collection
Fig. 36 British Museum 2001,1015,0.9. Purchase funded by Brooke Sewell Permanent Fund

Catalogue
Cat. 1 British Museum 2001,0315,0.2 © Nam June Paik Estate
Cat. 2 British Museum Book. NE 654.K6 1936 © DACS 2013.
Cat. 7 Private Collection © Yuan Yunpo
Cat. 31 British Museum 2009,3026.4 © International Olympic Committee
Cat. 40 British Museum 2006,0113,0.3.1-17 © Sano Hiroshi
Cat. 45 British Museum 2002,1001,0.2 © Song Shi-yop
Cat. 47 British Museum 2001,0607,0.10 © Kang Chŏng-nim
Cat. 49 British Museum 1992,0716,0.100 © Wu Junfa
Cat. 55 British Museum 2006, 0501, 0.26 © Chen Ziyun
Cat. 58 British Museum 2006,0119,0.2 © Okamoto Yaeko
Cat. 62 Private Collection © the children of Zhang Ding
Cat. 68 British Museum 1995,0507.2 © Sigmund Abeles

Index

Note: page numbers in **bold** refer to information contained in captions.